The Neural Basis of Reading

The Neural Basis of Reading

Edited by

Piers L. Cornelissen
University of York, UK

Peter C. Hansen
University of Birmingham, UK

Morten L. Kringelbach
University of Oxford, UK and Aarhus University, Denmark

Kenneth R. Pugh
Haskins Laboratories, USA

OXFORD
UNIVERSITY PRESS

2010

OXFORD
UNIVERSITY PRESS

Oxford University Press, Inc., publishes works that further
Oxford University's objective of excellence
in research, scholarship, and education.

Oxford   New York
Auckland   Cape Town   Dar es Salaam   Hong Kong   Karachi
Kuala Lumpur   Madrid   Melbourne   Mexico City   Nairobi
New Delhi   Shanghai   Taipei   Toronto

With offices in
Argentina   Austria   Brazil   Chile   Czech Republic   France   Greece
Guatemala   Hungary   Italy   Japan   Poland   Portugal   Singapore
South Korea   Switzerland   Thailand   Turkey   Ukraine   Vietnam

Published by Oxford University Press, Inc.
198 Madison Avenue, New York, New York 10016
www.oup.com

Oxford is a registered trademark of Oxford University Press

Library of Congress Cataloging-in-Publication Data

The neural basis of reading / edited by Piers L. Cornelissen . . . [et al.].
p.   cm.
Includes bibliographical references and index.
ISBN 978-0-19-530036-9
1. Reading disability.   2. Neurosciences.   I. Cornelissen, Piers L.
LB1050.5.N456 2010
616.85'53—dc22
2009030431

9 0 7 6 5 4 3 2 1

Printed in China
on acid-free paper

Contents

Contributors

Nicola Brunswick
Department of Psychology,
  Middlesex University,
  London, UK

Laurent Cohen
INSERM, CRICM, UMRS 975,
  Paris, France
AP-HP, Hôpital de la Salpêtrière,
  Department of Neurology,
  Paris, France
Université Paris VI,
  Faculté de Médecine Pitié-Salpêtrière,
  IFR 70,
  Paris, France

Piers Cornelissen
Department of Psychology,
  University of York, UK

Stanislas Dehaene
Collège de France,
  Paris, France
Inserm-CEA Cognitive Neuroimaging Unit,
  NeuroSpin Center,
  Saclay, France

Gina Della Porta
Haskins Laboratories,
  New Haven, CT, USA

Julie Fiez
Learning Research and Development Center,
  University of Pittsburgh,
  PA, USA

Stephen J. Frost
Haskins Laboratories,
  New Haven, CT, USA

Jonathan Grainger
CNRS & University of Provence,
  France

Peter C. Hansen
School of Psychology,
  University of Birmingham, UK

Argye Hillis
Department of Cognitive Science,
  Johns Hopkins University,
  Baltimore, MD, USA

Phillip Holcomb
Tufts University,
    MA, USA

Morten L. Kringelbach
Department of Psychiatry,
    University of Oxford, UK
CFIN,
    Aarhus University, Denmark

Nicole Landi
Haskins Laboratories,
    New Haven, CT, USA
Yale Child Study Center,
    New Haven, CT, USA

Ying Liu
University of Pittsburgh,
    PA, USA

W. Einar Mencl
Haskins Laboratories,
    New Haven, CT, USA

Dina Moore
Haskins Laboratories,
    New Haven, CT, USA
Southern Connecticut State University,
    New Haven, CT, USA

Kimihiro Nakamura
Cognitive Neuroimaging Unit,
    INSERM-CEA, NeuroSpin,
    CEA/SAC/DSV/I2BM,
    Gif/Yvette, France

Jessica Nelson
Learning Research and Development Center,
    University of Pittsburgh,
    PA, USA

Kristen Pammer
The Australian National University,
    Canberra, Australia

Charles Perfetti
Learning Research and
    Development Center,
    University of Pittsburgh,
    PA, USA

Kenneth R. Pugh
Yale University,
    New Haven, CT, USA
Haskins Laboratories,
    New Haven, CT, USA

Jay G. Rueckl
Haskins Laboratories,
    New Haven, CT, USA
University of Connecticut,
    Storrs, CT, USA

Rebecca Sandak
Haskins Laboratories,
    New Haven, CT, USA

John Stein
Department of Physiology,
    Anatomy and Genetics,
    University of Oxford, UK

Li-Hai Tan
Hong Kong University,
    China

Fabien Vinckier
INSERM U562, Service Hospitalier
    Frédéric Joliot, CEA/DSV,
    Orsay, France

Carol Whitney
Department of Linguistics,
    University of Maryland,
    College Park,
    MD, USA

Introduction

Reading is a unique human skill, and modern societies rely extensively on literacy skills. Reading disability can therefore have a profound personal, economic, and social impact. Yet, the scientific understanding of the neural basis of reading in the normal brain is still underdeveloped, and a better understanding of normal reading processes could potentially help individuals with developmental dyslexia (e.g., between 15–30 million people in the United States alone), and those with reading disabilities acquired through injury or disease.

Most people in the developed countries are, however, expert readers, but it is somewhat of an enigma that our brain can achieve expertise in such a recent cultural invention. Given that the first alphabetic scripts were only invented probably around 4,000 to 5,000 years ago, it is unlikely that evolution through natural and/or sexual selection has had time to develop cognitive modules dedicated to reading. Instead, it is likely that through extensive rehearsal, skilled readers develop specialized processes that utilize preexisting neural circuitry for visual object recognition and spoken language. However, details of the neurobiological implementation and nature of the processes that allow visual symbols to be mapped onto the speech sounds and meanings they represent remain somewhat unclear.

Neuroimaging offers a unique window on reading and has so far allowed us to reach profound insights about the neural correlates of reading in health and disease, but it has also raised important questions that have generated much scientific debate. This book is aimed at everyone interested in the reading brain, and it addresses some of the fundamental questions in reading research. These can roughly be divided into three classes according to which methods of investigation have been used: (1) behavioral data and modelling (with direct implications for neuroimaging), (2) neuroimaging, and (3) impaired reading, in which each of these classes obviously overlaps to some extent.

The first part of the book begins with a chapter by Grainger and Holcomb. They describe a functional architecture for word recognition focusing on how orthographic and phonological information cooperate in initial form-based processing of printed word stimuli. Computational mechanisms for orthographic processing and orthography-to-phonology translation are proposed based on behavioral data and computational considerations, as well as on electrophysiological recording of brain activity.

Chapter 2 by Pammer describes a model that suggests that the accurate perception of letters and features is intrinsic to good word recognition skills, and that visual sensitivity may be mediated by a preattentive visual search mechanism from the dorsal pathway. She explores the possibility that systematic exposure to reading and words leads to a functional specialisation of a part of the visual system, and, conversely, that a lack of exposure to reading due to other causes, such as poor phonological decoding for example, may impact on the gradual specialisation/development of the dorsal pathway.

In Chapter 3, Whitney show how the many asymmetries that have been observed in half-field studies of visual word recognition must originate at a prelexical level. In particular, she uses the SERIOL model of orthographic encoding to explain how and why an asymmetry arises in the visual processing of letter strings.

The second and largest section of the book is dedicated to the new insights that neuroimaging has brought to reading. In Chapter 4, Brunswick gives an overview of how neuroimaging has helped our understanding of the functional neuroanatomy of reading. This is further explored in Chapter 5 by Dehaene and Cohen, who review the evidence for a specialized "visual word form area" within the occipitotemporal cortex of literate human adults, and present a speculative model for how invariant visual word recognition might be implemented at the single-neuron level.

Cross-cultural differences in reading systems show how culture can shape the human brain. Chapter 6 by Perfetti, Nelson, Liu, Fiez, and Tan reviews the structure of writing systems, which is critical for understanding why they might matter, and then reviews some of the behavioral evidence for the effects of writing systems on reading. They follow with a review of the comparative (across writing system) neuroscience research and explore how the brain accommodates learning to read in a second writing system.

One example of what script-specific studies can tell us about general principles for reading is provided in Chapter 7 by Nakamura, who first reexamines several different forms of script-specific reading disorders reported in the neuropsychological literature of Japan. Functional brain imaging studies of Japanese have shown interesting intra- and interhemispheric brain differences between the two script systems (kanji and kana), as well as cross-script convergence, which could have important implications for the functional organization of the human mechanism of reading.

Visual word recognition is an important (and probably the best understood) component of reading. In order, however, to fully understand how visual word recognition is achieved, and how it may fail in developmental dyslexia, we need to identify not only the necessary and sufficient complement of nodes that comprise this network—its functional anatomy—but we also need to understand how information flows through this network with time and, indeed, how the structure of the network itself may adapt in both the short and long term. In Chapter 8, Cornelissen, Kringelbach, and Hansen take a historical approach to reviewing recent magnetoencephalography research that elucidates these temporal dynamics, focusing particularly on events within the first 500 ms of a visually presented word, and which should set crucial constraints on models of visual word recognition and reading.

The third and final section of the book considers what happens when reading is impaired. In Chapter 9, Cohen, Vinckier, and Dehaene review how the simple anatomical and functional scheme for the architecture of the reading system fits with multimodal data from patients with various deficits affecting the visual stages of word processing. They outline the proposed architecture for reading, then sketch an overview of peripheral dyslexias, and eventually consider how the model may account for behavioral, anatomical, and functional observations in patients with varieties of alexia.

In Chapter 10, Hillis reviews data from reading (and other lexical tasks) in patients with acute stroke and their implications for specific hypotheses regarding the neural basis of reading. The goal of this methodology is to determine those areas of the brain responsible for impairments of specific components of the reading process, before reorganization or recovery.

Chapter 11, by Pugh and colleagues, first reviews relevant behavioral studies of component processing in fluent reading, with particular emphasis on the role of early (sublexical) phonology; this operation appears to be most compromised in disabled readers. They discuss the current literature on the neurobiology of skilled and disabled reading, with an emphasis on phonological processing, adaptive learning, and complex tradeoffs and interactions. They also consider the crucial next steps (both technical and theoretical) in the emerging cognitive neuroscience of reading and its disorders.

Finally, in Chapter 12, Stein provides an overview of the reading networks and their implications for our understanding of developmental dyslexia. In particular, he focuses on the sublexical letter–sound conversion and the lexical direct visual–semantic routes for reading that rely greatly on accurate visual input. He proposes that the visual magnocellular system is crucial for this processing.

To conclude, we hope that the reader will appreciate that the whole field of reading research is very much a dynamic and growing one. In this book, a selection of scientists with long experience in reading research, each with their own view and voice, seek to provide some seasoned insights and to offer their insights into various conceptual and technical issues that continue to be discussed and developed. We hope this will be helpful and informative to everyone interested in reading.

Piers Cornelissen
Peter Hansen
Morten Kringelbach
Kenneth Pugh

I

BEHAVIORAL DATA

1

Neural Constraints on a Functional Architecture for Word Recognition

Jonathan Grainger and Phillip Holcomb

Visual Word Recognition

Understanding how literate adults can read single words has been one of the major objectives of cognitive psychology since the very beginning of this science. For many adults, reading is an everyday activity. We typically read millions of words in our lifetimes, and mastering this particular skill is often a prerequisite for successful integration into modern society. For cognitive psychologists, the speed and apparent ease with which individual words (either spoken or written) can be identified from around 50,000 or so possibilities in less than half a second has provided a continuing challenge for theorists in this field. In this chapter, we present a blueprint for a model of visual word recognition that has emerged as the best solution, given the multiple (behavioral, neurobiological, and computational) constraints imposed by a half century of research on this topic.

Skilled adult readers basically do two things with printed words. One is to read them silently for meaning, as part of the standard process of reading a text for oneself; and the other is to read them aloud, as a means of communicating the text to others. The process of *silent word reading* minimally requires two types of codes: *orthographic* (knowledge about letter identities and letter position) and *semantic* (knowledge about the meanings of words). The process of *reading aloud* minimally requires an orthographic code and a *phonological/ articulatory* code. Although no more than two critical codes are necessarily

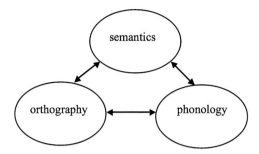

Figure 1.1 A generic architecture for word recognition, based on the "triangle" model of Seidenberg and McClelland (1989). Orthographic, phonological, and semantic codes mutually constrain the interpretation of a given orthographic or phonological input. In certain models, cross-code mappings are mediated by "hidden" units (not shown in the figure).

required for each task, it has become increasingly clear that all three types of codes (orthographic, phonological, and semantic) are automatically activated both in silent reading and reading aloud. These codes interact in the ongoing reading process, hence conjointly influence observed performance. This has led to the following generic architecture for word recognition (Fig. 1.1).

The minimalist architecture described in Figure 1.1 defines two routes to meaning given a visually presented word stimulus: a direct route from orthography to semantics, and an indirect route from orthography to phonology to semantics. This type of dual-route model (to be distinguished from classical dual-route theory; e.g., Coltheart, Rastle, Perry, Langdon, & Ziegler, 2001) will form the basis of the present approach. The architecture to be described and evaluated in this chapter can be seen as an extension of the generic model shown in Figure 1.1. It is an initial attempt to add hierarchical structure into this general framework by minimally distinguishing sublexical (i.e., smaller than words) and lexical (whole-word) levels of processing within each of the orthographic and phonological pathways (see Grainger, 2000, for a discussion of the relevance of this addition). This hierarchy also permits connections between orthography and phonology to be established at different points in each pathway. Although the generic model shown in Figure 1.1 has been useful in describing how orthographic, phonological, and semantic codes mutually constrain the process of learning to read words (e.g., Harm & Seidenberg, 1999), it remains quite limited as a description of the skilled reader. The additional structure that we propose to add to the generic model was motivated primarily on the basis of behavioral data obtained with skilled adult readers. In this chapter, we will show how such an extended architecture does well in accommodating both electrophysiologic and brain imaging results.

Before describing the extended architecture, first let us summarize two critical behavioral results that motivated Grainger and Ferrand's (1994) initial proposal for this extension. The first result concerns the role of phonological information during silent word reading. Critical evidence in favor of rapid, automatic phonological activation during the perception of printed word stimuli has been obtained using the masked priming paradigm. In this paradigm, pattern-masked prime stimuli are presented very briefly immediately prior to target word presentation, such that participants are usually only aware of the target stimulus (and produce a behavioral response to that stimulus according to the task required of them). Typical results show that prime stimuli that are phonologically related to target words (e.g., mayd-MADE) facilitate responding, compared to orthographically related control primes (e.g., mard-MADE). It is important to note that these phonological priming effects have been observed with very brief prime exposures, in conditions in which very little information about prime stimuli is available for conscious report (Ferrand & Grainger, 1992, 1993, 1994; Frost, Ahissar, Gotesman, & Tayeb, 2003; Lukatela & Turvey, 1994; Perfetti & Bell, 1991; Ziegler, Ferrand, Jacobs, Rey, & Grainger, 2000). These results all point to a processing mechanism that takes an orthographic description of the visual stimulus as input and generates the corresponding phonological description as output. This process operates rapidly enough to affect behavioral responses to printed words, and must occur sublexically (between graphemes and phonemes, for example).

The second critical result concerns an observed dissociation in the effects of lexical and sublexical phonology in these masked priming studies. Research using the masked priming paradigm has also shown that the lexical status of primes affects the pattern of orthographic and phonological priming observed (Ferrand & Grainger, 1996; Grainger & Ferrand, 1994). Homophone word primes (e.g., "made" as a prime for the heterographic homophone "maid") can either facilitate or inhibit target processing relative to unrelated word primes, depending on the extent to which participants are forced to rely on orthographic information when generating their response. This can be done when the task is lexical decision (word/nonword classification), by adding pseudo-homophone stimuli among the nonword targets (e.g., *brane* compared to *brone*). A "phonological" response strategy (i.e., respond "word" whenever a whole-word phonological representation is sufficiently activated) would generate too many false-positive errors to pseudohomophone targets. Thus, when a phonological response is possible (i.e., in the absence of pseudohomophone targets), then pseudohomophone primes generate standard facilitatory repetition priming (the prime is phonologically identical to the target). However, when a phonological response strategy is disabled by the inclusion of pseudohomophone targets, then standard inhibitory form priming is observed as the prime word's orthographic representation (e.g., made) competes for identification with the target word's orthographic representation (e.g., maid). However, this is not the case when prime stimuli are pseudohomophones. In this case, facilitatory priming is observed independently of whether pseudohomophone targets are present or not (Ferrand & Grainger, 1996). Grainger and Ferrand (1994) suggested that the pattern observed with homophone primes was evidence for the use of whole-word orthographic representations or whole-word phonological representations to generate a lexical decision. It is the reasoning based on these specific behavioral results that led to the development of the bimodal interactive-activation model (BIAM) to be described later in this chapter.

Variants of the architecture presented in Figure 1.2 have been described in previous work (e.g., Grainger & Ferrand, 1994; Grainger, Diependaele, Ferrand, Spinelli, & Farioli, 2003; Jacobs, Rey, Ziegler, & Grainger, 1998). In this architecture, a printed word stimulus, like all visual stimuli, first activates a set of visual features (V-features), which we assume are largely outside the word recognition system per se. Features in turn activate a sublexical orthographic code (O-units) that likely includes information about

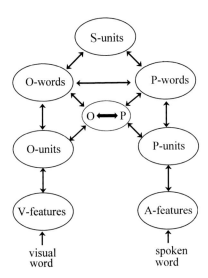

Figure 1.2 Architecture of a bimodal interactive activation model (BIAM) of word recognition in which a feature/sublexical/lexical division is imposed on orthographic (O) and phonological (P) representations. In this architecture, orthography and phonology communicate directly at the level of whole-word representations (O-words, P-words), and also via a sublexical interface (O↔P). Semantic representations (S-units) receive activation from whole-word orthographic and phonological representations (the details of inhibitory within-level and between-level connections are not shown).

letter identities and their relative positions (e.g., Grainger & Whitney, 2004). This early orthographic code then sends activation onto the central interface between orthography and phonology (O⇔P) that allows sublexical orthographic representations to be mapped onto their corresponding phonological representations, and vice versa. Thus a printed word stimulus rapidly activates a set of sublexical phonological representations (which we assume will include phoneme-sized units) that can influence the course of visual word recognition via their interaction with sublexical orthographic representations, or via the activation of whole-word phonological representations. In the following sections we discuss possible mechanisms involved in processing information in the orthographic and phonological pathways of the BIAM, and describe how they interact during word reading. The initial focus will be on orthographic processing, before moving on to discuss the role of phonology and its interaction with orthography during the reading process.

Orthographic Processing

On presentation of a printed word stimulus, an elementary analysis of its visual features is rapidly succeeded by the first stage of processing specific to letter string stimuli. Orthographic processing involves the computation of *letter identity* and *letter position*. There is strong evidence suggesting that each individual letter identity in a string of letters can be processed simultaneously, in parallel. The typical function linking letter-in-string identification accuracy and position-in-string is W-shaped (for central fixations), with highest accuracy for the first and last letters, and for the letter on fixation (Stevens & Grainger, 2003). A combination of two factors accurately describes this function: the decrease in visual acuity with distance from fixation, and the decreased lateral inhibition for outer letters (the first and last letter of a word). Admittedly, there is evidence for a small sequential component to this function (with superior identification for letters at the beginning of the string), but when collapsed over different fixation positions in the string, this sequential component tends to disappear (Stevens & Grainger, 2003).

This parallel independent processing of letter identities is the starting point for a description of orthographic processing. Grainger and van Heuven (2003) used the term "alphabetic array" to describe a bank of letter detectors that would perform such processing (Fig. 1.3.) These letter detectors are location-specific, with location referring to position relative to eye fixation position along a horizontal meridian. Letter detectors signal the presence of a particular configuration of visual features at a given location. Stimuli that are not aligned with the horizontal meridian are assumed to require a transformation of

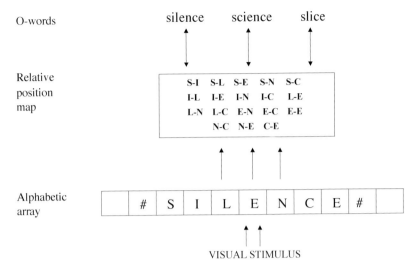

O-words   silence   science   slice

Relative
position
map

S-I	S-L	S-E	S-N	S-C
I-L	I-E	I-N	I-C	L-E
L-N	L-C	E-N	E-C	E-E
	N-C	N-E	C-E	

Alphabetic
array

| | # | S | I | L | E | N | C | E | # | |

VISUAL STIMULUS

Figure 1.3 Functional architecture for orthographic processing. Visual features extracted from a printed word feed activation into a bank of alphabetic character detectors (the alphabetic array). The next level of processing combines information from different processing slots in the alphabetic array to provide a relative position code for letter identities. These relative-position coded letter identities control activation at the level of whole-word orthographic representations (O-words) via bidirectional connections with all units at the relative position level.

retinotopic coordinates onto this special coordinate system for letter strings. This specialized mechanism for processing strings of letters is hypothesized to develop through exposure to print, and its specific organization will, of course, depend on the characteristics of the language of exposure (for simplicity, all examples in the present chapter are valid for languages with horizontal alphabetic orthographies read from left to right).

The alphabetic array codes for the presence of a given letter at a given location relative to eye fixation along the horizontal meridian. It does not say where a given letter is relative to the other letters in the stimulus, since each letter is processed independently of the others. Thus, processing at the level of the alphabetic array is insensitive to the orthographic regularity of letter strings. However, for the purposes of location-invariant word recognition, this location-specific map must be transformed into a "word-centered" code, such that letter identity is tied to within-string position independently of spatial location (cf. Caramazza & Hillis, 1990). This is the next stage in orthographic processing, involving the computation of what we refer to as *relative-position information*. Grainger and van Heuven (2003) summarized the different solutions adopted in currents models of visual word recognition and presented a tentative proposal of their own (see Fig. 1.3).

The central idea in Grainger and van Heuven's (2003) approach is that higher-level sublexical orthographic representations code for the presence of contiguous and noncontiguous letter sequences at lower levels of processing (i.e., the alphabetic array in Fig. 1.3). The principle of coding the relative position of nonadjacent letters is also used in Whitney's (2001) SERIOL model where, for example, the word CART is coded as the following set of bigrams: CA, CR, CT, AR, AT, RT. Thus, bigrams are formed across adjacent and nonadjacent letters in the correct order, the basis of what Grainger and van Heuven (2003) referred to as "open-bigram" coding. The critical difference between Grainger and van Heuven's account and the one developed by Whitney (2001) concerns the mechanism used to activate the appropriate open bigrams. Whitney (2001) described a method for translating acuity-dependent activations of letter representations into a monotonically decreasing gradient. Relative activation at the letter level is then transformed into activation of ordered bigram units. Our approach is more in the tradition of Mozer (1987), using a hierarchical, parallel activation mechanism, as shown in Figure 1.3. Open-bigram units receive activation from the alphabetic array, such that a given letter order, A-B, that is realized at any of the possible combinations of location in the alphabetic array activates the open bigram for that sequence. Thus, in recoding information represented in the alphabetic array, a location-specific map of letter identities is replaced by a location-independent, word-centered, relative-position code.

This model of orthographic processing provides a principled account of two key phenomena that the majority of alternative letter-position coding schemes cannot account for: *relative-position (RP) priming* and *transposed-letter (TL) priming*. RP priming is obtained under two conditions: (1) when a prime is formed by removing some of the target's letters (*subset priming*); and (2) when a prime is formed by inserting some irrelevant letters in the target stimulus (*superset priming*). In the masked priming paradigm, equivalent amounts of priming have been found for "relative-position" primes (e.g., "slene" as prime for the target "silence") and "absolute-position" primes (e.g., "s-len-e"), and these subset priming effects disappear when the order of letters is disrupted (e.g., "snele"; Grainger, Granier, Farioli, van Assche, & van Heuven, 2006; Humphreys, Evett, & Quilan, 1990; Peressotti & Grainger, 1999). In similar testing conditions, recent experimentation has shown that superset primes (e.g., "silmrence" for the target "silence") produce even stronger priming effects than subset primes (Van Assche & Grainger, 2006). TL priming, on the other hand, occurs when primes contain exactly the same letters as targets, but with small changes in letter order (e.g., "gadren" for the target "garden."). The appropriate control in this case is a prime stimulus in which the two transposed letters are replaced by different letters (e.g., "gabsen"). TL priming is robust for adjacent-letter transpositions, as in the preceding example (Perea & Lupker, 2003; Schoonbaert & Grainger, 2004) and nonadjacent transpositions (e.g., "caniso/casino"; Perea & Lupker, 2004). As pointed out by Grainger and Whitney (2004), the type of relative-position coding that is performed by an open-bigram scheme nicely accounts for both TL priming and RP priming. This can be demonstrated by simply calculating the amount of orthographic overlap, in terms of number of shared open bigrams, in the different priming conditions. For example, "gadren" shares all but one of the bigrams in "garden" (the "dr" bigram), whereas "gabsen" shares only six out of a total of 15. This coding scheme captures the critical fact that with subset RP primes, order is important. So, for example, the prime "slene" shares eight bigrams with the word "silence," whereas "snele" shares only five.

Electrophysiological Markers of Orthographic Processing

With respect to the general architecture for word recognition shown in Figure 1.2, the type of orthographic processing described in the preceding section occurs along the pathway from visual features to sublexical ortho-graphic representations onto whole-word orthographic representations. What could be the neural correlates of such processing? We have recently obtained evidence from electrophysiologic recordings, combined with the masked priming technique, that processing along this pathway generates a cascade of event-related potential (ERP) components that start as early as 90 ms post word onset and continue through to as late as 600 ms (Holcomb & Grainger, 2006). These ERP components are the P150, N250, P325, and N400, and in this section we will summarize the ERP research providing evidence for this time-course analysis and attempt to link it to relevant brain imaging research using functional magnetic reso-nance imaging (fMRI) and magnetoencephalography (MEG) (see also Grainger & Holcomb, 2009).

The first of these ERP effects is a very focal ERP positivity that we have labeled the *P150 effect* (Fig. 1.4). The P150 effect has a posterior scalp distribution focused over right occipital scalp sites (Fig. 1.4c) and is larger (i.e., more positive) to target words that are repetitions of the prior prime word, compared to targets that are unrelated to their primes (Fig. 1.4a).[1] We have now seen the P150 in two different studies using word stimuli, one in English (Fig. 1.4a) and one in French (Fig. 1.4b). Moreover, as suggested by the ERPs plotted in Figure 1.4a, the P150 is sensitive to the degree of overlap between the prime and target items, with greater positivities for targets that completely overlap their primes in every letter position and intermediate for targets that overlap in most but not all positions.

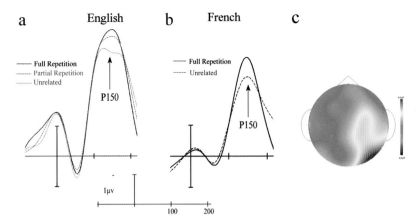

Figure 1.4 Event-related potentials (ERPs) at the right occipital electrode site for English words (a), French words (b), and scalp maps centered on the 150 ms epoch (c).

Several other masked priming studies using other types of stimuli suggest that this earliest of repetition effects is likely due to differential processing at the level of visual features (V-features in Fig 1.1). In one study (Petit, Midgley, Holcomb, & Grainger, 2006) using the same masked repetition priming parameters as the just described word studies, but using single letters as primes and targets, we found that the P150 was significantly larger to mismatches between prime and target letter case, but more so when the features of the lower- and uppercase versions of the letters were physically different compared to when they were physically similar (e.g., A-A compared to a-A vs. C-C compared to c-C; see Fig. 1.5).

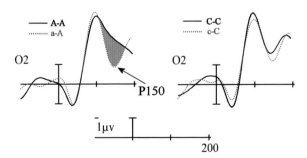

Figure 1.5 Occipital event-related potential (ERP) recordings for target letters in a masked letter priming task.
From Petit, J.P., Midgley, K.J., Holcomb, P.J., & Grainger, J. (2006). On the time-course of letter perception: A masked priming ERP investigation. *Psychonomic Bulletin & Review*, 13, 674–681. Used with permission of the publisher.

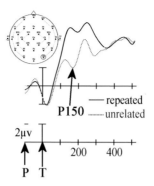

Figure 1.6 Event-related potentials (ERPs) to pictures of objects in a masked picture priming task.
From Eddy, M., Schmid, A., & Holcomb, P.J. (2006). A new approach to tracking the time-course of object perception: Masked repetition priming and event-related brain potentials, *Psychophysiology, 43*, 564–568. Used with permission of Wiley InterScience.

In another line of research using pictures as primes and targets (Eddy, Schmid, & Holcomb, 2006), we have been able to further test the domain specificity of the P150 effect for letters and words in masked priming. In both picture studies, we found an early positivity to pictures of objects that were physically different in the prime and target positions compared to repeated pictures (Fig. 1.6). This positivity had a similar scalp distribution (posterior right) and time course to the P150 that we found for word and letter targets. However, although the effect for letters and words was on the order of .5 to 1.0 μV in amplitude, the effect for pictures was greater than 2 μV. One possibility for this larger effect is that different prime and target pictures match or mismatch on a larger number of visual features than do single letters and five-letter words. Together, the results from these studies suggest that the P150 is sensitive to processing at the level of visual features (V-features in our model in Fig. 1.2) and that this process occurs in the time frame between 90 and 180 ms.

In a recent study (Kiyonaga, Grainger, Midgley, & Holcomb, 2007), we found that, following the P150, a subsequent negative-going wave that starts as early as 110 ms and peaks around 250 ms is also sensitive to masked repetition priming of words, being more negative to targets that are unrelated to the previous masked prime word than to those that are repeats of the prime (Fig. 1.7a). We referred to this as the *N250 effect* (by "effect" we mean the difference between repeated and unrelated target ERPs). Unlike the earlier P150 effect, the N250 has a more widespread scalp distribution, being largest over midline and slightly anterior left hemisphere sites (Fig. 1.7c). Also, unlike the P150, N250-like effects were not observed in our picture or letter studies, but they were apparent when targets were pseudowords (Fig. 1.7b).

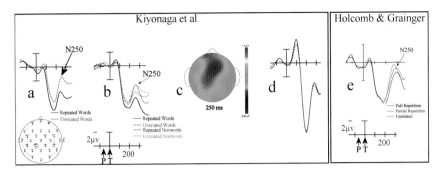

Figure 1.7 Event-related potentials (ERPs) to words in a masked word priming study (Kiyonaga et al., 2007) for visual word targets show an N250 effect (*a*), visual nonword targets show a similar effect (*b*), scalp maps of the N250 effect (*c*), no N250 was observed to auditory targets in cross-modal masked priming (*d*), and N250 effects were observed in a second study (Holcomb & Grainger, 2006) to both fully repeated words and partial word repetitions (*e*).

Finally, although the N250 was modulated when both primes and targets were visual letter strings, no such modulation was present when primes were visual and targets were auditory words (Fig. 1.7d).

In a second study (Holcomb & Grainger, 2006), the N250 effect also proved to be sensitive to the degree of prime-target orthographic overlap, being somewhat larger for targets that overlap their primes by all but one letter compared to targets that completely overlap with their primes (Fig. 1.7e). One interpretation consistent with this pattern of results is that the N250 is sensitive to processing at the interface between sublexical and whole-word representations (O-units and O-words on the visual side of the BIAM), where, because of resemblance to real-word neighbors, partial repetitions (e.g., teble-TABLE) and pseudoword repetitions benefit from orthographic overlap between prime and target.

In the second of these studies (Holcomb & Grainger, 2006), we also for the first time reported evidence for a second component that was sensitive to our masked priming manipulation. We referred to this component as the P325 effect, and as can be seen in Figure 1.8a, it intervened between the N250 and the later N400 effects, peaking near 350 ms. Evidence that this is actually a component independent from the surrounding negativities can be seen in Figure 1.8a. Although the N250 and N400 produced similar *graded* responses to the three levels of priming (most negative to Unrelated, intermediate to Partial Repetition, and least negative to Full Repetition), the P325 was more positive only in the Full Repetition condition (the Partial Repetition and Unrelated did not differ). This pattern of results is consistent with the hypothesis that the P325 effect is sensitive to processing within whole-word representations (O-words), being modulated only when prime and target words

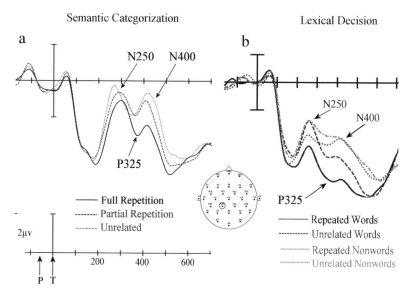

Semantic Categorization

Lexical Decision

Figure 1.8 Event-related potentials (ERPs) to visual targets in a masked priming paradigm when the task was semantic categorization (*a*) and lexical decision (*b*).

completely overlap. Further support for this hypothesis can also be seen in Figure 1.9b, where we have replotted the ERPs from Figure 1.7c, contrasting repetition effects for words and pseudowords on a longer time scale (through 700 ms). In this figure, the positivity we call the P325 effect can be clearly seen intervening between the N250 and N400. Moreover, although it is larger

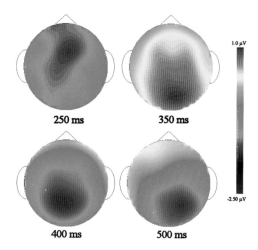

Figure 1.9 Scalp voltage maps for visual masked priming repetition effects in four different 50 ms time epochs.

for repeated compared to unrelated words, it does not differentiate repeated compared to unrelated pseudowords. This makes sense, given that pseudowords are not represented lexically and therefore should not produce repetition effects within whole-word representations themselves.

Following the N250 and P325 effects, we have also seen evidence for the modulation of the N400 component in our masked repetition priming experiments. In the two studies just mentioned (Kiyonaga et al., 2006; Holcomb & Grainger, 2006), N400s were larger to words that were unrelated to their primes (Fig. 1.8a,b), although this was not the case for pseudoword targets (Fig. 1.8b). As in our previous work using single-word paradigms and supraliminal priming (e.g., Holcomb, O'Rourke & Grainger, 2002; Holcomb, Anderson, & Grainger, 2005) we interpret this pattern of findings as being consistent with N400 repetition priming, reflecting interactions between levels of representation for whole words and concepts (the so-called "form-meaning interface"). In our view, the N400 reflects the amount of effort involved in forming links between these levels, with larger N400 effects indicating that more effort was involved.

Evidence for at least a partial independence of this array of components comes from their different patterns of scalp distribution. As seen in the voltage maps in Figure 1.9 (derived from subtracting Full Repetition ERPs from Unrelated ERPs), the ERPs in the time periods of all three components (N250, P325 and N400) have relatively widespread distributions across the scalp. Although the N250 tended to have a more frontal focus, the early phase of the N400 had a posterior and *left* lateralized focus, whereas the later phase of the N400 had an even more posterior and *right* lateralized focus. The P325 had, on the other hand, an even more posterior (occipital) midline focus.

The data presented thus far suggest that ERPs recorded in the masked repetition priming paradigm produce a series of components that are sensitive to the sequence of overlapping processes outlined in the BIAM. Figure 1.10 illustrates one possible scheme for how these early ERP effects might map onto the printed word side of the BIAM: Above a diagram of the BIAM is plotted an ERP difference wave that contrasts unrelated and repeated words. The time frame of each component is indicated by the dashed lines connecting the ERP wave to hypothesized underlying processes in the model. Starting with the P150, data presented above are consistent with this component, reflecting some aspect of the process whereby visual features are mapped onto abstract representations relevant to a specific domain of processing—in this case, letters and groups of letters. That the P150 reflects a domain-nonspecific process or family of processes is supported by our having found P150 effects for letters, letter strings, and pictures of objects. Following the P150 is the N250, which we have proposed reflects the output of a visual word-specific process—one whereby orthographic information is mapped

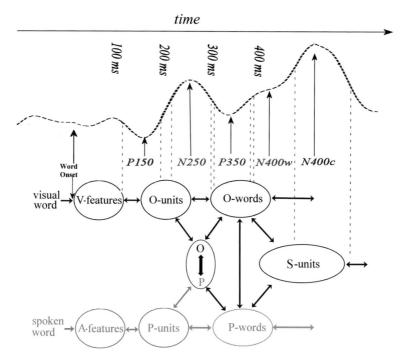

Figure 1.10 Event-related potential (ERP) masked repetition priming effects mapped onto the bimodal interactive activation model (note that we have turned the model on its side to better accommodate the temporal correspondence between the model and the ERP effects).

onto whole-word representations. Evidence for the domain-specificity of the N250 comes from the fact that we did not see evidence of such a component for spoken words or for pictures in our masked priming studies (described earlier). After the N250 comes the P325 effect, which we tentatively have suggested reflects processing within the lexical system itself (O-words). Finally, following the P325, come the two subcomponents of the N400. The N400w ("w" for word), we have suggested, reflects interactions between word- and concept-level processes (O-word to S-unit). We have further proposed that concept-to-concept processing (which would support higher-level sentence and discourse processing) is reflected in a later phase of the N400 (N400c, "c" for concept).

Where might the neural generators for these different ERP components be located? Although it is difficult to localize ERP effects with any certainty (Nunez, 1990), it is nevertheless tempting to speculate that, given its focal posterior distribution, the P150 might reflect neural activity in or around secondary visual areas (e.g., V2), which are know from unit work in monkeys to be important in early visual feature processing. This activity might also be similar to activity in the MEG signal that Cornelissen, Tarkiainen, Helenius, and Salmelin (2003) referred to as a Type I response. Second, the pattern of effects on the N250 suggest that it may reflect activity in the visual word form area (VWFA), a left fusiform gyrus region thought by some to house the neural mechanisms involved in orthographic processing of printed words (Cohen, Dehaene, Naccache, Lehericy, Dehaene-Lambertz, Henaff, & Michel, 2000; Dehaene, Le Clec'H, Poline, Le Bihan, & Cohen, 2002; McCandliss, Cohen, & Dehaene, 2003; Nobre, Allison, & McCarthy, 1994). Research using MEG has estimated that the VWFA becomes significantly active after about 200 ms post stimulus onset (Pammer, Hansen, Kringelbach, Holliday, Barnes, Hillebrand, Singh, & Cornelissen, 2004). This is the same time frame as the N250. Furthermore, there is growing evidence that the VWFA can be subdivided into a hierarchically organized network of increasingly abstract orthographic representations (Dehaene, Jobert, Naccache, Ciuciu, Poline, Le Bihan, & Cohen, 2004; Nobre et al., 1994; Tagamets, Novick, Chalmers, & Friedman, 2000). Our word-specific ERP components could tentatively be mapped onto the anterior-posterior subdivision of the VWFA highlighted in this work. The neural generators of our earliest word-specific repetition effects (those on the rising edge of the N250 between 100 to 200 ms), would be located in most posterior regions (possibly corresponding to Cornelissen and colleagues' [2003] Type II response), and our mid-latency effects (those encompassing the peak and trailing edge of the N250 between 200 and 300 ms) and later repetition effects (those associated with the P325 and N400w epoch between 300 and 450 ms) being located in progressively more anterior regions. There is some evidence from intracranial ERP studies that one source of the N400 is located along this pathway in medial anterior temporal areas (McCarthy, Nobre, Bentin, & Spencer, 1995).

Phonological Processing

The evidence summarized thus far is suggestive of a fast route from orthography to semantics that implements an approximate, fairly coarse-grained orthographic code. In the BIAM, this fast orthographic route is supplemented by a phonological route that requires a more fine-grained orthographic code as input. Given the sequential structure of spoken language (unlike the visual signal, the auditory signal unfolds over time), it seems likely that this phonological route would at least partially involve sequential processing mechanisms. This contrasts with the strictly parallel nature of processing in the orthographic route (cf. Coltheart and colleagues' [2003] dual-route model). It is also hypothesized that the distinction between vowels and consonants plays an important role in mapping from orthography to phonology along this pathway. Vowels provide critical information about syllabic structure, and a large amount of evidence suggests that syllabic representations are involved in both auditory and visual word recognition (e.g., Mehler, Dommergues, Frauenfelder, & Segui, 1981; Carreiras, Alvarez, & de Vega, 1993).

As noted at the beginning of this chapter, the BIAM was initially designed to account for rapid, automatic involvement of phonological information during visual word recognition (Ferrand & Grainger, 1992, 1993, 1994; Frost et al., 2003; Perfetti & Bell, 1991; Ziegler et al., 2000). According to the time-course analyses provided by Ferrand and Grainger (1993) and Ziegler and colleagues (2000), phonological code activation lags about 20–30 ms behind orthographic code activation. This provides strong evidence against two popular alternative architectures for word recognition. First, dual-route cascade (DRC) theory (Coltheart et al., 2001) cannot capture fast phonological influences on visual word recognition because sublexical phonology only influences visual word recognition very indirectly, via output phonology and the phonological output lexicon. Second, strong phonological theories (e.g., Frost, 1998), according to which silent reading is always phonologically mediated, are invalidated by any evidence for direct orthographic access to meaning.

The architecture of the BIAM is particularly well-suited for accommodating the time course of orthographic and phonological priming found by Ferrand and Grainger (1993). Orthographic overlap across prime and target (i.e., primes share letters with targets) has its influence along the orthographic pathway in Figure 1.2 (and described in Figure 1.3). Thus, assuming response read-out from whole-word orthographic representations in a standard visual lexical decision task or perceptual identification task (Grainger & Jacobs, 1996), then any preactivation of representations involved in orthographic processing will have the earliest influence on response times in such tasks. However, as soon as letter-level information is available, the process of mapping sublexical orthography onto sublexical phonology begins. Thus, phonological representations are rapidly activated following onset of a visually presented word and can modify the activation of whole-word orthographic representations either via direct connections with the sublexical orthography–phonology interface, or indirectly via the activation of whole-word phonological representations. The architecture of the BIAM therefore correctly predicts fast phonological priming effects that lag only slightly behind orthographic effects. Finally, as can be seen in Figure 1.11. Ferrand and Grainger found that both types of priming varied nonmonotonically as a function of prime exposure duration, with a clear maximum followed by a decline. The BIAM accounts for this in terms of the time necessary for within-level inhibition to develop across whole-word orthographic and phonological representations.

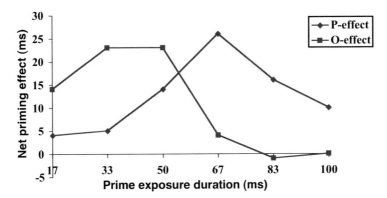

Figure 1.11 Time course of orthographic and phonological priming reported by Ferrand and Grainger (1993). Net priming effects for orthographically related primes are significant at 33 ms prime exposures and no longer significant at 67 ms exposures at about the same time as phonological priming emerges.

In recent research (Grainger, Kiyonaga, & Holcomb, 2006), we have found clear evidence in the ERP signal for early influences of phonology in visual word recognition. In this study, participants monitored target words for animal names, and critical (nonanimal) trials were primed by briefly presented (50 ms) pattern-masked pseudowords that varied in terms of their phonological overlap with target words but were matched for orthographic overlap (e.g., bakon-BACON vs. bafon-BACON). As shown in Figure 1.12,

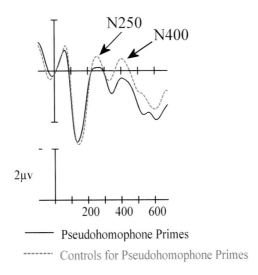

Figure 1.12 Event-related potentials (ERPs) generated by target words following masked presentation of pseuodhomophone primes (e.g., brane–BRAIN) versus orthographic control primes (e.g., brant–BRAIN).

phonological priming had its earliest influence starting around 225 ms post target onset, and caused a significant reduction in both N250 and N400 amplitudes compared to their orthographic controls. In a separate experiment comparing orthographically related primes (e.g., teble-TABLE) to unrelated primes, the earliest influence on ERPs generated by target words appeared at around 200 ms post target onset (see Fig. 1.8a; also, Holcomb & Grainger, 2006). Thus, if we accept that the "teble-table" priming is driven mainly by orthographic overlap, then we have an observed lag between orthographic and phonological priming effects in ERPs that fits remarkably well with Ferrand and Grainger's behavioral research.

Having established a relatively early and quite robust contribution of phonological information during visual word recognition, we can now turn to examine the precise nature of this phonological code and the manner in which it is derived from orthographic information. In attempting to answer these questions, we should keep in mind the critical distinction between the phonological code used to support silent word reading (*phonology for meaning*), and the phonological code used to generate an articulatory output during the process of reading aloud (*phonology for articulation*). These are not necessarily the same. The BIAM makes one clear prediction about the nature of phonological representations subtending silent reading: they should be the same, or at least derived from, the phonological representations that allow an acoustic signal to be mapped onto meaning during spoken word recognition. This follows from the simple fact that the process of learning to read involves (at least partly) the association of newly learned letters and letter clusters with the previously learned sounds of words (Ziegler & Goswami, 2005). So, what essence of the sequential nature of spoken language remains in the phonological code used during silent reading?

Carreiras, Ferrand, Grainger, and Perea (2005) used bisyllabic words to examine whether phonology is computed sequentially (from beginning to end) or in parallel (simultaneously across the whole word). The experiments used the masked priming technique in which target stimuli (to which participants respond) are preceded by briefly presented prime stimuli that participants are typically unaware of. They varied the phonological relationship between primes and targets. Bisyllabic target words were primed by pseudowords that shared either the first or the second phonological syllable of the target. In one of the experiments the participants had to decide whether the target stimulus was a word or a nonword (lexical decision), while in the other experiment they had to read the stimuli aloud as rapidly as possible (naming). Overlap of the first syllable only—not the second—produced facilitation in both the lexical decision and the naming tasks. These findings suggest that, for polysyllabic words, phonological codes are computed sequentially during silent reading and reading aloud.

The results of Carreiras and coworkers (2005) show that the type of phonological code used to support visual word recognition shares at least one characteristic with the phonological code used during spoken language processing—its sequential nature. Their results suggest that during the process of mapping orthography onto phonology, word beginnings are processed more rapidly than word endings. This result also suggests some commonalities in the phonological code used during silent reading and the code used during reading aloud, since both the lexical decision (silent reading) and naming (reading aloud) tasks showed priming from initial syllable overlap only. However, these two tasks were differentially sensitive to another type of sequential effect related to sublexical phonology. Primes that shared only their first letter/phoneme with target words facilitated performance relative to completely unrelated primes, but only in the naming task. This result corresponds to the *onset priming* effect found in previous masked priming studies (Forster & Davis, 1991; Grainger & Ferrand, 1996; Kinoshita, 2003; Schiller, 2004). Given that onset priming effects are only found in the naming task and depend on phonological and not orthographic overlap (e.g., *kos-car* just as effective as *cos-car*: see Kinoshita, 2003, for a review of this evidence), we argue that they reflect the rapid conversion of orthographic information into a phonological-articulatory code. Onset priming effects are observed with very brief prime exposure durations, shorter than those necessary to obtain priming from pseudohomophone priming (Grainger & Ferrand, 1996). This suggests that, by the time a sublexical phonological code has been generated at the sublexical O–P interface, and before that information has been sent on to influence processing at the level of whole-word representations, an articulatory code has also been generated. This could arise by letter-level activity being sent directly to units that code for articulatory output without having to first compute a more abstract phonological code (cf., Kinoshita, 2003).

A possible MEG correlate of this hypothesized rapid conversion of orthographic information into an articulatory code can be found in the work of Pammer and colleagues (2004). According to our account of orthographic processing (Fig. 1.3) and our general architecture for word recognition (Fig. 1.2), the earliest letter-string–specific activation should correspond to processing in the alphabetic array. Pammer and colleagues found such activation arising on average at about 150 ms post target onset in the left posterior fusiform gyrus, and therefore temporally and spatially coincident with the Type II response of Cornelissen and coworkers (2003), which we associate with processing at the level of independent letter detectors (alphabetic array). In our model, processing in the alphabetic array then feeds activation on to higher levels of orthographic processing and the central interface for orthography and phonology. Most important, to account for the behavioral evidence showing onset effects at brief prime exposures in the naming task, we hypothesized that activity in letter detectors in the alphabetic array is also directly sent to the representations involved in computing a set of articulatory motor commands (Grainger & Ferrand, 1996). This could well be occurring in the inferior frontal gyrus (IFG), the region where Pammer and colleagues found activity only slightly later (about 75 ms) than in the posterior fusiform, and prior to activation of more anterior fusiform regions (including the VWFA). Several studies have found greater activation of the left IFG during pseudoword reading, as opposed to word reading, and interpreted this as evidence for sublexical conversion of orthographic information into a phono-logical output code (e.g., Fiebach, Friederici, Müller, & von Cramon, 2002; Fiez & Petersen, 1998; Hagoort, Indefrey, Brown, Herzog, & Steiz, 1999; Pugh et al., 1996). This is consistent with the multiple-route architecture of our model, according to which whole-word phonological representations should dominate when reading aloud words (particularly high frequency words) compared to pseudowords. It is with the latter type of stimuli (and low frequency words) that overt pronunciation will be supported most by a sublexical conversion process. However, unlike previous interpretations of IFG activation, we suggest that this is not the only part of the brain involved in the sublexical conversion of orthography to phonology. We hypothesize that an equally important conversion process uses connections between the left fusiform region and other inferior temporal and lateral temporal regions (to be discussed in the following section) as one of the pathways from print to meaning.

Cross-modal Interactions

One critical aspect of the architecture described in Figure 1.2 is the predicted occurrence of strong cross-modal interactions during word recognition. According to this highly interactive architecture, information related to modalities other than that used for stimulus presentation (i.e., the auditory modality for a printed word) should rapidly influence stimulus processing. In the preceding sections, we presented evidence for the involvement of pho-nological variables during visual word recognition. This finding is perhaps not that surprising given the fact that the process of learning to read requires the deliberate use of phonologicalal information (children are taught to associate letters and letter clusters with their corresponding sounds). However, the BIAM also makes the less obvious prediction that spoken word recognition should be influenced by the orthographic characteristics of word stimuli. Is this the case?

Early research had shown orthographic influences on adult performance when judging if two words rhymed, such that orthographically different rhymes (e.g., RYE-TIE) were more difficult to match than orthographically identical rhymes (Seidenberg & Tanenhaus, 1979). Similarly, priming across two auditorily presented words was only found to be robust when the phonological overlap also involved orthographic overlap (Jakimik, Cole, & Rudnicky, 1985; see also Slowiaczek, Soltano, Wieting, & Bishop, 2003). Furthermore, Ziegler and Ferrand (1998) have shown that auditory lexical decision responses were longer to words with rhymes that can be spelled in different ways (e.g., in French, the phonological rhyme /o/ in the target word "dos" can be written os, ot, aux, eau, eaux) compared to words with rhymes having a unique spelling. Ventura, Morais, Pattamadilok, and Kolinsky (2004) replicated and extended this effect of sound-to-spelling consistency in spoken word recognition in Portuguese. In a similar line of investigation, Ziegler, Muneaux, and Grainger (2003) have shown that spoken word recognition is affected by the number of orthographic neighbors of target words, while controlling for their phonological neighborhood.

More direct demonstrations of cross-modal interactions in word recognition have been obtained recently using masked cross-modal priming. In this paradigm, a briefly presented, pattern-masked visual prime stimulus is immediately followed by an auditory target word. Subjects typically perform a lexical decision on target stimuli (Grainger et al., 2003; Kouider & Dupoux, 2001). In the first published application of the cross-modal version of the paradigm, Kouider and Dupoux (2001) found significant effects of masked visual primes on the recognition of auditorily presented target words with prime durations of 64 ms or longer. Grainger and colleagues (2003) extended this observation to even shorter prime durations, finding significant effects of visual primes on auditory target processing at prime exposure durations of only 50 ms. In the Grainger-led study, cross-modal effects of pseudohomophone primes (e.g., "brane" as a prime for "brain") emerged with longer exposure durations (67 ms), equivalent to the duration necessary for obtaining within-modality (visual-visual) pseudohomophone priming.

The predictions of the BIAM are best followed using the diagram in Figure 1.13, which represents the state of activation in the network after an initial feedforward flow of information and before any feedback has occurred. The amount of feedforward information flow is determined by prime duration (plus factors such as stimulus luminance and type of masking). The bimodal model successfully accounts for the key data patterns obtained so far with masked cross-modal priming:

- Within-modality repetition priming arises with shorter prime durations than across-modality repetition priming (Kouider & Dupoux, 2001).

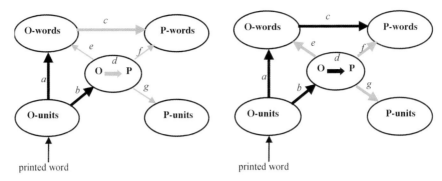

Figure 1.13 Hypothesized state of activation in the bimodal interactive-activation network (BIAM) following the brief visual presentation of a printed word followed by backward masking, with prime exposure duration increasing from the left-hand to the right-hand panel. The darkness and thickness of lines reflects the amount of activation flow, with strongest activation between O-units and O-words (*a*) and between O-units and the O-P sublexical interface (*b*). Intermediate levels of activation flow are hypothesized to arise between O-words and P-words (*c*), and at the sublexical O-P interface (*d*).

This is because, on presentation of a visual prime stimulus, whole-word orthographic representations are activated more rapidly (pathway "a" in Figure 1.13) than whole-word phonological representations (pathway "a-c").

- Across-modality repetition priming arises with shorter prime durations than across-modality pseudohomophone priming (Grainger et al., 2003). This is because pseudohomophones mostly activate whole-word phonological representations via the sublexical pathway (pathway "b-d-f"), compared to across-modality repetition priming, which is mostly subserved by the lexical route (pathway "a-c").
- Across-modality pseudohomophone priming emerges at the same prime exposures (67 ms) as are necessary to obtain within-modality pseudohomophone priming (Grainger et al., 2003); this is because within-modality and across-modality pseudohomophone priming are both mediated by the sublexical interface between orthography and phonology (pathways "b-d-e", "b-d-f").

In a recent study, we examined masked cross-modal priming using ERP recordings to visual and auditory target words and 50 and 67 ms prime exposures (Kiyonaga et al., 2006). As predicted by the bimodal architecture, we found that at the shorter (50 ms) prime exposures, repetition priming effects on ERPs arose earlier and were greater in amplitude when targets were in the same (visual) modality as primes. However, with slightly longer prime durations (67 ms), the effect of repetition priming on N400 amplitude was just as strong for auditory (across-modality) as for visual (within-modality) targets. The within-modality repetition effect had apparently already asymptoted at the shorter prime duration, whereas the cross-modal effect was evidently lagging behind the within-modality effect by a small amount of time. Figure 1.14 shows the change in cross-modal priming from 50 ms to 67 ms prime durations in the Kiyonaga study. This is exactly what one would predict on the basis of the time-course of information flow depicted in Figure 1.13. With sufficiently short prime durations (i.e., 50 ms in the testing condition of the Kiyonaga et al. study), then feedforward information flow from the prime stimulus has most of its influence in the orthographic pathway ("a", as shown in the left-hand figure), and it is only with a longer prime duration that feedforward activation from a visual prime stimulus can significantly influence activation in whole-word phonological representations (pathways "a-c" and "b-d-f", as shown in the right-hand figure). Furthermore, the BIAM correctly predicts that cross-modal transfer is dominated by lexical-level pathways, since we found very little evidence for any early (pre-N400) effects of cross-modal repetition even at the 67 ms prime duration.

Not surprisingly, very strong modulations of ERP amplitude are observed in cross-modal priming with supraliminal prime exposures (Anderson & Holcomb, 1995; Holcomb, et al., 2005). More important, however, is the fact that we observed a strong asymmetry in the size of cross-modal priming effects as a function of the direction of the switch (Holcomb et al., 2005). Visual primes combined with auditory targets were much more effective in

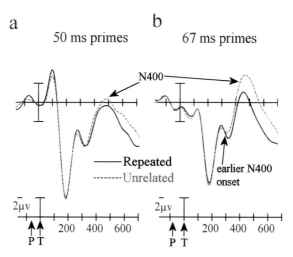

Figure 1.14 Across-modality (visual prime–auditory target) repetition priming at 50 ms and 67 ms prime durations in the study of Kiyonaga et al. (2007).

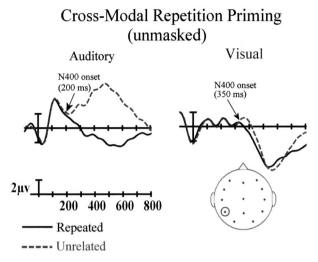

Figure 1.15 Supraliminal cross-modal repetition priming results of Holcomb et al. (2005, 200 ms SOA) showing asymmetry of effects as a function of modality (visual primes–auditory targets on the left, auditory primes–visual targets on the right).

reducing N400 amplitude during target word processing than were auditory primes combined with visual targets (Fig. 1.15).

This observed asymmetry in cross-modal priming effects might well reflect an asymmetry in the strength of connections linking orthography and phonology on the one hand, and phonology with orthography on the other. The process of learning to read requires the explicit association of newly learned orthographic representations with previously learned phonological representations, thus generating strong connections from orthography to phonology. These strong connections would allow the rapid generation of a phonological representation from the visual prime that would be activated during the processing of auditory targets, hence generating the observed priming effect. On the other hand, the association between phonology and orthography is learned explicitly for the purpose of producing written language, and these associations need not directly influence the perception of visually presented words. This can explain why the auditory-visual cross-modal priming effect shown in Figure 1.15 is much smaller than the corresponding visual-auditory effect. Furthermore, phonological representations that are rapidly activated by an auditory prime may have dissipated in activation level by the time equivalent representations are activated during the processing of visual targets.

What brain regions might be involved in such cross-modal interactions in word recognition? Cohen, Jobert, Le Bihan, and Dehane (2004) presented fMRI evidence for a brain region involved in the type of multimodal processing that is described in the BIAM. Using within- and across-modality repetition priming, they observed an area of lateral inferotemporal cortex that responded strongly to both visually and auditorily presented words. This region is located slightly anterior to the VWFA, which fits with our proposal of a processing hierarchy that takes orthographic information as input and connects it to the appropriate phonological code. It also fits with our ERP results showing that whole-word pathways dominate the earliest phases of cross-modal (visual-auditory) transfer.

Finally, concerning possible neural correlates of the type of sublexical and lexical representations of phonology hypothesized in the BIAM, the evidence at present points to lateral temporal cortex, and more precisely the superior temporal gyrus, as a possible locus for whole-word phonological representations involved in both spoken word recognition (e.g., Binder et al., 2000; Booth et al., 2002; Cohen et al., 2004; Howard et al., 1992) and possibly also visual word recognition (Sekiguchi, Koyama, & Kakigi, 2004). Sekiguchi and associates found that visually presented heterographic homophones (hair-hare) influenced cortical magnetic responses after 300 ms post target onset, and located the source to be in the superior temporal cortex. The lack of an earlier effect of homophone status in the study by Sekiguchi and associates fits with the ERP findings of Ziegler, Benraïs, and Besson (1997), and also fits with our suggestion that lexical-level processing is only starting to be fully established at around 300 ms post stimulus onset. As for possible loci of the sublexical conversion of orthography to phonology on the route to word meaning (the central O–P interface in our model), Cohen and colleagues (2004, see also Booth et al., 2002) found that a part of lateral inferior temporal cortex was always strongly activated by both visually and auditorily presented words. Furthermore, Booth and colleagues (2002) presented evidence that the supramarginal gyrus and the angular gyrus are involved in the conversion of orthography to phonology and vice versa. However, since word stimuli were used in these experiments, the multimodal regions that were isolated could correspond to lexical-level interactions between modalities. Further research could attempt to isolate multimodal regions specific to word stimuli, and other regions possibly specific to pseudoword stimuli.

Conclusion

In this chapter, we presented a functional architecture for word recognition constrained mainly by behavioral results and computational considerations. The architecture describes the key processing stages involved in reading isolated words, and how these processing stages are connected to the system designed to recognize spoken words during auditory language processing. The highly interactive nature of the architecture accounts for the increasing evidence in favor of cross-modal influences on both visual and auditory word recognition. Furthermore, behavioral evidence has allowed us to start to specify the mechanisms involved in each of the model's component processes, most notably the orthographic pathway and the sublexical conversion of spelling to sound. The model makes a clear distinction between an approximate orthographic code computed in parallel and used to rapidly access the meaning of words, and a more precise orthographic code with some sequential structure used to activate phonology. A further distinction is made between the type of phonological code that supports silent reading (for meaning) and reading aloud (articulation). Recent ERPs and brain imaging results were used as further constraints for specifying the precise time course of processing in the model, and as a further test of the basic assumptions of the model.

Author Note

The chapter was written while the first author was on sabbatical leave at Tufts University in 2005. The authors thank all the participants in the graduate seminar on the "Cognitive Neuroscience of Recognition" for all the very helpful discussions of this work. This research was supported by NICHD grants HD025889 and HD043251.

Note

1. Deciding whether a particular ERP effect is due to modulation of underlying negative-going or positive-going EEG activity is frequently difficult and is always, to some degree, arbitrary. In this regard, we could have just as easily referred to the effect illustrated in Figure 1.4a as an enhancement of the N1 because it clearly overlaps the exogenous N1. However, we have chosen to refer to this as a positive-going effect for two reasons. First, we think it likely that the mismatching unrelated targets are driving the differences between the unrelated and repeated ERPs in this epoch. Second, this nomenclature is also consistent with the naming scheme used for the N250 and N400, where it is the relative polarity of the ERP to the unrelated condition that is used to describe the polarity of the effect. Note however that we will violate this scheme when we introduce the P325 effect (referred to as the P325 in our later work, e.g., Grainger & Holcomb, 2009). Here we will argue that it is the repeated targets that drive the effect.

References

Anderson, J.E. & Holcomb, P.J. (1995). Auditory and visual semantic priming using different stimulus onset asynchronies: An event-related brain potential study. *Psychophysiology, 32,* 177–190.

Binder, J.R., Frost, J.A., Hammeke, T.A., Bellgowan, P.S.F., Springer, J.A., Kaufman, J.N., & Possing, E.T. (2000). Human temporal lobe activation by speech and nonspeech sounds. *Cerebral Cortex, 10*, 512–528.

Booth, J.R., Burman, D.D., Meyer, J.R., Gitelman, D.R., Parrish, T.B., & Mesulman, M.M. (2002). Functional anatomy of intra- and cross-modal lexical tasks. *NeuroImage, 16*, 7–22.

Caramazza, A. & Hillis, AE (1990). Spatial representation of words in the brain implied by studies of a unilateral neglect patient. *Nature, 346*, 267–269.

Carreiras, M., Alvarez, C.J., & de Vega, M. (1993). Syllable frequency and visual word recognition in Spanish. *Journal of Memory and Language, 32*, 766–780.

Carreiras, M., Ferrand, L., Grainger, J., & Perea, M. (2005). Sequential effects of masked phonological priming. *Psychological Science, 16*, 585–589.

Cohen, L., Dehaene, S., Naccache, L., Lehericy, S., Dehaene-Lambertz, G., Henaff, M., & Michel, F. (2000). The visual word form area: Spatial and temporal characterization of an initial stage of reading in normal subjects and posterior split-brain patients. *Brain, 123*, 291–307.

Cohen, L., Jobert, A., Le Bihan, D., & Dehaene, S. (2004). Distinct unimodal and multi-modal regions for word processing in the left temporal cortex. *Neuroimage, 23*, 1256–1270.

Coltheart, M., Rastle, K., Perry, C., Langdon, R., & Ziegler, J. C. (2001). DRC: A dual route cascaded model of visual word recognition and reading aloud. *Psychological Review, 108*, 204–256.

Cornelissen, P., Tarkiainen, A., Helenius, P., & Salmelin, R. (2003). Cortical effects of shifting letter position in letter strings of varying length. *Journal of Cognitive Neuroscience, 15*, 731–746.

Dehaene, S., Le Clec'H, G., Poline, J.B., Le Bihan, D., & Cohen, L. (2002). The visual word form area: A prelexical representation of visual words in the fusiform gyrus. *NeuroReport, 13*, 321–325.

Dehaene, S., Jobert, A., Naccache, L., Ciuciu, P., Poline, J.-B., Le Bihan, D., & Cohen, L. (2004). Letter binding and invariant recognition of masked words: Behavioral and neuroimaging evidence. *Psychological Science, 15*, 307–313.

Eddy, M., Schmid, A., & Holcomb, P.J. (2006). A new approach to tracking the time-course of object perception: Masked repetition priming and event-related brain potentials, *Psychophysiology, 43*, 564–568.

Ferrand, L. & Grainger, J. (1992). Phonology and orthography in visual word recognition: Evidence from masked nonword priming. *Quarterly Journal of Experimental Psychology, 45A*, 353–372.

Ferrand, L. & Grainger, J. (1993). The time-course of phonological and orthographic code activation in the early phases of visual word recognition. *Bulletin of the Psychonomic Society, 31*, 119–122.

Ferrand, L. & Grainger, J. (1994). Effects of orthography are independent of phonology in masked form priming. *Quarterly Journal of Experimental Psychology, 47A*, 365–382.

Ferrand, L. & Grainger, J. (1996). List context effects on masked phonological priming in the lexical decision task. *Psychonomic Bulletin and Review, 3*, 515–519.

Fiebach, C.J., Friederici, A.D., Müller, K., & von Cramon, D.Y (2002). fMRI evidence for dual routes to the mental lexicon in visual word recognition. *Journal of Cognitive Neuroscience, 14*, 11–23.

Fiez, J.A., & Petersen, S.E. (1998). Neuroimaging studies of word reading. *Proceedings of the National Academy of Sciences, USA, 95*, 914–921.

Forster, K.I. & Davis, C. (1991). The density constraint on form-priming in the naming task: Interference effects from a masked prime. *Journal of Memory and Language, 10,* 1–25.

Frost, R. (1998). Toward a strong phonological theory of visual word recognition: True issues and false trails. *Psychological Bulletin, 123,* 71–99.

Frost, R., Ahissar, M. Gotesman, R., & Tayeb, S. (2003). Are phonological effects fragile? The effect of luminance and exposure duration on form priming and phonological priming. *Journal of Memory and Language, 48,* 346–378.

Grainger, J. (2000). From print to meaning via words? In A. Kennedy, R. Radach, D. Heller, & J. Pynte (Eds.). *Reading As a Perceptual Process.* Oxford: Elsevier.

Grainger, J., & Ferrand, L. (1994). Phonology and orthography in visual word recognition: Effects of masked homophone primes. *Journal of Memory and Language, 33,* 218–233.

Grainger, J. & Ferrand, L. (1996). Masked orthographic and phonological priming in visual word recognition and naming: Cross-task comparisons. *Journal of Memory and Language, 35,* 623–647.

Grainger, J., Diependaele, K. Spinelli, E. Ferrand, L., & Farioli, F. (2003). Masked Repetition and Phonological Priming Within and Across Modalities, *Journal of Experimental Psychology: Learning, Memory and Cognition, 29,* 1256–1269.

Grainger, J., Granier, J.P., Farioli, F., Van Assche, E., & van Heuven, W. (2006). Letter position information and printed word perception: The relative-position priming constraint. *Journal of Experimental Psychology: Human Perception and Performance, 17,* 1021–1026.

Grainger, J. & Holcomb, P.J. (2009). Watching the word go by: On the time-course of component processes in visual word recognition. *Language and Linguistic Compass, 3,* 128–156.

Grainger, J. & Jacobs, A.M. (1996). Orthographic processing in visual word recognition: A multiple read-out model. *Psychological Review, 103,* 518–565.

Grainger, J. Kiyonaga, K., & Holcomb, P.J. (2006). The time-course of orthographic and phonological code activation. *Psychological Science, 17,* 1021–1026.

Grainger, J. & Van Heuven, W. (2003). Modeling Letter Position Coding in Printed Word Perception. In P. Bonin (Ed.), *The Mental Lexicon.* New York: Nova Science Publishers (pp. 1–24).

Grainger, J. & Whitney, C. (2004). Does the huamn mind raed wrods as a wlohe? *Trends in Cognitive Sciences, 8,* 58–59

Hagoort, P., Indefrey, P., Brown, C., Herzog, H., Steinmetz, H., & Steiz, R.J. (1999). The neural circuitry involved in the reading of German words and pseudowords: A PET study. *Journal of Cognitive Neuroscience, 11,* 383–398.

Harm, M. W., & Seidenberg, M. S. (1999). Phonology, reading acquisition, and dyslexia: Insights from connectionist models. *Psychological Review, 106,* 491–528.

Holcomb, P.J., O'Rourke, T., & Grainger, J. (2002). An event-related brain potential study of orthographic similarity. *Journal of Cognitive Neuroscience, 14,* 938–950.

Holcomb, P.J. Anderson, J., & Grainger, J. (2005). An electrophysiological investigation of cross-modal repetition priming. *Psychophysiology, 42,* 493–507.

Holcomb, P.J. & Grainger, J. (2006). On the time-course of visual word recognition: An ERP investigation using masked repetition priming. *Journal of Cognitive Neuroscience, 18,* 1631–1643.

Howard, D., Patterson, K., Wise, R., Brown, W.D., Friston, K., Weiller, C., & Frackowiak, R. (1992). The cortical localization of the lexicons. *Brain, 115,* 1769–1782.

Humphreys, G. W., Evett, L. J., & Quinlan, P. T. (1990). Orthographic processing in visual word recognition. *Cognitive Psychology, 22,* 517–560.

Jacobs, A.M., Rey, A., Ziegler, J.C., & Grainger, J. (1998). MROM-p: An interactive activation, multiple read-out model of orthographic and phonological processes in visual word recognition. In J. Grainger & A.M. Jacobs (Eds.), *Localist Connectionist Approaches to Human Cognition.* Hillsdale, NJ.: Erlbaum.

Jakimik, J., Cole, R. A., & Rudnicky, A. I. (1985). Sound and spelling in spoken word recognition. *Journal of Memory and Language*, *24*, 165–178.

Kinoshita, S. (2003). The nature of masked onset priming effects in naming: a review. In S. Kinoshita & S.J. Lupker (Eds.). *Masked Priming: The State of the Art.* New York: Psychology Press.

Kiyonaga, K. Midgley, K.J., Holcomb, P.J., & Grainger, J. (2007). Masked cross-modal repetition priming: An ERP investigation. *Language and Cognitive Processes*, *22*, 337–376.

Kouider, S., & Dupoux, E. (2001). A functional disconnection between spoken and visual word recognition: evidence from unconscious priming. *Cognition*, *82*, B35–B49.

Lukatela, G., & Turvey, M.T. (1994). Visual access is initially phonological: 2. Evidence from phonological priming by homophones, and pseudohomophones. *Journal of Experimental Psychology: General*, *123*, 331–353.

McCandliss, B.D., Cohen, L., & Dehaene, S. (2003). The visual word form area: expertise for reading in the fusiform gyrus. *Trends in Cognitive Sciences*, *7*, 293–299.

McCarthy, G., Nobre, A.C., Bentin, S., & Spencer D. (1995). Language-related field potentials in the anterior-medial temporal lobe: I. Intracranial distribution and neural generators. *Journal of Neuroscience*, *15*:1080–1089.

Mehler, J., Dommergues, J.-Y., Frauenfelder, U., & Segui, J. (1981). The syllable's role in speech segmentation. *Journal of Verbal Learning and Verbal Behavior*, *20*, 298–305.

Mozer, M. (1987). Early parallel processing in reading: A connectionist approach. In M. Coltheart (Ed.), *Attention and Performance XII*, Hillsdale, NJ.: Erlbaum.

Nobre, A.C., Allison, T., & McCarthy, G. (1994). Word recognition in the human inferior temporal lobe. *Nature*, *372*, 260–263.

Nunez, P.L. (1990). Localization of brain activity with electroencephalography. *Advances in Neurology*, *54*, 39–65.

Pammer, K., Hansen, P.C., Kringelbach, M.L., Holliday, I., Barnes, G., Hillebrand, A., Singh, K.D., & Cornelissen, P.L. (2004). Visual word recognition: the first half second. *NeuroImage*, *22*, 1819–1825.

Perea, M. & Lupker, S. J. (2003). Transposed-letter confusability effects in masked form priming. In S. Kinoshita and S. J. Lupker (Eds.), *Masked Priming: State of the Art.* Hove, UK: Psychology Press (pp. 97–120).

Perea, M. & Lupker, S. J. (2004). Can *CANISO* activate *CASINO*? Transposed-letter similarity effects with nonadjacent letter positions. *Journal of Memory and Language, 51,* 231–246.

Peressotti, F. & Grainger, J. (1999). The role of letter identity and letter position in orthographic priming. *Perception & Psychophysics*, *61*, 691–706.

Perfetti, C.A., & Bell, L.C. (1991). Phonemic activation during the first 40 ms of word identification: Evidence from backward masking and priming. *Journal of Memory and Language*, *30*, 473–485.

Petit, J.P., Midgley, K.J., Holcomb, P.J., & Grainger, J. (2006). On the time-course of letter perception: A masked priming ERP investigation. *Psychonomic Bulletin & Review*, *13*, 674–681.

Pugh, K.R., Shaywitz, B.A., Shaywitz, S.E., Constable, R.T., Skudlarski, P., Fulbright, R.K., Bronen, R.A., Shankweiler, D.P., Katz, L., Fletcher, J.M., & Gore, J.C. (1996). Cerebral organization of component processes in reading. *Brain, 119*, 1221-1238.

Schiller, N. O. (2004). The onset effect in word naming. *Journal of Memory and Language, 50*, 477–490.

Schoonbaert, S. & Grainger, J. (2004). Letter position coding in printed word perception: Effects of repeated and transposed letters. *Language and Cognitive Processes, 19*, 333–367.

Sekiguchi, T., Koyama, S., & Kakigi, R. (2004). The effect of phonological repetition on cortical magnetic responses evoked by visually presented words. *Journal of Cognitive Neuroscience, 16*, 1250–1261.

Seidenberg, M. S. & McClelland, J. L. (1989). A distributed, developmental model of word recognition and naming. *Psychological Review, 96*, 523–568.

Seidenberg, M. S. & Tanenhaus, M. K. (1979). Orthographic effects in rhyme monitoring. *Journal of Experimental Psychology: Human Learning and Memory, 5*, 546–554.

Sekiguchi, T., Koyama, S., & Kakigi, R. (2004). The effect of phonological repetition on cortical magnetic responses evoked by visually presented words. *Journal of Cognitive Neuroscience, 16*, 1250–1261.

Slowiaczek, L. M., Soltano, E. G., Wieting, S. J., & Bishop, K. L. (2003). An investigation of phonology and orthography in spoken-word recognition. *Quarterly Journal of Experimental Psychology, 56A*, 233–262.

Stevens, M. & Grainger, J. (2003). Letter visibility and the viewing position effect in visual word recognition. *Perception & Psychophysics, 65*, 133–151.

Tagamets, M.A., Novick, J.M., Chalmers, M.L., & Friedman, R.B. (2000). A parametric approach to orthographic processing in the brain: An fMRI study. *Journal of Cognitive Neuroscience, 12*, 281–297.

Van Assche, E. & Grainger, J. (2006). A study of relative-position priming with superset primes. *Journal of Experimental Psychology: Learning, Memory and Cognition, 32*, 399–415.

Ventura, P., Morais, J., Pattamadilok, C., & Kolinsky, R. (2004). The locus of the orthographic consistency effect in auditory word recognition. *Language and Cognitive Processes, 19*, 57–95.

Whitney, C. (2001). How the brain codes the order of letters in a printed word: The SERIOL model and selective literature review. *Psychonomic Bulletin & Review, 8*, 221–243.

Ziegler, J. C., Benraïs, A., & Besson, M. (1999). From print to meaning: An electrophysiological investigation of the role of phonology in accessing word meaning. *Psychophysiology, 36*, 775–785.

Ziegler, J. C. & Ferrand, L. (1998). Orthography shapes the perception of speech: The consistency effect in auditory word recognition. *Psychonomic Bulletin & Review, 5*, 683–689.

Ziegler, J., Ferrand, L., Jacobs, A.M., Rey, A., & Grainger, J. (2000). Visual and phonological codes in letter and word recognition: Evidence from incremental priming. *Quarterly Journal of Experimental Psychology, 53A*, 671–692.

Ziegler, J. C. & Goswami, U. C. (2005). Reading acquisition, developmental dyslexia and skilled reading across languages: A psycholinguistic grain size theory. *Psychological Bulletin, 131*, 3–29.

Ziegler, J.C., Muneaux, M., & Grainger, J. (2003). Neighborhood effects in auditory word recognition: Phonological competition and orthographic facilitation. *Journal of Memory and Language, 48*, 779–793.

2

Features Are Fundamental in Word Recognition

Kristen Pammer

Sensitivity to the features of letters and the position of letters within words is vital to reading. It exlpians the ablity to raed txet sUcH aS tHiS, it explains why we can navigate through a page of text which is otherwise simply a highly cluttered visual scene, and it explains why the FCUK[©] clothing label is so popular. However, most boxes-and-arrows models of visual word recognition and reading relegate the visual processing of text to a small box at the very top of the model, typically called something like "visual processing," within which, presumably, something magical occurs. One might easily be left with the impression that features, letters, and their positions within words play little part in word recognition and reading. The reality, however, is that efficient word recognition is dependent upon accurately encoding the visual features of words and correctly ordering them within the processing stream.

Let's consider for a moment the function of the visual system when reading. Assuming normal acuity, reading is fundamentally a spatio-temporal skill, such that accurate word recognition and fluent reading is dependent upon the fast temporal sequencing and spatial encoding of features. During a sentence of 12 words, and depending on the nature of the text, for example, the eyes may make nine saccades and fixations, and one regressive movement. Each fixation lasts between 150 and 300 ms, and the saccade velocity can be as high as 500° per second (Rayner, 1998). In other words, when reading, the eyes are moving fast—very, very fast—and during these fast jumps across the word or line, the visual system is processing lines, corners and edges, constructing letters, concatenating information to information already processed, and calculating what to process next. This information is integrated with higher cortical mechanisms (for example, memory, language, attention) because reading is also an example of cognitive pattern recognition. It is these more cognitive mechanisms that are generally the focus in models of reading; however, it is nevertheless undeniable that the front-end of this highly interactive system is spatio-temporal visual processing.

Word Recognition Is Dependent Upon Letters and Their Positions Within Words

The degree to which accurate word recognition and fluent reading is dependent upon feature analysis and spatio-temporal sequencing has been demonstrated empirically. For example, the bottleneck imposed on word recognition by accurate letter detection was demonstrated by Pelli, Farell, and Moore (2003). Here, they varied the contrast energy necessary to read words as predicted by a letter-by-letter approach to word recognition versus a whole-word approach. Reading was demonstrably better in the model in which the contrast energy-favored individual letters. Moreover, the energy required to detect words is dependent upon word length, such that threshold energy increases as words increase from 2 to16 letters, again as would be predicted if word recognition is limited by letter recognition. Therefore, letter detection is important in word recognition.

The findings demonstrating that word recognition is dependent upon sensitivity to individual letters does not seem, on the face of it, to be a particularly striking result. It would seem to be axiomatic that this should be the case. However, hundreds of studies show the processing superiority of the word over letters in terms of lexical access—the well-known Word Superiority Effect (WSE) (Reicher, 1969; Wheeler, 1970) being a point in case. Thus, our lexical system is sensitive to words as whole entities *and* individual letters. This implies highly distributed feedback and cascaded neural processes. However, if letters themselves are important in word recognition and reading, then the positions of letters within words are just as vital. Without an explicit ability to code position information we would have no way to distinguish "paternal" vs. "parental" "cat" vs. "act" or "trail" vs. "trial." However, once again we are faced with a contradiction. If position encoding is so important, then why is it that the "Cambridge University Effect" is so compelling (aoccdrnig to a rscheearch at Cmabrigde Uinervtisy, it deosn't mttaer in waht oredr the ltteers in a wrod are, the olny iprmoetnt tihng is taht the frist and lsat ltteer be at the rghit pclae . . .)? If letter position encoding is vital to word recognition, then the Cambridge University Effect should be unintelligible. So, what then is the evidence that position encoding is important in word recognition?

Priming studies consistently demonstrate that priming is more effective when the prime maintains the *relative* positions within words. Humphreys, Evett, and Quinlan (1990) found significant positive priming effects when prime and target letters respect their relative position in a target string while violating absolute position (e.g., BVK, but not TBVKU facilitates BLACK). Similarly, Peressotti and Grainger (1995) used a primed alphabetic decision task to test the extent to which letter-position coding is channel-specific. That is, whether separate units represent "A . . . Z" in the first position of a word/letter-string, "A . . . Z" in the second position, and so on. Peressoti and Grainger (1995; 1999) found evidence for both position-specific and cross-position priming. Specifically, priming effects were strongest when the primed letter occupied the same position within the prime and target strings. But, in addition, a prime string with a letter in one position could facilitate recognition of that same letter in a different position within a target (nonword) letter string. Therefore, these studies indicate that relative order among sets of letters, and not solely their absolute position, is important in letter-position coding. The same conclusions have evolved from the use of illusory words and letter migration errors. First demonstrated by Allport (1977), the illusory word phenomenon is the demonstration that the conjunction of features from two briefly presented words (e.g., LINE – LOVE) can result in a subject incorrectly reporting an illusionary new word (e.g., LIVE). It was initially believed that letters and features can migrate only so much as they can preserve their within-word position (Ellis, Flude, & Young, 1987), emphasizing the importance of specific position encoding. However, Davis and Bowers (2004) demonstrated that, assuming that the new illusory word could be a "real" word (i.e., does not violate orthographic constraints), then letters are just as likely to migrate to maintain relative positions in the new word. This supports Grainger and colleagues by suggesting that position encoding is important for word recognition, but that the coding mechanism is somewhat flexible, such that it appears to be the relative, rather than the absolute position of letters within words that is important.

The upshot of these findings is that efficient word recognition appears to be dependent upon our ability to *recognize* and accurately *sequence* the component letters, and this flies in the face of long-held models (not to mention neural parsimony) postulating that fluent word recognition must occur according to a whole-word process.

Removing Lexical Representation from the Equation

The research findings described thus far have at least one thing in common: they all use words or pseudowords. By using sequences of common letters as stimuli, one is necessarily faced with the likelihood that top-down lexical knowledge influences responding, particularly when the participants are fluent adult readers. The WSE described in all first-year psychology textbooks is the clearest example of this; letters are recognized faster in the context of a word, or even a nonword, than when presented alone. Thus, our sensitivity to letters and their positions within words may in fact simply be a *consequence* of our sensitivity to words. Therefore, the more stringent test of the hypothesis that letter position is important to reading is to remove the lexical aspects of the task, thereby avoiding the possible confound of lexical knowledge. If reading and word recognition is dependent upon the accurate recognition and sequencing of components of words, then one should be able to demonstrate that sensitivity to position encoding in structured stimuli should predict word recognition and reading ability.

The Symbols Task

In order to address this question, we designed a task that we believed measured the accuracy with which participants could discriminate the relative position of local items, but without using lexical knowledge (Pammer, Lavis, Cooper, Hansen, & Cornelissen, 2005; Pammer, Lavis, Hansen, & Cornelissen, 2004; Pammer, Lavis, & Cornelissen, 2004). In a standard lexical decision task, a participant is presented with a brief display of a word or a letter string and is required to indicate if the stimulus was a word or not. In other words, the subject is to make a "lexical decision" regarding the stimulus. The symbols task we designed was constructed to be as similar as possible to a standard lexical decision task, while removing any top-down influence from words. This was done by replacing strings of five alphabetic letters with strings of five nonalphabetic, but letter-like symbols. See Figure 2.1.

Thus, a symbol-string appeared briefly on screen, was masked, and then two alternative symbol-strings were displayed, one above the other. Participants were asked to pick which of the two alternatives they had just been shown; one was the same string, and the other was a string with the same symbols, but arranged in a different order (symbols position version). The correct choice appeared at random in either the upper or lower position, with equal probability. The stimulus comprised 26 symbols constructed from only vertical or horizontal lines and were designed to contain a similar number of line elements to actual letters. Thus, in order for the subject to successfully

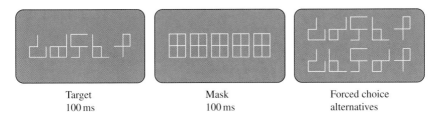

| Target | Mask | Forced choice |
| 100 ms | 100 ms | alternatives |

Figure 2.1 The sequence of events in the standard "symbols task" used by Pammer and colleagues (Pammer et al., 2005; 2004a, 2004b).

complete this task, the positions of the elements needed to be encoded. We believe that this task is analogous to a subject having to distinguish between "trail" and "trial" (for example), but without the lexical framework that would otherwise be used, thereby isolating bottom-up spatial encoding mechanisms. Our reading task was always a lexical decision task, but one in which we aimed to emphasize the spatial relationship between the letters. So, in this task, words were five-letter, high-frequency words, and the nonword foils were constructed as anagrams of the words used (HOUSE and HSUOE for example). Our aim over a series of experiments was to investigate the relationship between the symbols task and word recognition, such that if the ability to do the symbols task relies on the same perceptual resources as position encoding in word recognition, then there should be a correlation between the two tasks, and the symbols task should specifically predict word recognition accuracy.

What Do the Symbols Tasks Show Us?

We have demonstrated that sensitivity to solving the symbols tasks is consistently correlated with, and predicts word recognition as indexed by lexical decision. This suggests that being good at quickly processing the components and relative positions of items in a string of symbols is related to the ability to accurately recognize a familiar word compared to an anagram. Our assumption is that the same brain mechanisms are involved in processing the spatio-temporal components of text, as in processing the spatio-temporal components of the symbols task. However, both the symbols tasks and lexical decision share other processing demands, such as attention, being able to effectively process information presented in a fast temporal sequence, short-term memory, and a requirement for fixation stability. Any one of these other factors could account for the shared variability between the two tasks and could therefore explain the relationship between the two. Therefore, in a series of experiments we investigated this possibility. We first of all looked at attention—an attention dwell task was used as an index of divided attention and attentional engagement. There are many different "attention" tasks that could be used, but for this purpose we were interested in whether basic overt attentional behavior could explain performance in both the symbols task and the lexical decision task. While we found that both attention tasks were correlated with and predicted reading ability, we found no relationship between attention-dwell and lexical decision. We then tested subjects' ability to process information quickly—perhaps the symbols and lexical decision tasks are related because of a shared requirement for being able to quickly process fast presented displays. Here we used metacontrast—although the underlying theoretical model of the processes involved in metacontrast are peripheral to this question, the task itself requires a subject to process a detailed, masked display presented at much the same time sequences as the symbols task. If performance on the symbols task is dependent simply upon being able to quickly process rapidly changing displays, then there should be a correlation between metacontrast performance and the symbols task. We did not find this, and once again the symbols task predicted reading ability. Finally, we tested fixation stability and memory. These are two obvious possible links between the symbols task and lexical decision—fixation instability could result in poor performance in processing the component items of both the symbols and lexical decision tasks. Similarly, the symbols task clearly draws on memory resources: The subject must remember the two alternative symbol strings in order to compare them to the target. However, once again, there were no differences in fixation stability for subjects who were poor or good at the symbols task, and although memory is important for reading, it was not related to the symbols task. Thus, these results are entirely consistent with a model of word recognition that posits an early stage of feature processing such that the spatio-temporal sequencing of letters within words places limits on subsequent lexical access.

So, how can word recognition be so dependent upon the recognition and sequencing of individual letters? Surely this would advocate a position in which a long word would take a prohibitively long time to read, and indeed is a position that was rejected over 50 years ago. It is also reminiscent of a pattern of reading which characterizes some forms of acquired dyslexia (e.g., Damasio & Damasio, 1983; Patterson & Kay, 1982). The fact that word recognition is limited by letter recognition does not obviate subsequent parallel and cascaded processing, such that after the initial selection and assembly of the visual *pattern* of a word, the activation of letters and subsequent word recognition can proceed by any parallel and cascaded process, as advocated in any number of models of word recognition (e.g., Seidenberg & McClelland, 1989; Plaut, McClelland, Seidenberg, & Patterson, 1996). Indeed, we have neuroimaging data that demonstrates this cascaded processing very well (Pammer, Hansen,

Holliday, & Cornelissen, 2006). Mapping the time course of information flow through the reading network in a standard lexical decision task, we showed concurrent activation in disparate areas of the network, with, for example, language processing in Broca's area occurring concurrently with the onset of visual coding in the fusiform gyrus. This is a good example of how, when faced with the requirement for complex cognitive processing, the brain does not respond in an orderly, linear way, but instead processes in highly cascaded (subsequent areas activating before previous processing has finished) and interactive way. Thus, a dependence on the accurate encoding of individual letters is not the same thing as letter-by-letter reading, which is generally believed to be a serial process.

Dyslexia and Position Encoding

We have all heard the joke about the dyslexic agnostic who lay awake at night wondering if there was a DOG. But this is less a joke than a perceptual reality. If word recognition, and by extension, reading, is dependent upon accurate encoding of letters and their relative position within words, then this has profound implications for children learning to read and those children who fail to learn to read, challenging the long-held assumption that dyslexia is entirely the result of poor phonological representations. The wealth of data demonstrating that dyslexia is dependent on phonological skills is undeniable (refer to Snowling 2000 for a review). However there is evidence of a visual contribution to dyslexia as well. For example, Cornelissen and colleagues have shown correlations between tasks that explicitly demand accurate information about letter position and visual tasks like coherent motion detection (using random dot kinematograms) (Cornelissen et al., 1998a; Cornelissen, Hansen, Hutton, Evangelinou, & Stein, 1998b). For example, the probability of children misreading single words like VICTIM as VIKIM, or PERSON as PRESON was directly related to their coherent motion sensitivity. This result held even when children's reading ability, chronological age, IQ, and phonological skills were taken into account. Such orthographically inconsistent nonsense errors (or "letter" errors) would be expected to occur if "poor" motion detectors failed to encode letter position accurately (Cornelissen & Hansen, 1998). Similarly, Pammer and Kevan have consistently demonstrated that visual sensitivity predicts orthographic coding. Here we used a low-level visual task called the *visual frequency doubling task* (FDT) to predict reading skills. We have found that FDT sensitivity specifically predicts irregular word reading over nonword reading (Kevan & Pammer, 2008b; Pammer & Kevan, 2007). Moreover, pre-reading children who are at risk for dyslexia have lower sensitivity to FDT and coherent motion compared to an unselected sample of children of the same age (Kevan & Pammer, 2008b). The suggestion from these results is that visual sensitivity—particularly visual sensitivity specific to the magnocellular visual pathway—seems to be important to coding the visual qualities of words. In order to test this further, we used the symbols task to investigate the relationship between relative position sensitivity and reading ability in children (Pammer et al., 2004a). Here we demonstrated that relative position sensitivity is reduced in developmental dyslexic readers compared to age-matched control readers, and that sensitivity to the symbols task predicts individual variability in contextual reading. Similarly, in another study (Pammer et al, 2004b), we demonstrate that the symbols task is correlated with both single-word and contextual reading in children. The implications of these findings is that subtle visual impairments in reading-impaired children may cause a subjective uncertainty about letter position when they read, making it difficult to establish stable orthographic to phonological mappings.

Linking Behavior to Human Neurophysiology

A number of cognitive models have been proposed to accommodate position encoding in reading, and a number of excellent reviews of these models (e.g., Davis & Bowers, 2006) exist, thus the following section will discuss the possible underlying neurophysiology, rather than the cognitive models.

There appears to be a reasonable collection of research to support the proposal that good word recognition and subsequent reading skills are to some degree dependent upon how well we can recognize and sequence letters within words. In other words, fluent reading is reliant upon good spatial encoding skills. However, if this were truly the case, then there should be supporting neurophysiological evidence demonstrating a direct link between early spatial encoding and reading. Vidyasagar (Pammer & Vidyasagar, 2005; Vidyasagar, 1999; 2004) has proposed a theoretical framework that supports this link. The visual system is composed of at least two neural processing pathways: the dorsal pathway receiving input primarily from magnocellular cells, and the ventral pathway that receives information primarily from parvocellular cells. Each of the two pathways have different anatomical projections and different functional properties. For example, the dorsal pathway—fed primarily by magnocellular cells—is sensitive to high temporal frequency, low contrast, low spatial frequencies, and is color insensitive. Conversely, the ventral pathway is innervated primarily by the parvocellular cells and is sensitive to color and detail, and insensitive to motion (Merigan & Maunsell, 1993). There is neurophysiological evidence that the fast-processing magnocellular cells in the dorsal stream project to the right posterior parietal cortex to encode the spatial qualities of a visual scene (Shomstein & Behrmann, 2006). It has been suggested that then this "spatial map" is fed back to early visual processing centers such as the primary visual cortex and the ventral stream, allowing the selective "spotlighting" of salient aspects of a scene and subsequent detailed analysis. Thus, the magnocellular cells and dorsal pathway provide a mechanism for guided visual search, such that the dorsal stream highlights smaller parts of a cluttered visual scene that then undergo more detailed analysis by early and extrastriate visual centers. This selective spatial sampling obviates the need to sample the entire visual scene and thus consumes fewer neural resources. There is recent neurophysiological evidence for attentional modulation of early visual centers such as V1 by the dorsal stream (Saalmann, Pigarev, & Vidyasagar, 2007), and this seems a reasonable framework to understand how the dorsal deficit might contribute to reading.

The application of this for word recognition and reading is that the lines, edges, and curves in a word constitute a cluttered visual pattern—particularly if a word is imbedded in text, as is usually the case. Thus, the role of the dorsal pathway in word recognition and reading is to provide a preattentive spatial selection of the components of individual words, to be fed back to other visual centers such as VI and the ventral pathway, so that the elements imbedded within each selection can undergo further analysis and be assembled correctly by the ventral stream. If this is the case, then the link between our symbols task and reading is relatively clear: The symbols stimuli—when presented very quickly—poses a similar visual problem to word recognition. Just as accurate word recognition is dependent upon accurate visuospatial encoding of the individual letters, accurate recall of the symbols string is dependent upon accurate visuospatial encoding of the individual symbols. Therefore, it makes sense that the symbols task consistently predicts reading ability, because both tasks are likely to engage the same dorsally mediated early spatial selection.

There is cumulating evidence from human neuroimaging, psychophysics, and primate research to support this theoretical model. However, the application of the model to reading and word recognition remains speculative. Nevertheless, it provides a coherent and biologically plausible account for the behavioral findings, and provides a much-needed link between theories of reading and evidence of a magno-deficit in dyslexia. Moreover, we have recently (Pammer et al., 2006) tested this theory directly by using magnetoencephalographic neuroimaging. If the dorsal stream is directly involved in the early spatial selection of features within words, then we should be able to observe a pattern of activity in which the dorsal stream activates early (<200 ms) and that this activation becomes more pronounced when the dorsal stream is required to work harder. This is exactly what we found when we presented participants with normal words in a lexical decision task versus words in which the constituent letters had been spatially displaced. This provides good evidence to suggest that the dorsal pathway has a role in early spatial selection in word recognition. Moreover, this model provides a nice explanation for the evidence that deficits involving the magnocellular pathway seem to predict orthographic sensitivity rather than phonological awareness in word reading (Kevan & Pammer, 2008; Pammer & Kevan 2007).This makes sense if reading and word recognition are the result of the accurate synthesis of orthographic and phonological information—early visual encoding is most likely to influence orthographic sensitivity (our knowledge of how words look) rather than phonological sensitivity (our knowledge of how words sound). Similarly, the symbols task might be considered a correlate of orthographic sensitivity without the lexical associa-tion. The question arises however, how a deficit in early spatial coding mechanisms differentially affects word recognition to impair the lexical route more so than the phonological route? There is compelling evidence to suggest that there exists at least two different types of dyslexia. *Phonological dyslexia* is generally characterized by problems in sounding out words typified by difficulty in reading nonwords such as *polterink.* The underlying cognitive impairment here is believed to be a problem in applying accurate grapheme-to-phoneme correspondence rules (Castles & Coltheart, 1993). *Surface dys-lexia,* on the other hand, is a result of poor orthographic skills, indexed by problems in directly recognizing irregular words such as *yacht.* The question is then, if a visual processing deficit exists at the very earliest stages of word recognition, should it not affect word recognition per se, rather than irregular and nonwords differently? Take the following examples "colonel" an irregular word, and "kernel" a regular word. A simple example of disrupted orthogra-phical coding may disrupt internal position encoding to produce, for example, "kenrel" and "coolne" respectively. In the "kenrel" example no lexical entry is activated using either the phonological or lexical route. Presumably then a reevaluation of the word takes place supported by the application of GPC rules until the recognizable "kernel" is activated. Conversely, "coolne" pronounced phonetically is no more recognizable than "colonel," the application of GPC rules is unhelpful, and the reader must rely exclusively on orthographic information. Thus, impaired early visual processing may affect irregular word reading relatively more than regular word processing because in irre-gular words one must rely exclusively on accurate visual encoding without the added scaffolding of applicable GPC rules. Moreover, one could speculate that there may be less reliance on visual skills in languages with more regular grapheme-to-phoneme correspondences.

Another model that explicitly links orthographic processing to visuospatial coding is the visual attention-span hypothesis (Bosse, Tainturier, & Valdois, 2007; Prado, Dubois, & Valdois, 2007). Valdois and colleagues have suggested that reading occurs by implementing a "perceptual window." The size of the perceptual window can vary with task requirements, and the larger the window, the more likely that global, whole-word processing mechanisms are used in a parallel way. When a smaller perceptual window is used, then serial mechanisms are used to concatenate sequential elements of the words in order to assemble the word from its constituent components. Most familiar words and irregular words would be processed globally with a wider attentional window, whereas phonological decoding would require extracting the phonological elements, maintaining them in short-term memory, and then synthesizing them into a word. Orthographic irregularity then would require a large attentional window, parallel processing of word elements, and a spatial system capable of mapping the spatial area and extracting the word elements to be bound to represent a word—clearly a job for the dorsal pathway.

Continuing Challenges

The model presented here suggests that the accurate perception of letters and features is intrinsic to good word recognition skills. Moreover, such visual sensitivity may be mediated by a preattentive visual search mechanism from the dorsal pathway. However, it is equally plausible that causality may evolve the other way around, or at least be more dynamic than this, such that the very act of reading in fact results in dynamic changes in the visual system, and systematic exposure to reading and words leads to a functional specialization of a part of the visual system. Conversely, a lack of exposure to reading due to other causes, such as poor phonological decoding for example, may impact on the gradual specialization/development of the dorsal pathway.

All of these studies have used word recognition, and I have skirted around making a clear distinction between reading and word recognition. Clearly, reading is dependent upon word recognition, but we have yet to ascertain the degree to which feature analysis and relative position encoding is important in contextual reading. It might well be the case that because of the fast temporal synchronization required for contextual reading, the system is more dependent upon top-down modulation of word recognition compared to bottom-up stimulus features such as letters and their spatial sequence. Similarly, while we have behavioural evidence that the symbols task and work recognition share visuospatial resources, the next step is to evaluate this by looking at the neurophysiological architecture of each task. If the symbols task and word recognition share the same visuospatial resources and, by extension then, reading is dependent upon accurate letter-position encoding, then the same brain mechanisms should be involved in each task. Any model of reading and word recognition must be biologically plausible; thus, we need to confirm that the assumptions we make by linking the symbols task and lexical decision are valid. One would predict that the dorsal pathway, as indexed by the posterior parietal cortex, would be involved in both the symbols and lexical decision tasks within a time frame that would be consistent with preattentive visuospatial encoding. Such research has yet to be conducted.

We also have little knowledge regarding the developmental plasticity of the dorsal pathway—and by extension orthographic analysis—when learning to read. It may be the case that the dorsal pathway may not be sufficiently developed to cope with the visuospatial demands of reading before a certain age. A recent functional magnetic resonance imaging (fMRI) study has suggested delayed development of the dorsal pathway until at least after 6 years of age (Klaver et al., 2008). Similarly, is there an age at which dorsal sensitivity is "hardwired" such that the visuospatial requirements for reading are no longer plastic? These questions are closely tied to knowledge about the reciprocal nature of reading and neural development.

Finally, of course, are the implications for reading remediation. One of the aims of reading research is to understand the mechanisms involved in poor reading, and by virtue of this knowledge, have a sound theoretical framework for best practice in teaching children to read and helping children overcome reading problems. Presently, little research looks at the remedial implications of these findings. Knowledge about the developmental plasticity of the dorsal pathway, and the reciprocal influence of reading acquisition are vital components to understanding the reading network and designing appropriate reading intervention.

References

Allport, D. (1977). On knowing the meaning of words we are unable to report: The effects of visual masking. In S. Dornic (Ed). *Attention and performance VI*, pp 505–533. Hillsdale, NJ: Erlbaum.

Ans B., Carbonnel S., & Valdois S. (1998). A connectionist multiple-trace memory model for polysyllabic word reading. *Psychological Review, 105*, 678–723.

Bosse M.L., Tainturier M.J., & Valdois S. (2007). Developmental dyslexia: The visual attention span deficit hypothesis. *Cognition, 104*, 198–230.

Castles, A., & Coltheart, M. (1993). Varieties of developmental dyslexia. *Cognition, 47*, 149–180.

Cornelissen, P., & Hansen, P. (1998). Motion detection, letter position encoding, and single word reading. *Annals of Dyslexia, 48*, 155–188.

Cornelissen, P., Hansen, P., Gilchrist, I., Cormack, F., Essex, C., & Frankish, C. (1998a). Coherent motion detection and letter position encoding. *Vision Research, 38*, 2181–2191.

Cornelissen, P., Hansen, P., Hutton, J., Evangelinou, V., & Stein, J. (1998b). Magnocellular visual function and children's single word reading. *Vision Research, 38*, 471–482.

Damasio, A., & Damasio, H. (1983). The anatomic basis of pure alexia, *Neurology, 33,* 1573–1583.

Davis, C., & Bowers, J (2006). Contrasting five different theories of letter position coding: Evidence from orthographic similarity effects. *Journal of Experimental Psychology—Human Perception and Performance, 32,* 535–557.

Davis, C., & Bowers, J. (2004). What do letter migration errors reveal about letter position coding in visual word recognition. *Journal of Experimental Psychology; Human Perception and Performance, 30,* 923–941.

Ellis, A., Flude, B., & Young, A. (1987). Neglect dyslexia and the early visual processing of letters in words and nonwords. *Cognitive Neuropsychology, 4,* 439–464.

Humphreys, G., Evett, L., & Quinlan, P. (1990). Orthographic processing in visual word identification. *Cognitive Psychology, 22,* 517–561.

Kevan, A., & Pammer, K. (2008a). Visual processing deficits in preliterate children at familial risk for dyslexia. *Vision Research, 48,* 2835–2839.

Kevan, A., & Pammer, K. (2008b) Making the link between dorsal stream sensitivity and reading. *Neuroreport, 19,* 467–470.

Klaver, P., Lichtensteiger, J., Bucher, K., Dietrich, T., Loenneker, T. & Martin, E. (2008). Dorsal stream development in motion and structure-from-motion perception. *Neuroimage, 39,* 1815–1823.

Merigan, W., & Maunsell, J. (1993). How parallel are the primate visual pathways? *Annual Review of Neuroscience, 16,* 369–402.

Pammer, K., & Kevan, A. (2007). The contribution of visual sensitivity, phonological processing and non-verbal IQ to children's reading. *The Society for the Scientific Study of Reading. 11,* 33–53.

Pammer, K., Lavis, R., Cooper, C., Hansen, P., & Cornelissen, P. (2005). Symbol string sensitivity and adult performance in lexical decision. *Brain and Language, 94,* 278–296.

Pammer, K., Lavis, R., Hansen, P., & Cornelissen, P. (2004a). Symbol string sensitivity and children's reading. *Brain and Language, 89,* 601–610.

Pammer, K., Lavis, R., & Cornelissen, P. (2004b). Visual encoding mechanisms and their relationship to text presentation preference. *Dyslexia, 10,* 77–94.

Pammer, K., Hansen, P., Holliday, I., & Cornelissen, P. (2006). Attentional shifting and the role of the dorsal pathway in visual word recognition. *Neuropsychologia, 44,* 2926–2936.

Pammer, K., & Vidyasagar, TR. (2005) Integration of the visual and auditory networks in dyslexia: a theoretical perspective. *Journal of Research in Reading, 28,* 320–331.

Patterson, E., & Kay, J. (1982). Letter-by-letter reading: psychological description of a neurological syndrome, *Quarterly Journal of Experimental Psychology 34A,* 411–441.

Pelli, D., Farell, B., & Moore, D. (2003). The remarkable inefficiency of word recognition. *Nature, 42,* 6941, 752–756.

Peressotti, F., & Grainger, J. (1995). Letter-position coding in random consonant arrays. *Perception & Psychophysics, 57,* 875–890.

Peressotti, F., & Grainger, J. (1999). The role of letter identity and letter position in orthographic priming. *Perception & Psychophysics, 61,* 691–706.

Plaut, D., McClelland, J., Seidenberg, M., & Patterson, K. (1996) Understanding normal and impaired word reading: Computational principles in quasi-regular domains. *Psychological Review, 103,* 56–115.

Prado, C., Dubois, M., & Valdois, S. (2007). The eye movements of dyslexic children during reading and visual search: Impact of the visual attention span. *Vision Research, 47,* 2521–2530.

Rayner, K. (1998). Eye movements in reading and information processing: 20 years of research. *Psychological Bulletin, 124*, 372–422.

Reicher, G. (1969). Perceptual recognition as a function of meaningfulness of stimulus material. *Journal of Experimental Psychology, 81*, 274–280.

Saalmann, Y., Pigarev, I., & Vidyasagar T.R. (2007). Neural mechanisms of visual attention: How top-down feedback highlights relevant locations. *Science,* 316, 1612–1615.

Seidenberg, M. & McClelland, J. (1989) A distributed, developmental model of word recognition and naming. *Psychological Review, 96*, 523–568.

Shomstein, S., & Behrmann, M. (2006). Cortical systems mediating visual attention to both objects and spatial locations. *Proceedings of the National Academy of Sciences, 103*, 11387–11392.

Snowling, M. (2000). *Dyslexia,* Oxford: Blackwell.

Vidyasagar, T.R. (1999). A neuronal model of attentional spotlight: parietal guiding the temporal. *Brain Research Reviews, 30*, 66–76.

Vidyasagar, T.R. (2004). Neural underpinnings of dyslexia as a disorder of visuo-spatial attention. *Clinical Experimental Optometry, 87*, 4–10.

Wheeler, D. (1970). Processes in word recognition. *Cognitive Psychology, 1*, 59–85.

3

Semantic Asymmetries Must Originate in a Visual Asymmetry

Carol Whitney

Visual half-field studies, in which stimuli are presented to the right or left parafovea, are widely used in the investigation of visual word recognition and semantic processing. Due to the architecture of the visual system, information from the left visual field (LVF) initially projects to the right hemisphere (RH), while the right visual field (RVF) projects to the left hemisphere (LH). Therefore, observed asymmetries in half-field studies have been used to draw conclusions about specializations of the cerebral hemispheres. For example, based on lateralized studies of semantic priming, Burgess and Simpson (1988) said: "Results suggest that, while automatic processing occurs in both hemispheres, only the left hemisphere engages in controlled processing of ambiguous word meanings. In addition, the present results support the idea that the right hemisphere has a special role in ambiguity resolution and that the right hemisphere lexicon possesses a richer endowment than earlier thought." Also based on semantic priming, Koivisto and Laine (2000) said: "It is suggested that the left hemisphere automatically activates categorically related word meanings in both hemispheres. The right hemisphere contributes by maintaining the meanings active and by retrospectively integrating them to the context." Based on asymmetric N400 patterns in a lateralized event-related potential (ERP) study, Kutas and Federmeier (1999) said: "We propose that right hemisphere processing is best characterized as 'integrative'; new information is compared directly with context information.

In contrast, left hemisphere processing is better characterized as 'predictive'; the processing of context leads to an expectation about the semantic features of upcoming items and new information is compared with that expectation rather than directly with the context."

Such interpretations of hemispheric specialization are based on the underlying assumption that processing remains dominated by the hemisphere contralateral to the stimulus. That is, LVF presentation invokes RH-specific linguistic mechanisms, while RVF presentation invokes LH-specific linguistic mechanisms. However, this widespread assumption is inconsistent with the results of brain-imaging experiments. Magnetoencephalography (MEG) and functional magnetic resonance imaging (fMRI) studies have shown that for central presentation, processing becomes lateralized to the left fusiform gyrus, where a retinotopic representation of the string is converted into an abstract encoding of letter order in the visual word form area (VWFA) (Dehaene, Jobert, Naccache, Ciuciu, Poline, Le Bihan, & Cohen, 2004; McCandliss, Cohen, & Deheane, 2003; Tarkiainen, Helenius, Hansen, Cornelissen, & Salmelin, 1999). This left lateralization is present even for half-field presentation. That is, brain activation patterns are identical for LVF and RVF presentation at the level of the VWFA and beyond (Cohen, Dehaene, Naccache, Lehericy, Dehaene-Lambertz, Henaff, & Michel, 2000). Furthermore, patients suffering from isolated lesions to the splenium of the corpus callosum show pure alexia for words presented to the LVF/RH, but unimpaired reading for words presented to the RVF/LH (Cohen, Martinaud, Lemer, Lehericy, Samson, Obadia, Slachevsky, & Dehaene, 2003). This pattern of deficit shows that orthographic information going to the LVF/RH is normally transferred to the LH prior to lexical access. In sum, these studies indicate that an abstract encoding of letter order is created in the LH, and lexical access occurs in the LH, independently of presentation location. Therefore, processing at the lexical levels and above must be qualitatively the same for RVF or LVF presentation (Fig. 3.1).

If so, VF asymmetries must actually originate at a level of processing prior to this LH convergence. However, these are visual areas. How could visual processing create asymmetries in performance of lexical and semantic tasks? Based on the Sequential Encoding Regulated by Inputs to Oscillations within Letter units (SERIOL) model of the lexical route of visual word recognition, I have proposed that hemisphere-specific visual processing is required to form the abstract encoding of letter order and that such processing leads to VF-specific activation patterns at the pre-lexical level (Whitney, 2001). This difference in activation patterns affects lexical access, giving the *appearance* of qualitatively different performance patterns at the lexical level (Whitney, 2004). We (Whitney & Lavidor, 2004; 2005) have verified this account for asymmetries related to length and orthographic-neighborhood size (N) by

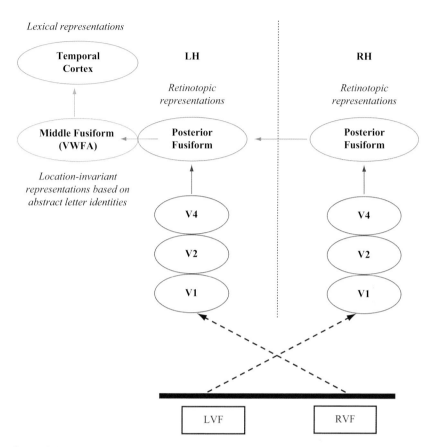

Figure 3.1 Emerging picture of visual processing of letter strings in normal readers, based on brain-imaging data (Cohen et al., 2000; Dehaene et al., 2004; Tarkiainen, et al. 1999). For both left visual field (LVF) and right visual field (RVF) presentation, information is funneled through left hemispheric (LH) fusiform areas, which encode a prelexical representation of the string. Any effect of VF would have to originate prior to this LH convergence.

using contrast adjustments to manipulate activation patterns, resulting in the reversal of the normal asymmetries.

Our experimental work thus far has focused on lexical properties (length and N). Semantic asymmetries would also have to originate at the visual level, but it is less obvious how activation patterns could affect this higher level of processing. This issue is the main focus of the present chapter.

In this chapter, I first the SERIOL model and the results of the length and N experiments. Then, I address VF effects in semantic priming and on N400 amplitude in the above ERP study (Kutas & Federmeier, 1999). The chapter concludes with a discussion of the implications of this work and brief comments on directions for future research.

SERIOL Model

It is well known that neural representations increase in abstractness as distance from the periphery increases. The SERIOL model offers a comprehensive theory of the representational transformations carried out by a skilled reader in the processing stream extending from primary visual cortex to lexical access (along the orthographic, lexical route). Here, an overview of the theory is presented, followed by a detailed examination of those levels relevant to VF asymmetries. For brevity, I do not include supporting experimental evidence for the model; such arguments can be found elsewhere (Whitney, 2001a; 2001b; 2002; Whitney & Berndt, 1999).

Overview

The SERIOL framework is comprised of five layers: edge, feature, letter, bigram, and word. Each layer is comprised of nodes, corresponding to neural assemblies. For the edge, feature, and letter layers, a letter's activation is taken to be the total amount of neural activity devoted to representing that letter. Thus, a letter's activation increases with number the of nodes activated by the letter, and their firing rate and firing duration.

The edge layer corresponds to the earliest levels of visual processing (V1, V2), where the representation of the string is split across the hemispheres, and receptive fields are small. Here, an activation pattern results from the acuity gradient. This gradient originates in the density of cones in the retina and is magnified into the cortex, such that the amount of cortical area representing a fixed amount of visual space is highest at fixation and falls off as eccentricity increases. Thus, in the model, letter activations are highest near fixation, and fall off as distance from fixation increases.

At the feature layer (V4, posterior fusiform), units are more broadly tuned to retinal location, while the representation of the string is still split across the hemispheres. As discussed in more detail later, I proposed that the acuity gradient is converted into an activation pattern, dubbed the *locational gradient*, in which activation level decreases across the string from left to right. For example, for the stimulus BIRD, B's features become the most highly activated, I's the next most activated, R's the next, and D's the least.

The letter layer (LH fusiform posterior to the VWFA) is comprised of nodes that synchronously oscillate in excitability (Hopfield, 1995; Lisman & Idiart, 1995). The interaction of the locational gradient with the variations in excitability induces sequential firing. That is, timing of firing depends on the amount of input to a letter node; a letter node receiving more input fires before one receiving less input. In our example, B fires, then I, then R, and then D. This conversion also results in varying letter activation levels. In general, letter activations are similar to their feature activations, except that activation increases at the final letter because its firing is not inhibited by a subsequent letter (Whitney & Berndt, 1999; Whitney, 2001a), as is consistent with the well-known final-letter advantage.

It is assumed that this serial representation of letter order serves separate lexical and phonological routes to the lexicon. The model focuses on the lexical route. The bigram layer (VWFA) is comprised of nodes that represent ordered letter pairs. That is, a bigram node is activated when its constituent letters fire in a certain order. Thus, bigram nodes BI, IR, and RD, as well as those corresponding to noncontiguous letter pairs (BR, BD, and ID), become activated in our example. A bigram node's activation level depends on the time lag between the firing of its constituent letters; bigram nodes activated by contiguous letters become more highly activated than those activated by noncontiguous letters.

Bigram nodes then activate the word layer (LH temporal areas) via weighted connections that record the bigram activation pattern resulting from each word. The input to a word unit is calculated in the usual way, as the dot-product of the input and weight vectors. Lateral inhibition within the word layer allows the most highly activated word node to become the winner.

In summary, the acuity gradient at the edge layer is transformed into the monotonically decreasing locational gradient at the feature layer. The locational gradient is converted into a serial encoding at the letter layer, which is then decoded into a set of ordered letter pairs at the bigram layer. Bigram nodes contact the word layer via weighted connections. Thus, the model specifies how the initial retinotopic representation is transformed into a location-invariant (serial) representation of letter order, and how this representation activates the word layer via a prelexical (bigram) encoding that is based on the relationship between letters, not on their absolute string position (Grainger & Whitney, 2004).

As discussed earlier, VF asymmetries must arise prior to the lateralized LH representation, namely in the edge and feature layers of the model. Indeed, creation of the locational gradient requires hemisphere-specific processing, as discussed next.

Locational Gradient Formation

The acuity gradient is converted into the locational gradient as edge nodes activate feature nodes. Note that the proposed locational gradient monotonically *decreases* from the first letter to the last letter, whereas the acuity gradient *increases* from the first letter to the fixated letter (i.e., in the LVF/ RH), and *decreases* from the fixated letter to the last letter (i.e., in the RVF/ LH) (Fig. 3.2). Therefore, the slope of the RH acuity gradient is in the opposite

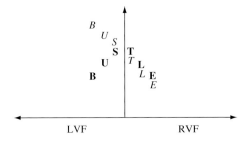

Figure 3.2 Acuity gradient (*boldface*) versus locational gradient (*italics*) for the fixated stimulus BUSTLE. The horizontal axis represents retinal location, whereas the vertical axis represents activation level.

direction as required for the locational gradient, while the slope of the LH acuity gradient is in the same direction. Thus, in the RH, the acuity gradient's slope must be inverted as features are activated. In contrast, the acuity gradient's slope can be maintained as features are activated in the LH. As a result, processing at the feature layer differs across hemispheres, with the RH performing a more extensive transformation. This hemisphere-specific processing is learned during reading acquisition, perhaps in response to a top-down attentional gradient.

First, we consider the RH processing. I propose that RH features become more highly activated by edge-level inputs than LH features, allowing the first letter's features to reach a high level of activation even if they are far from fixation. This could occur either via stronger learned connections from the edge to feature layers in the RH, or via stronger self-excitation within the RH feature layer. Within the RH feature layer, strong directional lateral inhibitory connections are learned, such that nodes inhibit other nodes having receptive-field locations to their right. Thus, inhibitory input increases as letter position increases, because more and more features send inhibition from the left. For example, consider the word BUSTLE as in Figure 3.2. B's features would input U's features, while B and U's features would inhibit S's features. This strong directional inhibition overrides the slope of the acuity gradient, inverting it. So, the features comprising the first letter attain a high level of activation (due to strong excitation and lack of lateral inhibition), and activation decreases toward fixation (due to sharply increasing lateral inhibition from the letters to the left).

In the LH, excitatory and lateral inhibitory connections are weaker, because the acuity gradient's slope is already in the correct direction. Thus, the acuity gradient is essentially maintained at the feature layer, although some directional inhibition may steepen its slope.

In addition to inhibition within hemispheres, there is also inhibition across hemispheres. The RH features inhibit the LH features, bringing the LH feature activations lower than those of the RH. Thus, the two halves of the locational gradient are meshed to create a strictly decreasing activation gradient from the first to the last letter.

In summary, hemisphere-specific processing is required to form the locational gradient, due to differing acuity patterns across the visual fields. In the RH, strong excitation and left-to-right lateral inhibition invert the acuity gradient to form the locational gradient. In the LH, the acuity gradient serves as the locational gradient.

Parafoveal Processing

The hemisphere-specific transformations that are required to create the locational gradient for a fixated word have ramifications for parafoveally presented words. Next we focus on the resulting activation patterns.

Note that the proposed stronger bottom-up activation to the RH implies that an initial letter should be better perceived in the LVF than the RVF, even if it is at a larger eccentricity in the LVF. This is indeed the case (Bouma, 1973; Estes, Allmeyer, & Reder, 1976). In contrast, a second or third letter at a given eccentricity is less well perceived in the LVF than the RVF (Wolford & Hollingsworth, 1974). This is explained by the strong LVF/RH left-to-right inhibition, indicating that this inhibition outweighs the effect of stronger bottom-up input. Moreover, mathematical modeling (Whitney, 2001) has shown that the theory of locational gradient formation explains detailed patterns of perceptibility in the interaction of eccentricity, visual field, and string position (Wolford & Hollingsworth, 1974).

These data and the modeling indicate the following activation feature–level patterns for half-field presentation. In the LVF/RH, strong inhibition from the first letter to the low-acuity second and third letters makes their activations quite low. However, as acuity increases for the final letters, lateral inhibition becomes insufficient, and their activations remain too high. Thus, there is a sharp decrease in activation across the early string positions, and then a flattening across the final letters (Fig. 3.3). In contrast, the locational gradient remains smoothly decreasing for RVF presentation, because it is largely based on the acuity gradient.

I propose that such differing activation patterns are the source of VF asymmetries. Recall that bigram activation levels depend on the firing patterns of the constituent letters, which depend on the locational gradient. It is assumed that learned bigram-to-word connection weights record the pattern of bigram activations for each word. Thus, the amount of bottom-up input reaching a word node depends on how well the bigram activation vector "matches" the learned weight vector. (More precisely, it depends on the angle between the activation and weight vectors, as well as the magnitude of those vectors.) When the LVF locational gradient is not smoothly decreasing,

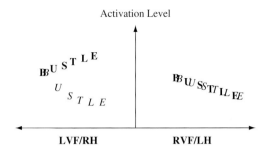

Figure 3.3 Activation patterns for parafoveal presentation. Boldface letters represent bottom-up excitation to the feature level, illustrating stronger excitation to the left visual field (LVF)/right hemisphere (RH). Lateral inhibition then forms the locational gradient (*italics*). In the LVF/RH, strong inhibition from the first letter has a large effect on the second and third letters; however, due to the relatively low activations of the initial letters and the increasing activation levels of the final letters, lateral inhibition fails to create a smoothly decreasing gradient near the end of the string. In the right visual field (RVF)/left hemisphere (LH), the locational gradient is equivalent to the bottom-up acuity gradient, so it remains smoothly decreasing.

it will create a bigram activation pattern that differs from the learned weight vector (which presumably is based on the activation pattern resulting from a smoothly decreasing gradient). Therefore, the bottom-up pattern does not match the learned pattern as well as for central or RVF presentation, reducing the amount of input to the corresponding word node.

Length Experiment

It is well known that there is a length effect in lexical decision for LVF, but not RVF, presentation (Ellis & Young, 1988; Young & Ellis, 1985). That is, reaction times (RTs) increase with string length for LVF presentation, but are independent of string length for RVF presentation (and central presentation, as well). As string length increases in the LVF, the locational gradient would become more and more non-smooth, increasing the mismatch with the learned weight vector, and creating a length effect. (See Whitney and Lavidor [2004] for a discussion of how a length effect could be absent for RVF and central presentation, despite serial processing at the letter level.)

This analysis suggests that it should be possible to abolish the LVF length effect by "fixing" the locational gradient (i.e., making it smoother). Therefore, we (Whitney & Lavidor, 2004) performed an experiment using position-specific contrast adjustments to manipulate bottom-up activation patterns. In the control condition, all letters were presented in light gray on a black background. In the adjust condition, the contrast of the second and third letters was increased by presenting those letters in white, and the contrast of the sixth

Figure 3.4 Left visual field (LVF)/right hemisphere (RH) locational gradient (*purple italics*) and corrective effect (*normal face*) of the contrast manipulation. Increased contrast is indicated in black (second and third letters), decreased contrast is shown in light gray (sixth letter), while unchanged contrast is shown in medium gray. The increased bottom-up input to the second and third letters raises their activation levels, and increases left-to-right lateral inhibition to the fourth, fifth, and sixth letters, decreasing their activation levels. Decreased bottom-up input to the sixth letter further lowers its activation level. The result is a more smoothly decreasing activation gradient.

letter (if present) was decreased by presenting it in medium gray, while letters at other positions remained light gray. Such an adjustment should smooth the gradient in the LVF as shown in Figure 3.4, thereby negating the length effect via facilitation for longer words (as compared to the control condition). Conversely, the same manipulation should degrade an otherwise smooth RVF gradient, creating a length effect. These predictions were confirmed, as shown in Figure 3.5. The LVF length effect was abolished, demonstrating that

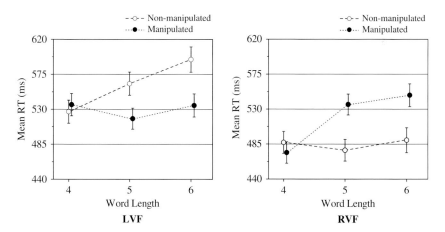

Figure 3.5 Experimental results of lexical-decision experiment from Whitney and Lavidor (2004). In the nonmanipulated condition, all letters were presented at the same contrast level. In the manipulated condition, the contrast of the second and third letters was increased, and the contrast of the sixth letter (if present) was decreased. Error bars represent one standard error of the mean.

a length effect is not an inherent attribute of LVF/RH processing. Therefore, the asymmetry of the length effect does not arise from hemisphere-specific modes of lexical access (Ellis & Young, 1988; Young & Ellis; 1985), but rather originates in activation patterns at the visual level.

N Experiment

Another VF asymmetry is related to the N effect. *N* refers to the number of orthographic neighbors, words that can be formed by changing one letter of the target word (Coltheart, Davelaar, Jonasson, & Besner, 1977). For example, BAND is a high-N word, with neighbors LAND, SAND, BEND, BIND, BARD, BALD, BANE, etc., while ONYX is a low-N word, with no neighbors. For CVF presentation of four-letter, low-frequency words under lexical decision, high-N words are responded to more quickly than low-N words (Andrews, 1997). Interestingly, this N effect is present for LVF, but not RVF, presentation (Lavidor & Ellis, 2002a,b). Note that this asymmetry goes in the opposite direction as the length effect; CVF presentation patterns with the LVF, not the RVF, indicate that the N-effect asymmetry cannot be attributed to less-efficient LVF processing.

Although the SERIOL model focuses on bottom-up processing, this is not to imply an absence of top-down processing, To explain the N effect, I assume that feedback occurs from the word layer to letter layer, and that lexical decision requires multiple oscillatory cycles (i.e., the sequence of letters fires multiple times). After the first oscillatory cycle, the activated word nodes then provide top-down input to the letter nodes. This feedback is also in the form a gradient, with the first letter receiving the most input, the second letter receiving the next most, etc. So, during the second oscillatory cycle, letter nodes receive both bottom-up input (from the feature level) and top-down input (from the word level).

Input levels to letter nodes directly affect the temporal evolution of word node activations. Because letters are activated sequentially, bigrams are activated sequentially. Increased input to letter nodes would speed their firing, and the firing of their respective bigram nodes. This would speed the activation of the target word node and decrease the amount of time that the target word node receives inhibition from competitor word nodes (Whitney, 2004), thus decreasing reaction times. Thus, additional, top-down input from orthographic neighbors could speed letter activations and decrease reaction times.

In English, most orthographic neighbors match the target word's body. For many four-letter words, this would correspond to the last three letters. Therefore, the second, third, and fourth letter nodes preferentially receive top-down input in the case of high N. Because the top-down input is in the form of a gradient, the second and third letters receive more top-down input than the fourth letter, so the internal letters are the most strongly affected by high N. For LVF presentation, this top-down activation gradient may also have the effect of smoothing the locational gradient across the last three letters, as the activation of the fourth letter's features may be relatively too high. This smoothing would also contribute to a facilitatory effect.

Why, then, is there no N effect for RVF presentation? Recall that the RVF locational gradient is based on the acuity gradient. It has been established that the acuity gradient becomes less steep as eccentricity increases (Westheimer, 1987). (While this seems contrary to the usual wisdom that "acuity falls off quickly outside the fovea," it is actually the case that acuity falls off most quickly *within* the fovea, so acuity is substantially reduced by the fovea/parafovea boundary.) Therefore, the RVF locational gradient across the first three letters will be shallower than for LVF or CVF presentation. See Figure 3.6 for a comparison of the proposed activation patterns for CVF, RVF, and LVF presentation. Due to this shallowness, the second and third letter nodes already fire as early as possible, so additional top-down input from high N has no effect. (See Whitney and Lavidor [2005] for details.)

Therefore, it should be possible to abolish the N effect (in the CVF and LVF) by increasing input to the internal letters (mimicking the top-down effect of high N), and to create the N effect (in the RVF) by decreasing input to the internal letters (mimicking the steeper LVF and CVF gradients).

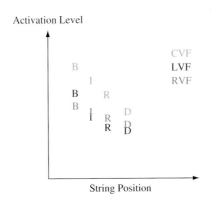

Figure 3.6 Comparison of proposed feature-layer activation patterns (locational gradients) for central visual field (CVF), left visual field (LVF), and right visual field (RVF) presentation of the stimulus BIRD. The CVF pattern is steeply and smoothly decreasing. The LVF pattern is non-smooth; it is steep across positions 1 to 3, and shallow across positions 3 to 4, because left-to-right inhibition becomes increasingly less effective as acuity increases. The RVF pattern is smooth and shallow, because it follows the acuity gradient, which is shallow in the parafovea.

For CVF and LVF presentation, input to the internal letters can be increased by slightly dimming the first letter, thereby reducing feature-level, left-to-right inhibition from the first letter to the internal letters. For the LVF in particular, dimming the last letter may help to smooth the locational gradient, reproducing the moderating effect of a top-down activation gradient (Fig. 3.7). A small change in contrast level should have little direct effect on the perception of the letter. Therefore, the dimming itself is not expected to increase RTs. For LVF and CVF presentation, such adjustments should mimic the compensatory effect of top-down input from high N. Therefore, responses to low-N words should be facilitated (as compared to a low-N control condition), making low-N words as fast as high-N words, and giving no N effect. The same manipulation in the RVF should have little effect.

Conversely, dimming the internal letters of an RVF string should mimic a steeper gradient, creating an N effect. That is, under such an adjustment, RTs for high-N words should be as fast as the control high-N condition (because the top-down input from high-N compensates for the reduced bottom-up input), but RTs should increase in the low-N condition (because there is no such compensation).

In summary, for lateralized presentation, dimming the outer letters should mimic the effect of top-down input from high-N, abolishing the LVF N effect via facilitation of low-N words. Dimming the inner letters should reproduce the LVF activation pattern in the RVF, creating an N effect via inhibition of low-N words. For the CVF, dimming the first letter should reproduce the effect of high-N, also abolishing the N effect via facilitation of low-N words.

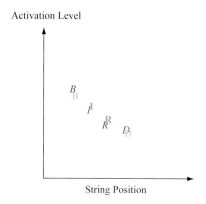

Figure 3.7 Left visual field (LVF)/right hemisphere (RH) locational gradient (*purple italics*) and effect (*normal face*) reducing the contrast of the first and fourth letters (indicated in light gray). The decreased bottom-up input to the first letter decreases its activation level. The decreased activation of the first letter decreases left to right lateral inhibition to the other letters, increasing their activations, while the decreased bottom-up input to fourth letter has the net effect of decreasing its activation. The result is a smoother, shallower locational gradient.

These predictions were confirmed in two lexical-decision experiments. In the first experiment, we focused on the asymmetry of the N effect, using lateralized presentation only. There were three presentation conditions: control, both outer letters dimmed, or both inner letters dimmed. In the control condition, all letters were presented in white on a dark gray background. A letter was dimmed by changing it to light gray. In the second experiment, we focused on negating the N effect for both the CVF and LVF. In this case, a single adjustment condition was tailored to specific locations. For lateralized presentation, both outer letters were dimmed; for the CVF, only the first letter was dimmed.

The results of the experiments are given in Figures 3.8 and 3.9. In both experiments, it is evident that dimming the outer letters had no effect in the RVF, but facilitated LVF low-N words in particular, abolishing the N effect. Note that this facilitation could not be a result of simply unmasking the internal letters at a very low level, as this effect was not present for the RVF. Thus, this manipulation had a VF-specific effect, as predicted. The second experiment shows that it is also possible to abolish the CVF N effect. The fact that low-N facilitation was achieved in the CVF indicates that the lack of facilitation in the RVF was not a result of more efficient processing in general.

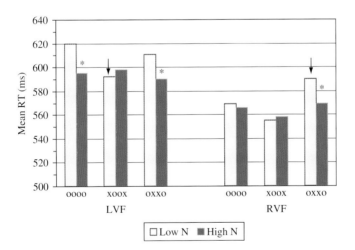

Figure 3.8 Experimental results for contrast adjustments for lateralized presentation of high-N versus low-N words in lexical decision. The presentation condition is indicated by **o**'s and **x**'s, which represent control and dimmed contrast levels, respectively, for the letter in the corresponding position. For example, **oooo** denotes the control condition, whereas **xoox** represents the condition in which the outer letters were dimmed. A statistically significant ($p < 0.5$) difference between high-N and low-N conditions is indicated with a star. A contrast-adjusted condition that significantly differed from its respective control presentation is indicated by an arrow.

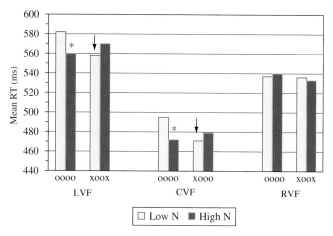

Figure 3.9 Experimental results for central visual field (CVF) and lateralized presentation of high-N versus low-N words. Presentation conditions and statistically significant differences are displayed in the same manner as in Figure 3.8.

The first experiment also shows that the N effect can be created in the RVF by dimming the internal letters, as predicted. These results firmly establish that the N effect depends on orthographic activation patterns. When top-down input can help the internal letters fire earlier, an N effect occurs. When they already fire as early as possible relative to each other (due to a shallow acuity/locational gradient), no N effect occurs.

Note also that, across experiments, the majority (10 of 14) of the adjusted conditions did not differ from their respective controls, confirming the assumption that dimming would have little direct effect on the processing of the affected letters. Rather, differences from the control condition only occurred in those cases in which the adjustment was predicted to modulate the effect of low N.

In summary, these experiments demonstrate that the asymmetries of the N and length effects do not arise from inherent differences in processing at the lexical level, because if that were the case, it would not be possible to reverse the asymmetries via visual manipulations. Rather, the N effect occurs when the slope of the locational gradient is sufficiently steep that top-down input can assist with the firing of the internal letters. The locational gradient is steeper for the LVF and CVF than for the RVF, explaining the pattern of the N effect. In contrast, the length effect occurs when the locational gradient is not smoothly decreasing. This only occurs for the LVF, explaining the pattern of the length effect.

This analysis suggests that it may be possible for top-down input from high N to compensate for a non-smooth LVF gradient in longer words. Indeed,

Lavidor and Ellis (2002b) showed that for high-N words of four to six letters, the LVF length effect was absent (but was present for low-N words). That is, the facilitatory effect of high N increased with length, canceling the length effect. These results show that performance under LVF presentation is very dependent on orthographic activation patterns, which can be adjusted via top-down input or contrast manipulations. Indeed, Chiarello (1985) demonstrated that centrally presented orthographic primes produced facilitation for LVF, but not RVF, target presentation (under automatic priming conditions where the probability of a prime–target relationship was low). This LVF sensitivity may also contribute to asymmetries in semantic priming, as discussed next.

Semantic Asymmetries

Thus far, we have examined theoretical arguments and experimental evidence for a sublexical source of VF asymmetries associated with lexical processing. Next, we consider how such a sublexical source could also lead to asymmetries in semantic processing. In the following, I characterize the effect of LVF presentation as providing impaired orthographic encoding and reduced bottom-up input. This subsumes all effects of differences in letter activations that lead to a reduced match to connection weights and/or slowed activation of the target word.

Semantic Priming

Various attributes of the prime–target relationship can be manipulated under hemifield presentation of the target. The prime can be presented to the CVF, to the same hemifield as the target, or to the opposite hemifield. The target can be related to the prime by association, (e.g., SPIDER and WEB), shared semantic category (e.g., BEET and TURNIP), or by both attributes (e.g. NURSE and DOCTOR). The strength of a such semantic or associative relationship can also be varied. If the prime or target is ambiguous in meaning, the related word can refer to either the dominant meaning (e.g., BANK and MONEY) or to the subordinate meaning (e.g., BANK and RIVER). Manipulations of these factors have yielded different patterns of visual field asymmetries. First, I review the major findings. All studies discussed here are lexical-decision experiments.

Burgess and Simpson (1988) used the central presentation of an ambiguous prime followed by the presentation of a target related to the prime's subordinate or dominant meaning. Under a stimulus onset asynchrony (SOA) of 750 ms, priming of a dominant target occurred for both LVF and RVF presentation, whereas priming of the subordinate target occurred only for LVF presentation. In another experiment (Faust & Lavidor, 2003), a pair of primes was centrally presented, and the targets were ambiguous. The primes were either both related to the target's dominant meaning, or both related to the subordinate meaning, or one was related to each meaning (mixed primes). For RVF targets, dominant primes were the most facilitatory of the three prime types; for LVF targets, mixed primes were the most facilitatory.

Chiarello, Burgess, Richards, and Pollock (1990) compared priming of associative-only, semantic-only, and associative-semantic relationships for primes and targets presented to the same hemifield under an SOA of 600 ms. Associative-only primes produced no facilitation, and associative-semantic priming was present for both VFs, whereas semantic-only priming was present for LVF, but not RVF, presentation.

However, a subsequent study revealed the opposite pattern for semantic-only primes. Using prime presentation to the same or opposite visual field as the target under SOAs of 250 or 450 ms, Abernathy and Coney (1996) found facilitation when the prime was presented to the RVF (independently of target location), whereas prime presentation to the LVF did not provide facilitation. Koviosto (1997), using SOAs of 165, 250, 500, and 750 ms, showed that these conflicting results were related to the differing SOAs. For 165 and 250 ms, facilitation was stronger for RVF primes, whereas for 750 ms, facilitation was stronger for LVF primes, with a nonsignificant LVF advantage for 500 ms.

Another study (Hutchinson, Whitman, Abeare, & Raiter, 2003) compared strongly associated pairs with more weakly associated pairs (where semantic similarity was not controlled). For 50 ms SOAs, priming was determined by the prime's presentation location—RVF primes gave facilitation for strong, but not weak, associates for target presentation to either VF, while LVF primes gave facilitation for both strong and weak associates. This pattern differs from semantic-only priming for brief SOAs, where priming was stronger for RVF primes. For 750 ms SOAs, LVF primes gave facilitation for strong associates only, although priming for weak associates just missed significance for the LVF/LVF prime–target condition.

In understanding the observed asymmetries, two separate issues are noted. When the prime is centrally presented, any VF differences must arise from differing influences of the prime on the activation of the target word. When the prime is laterally presented, VF effects can also arise from the way in which the primed word differentially interacts with other lexical and semantic representations in the lexicon.

Based on factors that we have already discussed, I address the resulting VF differences in both these cases. When the effect of the prime is held constant (central presentation), LVF target presentation can result in stronger priming because both semantic and orthographic priming are possible. That is, for RVF presentation, priming is limited to interactions between the semantic and lexical levels; for LVF presentation, interactions between the lexical and orthographic levels can lead to facilitation as well, resulting in greater total facilitation. We now consider how this proposal explains the experimental findings for ambiguous words.

I will assume that there are separate lexical representations for the different meanings of the word, and that there is a separate, semantic level of representation. Each lexical representation of the word inhibits unrelated meanings. The lexical representations of related words are primed via spreading activation within and between the semantic and lexical levels.

Figure 3.10 shows the proposed interactions for the results of Burgess and Simpson (1988). When the prime is presented, it activates both meanings at the lexical and semantic levels, as well as words associated with both meanings. Under a long SOA, the dominant meaning will inhibit the subordinate meaning, but words related to the subordinate meaning remain primed because they do not directly receive the inhibition related to the competition between the meanings.

When a subordinate target is presented to the RVF, there is no facilitation, because it takes extra energy to co-activate the corresponding semantic representation (which has been inhibited by the dominant meaning.) Thus, although the lexical node corresponding to the subordinate target is primed, this priming is not evident due to the interaction with the semantic level. For LVF presentation, the interaction between the semantic and lexical levels is the same as for RVF presentation. However, in this case, an opportunity for orthographic priming occurs. The primed lexical node provides top-down input to the orthographic level, smoothing the locational gradient, and facilitating responses. This type of priming does not occur for the RVF because the locational gradient is already smoothly decreasing. Thus, there is facilitation of the subordinate meaning for LVF, but not RVF, presentation.

Next we consider priming for an ambiguous target, as described by Lavidor and Faust (2003). LVF priming should be strongest when top-down input to the orthographic level is maximized. This would occur when both of the target's lexical nodes are primed, namely in the mixed-primes condition, as observed. In contrast, RVF priming is strongest for dominant primes because priming is limited to the semantic/lexical levels, and dominant primes provide the strongest semantic priming.

What is the effect of lateralization of the prime? Because activation levels are lower under lateralized primes and so top-down influence from the lexical to orthographic levels is reduced, priming is dominated by the VF of the prime, not the target. To consider the dynamics of lexical activation in more detail, when a prime is presented, the prime activates the corresponding lexical node, as well as exciting other semantic and lexical representations via spreading activation. However, lateral inhibition within the lexical level

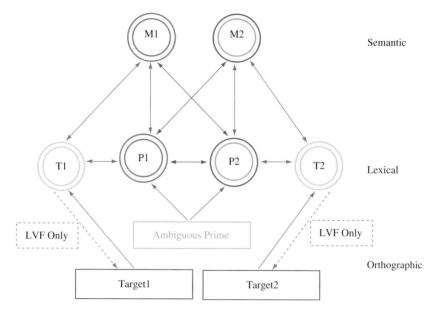

Figure 3.10 Illustration of proposed effect of 750 ms SOA in Burgess and Simpson (1988). Arrows represent net effect of interactions (*orange*, excitatory; *blue*, inhibitory). Inner node colors reflect the state of activation approximately 350 ms after prime presentation (*orange*, excited; *blue*, inhibited). Outer node colors represent the state of activation just before presentation of the target. When the prime is presented, it initially excites both meanings (P1, M1, dominant meaning; P2, M2, subordinate meaning), and spreading activation results in partial activation of word nodes of the related targets (T1, T2). Over time, the dominant meaning inhibits that subordinate meaning, so that, prior to target presentation, P2 and M2 are inhibited, but this inhibition does not directly affect T2. For a target related to the dominant meaning (*Target1*), the priming of T1 and M1 provide facilitation for presentation to either visual field. For right visual field (RVF) presentation of a word related to the subordinate meaning (*Target2*), top-down facilitation of the orthographic encoding is not possible, and the lack of excitatory support from M2 slows the rate of activation of T2, so that the net effect is no facilitation. For left visual field (LVF) presentation of Target2, top-down input from T2 provides orthographic priming, so that there is a net facilitatory effect.

will serve to inhibit the same lexical items that have been primed. For example, for the prime DOCTOR, the DOCTOR word node is directly excited, while the NURSE node is excited via spreading activation. However the DOCTOR node also inhibits the NURSE node, due to the usual competition within the lexical level (and the NURSE node inhibits the DOCTOR node, as well). Thus, related word nodes are both excited and inhibited.

Now recall that LVF presentation results in impaired orthographic encoding and decreased bottom-up input to corresponding word. This would have two contradictory effects. The reduced bottom-up input to the prime's word node would provide less excitation to drive spreading activation to related words. However, the reduced input would also decrease the inhibitory capacity of the prime's word node. The net effect of reduced bottom-up input on the activation of a related word node then depends on the relative levels of decreased excitation versus decreased inhibition.

The net result of the decreased inhibition, in turn, will vary with the difference between the activation levels of the related word and the prime. As this difference increases, the prime is inhibited less by the related word, so it can inhibit the related word relatively more. For example, if two competing nodes are well matched (little difference in activation levels), it will take a long time for one node to dominate. If the initial activation level of the more highly activated node is held constant, but the initial activation level of the other node is decreased, the more highly activated node will dominate more quickly. Therefore, the competitive interaction can be approximated as a one-way inhibitory connection from the more excited node to the less excited node, where the connection weight increases with the difference in their initial activations. Decreased bottom-up input to the prime can be considered to reduce the effective connection weight between the prime and related words.

As a result of these dynamics, the activation of a related word is a nonlinear function of prime activation. To illustrate, we consider a simple model in which the effect of spreading activation is given by a positive weight between the prime and related word node, and then the effect of competition is modeled via an inhibitory connection weight that is equal to the difference in activation between the prime and related word node. Let P denote the activation of the prime and E denote the excitatory weight: The initial activation of the related word node, R1, is then given by P*E. The inhibitory weight, I, is equal to P – R1, and the resulting activation of the related word node, R2, is given by R1 – P*I. For E = 0.5, as P increases from 0.2 to 0.6, R2 increases from 0.08 to 0.12. As P increases further (from 0.6 to 0.9), R2 *decreases* (from 0.12 to 0.045), as the effect of inhibition outweighs the effect of excitation. Thus, the related word activation (R2) initially increases as a function of prime activation (for P = 0.2 to 0.6), but then decreases as a function of prime activation (for P = 0.6 to 0.9).

In summary, the effect of LVF presentation of the prime depends on how the reduced bottom-up input levels affect the balance of inhibition and excitation on related word nodes. Due to feedback interactions, the activation of a related word may be a nonlinear function of the activation of the primed word node. As discussed next, this explains how VF asymmetries in priming effects could arise, and why VF asymmetries are dependent on SOAs and association strength.

First, we consider semantic-only primes. I assume that as SOA increases, activation continues to accumulate for the primed word node. That is, prime activation is an increasing function of SOA. I also propose that for RVF prime presentation for SOAs of less than 500 ms, the activation of a related word node is an increasing function of prime activation. Because LVF prime presentation results in less bottom-up input to the prime (i.e., less prime activation), the activation of the related word node is higher for RVF primes than LVF primes, giving an RVF priming advantage. This would correspond to P = 0.2 for LVF presentation and P = 0.6 for RVF presentation in the above example.

However, as SOA increases, RVF prime activations reach the level in which increased inhibition to the related word node outweighs increased excitation, and so the activation of the related word node decreases as prime activation increases. Thus for SOAs of greater than 500 ms, LVF primes result in higher related word activations than RVF primes, because the reduced LVF prime activations remain in the range at which related word activations are an increasing function of prime activation. This would correspond to P = 0.9 for RVF presentation and P = 0.6 for LVF presentation in the above example. See Figure 3.11.

Why, then, is LVF priming stronger than RVF priming at short SOAs for weakly associated primes (Hutchinson, Whitman, Abeare, & Raiter, 2003)? It may be the case that a weakly associated prime provides less excitation to the target than a semantic-only prime. In this case, inhibition would have a relatively stronger effect, and increased inhibition may outweigh the increased excitation, even at short SOAs. For example, consider E = 0.4 in the above example, corresponding to weaker excitatory effect. In this case, P = 0.2 gives R2 = 0.056, whereas P = 0.6 gives R2 = 0.024. So, for E = 0.4, R2 is a decreasing function of P in the range 0.2 to 0.6, whereas for E = 0.5, R2 was an increasing function of P in this range. So, it may be the case that a weakly associated prime corresponds to the lower value of E, where related node activations are a decreasing function of P even for low values of P. Therefore, an LVF prime advantage arises even at short SOAs. As SOA increases, priming should decrease because the increased values of P lead to relatively stronger inhibition. Indeed, for 750 ms SOA, weak associative priming was absent or nearly absent for LVF primes (Hutchinson, Whitman, Abeare, & Raiter, 2003).

Although these explanations of the various priming results may seem somewhat complex, they are based on the basic idea of a single mode of lexical access to a single lexicon. Under any model of visual word recognition, a delicate balance would have to exist between excitatory and inhibitory forces within and between processing levels. I claim that such complex, nonlinear interactions, modulated by the optimality of orthographic encoding, are sufficient to explain any VF differences. Even if the present explanations of the observed asymmetries are not precisely correct, they demonstrate in

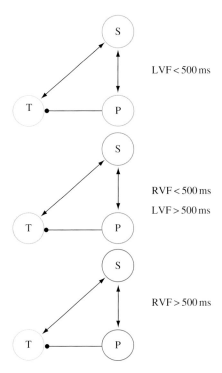

Figure 3.11 Proposed activation patterns for semantic-only primes by SOA and visual field. *P* and *T* denote lexical representations of the prime and target, respectively, whereas *S* represents semantic features common to both the prime and target. Activation level is depicted via the redness of the node (*yellowish*, lowest activation; *reddish*,= highest activation). Excitatory connections are shown by arrows, whereas an inhibitory relationship is shown by a closed circle, where the width of the line indicates the net inhibitory effect. For SOAs of <500 ms, the activation of the target increases with the activation of the prime. For SOAs of >500 ms, right visual field (RVF) prime activation reaches a level in which increased inhibition outpaces increased excitation of the target word.

principle how seemingly semantic asymmetries could arise from differences in orthographic encoding. In contrast, the usual explanation of semantic-priming asymmetries relies on separate modes of lexical access to separate lexicons. These more complicated assumptions are unnecessary, and are inconsistent with brain-imaging data.

   Shears and Chiarello (2003) characterize the semantic priming data as indicating that RVF presentation results in the rapid and narrow activation of related meanings, while LVF presentation results in a slower and broader activation of related meanings. This summary can be understood in a way that is consistent with a single route to the lexicon. LVF activation of lexical items (and related meanings) is slower due to an impaired orthographic encoding. LVF activation is broader because the reduced activation of the corresponding word decreases its inhibitory capacity, allowing related lexical items to remain activated.

This analysis suggests that it may be more difficult to use a contrast adjustment to get the LVF to look like the RVF for semantic asymmetries than in the length or N experiments. In those experiments, it was sufficient to change bottom-up input levels relative to *LVF* conditions in order to create the usual RVF RT pattern in the LVF. To abolish the length effect, the LVF six-letter RT had to be reduced to that of the LVF four-letter RT. To abolish the N effect, the LVF low-N RT had to be reduced to that of the LVF high-N RT. However, in semantic priming, the LVF contrast adjustment may need to mimic the input level of the *RVF* control condition in order to reproduce the RVF priming pattern. That is, the semantic priming pattern may depend on the *absolute* level of bottom-up input. Thus, if the LVF contrast adjustment is not sufficient to fully compensate for LVF presentation (i.e., if it does reduce the LVF RT all the way to the RVF control level), the RVF semantic-priming pattern may not be fully replicated. Conversely, if RVF bottom-up input levels are not degraded all the way to LVF levels, the LVF pattern may not appear in the RVF.

Indeed, our preliminary data from the application of contrast adjustments to the Faust and Lavidor (2003) task indicate that the adjustments give a priming pattern in both VFs that is intermediate between the control LVF and RVF patterns. That is, the manipulations seem to abolish this semantic asymmetry, rather than reverse it.

Asymmetry of the N400

Kutas and Federmeier (1999) have demonstrated an asymmetry that occurs with respect to the N400 effect in sentence processing. It is well known that the amplitude of the N400 is modulated by how well a word fits into the context of a sentence (Kutas & Hillyard, 1980). In general, expected words give lower (less negative) N400 amplitudes than unexpected words. Therefore, N400 amplitude has been taken to index the ease with which the meaning of a word can be integrated into the semantic representation of a sentence.

Federmeier and Kutas (1999) investigated this effect for three conditions: (a) an expected word; (b) an unexpected word within the same semantic category as the expected word (within-category violation); and (c) an unexpected word in a different, but related, semantic category (between-category violation). For example:

They wanted to make the hotel look more like a tropical resort, so along the driveway they planted rows of: (a) palms (b) pines (c) tulips.

Here *pines* and *tulips* are both unexpected, but pines are trees, like the expected word *palms*, whereas tulips are not.

For central presentation of all words in the sentence (including the critical word), they found that semantic similarity to the expected word modulated the N400: within-category violations gave smaller amplitudes than between-category violations (with expected words giving the smallest amplitudes). For lateralized presentation of the critical word (with central presentation of the sentential context), the same pattern arose for RVF presentation. For LVF presentation, the N400 amplitudes of expected words and between-category violations were the same as the RVF amplitudes, respectively, but the amplitude of within-category violations increased, making it equal to that of the between-category violation. Thus, in the LVF, there was no effect of the degree of similarity to the expected word. The authors interpreted this asymmetry as indicating that the two hemispheres specialize in different aspects of semantic integration, as quoted at the beginning of this chapter (Kutas & Federmeier, 1999).

Before explaining this asymmetry, we must first understand what the N400 is measuring. The Federmeier and Kutas (1999) result for central presentation indicates that the N400 is primarily sensitive not to how well a word fits into the sentence, but rather to its degree of semantic priming. That is, the semantic features activated by the expected word also preactivate related words to varying degrees, and the N400 indexes this priming. For example, *pines* shares more features with *palms* than does *tulips*, so *pines* is more highly primed than *tulips*, which is reflected in a reduced N400 component. This result is entirely consistent with the N400 effect in nonsentential contexts. For word lists, N400 amplitude decreases with a word's semantic similarity to previous words (Bentin, Kutas, & Hillyard, 1993).

However, N400 amplitude is also modulated by factors unrelated to semantic priming. For word lists and lexical decision, N400 amplitude is larger for low-frequency words than high-frequency words (Rugg & Doyle, 1992; Debruille, 1998). For words and nonwords in a lexical decision, N400 amplitude increases with orthographic neighborhood size (N), whereas N400 amplitude is higher overall for nonwords than words. For low-frequency words in a lexical decision, N400 amplitude is larger for words that resemble a higher-frequency word than for ones that do not (e.g., BRIBE vs. CIRCUS; BRIBE is similar to BRIDE while CIRCUS is not similar to any higher-frequency word) (Debruille, 1998). In a task where two stimuli (S1, S2) were successively shown, and the subject had to specify whether or not a probe stimulus was the same as S1 and/or S2, there was N400 priming of S2 even when it was a pseudoword that did not resemble a real word (a nonderivational pseudoword). That is, when S1 and S2 were the same nonderivational pseudoword, an N400 component was present for S1, but was completely absent for S2 (Deacon, Dynowska, Ritter, & Grose-Fifer, 2004).

Together, these results suggest that the N400 measures total lexical activation over the course of the activation of the target word, which depends on how efficiently the target word can inhibit its competitors. When a word is highly primed, it gets a head start on inhibiting competitors; total lexical activation and N400 amplitude are reduced as compared to unprimed targets. When a word has more neighbors, N400 amplitude increases because there are more highly activated competitors. A low-frequency word is less efficiently activated than a high-frequency word, so it inhibits competitors less efficiently, resulting in an increased N400 amplitude. When a low-frequency word is orthographically similar to a higher-frequency word, N400 amplitude is increased by the activation of the similar word. For nonwords in a lexical decision, total lexical activation and N400 amplitude are the highest, because there is no matching target to inhibit similar words. However, for repeated pseudowords, the N400 component is absent because lexical access is not even attempted, as the subject already knows that it is not a word (Deacon et al., 2004). In sum, I propose that the N400 component does not reflect semantic processing per se, but rather reflects lexical processing, where N400 amplitude is inversely related to how efficiently activation can be narrowed to a single word (the target).

Now we consider the source of the N400 asymmetry. As discussed earlier, LVF presentation would result in less bottom-up activation to the corresponding (target) word node. The amount of this decrease to the target would be larger than the decrease to word nodes that are orthographically similar to the target (i.e., the target has the most to lose). As a result, activation is less focused on the target. This would reduce the efficacy of inhibition from the target to orthographic competitors, and increase N400 amplitude. If so, why did LVF presentation only affect the within-category N400 (relative to RVF presentation)? As shown in Figure 3.12, such a pattern could arise if N400 amplitude is a nonlinear, sigmoid function of inhibition efficacy. The between-category and expected-word conditions give ceiling and floor effects, respectively, while the between-category condition falls in the more sensitive range. Furthermore, the level of preactivation of the highly expected word is independent of presentation location, so reduced input to an unexpected word would also affect its ability to inhibit the expected word. Therefore, the increased LVF N400 for the within-category violation may also reflect a reduced ability to compete with the expected word. (Again, the lack of a VF effect for the between-category violation may reflect a ceiling effect.)

Thus, I propose that the lack of an LVF similarity effect results from a decreased advantage for the target over competitors, arising from nonoptimal LVF visual encoding. However, Kutas and Federmeier (2002) have also shown a similar pattern of asymmetry when the target was presented as a picture, rather than a word (i.e., an N400 difference for violation conditions in

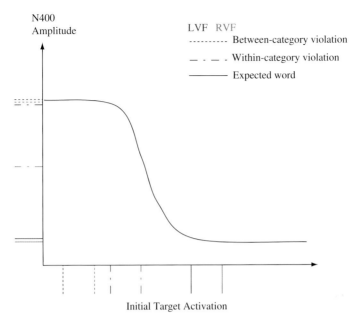

Figure 3.12 Proposed N400 patterns. The initial target activation for left visual field (LVF) presentation is reduced the same amount with respect to the corresponding right visual field (RVF) condition for all three types of target words. However, due to the shape of the N400 amplitude function, the resulting LVF N400 amplitude only differs from the corresponding RVF amplitude for the within-category violation.

the RVF, but not the LVF). They took this result as showing that the N400 asymmetry is purely semantic in nature, contrary to the claim I'm making here. However, in the picture experiment, the lack of a similarity effect in LVF arose because the between-category condition varied with VF. That is, the between-category amplitude decreased for the LVF, bringing it down to the level of the within-category violation. In contrast, in the word experiment, VF affected N400 amplitude for the *within*-category condition. This indicates that the lack of an LVF similarity effect in the picture experiment arose for a different underlying reason than in the word experiment. Therefore, the picture experiment by no means disproves the account offered here.

Conclusion

The implications of the brain-imaging evidence, the length and N experiments, and the present discussion of semantic asymmetries are quite straightforward. Visual half-field studies are inappropriate for making claims about hemispheric specializations at the lexical and/or semantic levels. Brain-imaging indicates a single lexical route to the lexicon (Cohen et al., 2000; Dehaene et al., 2004; Tarkiainen, et al. 1999), as would be expected on the basis of parsimony. That is, it would be inefficient to have separate modes of lexical processing for the LVF and RVF, and it is unclear how separate modes could be integrated together for a string crossing both VFs. Moreover, theoretical and experimental investigations based on the SERIOL model show that VF asymmetries can and do arise from orthographic activation patterns (Whitney, 2004; Whitney & Lavidor, 2004; Whitney & Lavidor, 2005). Therefore, it should be assumed that asymmetries in half-field studies reflect differences originating in prelexical, visual processing.

This is not to say that the usual strong RVF advantage for lexical processing is unrelated to the LH specialization for language. Consistent with the evidence for lateralization to the LH, I assume that orthographic information falling into the LVF/RH is transferred across the corpus callosum, activating LH representations encoding LVF retinal locations. Such callosal transfer could well affect the resulting LH activation pattern, changing absolute and relative activation levels across that portion of the string. For example, callosal transfer may further degrade the nonoptimal LVF/RH locational gradient for a left-to-right language. In a right-to-left language, the acuity gradient would be inverted for the RVF/LH, not the LVF/RH. In this case, the effect of acuity–gradient inversion may be reduced (relative to a left-to-right language) because the activation pattern does not also undergo callosal transfer, whereas the effect of callosal transfer alone on activation patterns (in the absence of acuity–gradient inversion in the LVF/RH) may create an LVF disadvantage (Lavidor & Whitney, 2005). The important point is that these influences originate pre-lexically. At lexical access and beyond, there are no *qualitative* differences in processing arising from presentation location or reading direction. Rather, the *quantitative* effects of callosal transfer and acuity–gradient inversion have repercussions at these higher levels of processing.

In closing, I have two suggestions regarding future experimental work into visual word recognition. First, the role of behavioral studies should not be neglected. Although brain imaging studies can localize *where* and *when* various stages of processing occur, they usually do not reveal *how* those brain areas carry out the processing being investigated. I believe that behavioral studies are actually more suitable for revealing the *how*. Due to the relative ease of running such studies, many different experimental conditions can easily be tested. In-depth analysis of the behavioral patterns can then inform us as to what algorithms the brain is using to perform a task. For example, the SERIOL model was developed primarily via consideration of priming, RT, and error patterns for letter and word recognition experiments. The proposed processing levels in the model fit well with brain imaging data that have since become available.

That said, I would also suggest that more emphasis be placed on performing half-field experiments in brain-imaging studies. The high spatial and temporal resolution provided by modern techniques may further clarify the point of callosal transfer of orthographic information, as well as the effects of visual manipulations. Such knowledge would help us to better understand how the brain carries out the task of visual word recognition.

References

Abernathy, M., & Coney, J. (1996). Semantic category priming in the left hemisphere. *Neuropsychologia, 34,* 339–350.

Andrews, S. (1997). The effect of orthographic similarity on lexical retrieval: Resolving neighborhood conflicts. *Psychonomic Bulletin and Review, 4,* 439–461.

Bentin, S., Kutas, M., & Hillyard, S.A. (1993). Electrophysiological evidence for task effects on semantic priming in auditory word processing. *Psychophysiology, 30,* 161–169.

Bouma, H. (1973). Visual interference in the parafoveal recognition of initial and final letters of words. *Vision Research, 13,* 767–782.

Burgess, C., & Simpson, G. B. (1988). Cerebral hemispheric mechanisms in the retrieval of ambiguous word meanings. *Brain and Language, 33,* 86–103.

Chiarello, C. (1985). Hemisphere dynamics in lexical access: automatic and controlled priming. *Brain and Language, 46,* 146–172.

Chiarello, C., Burgess, C., Richards, L., & Pollock, A. (1990). Semantic and associative priming in the cerebral hemispheres: some words do, some words don't … sometimes, some places. *Brain and Language, 38,* 75–104.

Coltheart, M., Davelaar, E., Jonasson, J.T., & Besner, D. (1977). Access to the internal lexicon. In S. Dornic (Ed.). *Attention and performance vi: the psychology of reading.* London: Academic Press.

Cohen, L., Dehaene, S., Naccache, L., Lehericy, S., Dehaene-Lambertz, G., Henaff, M.A., & Michel, F. (2000). The visual word form area: Spatial and temporal characterization of an initial stage of reading in normal subjects and posterior split-brain patients. *Brain,* 291–307.

Cohen, L., Martinaud, O., Lemer, C., Lehericy, S., Samson, Y., Obadia, M., Slachevsky, A., & Dehaene, S. (2003). Visual word recognition in the left and right hemispheres: anatomical and functional correlates of peripheral alexias. *Cerebral Cortex, 13,* 1313–1333.

Deacon, D., Dynowska, A., Ritter, W., & Grose-Fifer, J. (2004). Repetition and semantic priming of nonwords: Implications for theories of N400 and word recognition. *Psychophysiology, 41,* 60–74.

Debruille, J. B. (1998). Knowledge inhibition and N400: a study with words that look like common words. *Brain and Language, 62,* 202–220.

Dehaene, S., Jobert, A., Naccache, L., Ciuciu, P., Poline, J.B., Le Bihan, D., & Cohen L. (2004). Letter binding and invariant recognition of masked words: behavioral and neuroimaging evidence. *Psychological Science, 15,* 307–313.

Ellis, A. W., Young, A.W., & Anderson, C. (1988). Modes of word recognition in the left and right cerebral hemispheres. *Brain and Language, 35,* 254–273.

Estes, W. K., Allemeyer, D. H., & Reder, S. M. (1976). Serial position functions for letter identification at brief and extended exposure durations. *Perception & Psychophysics, 19,* 1–15.

Faust, M., & Lavidor, M. (2003). Semantically convergent and semantically divergent priming in the cerebral hemispheres: lexical decision and semantic judgment. *Cognitive Brain Research, 17,* 585–597.

Federmeier, K., & Kutas, M. (1999). A rose by any other name: long-term memory structure and semantic processing. *Journal of Memory and Language, 41,* 465–495.

Grainger, J., & Whitney, C. (2004). Does the huamn mnid raed wrods as a wlohe? *Trends in Cognitive Sciences, 8,* 58–59.

Holcomb, P.J., Grainger, J., & O'Rourke, T. (2002). An electrophysiological study of the effects of orthographic neighborhood size on printed word perception. *Journal of Cognitive Neuroscience, 14,* 938–950.

Hopfield, J.J. (1995). Pattern recognition computation using action potential timing for stimulus representation. *Nature, 376,* 33–36.

Hutchinson, A., Whitman, R.D., Abeare, C., & Raiter J. (2003). The unification of mind: Integration of hemispheric semantic processing. *Brain and Language, 87,* 361–368.

Koivisto, M. (1997). Time course of semantic activation in the cerebral hemispheres. *Neuropsychologia, 35,* 497–504.

Koivisto, M., & Laine. M. (2000). Hemispheric asymmetries in activation and integration of categorical information. *Laterality, 5,* 1–21.

Kutas, M., & Federmeier, K. D. (1999). Right words and left words: electrophysiological evidence for hemispheric differences in meaning processing. *Cognitive Brain Research, 8,* 373–392.

Kutas, M., & Federmeier, K. D. (2002). Picture the difference: electrophysiological investigations of picture processing in the two cerebral hemispheres. *Neuropsychologia, 40,* 730–747.

Kutas, M., & Hillyard, S. A. (1980). Reading senseless sentences: brain potentials reflect semantic incongruity. *Science, 207,* 203–205.

Lavidor, M., & Ellis, A. (2002a). Orthographic neighborhood effects in the right but not in the left cerebral hemisphere. *Brain and Language,* 80, 63–76.

Lavidor, M., & Ellis, A. (2002b). Word length and orthographic neighborhood size effects in the left and right cerebral hemispheres. *Brain and Language,* 80, 45–62.

Lavidor, M., & Walsh, V. (2003). A magnetic stimulation examination of orthographic neighborhood effects in visual word recognition. *Journal of Cognitive Neuroscience,* 15, 354–363.

Lavidor, M., & Whitney, C. (2005). Word length effects in Hebrew. *Cognitive Brain Research,* in press.

Lisman, J.E., & Idiart, M.A.P. (1995). Storage of 7 +- 2 short-term memories in oscillatory subcycles. *Science, 267,* 1512–1515.

McCandliss, B.D., Cohen, L., & Dehaene, S. (2003). The visual word form area: Expertise for reading in the fusiform gyrus. *Trends in Cognitive Science, 7,* 293–299.

Rugg, M.D., & Doyle, M.C. (1992). Event-related potentials and recognition memory for low- and high-frequency words. *Journal of Cognitive Neuroscience, 4,* 69–79.

Shears, C., & Chiarello, C. (2003). No go on neutrals? An interhemispheric account of semantic category priming. *Laterality, 8,* 1–23.

Tarkiainen, A., Helenius, P., Hansen, P.C., Cornelissen, P.L., & Salmelin R. (1999). Dynamics of letter string perception in the human occipitotemporal cortex. *Brain, 122,* 2119–2132.

Westheimer, G. (1987). Visual Acuity. In R.A. Moses and W.M Hart (Eds.). Adler's Physiology of the Eye, Clinical Applications (Chapter 17). St. Louis: The C.V. Mosby Company.

Whitney, C. (2001a). How the brain encodes the order of letters in a printed word: The SERIOL model and selective literature review. *Psychonomic Bulletin and Review, 8,* 221–243.

Whitney, C. (2001b). Position-specific effects within the SERIOL framework of letter-position coding. *Connection Science, 13,* 235–255.

Whitney, C. (2002). An explanation of the length effect for rotated words. *Cognitive Systems Research, 3,* 113–119.

Whitney, C. (2004). Hemisphere-specific effects in word recognition do not require hemisphere-specific modes of access. *Brain and Language, 88,* 279–293.

Whitney, C., & Berndt, R.S. (1999). A new model of letter string encoding: Simulating right neglect dyslexia. *Progress in Brain Research, 121,* 143–163.

Whitney, C., & Lavidor, M. (2004). Why word length only matters in the left visual field. *Neuropsychologia, 42,* 1680–1688.

Whitney, C., & Lavidor, M. (2005). Facilitatory orthographic neighborhood effects: The SERIOL model account. Submitted.

Wolford, G., & Hollingsworth S. (1974). Retinal location and string position as important variables in visual information processing. *Perception & Psychophysics, 16,* 437–442.

Young, A. W., & Ellis A.W. (1985). Different methods of lexical access for words presented to the left and right visual hemifields. *Brain and Language, 24,* 326–358.

II

NEUROIMAGING

4

The Functional Neuroanatomy of Reading

Nicola Brunswick

The Process of Reading

> To completely analyze what we do when we read would be the acme of a psychologist's achievements, for it would be to describe very many of the most intricate workings of the human mind, as well as to unravel the tangled story of the most remarkable specific performance that civilisation has learned in all its history.
>
> —Edmund Burke Huey (1908, p. 6)

Reading is one of the most important human cognitive skills. It is also one of the most artificial and complex, depending as it does on the automatic and accurate integration of visual word forms (orthography), auditory word sounds (phonology), and conceptual word meanings (semantics). Visual features are extracted from the printed image and combined to form individual letters. These individual letters and letter clusters are converted into whole words to which meaning must then be applied via successful lexical access. Once the semantic information stored in the lexicon has been retrieved, the meaning of individual words is combined within the context of the sentence to produce a coherent meaning.

Unlike speech, reading and writing have been identified as "latecomers" in evolutionary terms because of their artificially developed nature. Plato, for example, argued that writing "is inhuman, pretending to establish outside the mind what in reality can be only in the mind." Given the complexity and artificiality of the reading process, it is more likely that these skills are associated with numerous preexisting cortical systems that allow the processing of speech, visual processing, production of gestures, and verbal short-term memory. These interact in some remarkable way to enable us to read and derive meaning from individual letters, words, and sentences of increasing structural complexity.

This chapter describes and evaluates the application of neuroimaging and electrophysiological data to our current understanding of the functional neuroanatomy of reading. The studies reviewed will include data obtained from skilled readers and impaired readers using measures of glucose metabolism, oxygen consumption, and electrical activity, derived from techniques such as positron emission tomography (PET), functional magnetic resonance imaging (fMRI), magnetoencephalography (MEG), scalp-recorded electroencephalography (EEG), and event-related potentials (ERPs). It begins with a review of the currently most widely accepted model of single word reading: the dual-route model.

The Dual-Route Model of Single Word Reading

The dual-route model proposes that skilled reading in alphabetic languages such as English can be achieved in one of two ways (Fig. 4.1). One way involves the conversion of individual printed letters, or letter clusters (graphemes), into their corresponding sounds (phonemes) according to our knowledge of the grapheme–phoneme correspondence rules of the language. In this way, readers are able to access the pronunciations of words—regular words, unfamiliar words, and pronounceable nonwords (e.g., "callot")—without recourse to the lexicon. This is variously known as the grapho-phonological route to reading, the indirect route, the sublexical route, the nonlexical route, the assembled route, phonetic reading, or "reading by ear."

The alternative way involves recognizing visual word forms as whole entities in the lexicon. In this way, readers are able to access directly an associated phonological representation and semantic information for regular and irregular familiar words. As unfamiliar words have no representation in the lexicon, readers are unable to use this route to read words (or pseudo-words) that they have never previously encountered. This is variously known as the lexico-semantic route to reading, the direct route, the lexical route, the addressed route, whole-word reading, or "reading by eye."

The relative ease with which readers are able to apply grapheme–phoneme correspondence rules is dictated to a large extent by the level of transparency in a language (the depth of orthography). Languages such as Italian, Spanish, and Serbo-Croatian have an unequivocal mapping from graphemes to phonemes and have *shallow orthographies*. Italian readers, for example, must

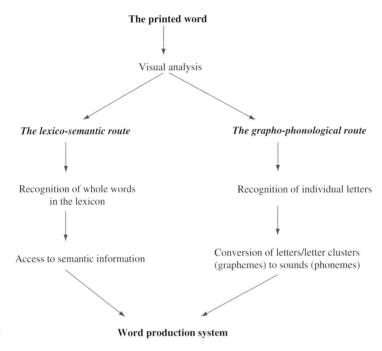

The printed word

Visual analysis

The lexico-semantic route   *The grapho-phonological route*

Recognition of whole words   Recognition of individual letters
in the lexicon

Access to semantic information   Conversion of letters/letter clusters
                                           (graphemes) to sounds (phonemes)

Word production system

Figure 4.1 Dual routes to single word reading.

learn to map just 33 graphemes onto the 25 phonemes that form their language. Therefore, novice readers of these languages, once they are familiar with the grapheme–phoneme correspondence rules, are quickly able to achieve a high level of accuracy in reading Italian, Spanish, or Serbo-Croatian text.

By contrast, English has a complex mapping between its graphemes, phonemes and whole word sounds, and has a *deep orthography*. This involves the often ambiguous mapping of 1,120 graphemes onto the 40 phonemes that constitute the English language. Consider, for example, the word pairs mint/pint, clove/love and gave/have. Just as the same letter sequences can have many pronunciations in English (e.g., the letter sequence "ough" in the words "cough," "bough," "hiccough," and "thorough"), the same sounds can be represented by numerous possible letter combinations (e.g., the sound /k/ can be represented by the single letter "k" [as in the word "walk"], by the letter "c" [as in "stoical"], by the letters "ch" [as in "stochastic"], or the letters "ck" [as in "pick"]).

If the grapho-phonological route was the only route to reading available, then readers of "deep" languages would be susceptible to making regularization errors—reading the irregular word "pint," for example, as if it rhymed with "mint." Readers of any alphabetic language would also be slowed by having to sound out each and every word. To circumvent such problems, the model posits that skilled readers are able to traverse the lexico-semantic route to access directly pronunciation and semantic information about regular and irregular words with which they are familiar. This route is, therefore, necessary for the reading of languages with deep orthographies.

The development of the dual-route model of reading arose largely from observation of patients with acquired dyslexia—those with reading impairment following brain injury (Marshall & Newcombe, 1966; see also Coltheart, Rastle, Perry, Langdon, & Ziegler, 2001). Patients with surface dyslexia (an example of an acquired dyslexia) are unable to read words based on their physical characteristics, but they are able to apply grapheme–phoneme correspondence rules. They are better able to read regular words and nonwords (e.g., "plank" and "trode") than irregular real words (e.g., "pint," which would be regularized to rhyme with "mint"). This pattern of errors suggests that these patients are relying exclusively on the grapho-phonological route to reading following impairment to the lexico-semantic route (Coltheart, Masterson, Byng, Prior, & Riddoch, 1983).

By contrast, patients exhibiting phonological dyslexia (another type of acquired dyslexia) are unable to read by applying grapheme–phoneme correspondence rules, but they are able to read familiar words as whole units, so they are better able to read regular and irregular familiar words (e.g., "cat" and "cough") than unfamiliar words, pseudowords (orthographically legal nonwords; e.g., "tonquil") or names (see Caccappolo-van Vliet, Miozzo, & Stern, 2004). This pattern of errors suggests that these patients are relying exclusively on the lexico-semantic route to reading following impairment to the grapho-phonological route (Patterson, 1982).

The dual-route model developed out of cognitive neuropsychological studies of patients with brain damage. A growing body of evidence from functional imaging and electrophysiology, however, suggests that the two routes that the model describes have actual counterparts in the healthy brain (e.g., Fiebach, Friederici, Müller, & von Cramon, 2002; Jobard, Crivello, & Tzourio-Mazoyer, 2003; Proverbio, Vecchi, & Zani, 2004).

Imaging the Dual Routes to Reading

In a meta-analysis of 35 neuroimaging studies of word and pseudoword reading by healthy adults, Jobard and colleagues (2003) found that the initial stage of visual word processing—the classification of word-like stimuli—was common to both words and pseudowords. This stage was associated with activity in the left occipitotemporal region, between the inferior temporal and fusiform gyri (a region previously labeled the visual word form area [VWFA];

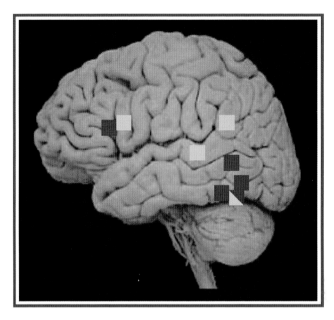

Figure 4.2 Brain regions associated with the dual routes to reading, as identified by Jobard and colleagues (2003). Regions associated with the grapho-phonological route are indicated by blue squares, those associated with the lexico-semantic route are indicated by red squares, the region associated with both routes is indicated by the red/blue square.

see Fig. 4.2. This region forms part of the ventral system identified by Pugh and colleagues (2000) discussed later.

Beyond this stage, the analysis supported the existence of two routes from print to meaning, with the grapho-phonological route being mediated by regions in the superior temporal gyrus, the supramarginal gyrus, and the opercular part of Broca's area. These regions are involved in phonological analysis and working memory, the latter process being necessary for the maintenance of information during the process of grapheme–phoneme conversion. The lexico-semantic route is mediated by regions at the occipitotemporal junction, the basal temporal cortex, the posterior part of the middle temporal gyrus, and the triangular part of Broca's area. These regions represent a direct pathway from prelexical processing (in the left occipitotemporal region) to semantic processing.

As this analysis and other studies suggest, areas in the left perisylvian regions appear to be important to the process of reading. Specific areas implicated include the anterior language area in the region of the left frontal operculum (Broca's area: Paulesu, McCrory, et al., 2000; Fiebach, et al., 2002); the posterior temporoparietal language area encompassing the posterior superior temporal gyrus (including Wernicke's area: Paulesu, McCrory, et al., 2000; McDermott, Petersen, Watson, & Ojemann, 2003), the supramarginal gyrus and the angular gyrus (Rumsey, Nace, Donohue, Wise, Maisog, & Andreason, 1997; Vandenberghe, Price, Wise, Josephs, & Frackowiak, 1996); and the posterior occipitotemporal language area including the posterior basal temporal cortex and the fusiform gyrus (Brunswick, McCrory, Price, Frith, & Frith, 1999; McCandliss, Cohen, & Dehaene, 2003).

These regions have been found to be activated during orthographic processing (processing the written form of letters and words), phonological processing (processing the spoken form of letter clusters and words), and semantic processing (processing the meaning of words and sentences). The relationship between these processes and the neural regions with which they are associated is considered next.

Imaging the Reading Process

It is now over 20 years since Petersen and colleagues' seminal functional imaging investigation of visual and auditory word processing in healthy adults (Petersen, Fox, Posner, Mintun, & Raichle, 1988). Using a series of hierarchical tasks, Petersen and colleagues associated "involuntary word-form processing" (during silent, passive word viewing) with activation in the primary visual cortex and bilateral striate and extrastriate cortices. Speech output (during reading aloud) was associated with activation in the cerebellum, the primary sensorimotor mouth cortex, the supplementary motor area, and the insula, whereas semantic processing (during verb generation) was associated with activation in the cerebellum, a region of the left inferior prefrontal cortex, and the anterior cingulate gyrus.

In a subsequent study by Petersen et al., the viewing of words was associated with activation in the left medial extrastriate visual cortex and in BA47, a left inferior frontal area anterior and inferior to Broca's area that is associated with semantic processing (Petersen, Fox, Snyder, & Raichle, 1990). Activation associated with the viewing of pseudowords (with their phonological but not semantic representations), was seen in the left medial extrastriate cortex but not in the left prefrontal cortex. Consonant letter strings and strings of false font (with neither semantic nor phonological representations) were not associated with activation in either the left medial extrastriate cortex or the left prefrontal cortex.

The authors suggested a link between activation in the left medial extrastriate cortex and the processing of words and pseudowords that obey the spelling rules of English. They identified this as a "word-form system" although this region has since been found to respond also to nonorthographic stimuli (Indefrey, Kleinschmidt, Merboldt, Kruger, Brown, Hagoort, & Frahm, 1997). Activation in the left prefrontal cortex was related to semantic processing, although subsequent failure by other researchers to replicate this finding has engendered considerable debate about the actual functional significance of this region for semantic processing (see Fiez, 1997; Thompson-Schill, Desposito, Aguirre, & Farah, 1997). No region of activation was specifically linked with phonological processing.

Orthography to Phonology

Studies designed to map the brain regions involved in the translation of orthography to phonology during reading have contrasted the reading/viewing of words with the naming/viewing of pictures (Bookheimer, Zeffiro, Blaxton, Gaillard, & Theodore, 1995; Menard, Kosslyn, Thompson, Alpert, & Rauch, 1996; Vandenberghe et al., 1996), the reading of pseudowords relative to regular and irregular words (Price, Wise, & Frackowiak, 1996; Rumsey et al., 1997), and the reading of Japanese Kana relative to Kanji (Law, Kanno, Fujita, Lassen, Miura, & Uemura, 1991). Kana is a perfectly regular orthography, the reading of which relies upon orthographic to phonological translation without need of recourse to the lexical access route, whereas Kanji does not rely on orthographic–phonological translation (although the suggestion that Kana is read entirely without lexical access has been challenged; see Ischebeck, Indefrey, Usui, Nose, Hellwig, & Taira [2004]). These studies suggest that the translation of orthography to phonology recruits the left supramarginal gyrus (BA40) and the anterior inferior parietal cortex.

Greater activation in the left inferior frontal cortex and occipitotemporal cortex has been found during the reading of pseudowords than during the reading of regular words (Ischebeck et al., 2004; Price, Wise, & Frackowiak, 1996; Rodriguez-Fornells, Rotte, Heinze, Nösselt, & Münte, 2002) and during the reading of words than during the viewing of consonant letter strings (Price & Friston, 1997). Others have specifically associated the reading of pseudowords and irregularly spelled real words with increased activation in the left inferior frontal gyrus, and the reading of regular words and letter strings with increased activation in the occipitotemporal cortices and the posterior left middle temporal gyrus (Fiebach et al., 2002; Herbster, Mintun, Nebes, & Becker, 1997; see also Simos et al., 2002). This consistent involvement of the left inferior frontal cortex in tasks involving rule–based orthographic-phonological conversion suggests that this region may play a role in segmented phonology (e.g., breaking the letter "g" down into the sounds /g/ and /ee/) and form part of the grapho-phonological route to reading (Fiebach et al., 2002; Paulesu, Frith, et al., 1996; Proverbio et al.,

2004). The left posterior middle temporal gyrus has been identified as playing a role in whole-word phonology (e.g., recognizing the letter "g" as a single complete entity), and may form part of the lexico-semantic route to reading (Simos et al., 2002) along with the occipitotemporal cortex, which is associated with the recognition of visual word forms (Cohen et al., 2000; Fiebach et al., 2002).

Further support for this suggestion derives from studies of language systems in different alphabetic orthographies (e.g., Paulesu, McCrory et al., 2000). This PET study of English and Italian skilled readers found that the reading of English resulted in activation in regions implicated in object/word naming and semantic processes (left posterior inferior temporal cortex and the anterior inferior frontal gyrus, BA45). The reading of Italian was associated with activation in regions implicated in phonological processing (left superior temporal gyrus and inferior parietal cortex). These findings (Fig. 4.3) can be interpreted as reflecting the different processes that underlie reading in a deep orthography (English) and in a shallow orthography (Italian). Whereas readers

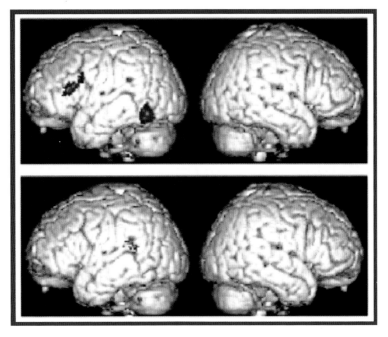

Figure 4.3 Regions in which English readers produced significantly greater activation than Italian readers during the reading of nonwords relative to rest (*top row*) and regions in which Italian readers produced significantly greater activation than English readers during the reading of words and nonwords relative to rest (*bottom row*).

From Paulesu, E., McCrory, E., Fazio, F., Menoncello, L., Brunswick, N., Cappa, S.F., et al. (2000). A cultural effect on brain function, *Nature Neuroscience, 3,* 1, 91–96. Reprinted by permission from Macmillan Publishers Ltd.

of English seem to activate the orthographic lexicon to allow them to select the correct pronunciation of words and nonwords, readers of Italian do not need to look up words or nonwords in the orthographic lexicon to find their pronunciation, instead they can rely on grapheme–phoneme conversion. This study shows how the involvement of orthographic and phonological processes in skilled reading is dependent on the transparency of the orthography, which in turn can shape neurophysiological systems.

Semantic Processing

As highlighted in the study by Paulesu, McCrory, and colleagues (2000), the left prefrontal/inferior frontal cortex is implicated in semantic processing, as well as in phonological processing (Demb, Desmond, Wagner, Vaidya, Glover, & Gabrieli, 1995; Kapur et al., 1994; Shaywitz, Shaywitz, Pugh, et al., 1995). However, when phonological processing is controlled for, activity in this region is either attenuated or eliminated (Démonet et al., 1992; Price, Moore, Humphreys, & Wise, 1997). Other studies have also failed to find activation in BA47 during semantic processing (Herbster et al., 1997; Price et al., 1996; Rumsey et al., 1997). A possible explanation for this finding may be that any form of semantic processing automatically activates phonological processes as well, so attempts at disentangling the brain correlates of the two processes are bound to be problematic (see Poldrack, Wagner, Prull, Desmond, Glover, & Gabrieli, 1999).

In one attempt to tease apart the relative involvement of the prefrontal regions in semantic and phonological processing, Gabrieli, Poldrack, and Desmond (1998) asked participants to perform a series of semantic and phonological tasks. They found a functional dissociation between regions within the left prefrontal cortex: while the more anterior frontal regions (in the region of BA47) were associated with semantic classification, the slightly more posterior frontal activations (in the regions of BA44 and BA45) were associated with phonological processes, such as rhyming and subvocal articulation (Gabrieli, Poldrack, & Desmond, 1998; see also Paulesu et al., 1996 and Fiebach et al., 2002).

Support for this dissociation comes from McDermott and colleagues (2003). During semantic processing, they observed activation in the left anterior/ventral inferior frontal gyrus (BA47), the left posterior/dorsal inferior frontal gyrus (BA44/45), the left superior/middle temporal cortex (BA22/21), the left fusiform gyrus (BA37), and the right cerebellum. During phonological processing, the left inferior frontal cortex (BA6/44, posterior to the semantic inferior frontal gyrus regions) and bilateral inferior parietal cortex (BA40) and precuneus (BA7) were activated (McDermott et al., 2003).

The identification of the left inferior frontal cortex (BA47) as a key player in semantic classification is consistent with the labelling of this region as part of a *semantic system* that allows the individual to access the meaning of written words. The semantic system also includes the left inferior temporal and posterior inferior parietal cortices. Activation in the left inferior temporal and posterior inferior parietal areas (BAs 38 and 39) was greater in response to sentences than to individual, unrelated words (Bottini et al., 1994) and greater in response to stories than to individual, unrelated sentences (Fletcher, Happé, Frith, Baker, Dolan, Frackowiak, & Frith, 1995). BA47 is thought to undertake an executive role, controlling the retrieval of semantic information from the more posterior regions (Fiez 1997).

In a review of nine neuroimaging studies of reading aloud single words, Fiez and Petersen (1998) concluded that, within the left hemisphere, the inferior occipitotemporal border in the fusiform and lingual gyri (BAs 18 and 37) was consistently associated with visual analysis specific to reading, whereas activation in the anterior superior temporal cortex (BA22/41) was associated with the stimulation of hearing one's own voice reading aloud. Semantic analysis was associated with activations near the border of the superior and middle temporal gyri (BA22/21). Speech production was associated with activations in the post-central gyrus (the motor cortex, near BA4), in the region of the supplementary motor area (the medial frontal gyrus), and in the cerebellum.

Anterior and Posterior Reading Systems

On the basis of these and similar data, Pugh and colleagues (2000) have suggested that three separate cortical circuits underlie skilled alphabetic reading—one anterior system and two posterior systems with dorsal and ventral streams (Fig. 4.4). The anterior system is localized in the region around the inferior frontal gyrus (including Broca's area), and is active during silent reading and naming; it is also engaged more in response to low-frequency words and pseudowords than to high-frequency words. Pugh and colleagues have suggested that this anterior system functions in union with the dorsal temporoparietal system to support normal reading development.

The dorsal stream of the posterior system comprises the angular gyrus and the supramarginal gyrus in the inferior parietal cortex, and the posterior part of the superior temporal gyrus, including Wernicke's area. Neuroimaging data have shown that, in early readers, this dorsal system predominates over the ventral system during the effortful reading of printed text, whereas in skilled readers, the dorsal system responds more strongly to pseudowords and

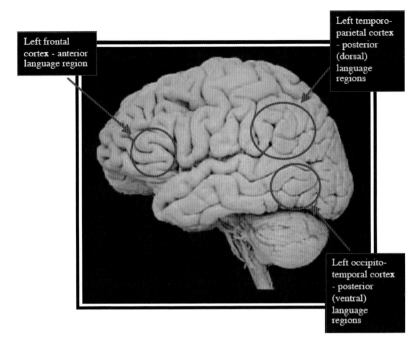

Left frontal cortex - anterior language region

Left temporo-parietal cortex - posterior (dorsal) language regions

Left occipito-temporal cortex - posterior (ventral) language regions

Figure 4.4 Areas of the left hemisphere that underlie skilled alphabetic reading.

to low-frequency words than to familiar words (Pugh et al., 2001). Furthermore, measures of regional cerebral blood flow in the left hemisphere superior temporal cortex have been found to be positively related to behavioral accuracy on an orthographic task (Flowers, Wood, & Naylor, 1991).

In a follow-up study using the same task, blood flow in Wernicke's area increased in adults who had been good childhood readers but decreased in adults who had been poor childhood readers. This effect was eliminated when task performance was controlled for. Blood flow in the angular gyrus, however, decreased (or did not increase) in those who had been good childhood readers, whereas it increased (or did not decrease) in those who had been poor childhood readers. This latter finding was independent of task performance (Flowers et al., 1991). On the basis of such evidence, the regions comprising this system have been linked with slow, rule–based reading involving grapheme-phoneme recoding and with mapping these orthographic and phonological representations onto their corresponding morphological and semantic associates (Pugh et al., 2001; Shaywitz, Shaywitz, Pugh, et al., 2002).

The ventral stream of the posterior system comprises the lateral extrastriate cortex and the left occipitotemporal junction (including the middle and inferior temporal gyri). In skilled readers, this stream is more significantly activated by familiar words than pseudowords and by pronounceable pseudowords more than unpronounceable nonwords (Brunswick et al., 1999; Tagamets, Novick, Chalmers, & Friedman, 2000). After an initial period of reading instruction, early readers show increased activation within the ventral system commensurate with their increased reading proficiency (Shaywitz et al., 2002). Taken together, these data indicate the importance of the ventral stream for skilled, automatic word recognition (Pugh et al., 2001; Shaywitz et al., 2002).

Anterior and posterior systems work together to support reading but the involvement of each system is dependent on the task demands (e.g., skilled reading of highly familiar words or the rather more effortful reading of pseudowords or letter strings) and the reader's level of skill. Individuals with developmental dyslexia show abnormal activation in the ventral stream (this is discussed later).

Reading Sentences

The majority of studies discussed so far have investigated the functional neuroanatomy of component processes involved in single-word reading. Some researchers have argued, however, that this "cherry-picking" of individual subcomponents necessarily leads to the administration of overly simplistic and "cognitively unnatural" tasks that are removed from the way in which reading normally occurs (Poeppel, 1996). For this reason, a number of researchers have undertaken studies to investigate the neural basis of sentence reading (Bavelier et al., 1997; Carpenter, Just, Keller, Eddy, & Thulborn, 1999; Kiehl, Laurens, & Liddle, 2002).

The reading of whole sentences has been associated with activation in Broca's area, Wernicke's area, the angular gyrus, and the anterior and middle regions of the superior temporal cortex. This pattern of activation may reflect, respectively, the syntactic and semantic analysis of words within the context of the sentence (Bavelier et al., 1997). Further activation in the dorsolateral prefrontal cortex may reflect this region's role as a "modulator" of activity within structures involved in semantic processing, such as Wernicke's area (see Frith, Friston, Liddle, & Frackowiak, 1991). This finding of activity within the anterior and middle superior temporal cortex is not reliably reported for the reading of single words, but it is a robust finding for the reading of sentences (Bavelier et al., 1997; Just, Carpenter, Keller, Eddy, & Thulborn, 1996; Mazoyer et al., 1993).

In an attempt to track the time course of reading comprehension, Carpenter and colleagues undertook an event-related fMRI investigation of functional activation during the reading of sentences that required participants to make spatial judgments. For example, a sentence would read "It is not true that the star is above the plus" and the picture that followed would show a star above a dollar sign. Participants had to press one of two buttons to indicate if the sentence was true or false (Carpenter et al., 1999). Within an average of 1 second of the individuals beginning to read each sentence, activation was observed in the left posterior temporal gyrus, possibly reflecting the coordination of representations used in interpreting spoken language and written text. Activation observed in the bilateral parietal cortices, in the region of the intraparietal sulcus, in the superior parietal gyrus, and the angular gyrus was interpreted as reflecting visuospatial processing.

An investigation of sentence comprehension found significantly greater activation in bilateral inferior frontal cortices, most significantly in the left dorsolateral prefrontal cortex, during the reading of incongruent sentences ("They called the police to stop the soup") than during the reading of congruent sentences ("The dog caught the ball in his mouth") (Kiehl et al., 2002). Activation in other regions believed to be involved in semantic processing at the level of the sentence—in the bilateral anterior medial temporal cortices and in the left posterior fusiform gyrus—was also reported. These regions— the anterior temporal lobe and the lateral frontal cortex—have been identified as possible sources of the language-related N400 ERP component.

The Time Course of Skilled Reading

Although data from studies using PET and fMRI have revealed a great deal about which cortical regions are active during the processing of spoken and written language, they are unable to provide information about the real-time course of these activations. To this end, electrophysiological techniques such as MEG, EEG, and ERPs can be useful research supplements.

An early MEG study of the silent reading of single words and pseudowords reported activation in regions associated with object/word naming, in left hemisphere inferior temporo-occipital cortex, within 200 ms of the words being presented (Salmelin, Service, Kiesilä, Uutela, & Salonen, 1996). A follow-up study by the same group found that specific time windows were associated with different levels of word processing (Salmelin, Schnitzler, Schmitz, & Freund, 2000). Within 100–150 ms of the words being presented, activation was observed in regions responsible for visual analysis of the written word, in the occipital and parieto-occipital cortices. Between 150 and 200 ms after word presentation, activation was observed in regions responsible for letter-string specific analysis, in left and right hemisphere occipitotemporal cortex. This was followed, between 200 and 600 ms, by activation in regions responsible for articulatory phonological processing/ subvocal rehearsal (left inferior frontal cortex) and semantic processing (left middle superior temporal cortex). Between 200 and 800 ms, activation was observed in regions associated with phonological aspects of language processing (in left hemisphere posterior parietal cortex) and attentional aspects of visual perception (right hemisphere posterior parietal cortex). Finally, from 200 ms onward, activation associated with the vocalization of words was observed in the bilateral motor cortices and the supplementary motor area.

These data show that, within 400 ms of the presentation of a printed word, activation specific to the letter-string starts in the left posterior brain regions; this is followed quickly by articulatory activation in the left inferior frontal cortex and semantic activation in the left superior temporal cortex. Together, these patterns of activity are interpreted as reflecting the process of orthographic–phonological recoding during reading.

Further electrophysiological support for the distinction between anterior and posterior semantic regions comes from data indicating the early involvement of frontal regions in lexical semantics and the later involvement of posterior regions in sentence processing (Posner & Pavese, 1998).

ERP studies of semantic processing have generally employed paradigms designed to elicit the N400 (Kutas & Federmeier, 2000), a negative-going peak occurring at approximately 400 ms after stimulus presentation. This typically occurs after participants read grammatically legal sentences that end either incongruously ("The dog ran up the sun") or unexpectedly ("The man had a drink of table"). The more incongruous or unexpected the sentence ending, the larger the N400 (Kutas & Hillyard, 1984), a finding that is thought to reflect the level of difficulty of integrating the terminal word within the sentence that preceded it (Kutas, Federmeier, Coulson, King, & Münte, 2000). The finding of larger N400s to semantically inappropriate sentence endings than to semantically appropriate endings has been recorded most consistently from the temporoparietal cortex (Connolly, Byrne, & Dywan, 1995; Helenius, Salmelin, Service, & Connolly, 1998), supporting this region's involvement in mapping among orthographic, phonological, and semantic representations of words (discussed earlier).

The studies discussed up to this point have associated specific left hemisphere brain regions with the subcomponents of alphabetic reading: visual word processing, grapheme–phoneme conversion, and semantic processing. These regions are situated in inferior frontal cortex (an anterior language system), in temporoparietal cortex (a posterior dorsal system), and in occipitotemporal cortex (a posterior ventral system). The observation that these, and other, brain regions are differentially involved in early reading and in skilled reading leads us to question the extent to which patterns of brain activation seen in good readers are reflected in the functional activations of children and adults with developmental dyslexia. This is considered in the next section.

Developmental Dyslexia

Developmental dyslexia has classically been defined as "a disorder manifested by difficulty in learning to read despite conventional instruction, adequate intelligence, and sociocultural opportunity" (World Federation of Neurology, 1968). It is characterized by unexpected impairments in reading and spelling, and by difficulties with processing speech sounds (e.g., recognizing rhyming words or repeating nonwords), with short-term memory for verbal material (e.g., remembering telephone numbers or directions), and with rapid verbal naming (see, for example, Frith, 1997; and Brunswick, 2009).

Over the years, a growing number of functional neuroimaging studies have identified brain regions that underlie the cognitive processes that are compromised in dyslexic readers (Brunswick, 2003; Paulesu, Brunswick & Paganelli, 2010). Three key brain regions have been found to distinguish between dyslexic and unimpaired readers: the left frontal cortex (particularly around the inferior frontal gyrus); the left temporoparietal cortex (particularly in the supramarginal gyrus and the posterior superior temporal gyrus); and the left posterior basal temporal cortex (the occipitotemporal region). Of these three regions—which correspond to the anterior and posterior pathways involved in reading described earlier—the left hemisphere occipitotemporal region is the one which shows the most consistent differences between dyslexic and unimpaired readers (Brunswick et al., 1999; McCrory, Mechelli, Frith, & Price, 2005; Paulesu, Démonet, Fazio, et al., 2001; Rumsey et al., 1997; Salmelin et al., 1996; Shaywitz et al., 2002).

Reduced Activation in Posterior Language Regions

Impairment of the dorsal pathway is revealed by studies employing rhyming tasks (Paulesu et al., 1996; Rumsey, Andreason, et al., 1992;), phonological processing (Shaywitz, Shaywitz, Pugh, et al., 1998), pronunciation and decision making (Rumsey et al., 1997), reading (Horwitz, Rumsey, & Donohue, 1998) and spelling (Flowers et al., 1991). Impaired functioning of the ventral pathway in dyslexia is evident in studies employing the silent reading of letter strings (Helenius, Tarkiainen, Cornelissen, Hansen, & Salmelin, 1999), the passive viewing of concrete and abstract words (Salmelin et al., 1996), nonword reading and phonological manipulations (Georgiewa, Rzanny, Hopf, Knab, Glauche, Kaiser, & Blanz, 1999), word reading and picture naming (McCrory et al., 2005), and explicit and implicit reading (Brunswick et al., 1999).

One MEG study found that, whereas unimpaired readers activated the left inferior occipitotemporal cortex within 200 ms of seeing words, dyslexic readers failed to activate this region within this time. Even within 700 ms, there was significantly less activation in this group than in unimpaired readers (Salmelin et al., 1996). These findings support the hypothesis that impaired phonological processing is associated with a functional disruption in the posterior neural system responsible for phonological processing (Georgiewa et al., 1999; Paulesu et al., 1996; Shaywitz et al., 1998).

The persistence of this functional disruption, even in behaviorally compensated adult developmental dyslexic readers, has also been noted in French and Italian dyslexic readers (Paulesu et al., 2001). During the performance of explicit and implicit reading tasks, dyslexic readers showed a consistent pattern of reduced left hemisphere activation, with a maximum peak in the middle temporal gyrus and additional peaks in the inferior and superior temporal gyri and middle occipital gyrus.

An important aspect of this study, not considered in some earlier studies of dyslexia (e.g., Rumsey et al., 1997; Salmelin et al., 1996), is that the dyslexic readers and the unimpaired readers performed the same task equally accurately. Differences in the patterns of neural activation found between the groups could not, therefore, be attributed to differences in task performance. Similar differences in activation, but with no differences in behavioral measures, have also been reported by others (Brunswick et al., 1999; McCrory, Frith, Brunswick, & Price, 2000; McCrory et al., 2005).

During explicit reading, the dyslexic readers again showed reduced activation in the left basal temporal gyrus (BA37), the cerebellum, and the medial lingual/occipital gyrus (Brunswick et al., 1999; Fig. 4.5). As mentioned earlier, these regions appear to represent a neural system involved in modality-independent phonological retrieval (Price & Friston, 1997). During the implicit reading task, in which participants made judgments about the physical forms of word, pseudoword and false font stimuli, the dyslexic readers again showed lower levels of activation than the unimpaired readers in left hemisphere temporoparietal regions: inferior parietal cortex (BA40/7) and middle temporal, inferior temporal, and posterior basal temporal cortices (Brunswick et al., 1999). Reduced activation in the left middle/basal temporal region, which was consistently underactivated in dyslexic readers relative to unimpaired readers, suggests a selective impairment in lexical phonological retrieval. This component of the language system is likely to be the source of a primary impairment in developmental dyslexia. Evidence from tasks requiring phonological retrieval (e.g., Spoonerism tasks, rapid naming, phoneme fluency) support the suggestion that dyslexia involves a core deficit in accessing phonological codes (Swan & Goswami, 1997).

McCrory and colleagues (2005) note that, although previous studies have shown that dyslexic readers produce little or no activation of the occipitotemporal cortex, their study—using word reading and picture naming tasks—found that good and dyslexic readers both showed activation in the occipitotemporal cortex,

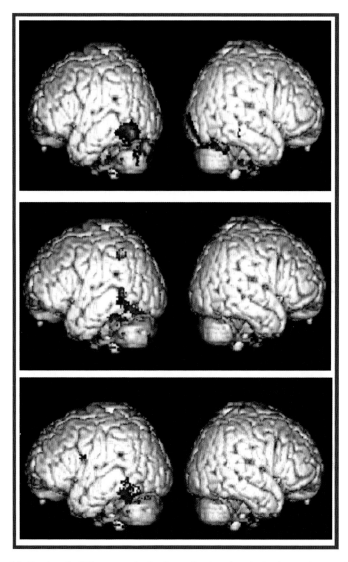

Figure 4.5 Regional differences in brain activation by dyslexic readers and skilled readers. Regions of reduced activation in dyslexic readers relative to skilled readers during explicit reading (*top row*), during implicit reading (*middle row*), and during both explicit and implicit reading (*bottom row*).

From Brunswick, N., McCrory, E., Price, C., Frith, C.D., & Frith, U. (1999). Explicit and implicit processing of words and pseudowords by adult developmental dyslexics: a search for Wernicke's Wortschatz? *Brain, 122,* 1901–1917. Reprinted with permission from Oxford University Press.

but dyslexic readers showed relatively less activation than the unimpaired readers. As this region is located between the visual cortex and the anterior temporal cortex, and has connections to the frontal cortex, this may be where visual, phonological, and semantic information is integrated (McCrory et al.,

2005). Dysfunction of this region might, therefore, reflect an impairment in this integrative process and may explain the reading and naming deficits of dyslexic readers.

During McCrory et al.'s (2000) word/pseudoword repetition study, dyslexic readers showed less activation than unimpaired readers in the right superior temporal cortex (BA22), the right postcentral gyrus, and in the left cerebellum irrespective of word type. The explicit/implicit reading study of Brunswick and colleagues (1999) had previously shown that dyslexic readers activated these regions normally when reading, suggesting that this observed neural manifestation of dyslexia is task-specific (i.e., functional and not structural). Other studies with skilled readers have associated attending to the phonetic structure of speech with a decrease in right hemisphere activity (Zatorre, Meyer, Gjedde, & Evans, 1996). It is arguable, therefore, that in this dyslexic sample, lower right hemisphere activation indicates reduced processing of nonphonetic aspects of speech, allowing greater salience to be afforded to phonological aspects of attended speech.

Dyslexia and Disconnection

As well as suggesting specific regions of neural dysfunction in dyslexic readers, functional imaging studies have provided evidence of poor connectivity within the brain's language systems. Whereas unimpaired readers have been found to activate anterior and posterior language regions (Broca's area and Wernicke's area) and the insula (irrespective of whether they were performing a short-term memory task or a visual rhyme judgment task), during a short-term memory task dyslexic readers activated only Wernicke's area (Paulesu et al., 1996). During the rhyme judgement task they activated only Broca's area. In neither condition did they activate the insula. This lack of connection between the anterior and posterior language regions, via the insula, may reflect a lack of automaticity in the processing of language by dyslexic readers.

Similarly, Horwitz and colleagues reported an absence of activation in the angular gyrus, the inferior frontal region, and the fusiform or lingual gyri in dyslexic readers (Horwitz et al., 1998). Unimpaired readers, by contrast, activated the left angular gyrus and extrastriate visual areas in the occipital and temporal cortex. Thus, it would appear that the angular gyrus is functionally disconnected from the left hemisphere language system in developmental dyslexia. (It is important to note that functional disconnection is not the same as anatomical, physical disconnection; two brain areas may be physically connected but functionally disconnected.) Abnormal activation of the angular gyrus is widely reported in dyslexic readers, and while the level of activity in this region is reported to correlate positively with reading ability in unimpaired readers, these two measures correlate negatively in dyslexic readers (Flowers et al., 1991; Shaywitz et al., 1998).

It is also interesting to note that anatomical differences (number and thickness of axons and amount of myelin) within the white matter of the temporoparietal region have been reported between dyslexic and unimpaired readers (Klingberg et al., 2000). Furthermore, a significant correlation is reported between the microstructure of this white matter in the left hemisphere temporoparietal cortex and reading ability. These functional anomalies within the angular gyrus and the structural anomalies within the temporoparietal cortex—regions that represent the dorsal pathway to reading—may be related to dyslexic readers' core phonological deficit. As this pathway is predominantly used by inexperienced readers and by skilled readers during "effortful" reading (i.e., during the reading of pseudowords and low-frequency words), it might be that abnormalities within this region lead to a developmental reading impairment.

Increased Activation in Anterior Language Regions

A correlate of reduced activation in posterior language regions during phonological processing is a relative increase in activation of inferior frontal regions in dyslexic readers (Brunswick et al., 1999; Pugh et al., 2000; Salmelin et al., 1996; Shaywitz et al., 1998). The occipitotemporal cortex and the left frontal operculum/insula are normally activated in concert as part of the modality-independent naming system associated with lexical phonological retrieval. This system is important either for the specification or the retrieval of phonological information (Price & Friston, 1997). It is possible, therefore, that greater activation of the inferior frontal cortex may be a by-product of weak connectivity between the anterior and posterior parts of the language system (as reported by Paulesu et al., 1996).

Others have suggested that enhanced frontal activation, along with a similar increase in activation observed in the right hemisphere posterior language regions during phonological processing (Grünling et al., 2004; Pugh et al., 2000; Shaywitz et al., 1998), may reflect the execution of compensatory mechanisms by dyslexic readers to support the impaired functioning of the posterior left hemisphere brain regions. In right hemisphere regions this compensation may be in the form of nonphonological visual pattern recognition (Shaywitz et al., 2002) whereas in inferior frontal regions it may be provided in the form of articulatory coding—the individual may be silently articulating the words to aid his or her performance of the task (Démonet et al., 1992; Grünling et al., 2004). Thus, these findings support neuropsychological evidence that both dyslexic and unimpaired readers employ a common language system for reading, but they activate anterior and posterior parts of this system differently, even when reading successfully.

Anterior and Posterior Abnormalities
—Evidence from Electrophysiology

EEG studies involving reading-relevant stimuli have associated dyslexia with increased levels of alpha activity (relative to unimpaired readers) in frontal regions during phonological processing (Rippon & Brunswick, 1998); in left frontal, midtemporal, and posterior frontocentral regions during speech perception, reading, and the processing of nonsense syllables (Duffy, Denckla, Bartels, & Sandini, 1980); and in temporoparietal regions during auditory phonemic discrimination (Ortiz, Exposito, Miguel, Martin-Loeches, & Rubia, 1992). As task-related alpha suppression is associated with attention (Ray & Cole, 1985), these findings may indicate reduced "cortical readiness" in dyslexic readers during these language tasks.

One study reported significantly increased levels of theta activity in the frontal cortex of dyslexic children during phonological processing but not during visual processing, while unimpaired readers showed a task-related decrease in their level of theta (Rippon & Brunswick, 2000). The dyslexic readers also showed a marked parieto-occipital asymmetry in beta amplitude (greater in the right hemisphere than in the left) irrespective of task; this contrasted with the pattern of task-related amplitude reduction displayed by the unimpaired readers. These findings once again seem to reflect differences in cognitive effort and strategy between dyslexic readers and unimpaired readers.

Theta amplitude is generally thought to reflect cognitive skill such that it decreases with practice and with the reduced attentional demands that accompany the skilled performance of a task (Rippon & Brunswick, 1998). Greater frontal theta activity in dyslexic readers during the phonological task would, therefore, seem to reflect the relatively greater effort expended by the dyslexic readers. The successful performance of the dyslexic group during the visual task suggests that no greater effort or attention was expended during this type of processing. The other finding—greater right than left hemisphere beta activity in the parieto-occipito cortex of the dyslexic and unimpaired readers during the visual and the phonological tasks—suggests that the dyslexic and unimpaired readers adopted similar cognitive strategies for the performance of the visual task. It also seems to indicate that the two groups of readers adopted dissimilar (or less proficient) cognitive strategies for the performance of the phonological processing task.

Similar anomalies have been reported from ERP studies of dyslexia. Significantly larger N100 amplitudes have been recorded in the left temporal region of unimpaired readers than in dyslexic readers during dichotic listening. The dyslexic group displayed comparatively bilateral activity (Brunswick & Rippon, 1994). While unimpaired readers tend to show greater levels of activity in the left hemisphere than in the right during language processing, dyslexic readers are often reported to show either no difference in activity between the left and right hemispheres (as in the study by Brunswick and Rippon), or greater activation in the right hemisphere than in the left (i.e., reversed asymmetry) in the language regions (Shucard, Cummins, & McGee, 1984).

In addition to these differences in amplitude, dyslexic and skilled readers often differ in terms of their ERP latencies (reflecting differences in the speed of processing of the two groups). Dyslexic readers, for example, are reported to display longer N200 latencies than unimpaired readers during lexical decision tasks (Taylor & Keenan, 1990); similarly, they display longer N140 and N230 latencies than control readers during auditory and visual recognition tasks (Neville, Coffey, Holcomb, & Tallal, 1993). Others have reported no inter-hemispheric differences in ERP activation in dyslexic readers during the processing of verbal and nonverbal stimuli (Chayo-Dichy & Ostrosky-Sollis, 1990). These patterns of symmetry/reversed asymmetry appear to be the result of lesser involvement of the dyslexic readers' left hemisphere rather than greater involvement of the right hemisphere. The differences in these waveforms, which occur approximately 100–200 ms post stimulus onset, are interpreted as reflecting differences in sensory/attentional processes in the dyslexic and skilled readers even at the earliest stages of visual and auditory language processing.

Dyslexic and unimpaired readers are also distinguishable on the basis of later ERP waveforms. Smaller amplitude/longer latency P300 waveforms, for example, have been observed in dyslexic readers relative to unimpaired readers (Taylor & Keenan, 1990; Grünling et al., 2004). The same has been reported for dyslexic men with a history of attention deficit and hyperactivity disorder (ADHD; Duncan, Rumsey, Wilkniss, Denckla, Hamburger, & Odou-Potkin, 1994). In this latter study, no differences in P300 amplitude were found between dyslexic readers without ADHD and unimpaired readers. Differences were found, however, between the dyslexic readers (with and without ADHD) and the unimpaired readers on the basis of their auditory P300 scalp distribution. Relative to the unimpaired readers, the dyslexic readers showed a more asymmetric P300 distribution (right hemisphere greater than left) at the frontal sites, while the unimpaired readers showed a more asymmetric distribution (again, right greater than left) at the parietal sites. These differences in the P300 waveform—an ERP associated with stimulus

evaluation and memory updating—have been interpreted as reflecting inefficient cognitive processing by dyslexic readers and an ineffective allocation of
attentional resources (Duncan et al., 1994; Rüsseler, Johannes, Kowalczuk,
Wieringa, & Münte, 2003).

Finally, the N400 is a measure of semantic processing that has shown
numerous, but seemingly inconsistent, differences between dyslexic readers
and unimpaired readers. Some researchers have observed an attenuated N400
in dyslexic readers (Grünling et al., 2004; Stelmack & Miles, 1990; Johannes,
Mangun, Kussmaul, & Münte, 1995), while others have reported an enhanced
N400 in dyslexic children (Neville et al., 1993). As the N400 provides an
indication of the ease with which individuals are able to integrate semantic
information within a context, this latter finding suggests that dyslexic readers
are experiencing greater difficulty than unimpaired readers with this process,
but taken together, these data may reflect the dyslexic readers' more subtle
difficulties with semantic integration.

A Note About Visual Processing

Although the majority of neuroimaging and electrophysiological studies of
dyslexia to date have focussed on the neurobiology that underpins language
processing in these readers, the last few years have witnessed a growing
interest in the contribution of visual perceptual skills to reading ability in
dyslexic readers. Dyslexic participants perform poorly on some visuo-spatial
tasks involving the copying of complex figures (Eden, Stein, Wood, & Wood,
1993; McManus, Chamberlain, Loo, Rankin, Riley, & Brunswick, in press;
although see also Brunswick & Martin, 2010; and Winner et al., 2001), the
counting of rapidly presented dots (Eden et al., 1993), and the mental rotation
of shapes (Winner et al., 2001) and letters (Rusiak, Lachmann, Jaskowski &
van Leeuwen, 2007). Such errors are not the result of a gross visual impairment; instead they have been linked to more subtle deficits in fundamental
aspects of visual processing including the functioning of the transient visual
system (Livingstone, Rosen, Drislane, & Galaburda, 1991; Lovegrove, 1993).
This system, which forms part of the magnocellular pathway of the lateral
geniculate nucleus (LGN) and projects onto area V5 of the visual cortex,
includes cells specialized for the detection of orientation, movement, direction, and depth perception (Lehmkuhle, Garzia, Turner, Hash, & Baro, 1993).

Structural or functional anomalies in the magnocellular pathway would be
expected to impair the efficiency of visual motion processing that would be
reflected in abnormal activation of area V5 (Eden, VanMeter, Rumsey,
Maisog, Woods, & Zeffiro, 1996). Evidence from anatomical postmortem
studies (Livingstone et al., 1991) and psychophysics (Cornelissen, Bradley,

Fowler, & Stein, 1994; Willows, Kruk, & Corcos, 1993) has suggested the existence of such abnormalities, and of a selective impairment in the magno-cellular systems of dyslexic readers. A growing body of evidence has linked these magnocellular abnormalities with delays in learning to read (Cornelissen et al., 1994; Talcott, Witton, McClean, Hansen, Rees, Green, & Stein, 2000).

The subtlety of the behavioral deficits and the specificity of the neural abnormality that underlies them is highlighted by Eden and colleagues' finding that coherently moving low-contrast dots failed to activate V5 in dyslexic readers, while they did activate this region bilaterally in unimpaired readers (Eden et al., 1996). No differences in activation were observed between the two groups in regions V1 (primary visual cortex) or V2 in response to stationary, high-contrast, patterns. Regions V1 and V2 receive information about direction of movement from the magnocellular layers of the LGN and transfer this information to region V5. These findings suggest a neurophysiological basis for the subtle visuoperceptual processing deficits associated with dyslexia (Stein & Walsh, 1997).

As reported previously for the functioning of the occipitotemporal cortex, however, it appears that dyslexic readers are able to activate region V5, but that activations in this region are abnormal when compared to those of unimpaired readers. Demb and colleagues, for example, observed activation in V5 in the brains of dyslexic readers, as well as in unimpaired readers in response to moving dots, although the unimpaired readers produced higher levels of activation than the dyslexic readers in regions V5 and also in V1 (Demb, Boynton, & Heeger, 1998). No significant group differences were observed in response to moving stimuli of high mean luminance. Given that the lower the luminance of a visual stimulus the greater the relative respon-siveness of the magnocellular system, this offers some support for the mag-nocellular pathway deficit hypothesis of dyslexia.

Although there is a core body of evidence in support of a magnocellular theory of dyslexia, this theory remains controversial. There is almost universal agreement that a fundamental deficit in developmental dyslexia is impaired phonological processing (Habib, 2000), but visual processing impairments are not always found in dyslexic readers (Skottun, 2000; Stein, Talcott, & Walsh, 2000). On the basis of their review of phonological, auditory, and visual abilities in adult developmental dyslexic readers, Ramus and colleagues reported that whereas all of their dyslexic participants had phonemic difficul-ties, very few exhibited visual difficulties (Ramus et al., 2003). It is possible, however, that studies such as this one that report normal visuospatial processing in developmental dyslexic readers simply fail to tap into the extremely subtle deficits that manifest abnormal functioning of the magno-cellular system (Démonet, Taylor, & Chaix, 2004; Habib, 2000). It is also possible that abnormal patterns of activation in area V5 once again reflect a lack of functional connectivity within the dyslexic brain. As reported earlier, neuroimaging evidence has indicated a lack of connectivity between the left angular gyrus and the occipitotemporal cortex, including V5 in dyslexic brains (Horwitz et al., 1998). Further neuroimaging studies of the specific function of V5, of the link between the functioning of this area and an individual's reading ability, and of the interrelationships between the neural substrates of linguistic and visual processing will help to disentangle these findings.

Conclusion

Evidence from neuroimaging and electrophysiological studies has identified anterior and posterior language systems in the brain. Behavioral data have associated these regions with the processing of phonological, semantic, and orthographic information. These systems work in concert to support the development of skilled reading, and their contributions to this process may be explained according to the dual-route model of reading. Functional impairments within these systems (e.g., hypoactivation in posterior regions and hyperactivation in anterior regions) and disconnection between these systems, have been associated with the cognitive and behavioral deficits that characterize developmental dyslexia. Once again, these may be explained according to the dual-route model and help to support evidence of the functional significance of particular regions gleaned from studies with skilled readers.

However, it is necessary to strike a note of caution when interpreting neuroimaging and electrophysiological data. Although these techniques have been used widely to investigate the neural correlates of the component processes of reading, it must be remembered that measures of blood flow, oxygen consumption or glucose metabolism are not measures of a neuron's activity but of processes associated with neural activity.

Increases in activation using any one technique might also be interpreted as reflecting the greater (and more effective) contribution of that region to a particular type of processing; this is not necessarily the case. Studies have linked "normal" levels of activation in specific brain regions with impaired cognitive function (Behrmann, Marotta, Harel, & Hasson, 2002), whereas others have associated lower levels of activation with greater ease of processing and familiarity with a particular type of stimulus. For example, Brunswick and colleagues (1999) associated the reading of pseudowords by dyslexic and skilled readers with relatively greater activation in language areas than the reading of words. Similarly, Briellman and colleagues used fMRI to measure blood flow in quadrilingual participants who were asked to generate nouns in each of their four languages (Briellmann, Saling, Connell, Waites, Abbott, & Jackson, 2004). They found that activation was dependent on language proficiency such that the more proficient the participant, the less the activation in the language areas.

Furthermore, the temporal and spatial limitations of PET, EEG, and fMRI have been widely acknowledged (e.g., Mazziotta, 1996; Volkow, Rosen, & Farde, 1997): whereas PET and fMRI show activation to within a few millimeters of the brain region being studied (i.e., they have good spatial resolution), EEG is not particularly good at localizing activation (it has poor spatial resolution). Conversely, EEG allows recordings to be made in milliseconds (i.e., it has excellent temporal resolution), whereas fMRI and PET involve measurements taken across hundreds of milliseconds and minutes, respectively (they have poor temporal resolution).

As we gain a greater understanding of the relationship between patterns of brain activation and function, future studies could overcome many of these technical and methodological limitations by combining techniques to maximize spatial and temporal resolution—by combining fMRI with MEG and/or EEG, for example, to obtain images with excellent spatial resolution in virtual real time—and by designing tasks that can reliably be used with different imaging techniques to allow comparisons to be made across the methodologies.

Using these techniques, it may prove enlightening to undertake longitudinal investigations of children's brains during reading development to identify the relative contributions of different language regions at different stages of learning. Studies in which individuals are scanned before and after receiving training in different cognitive skills involved in reading (e.g., phonological processing) might also reveal the specific effects that this training has at the neural level (as studies of aphasic patients have done; Cappa et al., 1997; Musso, Weiller, Kiebel, Müller, Bülau, & Rijntjes, 1999).

In one such study, dyslexic children were scanned before and after a period of training in auditory processing and oral language processing (Temple et al., 2003). The authors of this study observed that not only did this training improve the children's reading performance, it also resulted in increased activation in brain regions including the left temporoparietal cortex and inferior frontal gyrus. Similarly, Small and colleagues used fMRI to study brain reorganization in a stroke patient (who had acquired phonological dyslexia) before and after therapy involving the teaching of grapheme–phoneme correspondences (Small, Flores, & Noll, 1998). These authors found that prior to therapy the patient's brain activation was predominantly in the left angular gyrus (indicative of lexical reading) whereas after therapy her activation was predominantly in the left lingual gyrus, suggesting that she was using a sublexical reading strategy.

Future studies of this kind, using combinations of imaging techniques and carefully selected tasks, can only serve to enhance our knowledge and understanding of the neuroanatomy of skilled and impaired reading.

References

Bavelier, D., Corina, D., Jezzard, P., Padmanabhan, S., Clark, V. P., Karni, A., et al. (1997). Sentence reading: a functional MRI study at 4 tesla. *Journal of Cognitive Neuroscience, 9*, 5, 664–686.

Behrmann, M., Marotta, J.J., Harel, M., & Hasson, U. (2002). Activation in fusiform gyrus is not correlated with face recognition: normal cortical activation with impaired face recognition in congenital prosopagnosia. *Vision Sciences Society, Journal of Vision, 2*, 7, 562.

Bookheimer, S.Y., Zeffiro, T. A., Blaxton, T., Gaillard, W.D., & Theodore, W. H. (1995). Regional cerebral blood flow during object naming and word reading. *Human Brain Mapping, 3*, 2, 93–106.

Bottini, G., Corcoran, R., Sterzi, R., Paulesu, E., Schenone, P., Scarpa, P., et al. (1994). The role of the right hemisphere in the interpretation of figurative aspects of language: a positron emission tomography activation study. *Brain, 117*, 1241–1253.

Briellmann, R. S., Saling, M. M., Connell, A. B., Waites, A. B., Abbott, D. F., & Jackson, G. D. (2004). A high field functional MRI study of quadri-lingual subjects. *Brain and Language, 89*, 531–542.

Brunswick, N. (2003). Developmental dyslexia: Evidence from brain research. In T. Nunes & P. Bryant (Eds.). *Handbook of Children's Literacy*. Dordrecht, the Netherlands: Kluwer Press.

Brunswick, N. (2009). *Dyslexia. A Beginner's Guide*. Oxford: Oneworld Publications.

Brunswick, N. & Martin, G. N. (2010). Dyslexia and visuospatial ability: is there a causal link? In N. Brunswick (Ed.) *The Dyslexia Handbook 2009/10*. Bracknell: British Dyslexia Association.

Brunswick, N., McCrory, E., Price, C., Frith, C.D., & Frith, U. (1999). Explicit and implicit processing of words and pseudowords by adult developmental dyslexics: a search for Wernicke's Wortschatz? *Brain, 122,* 1901–1917.

Brunswick, N., & Rippon, G. (1994). Auditory event-related potentials, dichotic listening performance and handedness as indices of lateralization in dyslexic and normal readers. *International Journal of Psychophysiology, 18,* 265–275.

Caccappolo-van Vliet, E., Miozzo, M., & Stern, Y. (2004). Phonological dyslexia. A test case for reading models. *Psychological Science, 15,* 9, 583–590.

Cappa, S. F., Perani, D., Grassi F., Bressi, S., Alberoni, M., Franceschi, M., et al. (1997). A PET follow-up study of recovery after stroke in acute aphasics. *Brain and Language, 56,* 55–67.

Carpenter, P. A., Just, M. A., Keller, T. A., Eddy, W. F., & Thulborn, K. R. (1999). Time course of fMRI-activation in language and spatial networks during sentence comprehension. *Neuroimage, 10,* 2, 216–224.

Chayo-Dichy, R., & Ostrosky-Sollis, F. (1990). Neuroelectric correlates of dyslexia, *Revista Mexicana de Psicologia, 7,* 1, 109–119.

Cohen, L., Dehaene, S., Naccache, L., Lehéricy, S., Dehaene-Lambertz, G., Hénaff, M. A., & Michel, F. (2000). The visual word form area: spatial and temporal characterization of an initial stage of reading in normal subjects and posterior split-brain patients. *Brain, 123*, 291–307.

Coltheart, M., Masterson, J., Byng, S., Prior, M., & Riddoch, J. (1983). Surface dyslexia. *Quarterly Journal of Experimental Psychology, 37A, 469–495.*

Coltheart, M., Rastle, K., Perry, C., Langdon, R., & Ziegler, J. (2001). The DRC model: A model of visual word recognition and reading aloud. *Psychological Review, 108,* 204–256.

Connolly, J. F., Byrne, J. M., & Dywan, C. A. (1995). Assessing adult receptive vocabulary with event-related potentials: An investigation of cross-modal and cross-form priming. *Journal of Clinical and Experimental Neuropsychology*, *17,* 4, 548–565.

Cornelissen, P., Bradley, L., Fowler, S., & Stein, J. (1994). What children see affects how they spell. *Developmental Medicine and Child Neurology, 36*, 8, 716–726.

Demb, J. B., Boynton, G. M., & Heeger, D. J. (1998). Functional magnetic resonance imaging of early visual pathways in dyslexia, *Journal of Neuroscience*, *18,* 6939–6951.

Demb, J. B., Desmond, J. E., Wagner, A. D., Vaidya, C. J., Glover, G. H., & Gabrieli, J. D. E. (1995). Semantic encoding and retrieval in the left inferior prefrontal cortex: a functional MRI study of task difficulty and process specificity. *Journal of Neuroscience*, *15, 9,* 5870–5878.

Démonet, J. F, Chollet, F., Ramsay, S., Cardebat, D., Nespoulous, J. L., Wise, R., et al. (1992). The anatomy of phonological and semantic processing in normal subjects. *Brain, 115*, 1753–1768.

Démonet, J.-F., Taylor, M. J., & Chaix, Y. (2004). Developmental dyslexia. *Lancet, 363*, 1451–1460.

Duffy, F., Denckla, M., Bartels, P., & Sandini, G. (1980). Dyslexia: regional differences in brain electrical activity by topographic mapping. *Annals of Neurology*, *7,*412–420.

Duncan, C.C., Rumsey, J.M., Wilkniss, S.M., Denckla, M.B., Hamburger, S.D., & Odou-Potkin, M. (1994). Developmental dyslexia and attention dysfunction in adults: brain potential indices of information processing. *Psychophysiology*, *31, 4,* 386–401.

Eden, G. F., Stein, J. F. Wood, M. H., & Wood F. B. (1993). Dyslexia: a study of preserved and impaired visuospatial and phonological functions. *Annals of the New York Academy of Sciences*, *682*: 335–8.

Eden G.F., VanMeter J.W., Rumsey J.M., Maisog J.M., Woods R.P., & Zeffiro T.A. (1996). Abnormal processing of visual motion in dyslexia revealed by functional brain imaging. *Nature, 382*, 66–69.

Fiebach, C. J., Friederici, A. D., Müller, K., & von Cramon, D. Y. (2002). fMRI evidence for dual routes to the mental lexicon in visual word recognition. *Journal of Cognitive Neuroscience*, *14,* 11–23.

Fiez, J. A. (1997). Phonology, semantics and the role of the left inferior prefrontal cortex. *Human Brain Mapping*, *5,* 79–83.

Fiez, J. A., & Petersen, S. E. (1998). Neuroimaging studies of word reading. *Proceedings of the National Academy of Sciences of the United States of America*, *95,* 914–921.

Fletcher, P. C., Happé, F., Frith, U., Baker, S. C., Dolan, R. J., Frackowiak, R.S.J., & Frith, C. D. (1995). Other minds in the brain: a functional imaging study of "theory of mind" in story comprehension. *Cognition, 57,* 2, 109–128.

Flowers, D. L., Wood, F.B., & Naylor, C. E. (1991). Regional cerebral blood flow correlates of language processes in reading disability. *Archives of Neurology*, *48,* 637–643.

Frith, C. D., Friston, K. J., Liddle, P. F., & Frackowiak, R. S. J. (1991). Willed action and the prefrontal cortex in man: a study with P.E.T. *Proceedings of the Royal Society of London*, *244,* 241–246.

Frith, U. (1997). Brain, mind and behaviour in dyslexia. In C. Hulme and M. Snowling (Eds.). *Dyslexia. Biology, Cognition and Intervention*. London: Whurr Publishers Ltd.

Gabrieli, J. D. E., Poldrack, R. A., & Desmond, J. E. (1998). The role of left prefrontal cortex in language and memory. *Proceedings of the National Academy of Sciences of the United States of America*, *95,* 906–913.

Georgiewa, P., Rzanny, R., Hopf, J., Knab, R., Glauche, V., Kaiser, W., & Blanz, B. (1999). fMRI during word processing in dyslexic and normal reading children. *NeuroReport*, *10*, 3459–3465.

Grünling, C., Ligges, M., Huonker, R., Klingert, M., Mentzel, H.-J., Rzanny, R., et al. (2004). Dyslexia: the possible benefit of multimodal integration of fMRI and EEG data. *Journal of Neural Transmission*, *111*, 951–969.

Habib, M. (2000). The neurobiological basis of developmental dyslexia. *Brain*, *123*, 2373–2399.

Helenius, P., Salmelin, R., Service, E., & Connolly, J. (1998). Distinct time courses of word and context comprehension in the left temporal cortex. *Brain*, *121*, 1133–1142.

Helenius, P., Tarkiainen, A., Cornelissen, P., Hansen, P. C., & Salmelin, R. (1999). Dissociation of normal feature analysis and deficient processing of letter-strings in dyslexic adults. *Cerebral Cortex*, *4*, 476–483.

Herbster, A. N., Mintun, M. A., Nebes, R. D., & Becker, J. T. (1997). Regional cerebral blood flow during word and nonword reading. *Human Brain Mapping*, *5*, 84–92.

Horwitz, B., Rumsey, J. M., & Donohue, B. C. (1998). Functional connectivity of the angular gyrus in normal reading and dyslexia. *Proceedings of the National Academy of Sciences of the United States of America*, *95*, 8939–8944.

Huey, E.B. (1908). *The psychology and pedagogy of reading. with a review of the history of reading and writing and of methods, texts, and hygiene in reading*. New York: Macmillan.

Indefrey, P., Kleinschmidt, A., Merboldt, K. D., Kruger, G., Brown, C., Hagoort, P., & Frahm, J. (1997). Equivalent responses to lexical and nonlexical visual stimuli in occipital cortex: a functional magnetic resonance imaging study. *Neuroimage*, *5*, 78–81.

Ischebeck, A., Indefrey, P., Usui, N., Nose, I., Hellwig, F., & Taira, M. (2004). Reading in a regular orthography: an FMRI study investigating the role of visual familiarity. *Journal of Cognitive Neuroscience*, *16*, 5, 727–41.

Jobard, G., Crivello, F., & Tzourio-Mazoyer, N. (2003). Evaluation of the dual route theory of reading: a metanalysis of 35 neuroimaging studies. *Neuroimage*, *20*, 693–712.

Johannes, S., Mangun, G. R., Kussmaul, C., & Münte, T. F. (1995). Brain potentials in developmental dyslexia: differential effects of word frequency in human subjects. *Neuroscience Letters*, *195*, 183–186.

Just, M. A., Carpenter, P. A., Keller, T. A., Eddy, W. F., & Thulborn, K. R. (1996). Brain activation modulated by sentence comprehension. *Science*, *274*, 114–116.

Kapur, S., Rose, R., Liddle, P. F., Zipursky, R. B., Brown, G. M., Stuss, D., et al. (1994). The role of the left prefrontal cortex in verbal processing: semantic processing or willed action? *Neuroreport*, *5*, 16, 2193–2196.

Kiehl, K. A., Laurens, K. R., & Liddle, P. F. (2002). Reading anomalous sentences: An event-related fMRI study of semantic processing. *Neuroimage*, *17*, 2, 842–850.

Klingberg, T., Hedehus, M., Temple, E., Salz, T., Gabrieli, J., Moseley, M., & Poldrack, R. (2000). Microstructure of temporo-parietal white matter as a basis for reading ability: evidence from diffusion tensor magnetic resonance imaging. *Neuron*, *25*, 493–500.

Kutas, M., & Federmeier, K. D. (2000). Electrophysiology reveals semantic memory use in language comprehension. *Trends in Cognitive Sciences*, *4*, 463–470.

Kutas, M., & Hillyard, S. A. (1984). Brain potentials during reading reflect word expectancy and semantic association. *Nature*, *307*, 161–163.

Kutas, M., Federmeier, K. D., Coulson, S., King, J. W., & Münte, T. F. (2000). Language. In J. T. Cacioppo, L. G. Tassinari, and G. G. Bernston (Eds.). *Handbook of psychophysiology* (pp.576–601). Cambridge: Cambridge University Press.

Law, I., Kanno, I., Fujita, H., Lassen, N., Miura, S., & Uemura, K. (1991). Left supramarginal/ angular gyri activation during of syllabograms in the Japanese language. *Journal of Neurolinguistics, 6*, 243–251.

Lehmkuhle, S., Garzia, R. P., Turner, L., Hash, T., & Baro, J. A. (1993). A defective visual pathway in children with reading-disability. *New England Journal of Medicine, 328*, 14, 989–996.

Livingstone, M., Rosen, G., Drislane, F., & Galaburda, A. (1991). Physiological and anatomical evidence for a magnocellular defect in developmental dyslexia, *Proceedings of the National Academy of Sciences of the United States of America, 88*, 7943–7947.

Lovegrove, W. (1993). Do dyslexics have a visual deficit? In S.F. Wright and R. Groner (Eds.). *Facets of dyslexia and its remediation.* Amsterdam: Elsevier Science Publishers.

Marshall, J.C., & Newcombe, F. (1966). Syntactic and semantic errors in paralexia. *Neuropsychologia, 4*, 169–176.

Mazoyer, B. M., Dehaene, S., Tzourio, N., Frak, V., Murayama, N., Cohen, L., et al. (1993). The cortical representation of speech. *Journal of Cognitive Neuroscience, 4*, 467–479.

Mazziotta, J. C. (1996). Time and space. In A. W. Toga and J. C. Mazziotta (Eds.). *Brain mapping: the methods* (pp. 389–406). London: Academic Press.

McCandliss, B. D., Cohen, L., & Dehaene, S. (2003). The visual word form area: expertise for reading in the fusiform gyrus. *Trends in Cognitive Sciences, 7,* 293–299.

McCrory, E., Frith, U., Brunswick, N., & Price, C. (2000). Abnormal functional activation during a simple word repetition task: A PET study of adult dyslexics. *Journal of Cognitive Neuroscience, 12*, 753–762.

McCrory, E., Mechelli, A., Frith, U., & Price, C. (2005). More than words: a common neural basis for reading and naming deficits in developmental dyslexia? *Brain, 128*, 261–267.

McDermott, K.B., Petersen, S.E., Watson, J.M., & Ojemann, J.G. (2003). A procedure for identifying regions preferentially activated by attention to semantic and phonological relations using functional magnetic resonance imaging. *Neuropsychologia, 41*, 293–303.

McManus, I.C., Chamberlain, R., Loo, P.-W., Rankin, Q., Riley, H. & Brunswick, N. (in press). Art students who cannot draw: An exploration of the relations between personality, dyslexia, perceptual problems and drawing skills. *Psychology of Aesthetics, Creativity, and the Arts.*

Menard, M. T., Kosslyn, S. M., Thompson, W. L., Alpert, N. L., & Rauch, S. L. (1996). Encoding words and pictures: A positron emission tomography study. *Neuropsychologia, 34*, 185–194.

Musso, M., Weiller, C., Kiebel, S., Müller, S. P., Bülau, P., & Rijntjes, M. (1999). Training-induced brain plasticity in aphasia. *Brain, 122*, 1781–1790.

Neville, H. J., Coffey, S. A., Holcomb, P. J., & Tallal, P. (1993). The neurobiology of sensory and language processing in language impaired children. *Journal of Cognitive Neuroscience, 5,* 235–253.

Ortiz, T., Exposito, F. J., Miguel, F., Martin-Loeches, M., & Rubia, F. J. (1992). Brain mapping in dysphonemic dyslexia: in resting and phonemic discrimination conditions. *Brain and Language, 42, 3*, 270–285.

Patterson, K. E. (1982). The relation between reading and phonological coding: further neuropsychological observations. In A. W. Ellis (Ed.). *Normality and pathology in cognitive functions* (pp. 77–111). London: Academic Press.

Paulesu, E., Brunswick, N., & Paganelli, F. (2010). Cross-cultural differences in unimpaired and dyslexic reading: Behavioural and functional anatomical observations in readers of regular and irregular alphabetic orthographies. In N. Brunswick, S. McDougall & P. de Mornay Davies (Eds.) *Reading and dyslexia in different orthographies*. London: Psychology Press.

Paulesu, E., Démonet, J. F., Fazio, F., McCrory, E., Chanoine, V., Brunswick, N., Cappa, S. F., et al. (2001). Dyslexia: cultural diversity and biological unity. *Science, 16*, 291, 2064–5.

Paulesu, E., Frith, U., Snowling, M., Gallagher, A., Morton, J., Frackowiak, R. S. J., & Frith, C. (1996). Is developmental dyslexia a disconnection syndrome? Evidence from PET scanning. *Brain, 119*, 143–157.

Paulesu, E., McCrory, E., Fazio, F., Menoncello, L., Brunswick, N., Cappa, S.F., et al. (2000). A cultural effect on brain function, *Nature Neuroscience, 3*, 1, 91–96.

Petersen, S.E., Fox, P.T., Posner, M.I., Mintun, M.A., & Raichle, M.E. (1988). Positron emission tomographic studies of the cortical anatomy of single-word processing, *Nature, 331*, 6157, 585–589.

Petersen, S.E., Fox, P.T., Snyder, A.Z., & Raichle, M.E. (1990). Activation of extrastriate and frontal cortical areas by visual words and word- like stimuli, *Science, 249*, 1041–1044.

Poeppel, D. (1996). A critical review of PET studies of language. *Brain and Language, 55*, 317–351.

Poldrack, R. A., Wagner, A. D., Prull, M. W., Desmond, J. E., Glover, G. H., & Gabrieli, J. D. E. (1999). Functional specialization for semantic and phonological processing in the left inferior prefrontal cortex. *Neuroimage, 10*, 15–35.

Posner, M. I., & Pavese, A. (1998). Anatomy of word and sentence meaning. *Proceedings of the National Academy of Sciences of the United States of America, 95*, 899–905.

Price, C. J., & Friston, K. J. (1997). Cognitive conjunctions: a new approach to brain activation experiments. *Neuroimage, 5*, 261–270.

Price, C. J., Moore, C. J., Humphreys, G. W., & Wise, R. J. S. (1997). Segregating semantic from phonological processes during reading. *Journal of Cognitive Neuroscience, 6*, 727–733.

Price, C. J., Wise, R. J. S., & Frackowiak, R. S. J. (1996). Demonstrating the implicit processing of visually presented words and pseudowords. *Cerebral Cortex, 6*, 62–70.

Proverbio, A. M., Vecchi, L., & Zani, A. (2004). From orthography to phonetics: ERP measures of grapheme-to-phoneme conversion mechanisms in reading. *Journal of Cognitive Neuroscience, 16*, 2, 301–317.

Pugh, K. R., Mencl, W. E., Jenner, A. R., Katz, L., Frost, S. J., Lee, J. R., et al. (2001). Neurobiological studies of reading and reading disability. *Journal of Communication Disorders, 34*, 6, 479–492.

Pugh, K.R., Mencl, W.E., Jenner, A.J., Katz, L., Lee, J.R., Shaywitz, S.E., & Shaywitz, B.A. (2000). Functional neuroimaging studies of reading and reading disability (developmental dyslexia). *Mental Retardation and Developmental Disabilities Review, 6*, 3, 207–213.

Ramus, F., Rosen, S., Dakin, S. C., Day, B. L., Castellote, J. M., White, S., & Frith, U. (2003). Theories of developmental dyslexia: insights from a multiple case study of dyslexic adults. *Brain, 126*, 841–865.

Ray, W.J., & Cole, H.W. (1985). EEG alpha activity reflects attentional demands and beta activity reflects emotional and cognitive demands. *Science, 228*, 750–752.

Rippon, G.M.J., & Brunswick, N. (1998). EEG correlates of phonological processing in dyslexic children. *Journal of Psychophysiology, 12*, 261–274.

Rippon, G., & Brunswick, N. (2000). State and trait EEG indices of information processing in developmental dyslexia. *International Journal of Psychophysiology, 36*, 3, 251–265.

Rodriguez-Fornells, A., Rotte, M., Heinze, H.-J., Nösselt, T., & Münte, T. (2002). Brain potential and functional MRI evidence for how to handle two languages with one brain. *Nature, 415*, 1026–1029.

Rumsey, J. M., Reason, P., Zametkin, A. J., Aquino, T., King, A., Hamburger, S., et al. (1992). Failure to activate the left temporoparietal cortex in dyslexia. An oxygen 15 positron emission tomographic study. *Archives of Neurology, 49,* 527–534.

Rumsey, J. M., Nace, K., Donohue, B., Wise, D., Maisog, M., & Andreason, P. A. (1997). A positron emission tomographic study of impaired word recognition and phonological processing in dyslexic men. *Archives of Neurology, 54*, 562–573.

Rusiak, P., Lachmann, T., Jaskowski, P., & van Leeuwen, C. (2007). Mental rotation of letters and shapes in developmental dyslexia. *Perception, 36*, 617–631.

Rüsseler, J., Johannes, S., Kowalczuk, J., Wieringa, B. M., & Münte, T. F. (2003). Developmental dyslexics show altered allocation of attention in visual classification tasks. *Acta Neurologica Scandinavica, 107,* 1, 22–30.

Salmelin, R., Service, E., Kiesilä, P., Uutela, K., & Salonen, O. (1996). Impaired visual word processing in dyslexia revealed with magnetoencephalography. *Annals of Neurology, 40,* 157–162.

Salmelin, R., Schnitzler, A., Schmitz, F., & Freund, H-J. (2000). Single word reading in developmental stutterers and fluent speakers. *Brain, 123*, 1184–1202.

Seymour, P., & Evans, H. (1994). Levels of phonological awareness and learning to read. *Reading and Writing, 6*, 221–250.

Shaywitz, S. E., Shaywitz, B. A., Pugh, K. R., Fulbright, R. K., Constable, R. T., Mencl, W.E., et al. (1998). Functional disruption in the organization of the brain for reading in dyslexia. *Proceedings of the National Academy of Sciences of the United States of America, 95*, 2636–2641.

Shaywitz, B. A., Shaywitz, S. E., Pugh, K. R., Constable, R. T., Skudlarski, P. Fulbright, R. K., et al. (1995). Sex differences in the functional organization of the brain for language. *Nature, 373*, 607–609.

Shaywitz, B. A., Shaywitz, S. E., Pugh, K. R., Mencl, W. E., Fulbright, R. K., Skudlarski, P., et al. (2002). Disruption of posterior brain systems for reading in children with developmental dyslexia. *Biological Psychiatry, 52*, 2, 101–110.

Shucard, D.W., Cummins, K.R., & McGee, M.G. (1984). Event-related brain potentials differentiate normal and disabled readers. *Brain and Language, 21*, 318–334.

Simos, P.G., Fletcher, J.M., Bergman, E., Breier, J.I., Foorman, B.R., Castillo, E.M., et al. (2002). Dyslexia-specific brain activation profile becomes normal following successful reacprofial training. *Neurology, 58*, 1203–1213.

Skottun, B. C. (2000). The magnocellular deficit theory of dyslexia: the evidence from contrast sensitivity, *Vision Research, 40*, 111–127.

Small, S. L., Flores, D. K., & Noll, D. C. (1998). Different neural circuits subserve reading before and after therapy for acquired dyslexia. *Brain and Language, 62*, 298–308.

Stein, J., & Walsh, V. (1997). To see but not to read; the magnocellular theory of dyslexia. *Trends in Neuroloscience, 20*, 147–152.

Stein, J., Talcott, J., & Walsh, V. (2000). Controversy about the visual magnocellular deficit in developmental dyslexics. *Trends in Cognitive Sciences, 4*, 209–211.

Stelmack, R.M., & Miles, J. (1990). The effect of picture priming on event-related potentials of normal and disabled readers during a word recognition memory task. *Journal of Clinical and Experimental Neuropsychology, 12*, 887–903.

Swan D., & Goswami U. (1997). Picture naming deficits in developmental dyslexia: the phonological representations hypothesis. *Brain and Language, 56*, 334–353.

Tagamets, M. A., Novick, J. M., Chalmers, M. L., & Friedman, R. B. (2000). A parametric approach to orthographic processing in the brain: An fMRI study. *Journal of Cognitive Neuroscience, 12, 2*, 281–297.

Talcott, J.B., Witton, C., McClean, M.F., Hansen, P.C., Rees, A., Green, G.G.R., & Stein, J. F. (2000). Dynamic sensory sensitivity and children's word decoding skills. *Proceedings of the National Academy of Sciences of the United States of America, 97*, 2952–2957.

Taylor, M. J., & Keenan, N. K. (1990). ERPs to reading-related tasks in normal and dyslexic children. *Psychophysiology, 27*, 318–327.

Temple, E., Deutsch, G. K., Poldrack, R. A., Miller, S. L., Tallal, P., Merzenich, M. M., & Gabrieli, J. D. E. (2003). Neural deficits in children with dyslexia ameliorated by behavioral reacprofiation: Evidence from functional MRI, *Proceedings of the National Academy of Sciences of the United States of America, 100, 5*, 2860–2865.

Thompson-Schill, S. L., Desposito, M., Aguirre, G. K., & Farah, M. J. (1997). Role of left inferior prefrontal cortex in retrieval of semantic knowledge: a reevaluation. *Proceedings of the National Academy of Sciences of the United States of America, 94*, 14792–14797.

Vandenberghe, R., Price, C., Wise, R., Josephs, O., & Frackowiak, R. S. J. (1996). Functional anatomy of a common semantic system for words and pictures. *Nature, 383*, 254–256.

Volkow, N. D., Rosen, B., & Farde, L. (1997). Imaging the living human brain: Magnetic resonance imaging and positron emission tomography, *Proceedings of the National Academy of Sciences of the United States of America, 94, 7*, 2787–2788.

Willows, D.M., Kruk, R.S., & Corcos, E. (1993). *Visual processes in reading and reading disabilities*. Hillsdale, NJ: Lawrence Erlbaum Associates, Inc.

Winner, E., von Károlyi, C., Malinsky, D., French, L., Seliger, C., Ross, E., & Weber, C. (2001). Dyslexia and visual-spatial talents: Compensation vs deficit model. *Brain and Language, 76, 1*, 81–110.

World Federation of Neurology (1968). Report of research group on developmental dyslexia and world illiteracy. *Bulletin of the Orton Society, 18*,21–22.

Zatorre, R. J., Meyer, E., Gjedde, A., & Evans, A. C. (1996). PET studies of phonetic processing of speech: review, replication, and re-analysis. *Cerebral Cortex, 6*, 21–30.

5

Neural Coding of Written Words in the Visual Word Form Area

Stanislas Dehaene and Laurent Cohen

The efficiency of reading in literate adults rests on the ability to quickly identify visual words across large variations of irrelevant parameters such as position, size, color, font, or case. This perceptual expertise requires no less than 5 years of academic training in a specific writing system (Aghababian & Nazir, 2000). The outcome of this perceptual normalization process is an abstract representation of letter identities that has been termed the *visual word form* (VWF; Warrington & Shallice, 1980).

We formulated the idea that an area located in the mid-portion of the left fusiform gyrus, which activates whenever literate subjects are presented with strings of letters, contributes crucially to the cerebral basis of the VWF. Accordingly, we have proposed to label this left fusiform region the *visual word form area* (VWFA) (Cohen & Dehaene, 2000). This hypothesis is based both on neuroimaging studies of reading and on anatomo-clinical correlations in patients with pure alexia, an acquired deficit of reading that follows left occipitotemporal lesions (McCandliss, Cohen, & Dehaene, 2003). The VWFA hypothesis should be considered within the broader context of recent studies of functional specialization within the human ventral visual stream, which have identified several areas specialized for other classes of visual stimuli such as faces, places, or body parts (Downing, Jiang, Shuman, & Kanwisher, 2001; Hasson, Harel, Levy, & Malach, 2003; Haxby et al., 2001; Kanwisher, McDermott, & Chun, 1997).

The purpose of the present chapter is twofold. First, after a brief consideration of the major computational problems that must be resolved by the visual stages of reading, we review the evidence for or against the hypothesis that part of the left inferotemporal cortex functions as a specialized "visual word form area" in literate adults. We particularly address the criticisms that were recently raised against this hypothesis by Cathy Price and colleagues (Price & Devlin, 2003; Price, Winterburn, Giraud, Moore, & Noppeney, 2003); this part largely relies on arguments first presented in Cohen and Dehaene (2004).

Second, assuming that this area does indeed contain neurons that have become attuned to visual word recognition, we ask how these neurons might be organized. Considering that word recognition probably arises from a minimal "recycling" of the preexisting visual object recognition system, we present a hypothetical model, first presented in Dehaene, Cohen, Sigman, and Vinckier (2005), according to which a hierarchy of local combination detector (LCD) neurons, inspired from the known architecture of the primate inferotemporal cortex, collectively implement an invariant neural code for written words.

The Necessity of Specialization for Visual Word Recognition

Let us start with a computational analysis of the visual word recognition process. What type of problems does the visual system of a literate person routinely solve? A first problem is invariance. We are able to recognize words across considerable changes in *font,* CASE, [location] and size. Even unfamiliar word forms, such as mIxEd CaSe, pose only minor difficulties to our visual system (Besner, 1989; Mayall, Humphreys, & Olson, 1997; Paap, Newsome, & Noel, 1984). This implies that the visual word recognition process is highly efficient in "normalizing" and computing an invariant representation that discards irrelevant variations in the visual input. At the same time, however, very small details that are relevant to reading are maintained and even amplified. Consider the words "eight" and "sight." We are immediately aware of their radically different meanings and pronunciation, but it takes some time to realize that visually speaking, those words differ only by a very small amount. Our visual system is attuned to the minute difference between "eight" and "sight," which it amplifies so that we ultimately address completely different regions of semantic space, while it discards the much greater differences between "eight" and "EIGHT." Those computational requirements are largely common to the recognition of any type of visual objects: Tools, buildings, or faces can all appear with huge variations in their appearance, including size, location, orientation, etc. As with words, the visual system must both compensate for irrelevant variations in the input and exploit specific details that are critical for object identification (Riesenhuber & Poggio, 1999).

In the case of reading, crucial aspects of this capacity of invariant recognition must be learned. A general process of size invariance may suffice to recognize the identity of, say the letters "o" and "O." In general, however, what constitutes a significant visual difference and what does not is defined culturally rather than visually. Many of the mappings between upper- and lowercase, for instance, are arbitrary. The shape "e" might have been selected as the lower case of "A"—it is only a historical accident if the shape "a" was chosen. Thus, the fast mapping of "A" and "a" onto the same abstract letter identity cannot be explained by generic features of the organization of the visual system. Rather, the case invariance observed in several psychological experiments (e.g., Besner, Coltheart, & Davelaar, 1984; Bowers, Vigliocco, & Haan, 1998) must arise from specialization resulting from a learning process. Indeed, readers of the Latin script, who immediately perceive a difference between the letters e and c, may not know that the Hebrew letters ח and ה are distinct, something that will be obvious to any reader of that script.

Beyond case invariance, other psychological findings provide evidence for a functional tuning in reading. The word superiority effect is the fact that, when asked to detect the presence of a letter, subjects typically show superior performance when the letter is embedded in a visual string that respects the structure of the learned language than when it is embedded in a random string. For instance, subjects are faster and more accurate in detecting the letter "w" in "show" than in "ohsw" (Reicher, 1969). The word superiority effect is found with real words, pseudowords (Spoehr & Smith, 1975), and even non-words sufficiently similar to words such as SPCT (Rumelhart & McClelland, 1982). It implies the existence of a mechanism tuned to the possible structures of visual words.

Also remarkable is the absence of any effect of word length in reading. Within a range of about three to six letters, visual word recognition takes a constant time regardless of the number of letters composing that word (Lavidor & Ellis, 2002; Weekes, 1997). This suggests the presence of a parallel apprehension mechanism specialized for reading. Note that the absence of a length effect is found only when the words are presented in the familiar horizontal format and within a restricted region of the fovea and right hemifield (Lavidor, Babkoff, & Faust, 2001; Lavidor & Ellis, 2002). This suggests that at least part of the specialization for letter and word recognition occurs at retino-topically organized stages of visual processing (Nazir, 2000).

All in all, both computational arguments and experimental psychological data point to specialization for visual word recognition in skilled readers. It is not just that reading is more complex and imposes greater demands on visual processing than identifying pictures, faces, or colors. Rather, reading poses particular problems to the visual system, some of which (such as case invariance) are specific to reading in a given script. A generic visual recognition device is simply insufficient to account for the notation-dependent operations that are observed in skilled readers.

Three Forms of Specialization

How, then, is invariant visual word recognition implemented in neural tissue? When considering the mapping from a psychological function to its cortical implementation, and the extent to which it is implemented by "domain-specific" regions, we argue that three distinct theoretical possibilities must be carefully distinguished: functional specialization, reproducible localization, and regional selectivity. These can be considered as increasingly local forms of cortical specialization.

Functional specialization refers to the possibility that the visual system has become, at least in part, attuned to the requirements of reading in a given script. For instance, if some visual neurons fired identically to "A" and "a," but not to other letters, this would indicate abstract case-invariance and would constitute evidence of functional specialization for reading in Latin script. Likewise, if some neurons responded to various forms of the letter ה, but did not respond to ד, this would constitute functional specialization for reading in Hebrew. Note, however, that the hypothesis of functional specialization need not be associated with any hypothesis about the localization of such processes. It is logically possible that case-invariant neurons are present throughout the visual system, without any particular localization.

An alternative hypothesis is that such neurons tend to be grouped together in some fixed regions of visual cortex. We call this the *reproducible localization* hypothesis. Importantly, this hypothesis only claims that neurons engaged in the reading process are not localized randomly; it makes no claim about the localization of neurons engaged in other processes such as face, object, or color processing. The same neurons could be involved, or a different subset of neurons within the same region, or an entirely different patch of cortex.

Yet a third logically independent hypothesis is what we call the *regional selectivity* hypothesis. This is the postulate that certain regions of cortex are devoted solely to word reading. According to the regional selectivity hypothesis, at a suitably small scale (e.g., 1 or 2 mm), it should be possible to identify patches of cortex that respond exclusively to letters or words, and do not respond at all to stimuli such as faces or objects that do not contain features of letters or words.

The Hypothesis of the Visual Word Form Area

With those distinctions in mind, we can now state our position quite clearly. We propose that there is *functional specialization* for reading in the brain of literate human subjects, namely specialized neurons attuned to the requirements of visual word recognition in a specific script. We also propose that there is *reproducible localization* of the neural circuits that are attuned to the reading process. In particularly, within the visual system, we claim that whenever subjects read a word, a reproducible portion of the left occipito-temporal sulcus is activated and hosts functionally specialized circuits for letter and word recognition. We further claim that this area can be reproducibly observed in all cultures, even in readers of nonalphabetic scripts.

We suggest that this reproducible localization constitutes sufficient grounds for christening this region the VWFA. We do *not*, however, believe that there is complete *regional selectivity* for word recognition. Even the voxels that respond optimally to words tend to be also activated by other stimuli such as pictures or line drawings of objects. This should not be surprising, because the functional specialization for reading arises from a partial preemption or "recycling" of visual cortex that evolved for other purposes during phylogenesis (Dehaene, 2005). This cortex is partially plastic and can, during ontogenesis, become progressively attuned to the requirements of reading (McCandliss et al., 2003). In the most expert readers, one might perhaps identify patches of cortex that respond to written words more than to any other visual stimuli. In most subjects, however, the specialization for words is likely to be only partial. There may be columns of neurons specialized for the recognition of letters, graphemes, or words, but they are likely to be intermixed with other neurons involved in object and face recognition (Allison, Puce, Spencer, & McCarthy, 1999). Therefore, at the scale accessible to human neuroimaging, most if not all of the cortical surface is likely to respond jointly to words, faces, and objects with smooth but systematic changes in local selectivity (Haxby et al., 2001).

Importantly, such overlap between activations to words, objects, and faces does not preclude studying the functional contribution of inferior temporal cortex to reading per se. The issue of the nature of the contribution of a given cortical sector to reading (e.g., Is it case-independent? Is it location-invariant? Does it code for single letters, or for graphemes, syllables, or morphemes?) can be address completely independently of the orthogonal issue of whether neurons in this cortical sector also contribute to object or face recognition.

The term "visual word form area" was introduced to refer to the simple fact that a reproducible cortical region is active during visual word recognition and appears to possess properties of location and case invariance that suggest functional specialization for reading (Cohen et al., 2000; Cohen et al., 2002; Dehaene et al., 2001). Our use of the word "area" may have caused some confusion. "Area" is used here solely as a synonym for "location." It is *not* meant in the more technical sense of a distinct cortical sector distinguished by its layer, cellular, or receptor structure, as used, for instance, in the term "Brodmann area." We do not believe that there is a cytoarchitectonically defined subpart of the visual system that responds to visual words. We also consider it rather unlikely that the visual word area would have sharp borders that would delineate it qualitatively from other neighboring areas involved in face or object recognition. Rather, the density of neurons activated during reading probably varies continuously, although nonrandomly, across the surface of the ventral occipitotemporal cortex, thus creating a landscape of local preference for various categories of objects (Hasson, Levy, Behrmann, Hendler, & Malach, 2002; Haxby et al., 2001). Finally, it is likely that the rather large occipitotemporal region that we have termed VWFA can be further subdivided into, for instance, a posterior location-specific sector and a more anterior location-invariant sector (Dehaene et al., 2004). None of this, however, detracts from the usefulness of having a single term to refer to the anatomically reproducible ventral visual region that activates focally during word reading.

Evidence for Reproducible Localization

A large number of neuroimaging studies, using various methods, have evidenced a reproducible activation of the left fusiform gyrus during reading. Activation in this region can be identified merely by contrasting word reading relative to rest, either with positron emission tomography (PET) or with functional magnetic resonance imaging (fMRI) (Beauregard et al., 1997; Brunswick, McCrory, Price, Frith, & Frith, 1999; Dehaene, Le Clec'H, Poline, Le Bihan, & Cohen, 2002; Fiez, Balota, Raichle, & Petersen, 1999; Paulesu et al., 2000; Wagner et al., 1998). This region appears as a likely source of electrical and magnetic fields that are recorded over the left ventral occipitotemporal region, with a latency of about 150–200 ms, whenever subjects see words (Allison, McCarthy, Nobre, Puce, & Belger, 1994; Allison et al., 1999; Cohen et al., 2000; Marinkovic et al., 2003; A. C. Nobre, Allison, & McCarthy, 1994; Pammer et al., 2004; Salmelin, Service, Kiesilä, Uutela, & Salonen, 1996; Simos et al., 2002; Tarkiainen, Helenius, Hansen, Cornelissen, & Salmelin, 1999).

   When word reading is contrasted to a resting period, the active regions obviously comprise a large unspecific component of visual activity. However, simple subtractions allow a more specific delineation of the VWFA. For instance, Price and colleagues (1996) have obtained stronger activations to strings of consonants than to strings of pseudoletters at coordinates close to the VWFA. In one study, we isolated the VWFA using a spatial invariance criterion: contrary to more posterior retinotopic areas, the VWFA is activated by words presented in either the left or the right hemifield (Cohen et al., 2000). In another, we further required this region to respond more to strings of letters than to checkerboards presented in either hemifield (Cohen et al., 2002). Other investigators have subtracted the activations induced by foveal words and by pictures of faces, textures, or buildings (Gauthier et al., 2000; Hasson et al., 2002; Puce, Allison, Asgari, Gore, & McCarthy, 1996). There is good convergence to the same approximate Talairach coordinates across those studies (Cohen et al., 2000).

Several fMRI papers have further shown that this area can be identified in single subjects (Cohen et al., 2000; Cohen et al., 2002; Dehaene et al., 2002; Gauthier et al., 2000; Puce et al., 1996). This allows quantification of the interindividual variability, which is remarkably low. The VWFA is found at the same location in Talairach space (approximately –43, –54, –12) with a standard deviation of only about 0.5 cm.[1] Essentially all subjects show word-induced activation in the left hemisphere, whereas a symmetrical right-sided activation is only found in a few subjects and at a weaker level. Similar results have been obtained using single-subject magnetoencephalography (MEG) (Tarkiainen et al., 1999) and intracranial recordings (Allison et al., 1999).

Pure Alexia and Reproducible Localization

Evidence from neuropsychology corroborates the above neuroimaging evidence for a reproducible association of the left occipitotemporal region with word recognition processes (for a more extensive discussion, see Chapter 9). The syndrome of pure alexia, also known as alexia-without-agraphia, word blindness, or agnosic alexia, is characterized by the breakdown of reading following left occipitotemporal lesions in literate adults. Such patients typically show intact production and comprehension of oral language, and they can write normally either spontaneously or to dictation. However, they show various degrees of impairment in word reading. In the most severe cases, known as *global alexia*, they cannot even identify single letters (Dejerine, 1892). More frequently, pure alexic patients show relatively preserved, albeit slow, letter identification abilities and resort to letter-by-letter reading strategies (for references, see Montant & Behrmann, 2000).

The simplest account of pure alexia is that it reflects a breakdown of the visual word form system (Cohen et al., 2000; Warrington & Shallice, 1980). Indeed, although many patients show extensive left posterior cerebral artery infarction, some have much narrower lesions. To take but one example, Beversdorf and colleagues (1997) report a case with a limited surgical excision and demonstrative postmortem data. The lesion affected the expected region of the left mid-fusiform cortex, with an extension to the lateral edge of the lingual gyrus. The combination of lesions from multiple patients also permits to identify the necessary and sufficient regions that are reproducibly associated with pure alexia. Such work was done by Damasio and Damasio

(1983), Binder and Mohr (1992), and more recently by our group (Cohen et al., 2003), with a good agreement of these studies on the lateral edge of the left fusiform gyrus. For instance, Binder and Mohr (1992) delineated a critical region by comparing the lesions of alexic patients with those of patients with a left posterior cerebral artery infarct and no reading impairment, including patients with lesions to the lingual gyrus or the cuneus. The critical region fell within the left middle fusiform gyrus. Although it appears slightly more anterior than the VWFA, methodological differences in the reconstruction of lesions may be sufficient to account for this discrepancy.

In our recent work, we also found a similar region of lesion overlap in the fusiform gyrus. Although this region was admittedly larger than the VWFA strictly defined, it precisely encompassed the region of activation to words identified in fMRI studies of reading (Cohen et al., 2003). Thus, although the precision of the correlations should still be improved, there is good convergence toward the site of the VWFA as the anatomical correlate of pure alexia.

A factor that may blur anatomo-functional correlations is the role of white matter lesions. Our hypothesis implies that pure alexia should result either from a disruption of the VWFA itself, or from impaired projections to or from this system. The clearest example of such a deafferentation is the alexia restricted to the left half of the visual field, which results from lesions of posterior callosal pathways (Suzuki et al., 1998). In such cases, we observed reduced activations of the VWFA for words presented in the left hemifield (Cohen et al., 2000; Molko et al., 2002). Similarly, a few cases of alexia restricted to the right visual field (RVF) have been reported, and may be due to left intrahemispheric lesions deafferenting the VWFA but sparing low-level visual regions (Castro-Caldas and Salgado, 1984). Finally, the anatomical case reported by Greenblatt (1973) may be an instance of complete deafferentation of an intact fusiform cortex (see also Cohen, Henry et al., 2004).

Conversely, output projections from the VWFA to lateral language areas may be interrupted during their course in the parietal white matter, providing a plausible account for the so-called *subangular alexia* (Greenblatt, 1976; Iragui & Kritchevsky, 1991; Pirozzolo et al., 1981). Altogether, simple considerations on the input and output pathways of the VWFA provide a detailed and consistent explanation for the variety of visual alexias seen in adult neuropsychological cases (Cohen et al., 200; Chapter 9, this volume).

Evidence for Partial Regional Selectivity

In their critique of the VWFA hypothesis, Price and Devlin (2003) do not deny the reproducibility of fusiform activations during reading, but they claim that the same voxels are activated in a broad set of experimental conditions, including reading, but also auditory words processing, object perception, naming, perception of "socially interactive" movements, and the like. On this basis, they argue against a specialization for reading in this region.

Unfortunately, Price and Devlin's argument relies almost exclusively on the overlap of data from different groups of subjects, often scanned with PET. However, such data are typically generated with a spatial smoothness of 10 or even 15 mm. In this context, the finding of overlap between word-related and non–word-related (e.g., color or object processing) tasks is not conclusive, as it seems likely that even cortical territories known to be distinct would be found to overlap using this method. This is especially true when the method is applied across different groups of subjects, whereas individual sulci are known to vary at least up to 1 cm (Sowell et al., 2002; Thompson, Schwartz, Lin, Khan, & Toga, 1996).

Many higher-resolution studies, using either fMRI or intracranial recordings, have reported a partial selectivity for visual words within the ventral fusiform region. As noted earlier, we should perhaps not expect to find entire voxels solely responsive to visual words and not to any other category of stimuli. Nevertheless, the available evidence reveals systematic and reproducible activations that are greater to visual words than to other control stimuli.

Puce and colleagues (1996) report single-subject fMRI activations during passive presentation of visual words, faces, and textures. Nine out of twelve subjects showed greater activation to words than to faces in the left occipitotemporal sulcus, while a neighboring but slightly more mesial site conversely showed preferential activation to faces than to words. This systematic topographical organization was reproduced by Gauthier and colleagues (2000). Hasson and coworkers (2002) also contrasted fMRI activations to words, houses, and faces. Again, a site with greater responsivity to words than to either faces or buildings was found in the left occipitotemporal sulcus, lateral to face- and building-related activations. This region showed the same selectivity whether the stimuli were presented foveally or peripherally, confirming a previous demonstration of location-invariance in this region (Cohen et al., 2000). Hasson and coworkers (2003) suggest that the visual word-related activation always falls at a systematic location at the boundary between object-selective and face-selective regions in a large-scale map of object preference.

A similar although slightly more complex picture emerges from intracranial recordings in epileptic patients (Allison et al., 1999; A. C. Nobre et al., 1994; Puce, Allison, & McCarthy, 1999). Using subdural electrode arrays, Allison and colleagues (1999) observed sites that showed fast P150 or N200 waveforms that were larger, or occasionally exclusive for letter strings, compared to a variety of control stimuli such as phase-scrambled strings, flowers, faces, or geometrical shapes. The anatomical distribution of those sites was concentrated in the left occipitotemporal region, although with a greater spatial dispersion than suggested by comparable fMRI studies. On the basis of these data, Puce and colleagues (1999) suggest a theoretical model of spatially segregated cortical columns, each selective to a different type of visual stimuli, organized in local patches a few millimeters aside. Single-neuron studies (e.g., Kreiman, Koch, & Fried, 2000) will be needed to assess whether there is absolute selectivity for words in some patches, or whether there is partial intermixing at the microscopic level, as suggested by optical imaging studies in monkeys (e.g., Wang, Tanaka, & Tanifuji, 1996). However, in the present state of knowledge it cannot be denied that small subregions of visual cortex show at least partial selectivity for letter strings.

Top-down Recruitment of the Visual Word Form Area?

An alternative critique has to do with whether the VWFA is involved only in *visual* word processing—the alternative being that the VWFA is involved in multimodal lexical or semantic processing. Indeed, in Cohen et al. (2002), we listed a number of studies that reported ventral fusiform activation during spoken word processing. Do these findings, however, imply a rejection of the VWFA hypothesis? Before reaching this extremity, two alternative explanations must be examined. First, do these nonvisual activations really overlap with the VWFA? Second, if they do, could they correspond to late and nonobligatory top-down reactivations of the visual system?

Cohen and colleagues (2002) reviewed existing studies of ventral temporal activations by visual and nonvisual words. As already noted by Büchel and associates (1998), words in modalities other than the visual yielded activations more anterior (average y = –43) than those typical of the visual word form (average y = –60). Furthermore, the anterior activations were sensitive to the semantic demands of the task, whereas the posterior activations were observed even for visual pseudowords relative to random letter strings. Thus, we suggest that the VWFA must be carefully distinguished from more anterior regions that are increasingly cross-modal and engaged in semantic computations. Such a distinction is supported by several neuroimaging studies (e.g., Booth et al., 2002; see review in Giraud & Price, 2001), as well as by intracranial recordings (A. C. Nobre et al., 1994; A.C. Nobre, Allison, & McCarthy, 1998).

In this debate, it is crucial to keep in mind the spatial limitations of imaging methods. High-resolution single-subject studies are needed to evaluate the claim that the very same region is activated in both cases. Recently, we performed a study analogous to Booth and colleagues' (2002; 2003), using an orthogonal design with factors of modality (visual or auditory words) and task (phoneme or grapheme detection) (Cohen, Jobert, Le Bihan, & Dehaene, 2004). We indeed observed a left posterior inferotemporal activation even when spoken words were presented, and with a greater intensity during the grapheme task than during the phoneme task. In a group analysis, this activation overlapped with the VWFA, as defined by a left inferior temporal activation that was greater to visual than to spoken words. However, in single subjects, the two regions appeared as distinct but very close. The left occipitotemporal sulcus (average coordinates –44, –68, –4) was activated only by visual words, not by spoken words. Another more lateral and slightly more anterior inferotemporal region (–48, –60, –16) was activated also by spoken words, with modulation by the graphemic task (we called this region the *left inferotemporal multimodal area* [LIMA]).

This study thus points to a major pitfall of inferences based on the intersection of fMRI activation from different studies: this method is inherently limited by image resolution and can lead to inappropriate generalizations about the function of a given patch of cortex. It is likely that, as our ability to image this region evolves, more subdivisions will appear within what we currently think of as a single VWFA.

In another study, we contrasted the processing of written and spoken words within single subjects during a same–different task (Dehaene et al., 2002). In agreement with our hypotheses, in every subject, the left occipitotemporal gyrus was activated by visual words but there was no trace of activation by spoken words. Thus, this region is not automatically activated during auditory word processing and does not appear to be a supramodal area.

This does not, however, preclude the possibility of its top-down activation by auditory words in some particular tasks. For instance, Booth and colleagues (2002; 2003) observed an activation, which might correspond to the VWFA or to the LIMA, when subjects engaged in a spelling task on auditory words, but not when they engaged in a rhyming task on the same stimuli. Those results suggest that posterior inferotemporal activations during auditory word processing are optional and contingent on the engagement of the subject in orthographic processing.

Similarly, Burton and colleagues (2000) observed a left inferotemporal activation (TC –58, –56, –8) when subjects performed same–different judgments on spoken syllables, but only when they had to extract the first phoneme of the syllable, not when they could base their decisions on the syllable as a whole. Again, the activation might overlap with VWFA, although most likely it corresponds to the LIMA (Cohen, Jobert et al., 2004).

More work will be needed to understand which experimental conditions cause top-down orthographic recruitment, and when such top-down effects reach the LIMA or the VWFA. For instance, Price and coworkers (2003) observed left fusiform activation with PET during the repetition of spoken words, relative to a baseline condition of saying "OK" to auditory noises. Is it implausible, however, that spoken word repetition causes a small top-down activation of orthographic representations? We think that this is not so unlikely. It is known that the acquisition of literacy modifies the brain network involved in speech repetition (especially for pseudowords, see Castro-Caldas, Petersson, Reis, Stone-Elander, & Ingvar, 1998). Furthermore, a dramatic interference of orthography on speech perception has been evidenced in a variety of behavioral tasks, including rhyme detection (Donnenwerth-Nolan, Tanenhaus, & Seidenberg, 1981), syllable monitoring (Taft & Hambly, 1985), lexical decision (Ziegler & Ferrand, 1998), and phoneme monitoring. For instance, the interference of orthography prevents the detection of the phoneme "p" in the spoken French word "absurde" (Hallé, Chéreau, & Segui, 2000).

In the final analysis, PET and FMRI studies are ill-adapted to resolve the issue of top-down or bottom-up posterior inferotemporal activations, because they cannot resolve the fine temporal dynamics of neural activity, and hence cannot distinguish feedforward and feedback waves of activation. However, recent work using MEG has directly compared spoken and written word processing (Marinkovic et al., 2003). The results confirm that posterior inferior temporal activation is present early on (~170 ms) when reading words, but is absent or confined to the late part of the epoch when hearing words (Marinkovic et al., 2003, Figures 1 and 4).

Pure Alexia and Regional Selectivity

Does evidence from cognitive neuropsychology also support some selectivity for visual word recognition in the left inferotemporal cortex? Patients with pure alexia sometimes exhibit visual deficits beyond the domain of reading. However, such associations of deficits are known to provide only a weak source of constraints (Shallice, 1988). Given that the VWFA may contain intermixed cortical columns for word and object processing (Puce et al., 1999), it is likely that a disruption of the VWFA would induce some degree of impairment beyond reading (Behrmann, Nelson, & Sekuler, 1998). Even assuming that there is a cortical sector highly selective for the perception of alphabetic stimuli, it would be unlikely that a spontaneous lesion should affect this region with perfect selectivity while sparing the adjacent cortex. Thus, it is hardly surprising, from our point of view, that some degree of associated visual impairment is evident in most alexic patients.

Nevertheless, some authors argue that such associations of deficits refute a specialization for visual word recognition (Behrmann et al., 1998). We contend that any such attempt to account for pure alexia in terms of a "general visual problem" (Price & Devlin, 2003) is very unlikely to succeed. The breakdown of parallel letter processing in pure alexia has been attributed to a general inability to represent multiple object parts (Farah & Wallace, 1991), or to an increased sensitivity to visual object complexity (Behrmann et al., 1998). However, it is unclear how this may account for the frequent sparing of the recognition of complex multipart objects, faces, or digit strings in pure alexic patients. For instance, as an argument against a general impairment of parallel visual processing, Warrington and Shallice (1980) and Patterson and Kay (1982) showed that patients with letter-by-letter reading could accurately report digits flanking a letter string (e.g., 6APPLE4), even when such stimuli were flashed for 150 ms and comprised as many as eight intervening letters. It has been suggested that "reading is more complex and imposes greater demands on visual processing" than other forms of object recognition (Price & Devlin, 2003). However, a unidimensional axis of complexity or "demands" will not suffice to account for double dissociations, such as object agnosia without alexia (Albert, Reches, & Silverberg, 1975; Gomori & Hawryluk, 1984) or prosopagnosia without alexia (e.g., McNeil & Warrington, 1993).

In fact, even single-letter identification is frequently impaired in pure alexia. The deficit with isolated letters can range in severity from complete global alexia to the occurrence of occasional errors with a significant slowing down of letter naming (for a review, see Behrmann et al., 1998; e.g., Hanley & Kay, 1996). This symptom presents a real challenge to nonspecific theories of pure alexia, because it is difficult to argue that single letters are in any sense more complex than faces or drawings of objects. It seems much more likely that there is a partial specialization of cortical territories and their connections for letters and words, which is affected in pure alexia.

Evidence for Functional Specialization

Aside from the issue of regional selectivity, is there also evidence for functional specialization for visual word recognition? To demonstrate functional specialization, one should exhibit a pattern of brain activity that cannot be reduced to generic visual processes, but necessarily reflects regularities of the writing system. Evidence of this type has been presented by several investigators.

First, there are indications that the VWFA is tuned to the shape of letters, relative to visually equivalent pseudoletters. Following up on the initial insight of Petersen and colleagues (1990), Price and associates (1996) observed stronger activation in the left fusiform gyrus to strings of consonants than to strings of false-font characters. There is also evidence that strings of letters cause greater left fusiform activation than visually equivalent strings of digits (Polk et al., 2002). Indeed, intracranial recording suggest that there maybe specialized subregions for letters versus digits in the ventral occipito-temporal cortex (Allison et al., 1994). Such a fine-grained specialization cannot be explained by a generic visual process.

Second, the VWFA responds more to words or to pseudowords than to random consonant strings that violate orthographic constraints (Beauregard et al., 1997; Büchel et al., 1998; Cohen et al., 2002; Price et al., 1996; Rees, Russell, Frith, & Driver, 1999; Xu et al., 2001).[2] This suggests that it has become sensitive to orthographic rules in the subject's language, which are a matter of cultural convention.

Third, there is also evidence that the VWFA computes the arbitrary mapping between upper- and lowercase letters. The VWFA shows equally robust fMRI responses when words are presented in a familiar format or in a mixed-case format (e.g., "tAbLe") (Polk & Farah, 2002). Furthermore, the VWFA shows repetition priming whenever a target word is preceded by a subliminal presentation of the same word, whether the two words are printed in the same or in a different case (e.g., table followed by TABLE) (Dehaene et al., 2001). Such case-invariant priming in the VWFA was recently replicated with words made only of visually dissimilar letters that are related only by arbitrary cultural convention (e.g., a and A, g and G) (Dehaene et al., 2004). This indicates that processing in the VWFA goes beyond generic processes of size and location normalization and is capable of establishing the arbitrary links between upper- and lowercase letters. We take these results to indicate that, during the acquisition of literacy, perceptual learning in the VWFA progressively internalizes script- and language-specific regularities of the writing system.

Functional Specialization in Pure Alexia

According to the functional specialization hypothesis, disruption of the VWFA should result in the loss of the knowledge of regularities unique to the reading system. Several observations from pure alexia support this hypothesis. For instance, the patient studied by Miozzo and Caramazza (1998) was severely impaired at naming single letters, and she was unable to decide whether an uppercase and a lowercase letter had the same name or not. However, she could accurately discriminate real letters from visually equivalent pseudoletters, as well as normally oriented letters from mirror-reversed letters. This suggests a loss of abstract orthographic knowledge, with preservation of a basic familiarity with individual letter shapes.

Chanoine and coworkers (1998) reported closely similar findings in another patient. They also observed that, whenever the distractors were digits or simple geometrical shapes, the patient could easily match lower- and upper-case letters, or pick out a printed letter named by the examiner, whereas these tasks were severely impaired when the distractors were other letters. This dissociation between letters and digits in pure alexia dates back to Dejerine's observation, as he noted that "the patient recognizes very well all digits," while "he cannot recognize a single letter" (Cohen & Dehaene, 1995; Dejerine, 1892; Holender & Peereman, 1987; for imaging data see also Pinel, Dehaene, Riviere, & LeBihan, 2001; Polk et al., 2002).

Obviously, the dissociations between letters and other closely matched shapes such as digits cannot be accounted for on the basis of a nonspecific visual impairment. Rather, it implies the breakdown of the functional specialization incorporated during the acquisition of literacy, including knowledge of the finite set of characters, the links between upper- and lowercase letters, and the organization in arbitrary subsets of symbols such as letters and digits.

Cultural Recycling of Occipitotemporal Cortex

In summary, psychological, neuropsychological, and neuroimaging data converge to suggest that the human brain of literate subjects contains specialized mechanisms for visual word recognition (functional specialization), which map in a systematic way onto the properties of a cortical subregion of the left posterior occipitotemporal sulcus (reproducible localization). We claim that this constitutes sufficient evidence to label this region the VWFA, even if, at present, the evidence for the third type of cortical specialization (regional selectivity) is not definitive. The region that activates to visual words is well delimited and occupies a fixed location relative to other regions that preferentially respond to faces, houses, or objects (Hasson et al., 2003; Hasson et al., 2002; Puce et al., 1996). Nevertheless, most cortical patches that respond to words also activate to other stimuli, such as pictures or drawings. Thus, the evidence to date favors a model of partially distributed and overlapping representation of visual categories (Haxby et al., 2001; Haxby, Ishai, Chao, Ungerleider, & Martin, 2000), with a landscape of partial but not absolute preferences across the ventral cortical surface.

One puzzling issue remains: Why is there a reproducible cortical site responsive to visual words? Reading is a recent cultural activity of the human species. The 5,400 years that have elapsed since its invention are too short to permit the evolution of dedicated biological mechanisms for learning to read. Thus, visual word recognition must make use of the preexisting primate circuitry for object recognition. We speculate that, if the human brain can learn to read, it is only because part of the primate visual ventral object recognition system already accomplishes operations closely similar to those required in word recognition, and possesses sufficient plasticity to adapt itself to new shapes, including those of letters and words. During the acquisition of reading, part of this system becomes highly specialized for the visual operations underlying location- and case-invariant word recognition. It occupies a reproducible location within the left occipitotemporal sulcus because the neurons at this location possess intrinsic properties that render them most suited for this acquisition. Thus, reading acquisition proceeds by selection and local adaptation of a preexisting neural region, rather than by de novo imposition of novel properties onto that region.

To describe how recent cultural invention invades evolutionary ancient cerebral circuits, the term "neuronal recycling" has been proposed (Dehaene, 2005). This view assumes that the human ability to acquire new cultural objects relies on a neuronal "reconversion" or "recycling" process whereby those novel objects invade cortical territories initially devoted to similar or sufficiently close functions. According to this view, our evolutionary history, and therefore our genetic organization, has created a cerebral architecture that is both constrained and partially plastic, and that delimits a space of learnable cultural objects. New cultural acquisitions are therefore possible only inasmuch as they are able to fit within the preexisting constraints of our brain architecture.

The present hypothesis bears considerable similarity with a classical Darwinian concept that has been called "tinkering" by François Jacob (1977) or "exaptation" by Gould and Vrba (1982)—the reutilization, during phylogenesis, of biological mechanisms for a new function different from the one for which they evolved. In the case of cultural objects, however, this process takes place at a shorter time scale of weeks, months, or years, through epigenetic mechanisms that do not require any change in the genome. During the lifetime of the individual, each cultural acquisition must find its ecological niche in the human brain, a circuit whose initial role is close enough and whose flexibility is sufficient to be reconverted to this new role.

The term "recycling" should not imply that, prior to cultural acquisition, some brain areas are completely useless. On the contrary, neuronal recycling transforms what was, in our evolutionary past, a useful function into another function that is currently more important within the present cultural context. Thus, the neuronal tissue that supports cultural learning is not a blank slate, but possesses prior properties (although perhaps only in the form of small biases). Not any kind of object can be made of recycled glass or paper: Those materials possess intrinsic physical properties that make them more suitable for some uses than for others. Likewise, each cortical region or network possesses intrinsic properties that are adapted to the function it evolved for, and these properties are only partially modifiable during the cultural acquisition process. Cultural learning in humans may never totally overturn such preexisting biases, but rather changes them minimally as needed. Thus, cultural objects such as writing systems may not be infinitely malleable, and should in fact often reflect intrinsic constraints of the underlying neural networks.

What Is the Neural Code for Written Words?

The neuronal recycling model opens up the exciting possibility of using the considerable neurophysiological information available on the primate visual cortex to inform models of reading and its acquisition. Indeed, if this view is correct, the same neural mechanisms that underlie visual object recognition in monkeys are still at work, with minimal change, in the human brain of a literate subject recognizing words.

In particular, electrophysiological studies in primates might help answer a question that is, currently at least, beyond the reach of human neuroimaging methods: What is the neural code for written words? The VWFA is thought to play a pivotal role in informing other temporal, parietal, and frontal areas of the identity of a visual letter string for the purpose of both semantic access and phonological retrieval. To accomplish this function, it must provide a compact "neural code" for visual words; that is, an assembly of active neurons whose composition is unique to each word, yet invariant under changes in location, size, case, and font.

Cracking the cerebral code for visual words has become an active topic of experimental (Davis & Bowers, 2004; Humphreys, Evett, & Quinlan, 1990; Peressotti & Grainger, 1999; Schoonbaert & Grainger, 2004; Whitney & Lavidor, 2004) and theoretical (Grainger & Whitney, 2004; Whitney, 2001) investigations in cognitive psychology. Although many connectionist models of reading have been proposed, however, most have focused on the interactions between orthography, phonology, and semantics, hence ignoring the "front end" of visual word recognition. As a result, these models often presuppose a case- and location-invariant representation. Furthermore, they have tended to use an abstract approach, based more firmly on computer science than on a genuine consideration of neurophysiological data.

For instance, a classical scheme, called *slot-coding*, has been used in most models (Ans, Carbonnel, & Valdois, 1998; Coltheart, Rastle, Perry, Langdon, & Ziegler, 2001; Grainger & Jacobs, 1996; Harm & Seidenberg, 1999; McClelland & Rumelhart, 1981; Zorzi, Houghton, & Butterworth, 1998). It consists of a spatial array of case-independent letter detectors: an entire bank of units coding for every possible letter is replicated at each location or "slot." Thus, a simpler word such as "CAN" is represented by activating unit C in slot 1, unit A in slot 2, and unit N in slot 3.

Although this scheme is simple, it bypasses entirely the issue of location and case invariance: The inputs are merely supposed to be case-independent and spatially justified. Indeed, the code is radically changed whenever a word is shifted by one letter location. Although various alignment schemes have been proposed—alignment on the first letter (Coltheart et al., 2001), the preferred viewing position (Ans et al., 1998), or the first vowel (Zorzi et al., 1998), possibly with syllabic structuring of consonants into onset and coda (Harm & Seidenberg, 1999)—all suffer from a lack of generalization across locations. As a consequence, most slot-coding schemes provide no explanation for the known similarity of words with transposed letters (e.g., ANSWER–ANWSER), shared letter sequences (e.g., LEGAL–GALA), or morphemes (e.g., REPLAY–PLAY) if they are misaligned (Davis & Bowers, 2004).

The need to encode relative rather than absolute letter location led to the invention of *wickelcoding*, in which a word is encoded by its triplets of letters (Johnson & Pugh, 1994; Mozer, 1987; Plaut, McClelland, Seidenberg, & Patterson, 1996; Seidenberg & McClelland, 1989). For instance, the word "JUMP" is encoded by units sensitive to the substrings #JU, JUM, UMP, and MP#. However, wickelcoding fails to account for the similarity metric of visual words. For instance, the words COP and CAP are coded by entirely distinct units. The problem can be mitigated by using more flexible wickelcodes, for instance one in which a unit is dedicated to the sequence C_P, where _ stands for any intermediate letter (Mozer, 1987). Again, however, this code is merely stipulated to be case-invariant and location-invariant.

Only a single simulation model (Mozer, 1987) included a hierarchical processing stream capable of extracting a location-invariant code from a simulated retinal input (although no solution was proposed for case-invariance). The rest of this chapter is dedicated to the presentation of a neurophysiological model of invariant word recognition that bears much similarity to Mozer's original proposal, although it is derived more directly from the known physiological constraints of the primate visual system.

A Neurobiological Framework for Visual Word Recognition

Although space precludes any extensive review, the properties of the primate visual system that we view as essential for reading are the following:

1. *Hierarchical organization.* The ventral visual pathway is organized as a hierarchy of areas connected by both feedforward and feedback pathways. From posterior occipital to more anterior inferotemporal regions, the size

of the neurons' receptive fields increases by a factor of 2–3 (Rolls, 2000). This is accompanied by a systematic increase in the complexity of the neurons' preferred features, from line segments to whole objects, and a corresponding increase in invariance for illumination, size, or location.

2. *Shape selectivity.* Columns of neurons in the inferotemporal region form a broad repertoire of shape primitives, including simple letter-like shapes such as T or L, which are collectively capable of representing many objects (Tsunoda, Yamane, Nishizaki, & Tanifuji, 2001). Their selectivity is thought to arise from the neurons' capacity to integrate, in a spatial-specific manner, inputs from multiple, hierarchically lower neurons, each selective to more elementary view or contour elements (Brincat & Connor, 2004). This mechanism is also thought to contribute to spatial invariance, through pooling of multiple local detectors (Riesenhuber & Poggio, 1999; Rolls, 2000).

3. *Plasticity and perceptual learning.* Inferotemporal neurons are plastic and, through training, can become attuned to any image (Logothetis & Pauls, 1995; Logothetis, Pauls, Bulthoff, & Poggio, 1994). A single neuron may also become responsive to several arbitrary images that are repeatedly presented in temporal association (Miyashita, 1988). This mechanism might play a role in the acquisition of multiple representations of the same letters (e.g., upper- and lowercase).

4. *Large-scale visual biases.* fMRI has revealed that the human occipito-temporal region is traversed by a large-scale gradient of eccentricity bias (Malach, Levy, & Hasson, 2002), with lateral regions being more responsive to small foveal objects, and mesial regions to the periphery of the visual field. Written words and faces, which are both visually detailed and require foveation, tend to lie within foveally biased visual cortex (Malach et al., 2002). Retinotopic gradients, together with hemi-spheric asymmetries in downstream language areas, might bias the visual cortex and help explain why different categories of objects, including words, are associated with reproducible inferotemporal sub-regions in all individuals.

The Local Combination Detector Model

Can those data help sketch a neurobiological model of visual word recognition? From a neurobiological standpoint, cognitive psychological models of reading are least realistic in their attempt to achieve location invariance in a single step, by a sudden jump for location-specific letter detectors to larger location-independent units. In reality, as one moves up the visual hierarchy, receptive fields do not suddenly encompass the entire visual field, but progressively become larger, in parallel to an increase in the complexity of the neuron's preferred features (Riesenhuber & Poggio, 1999; Rolls, 2000).

Based on this consideration, we have proposed a tentative neurobiological scheme called the *local combination detectors* (LCD) model (Dehaene et al., 2005). As shown in Figure 5.1, the model assumes that a hierarchy of increasingly broader and more abstract neurons, each sensitive to a local combination of features, underlies invariant word recognition.

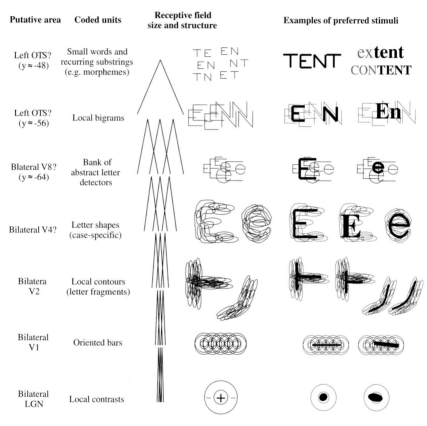

Figure 5.1 Model of invariant word recognition by a hierarchy of local combination detectors (LCDs). The model is inspired from neurophysiological models of invariant object recognition. Each neuron is assumed to pool activity from a subset of neurons at the immediately lower level, thus leading to an increasing complexity, invariance, and size of the receptive field at each stage. Note that only the excitatory components of the receptive fields are sketched here; however, both feedforward (e.g., center-surround) and lateral inhibition are likely to contribute significantly to define selective responses. The anatomical localizations are only tentative and should be submitted to further experimental testing. OTS, occipitotemporal sulcus; LGN, lateral geniculate nucleus; y, approximate anteroposterior coordinate relative to the human Montreal Neurological Institute template.

At the lower level, combinations of local-oriented bars can form local shape fragment detectors, which already have some small tolerance over displacements and changes in size. At the next stage, combinations of fragments can then be used to form local shape detectors. These neurons can detect a letter, but only in a given case and shape. Abstract letter identities can be recognized at the next stage, by pooling activation from populations of shape detectors coding for the different upper- and lowercase versions of a letter.

Because their receptive fields remain small, such letter detectors have a moderate tolerance for changes in size and location. Multiple letter detectors have to be replicated at several locations, thus forming the bank of case-invariant letter detectors postulated in many models.

Crucially, the natural subsequent stage is not location-independent bigram units, but neurons sensitive to *local* combinations of letters. One neuron, for instance, might respond optimally to "N one or two letters left of A, both around 0.5 degree right of fixation." Because receptive field size increases by a factor of two or three, we might in fact expect to find neurons coding for any sequence of one, two, or three letters. However, there is a trade-off here between location invariance and selectivity. A neuron coding for a triplet of letters would only be able to do so at a specific location. Conversely, a neuron coding for a single letter at any of three locations would provide no information about its precise location relative to other letters. While it is possible that such units contribute to word recognition, bigrams appear to provide the best compromise between the need to achieve location invariance and to preserve letter order. As shown in Figure 5.1, bigrams can be detected while allowing some tolerance for the exact location of the component letters. This can be achieved by pooling over partially overlapping letter detectors, thus allowing neurons responsive to the pair "NA" to have a broader receptive field than that of their component letter detector neurons for "N" and "A."

The notion that visual words can be encoded by bigrams was first proposed in the context of cognitive psychological studies of reading, where it has met with a good degree of experimental success (Grainger & Whitney, 2004; Schoonbaert & Grainger, 2004; Whitney, 2001). Crucially, Grainger and colleagues have had to assume a coding by "opens bigrams." The idea is that words are coded by the list of ordered letter pairs that they contain, but that these letters do not have to be consecutive. They can be separated by a few intermediate letters. The open bigram detector for the pair "G–R," for instance, reacts to the presence, anywhere on the retina, of a letter G to the left of a letter R, even if a few letters are present in between.

One of the key findings in support of this coding scheme is that a word can be primed by a subset of its letters, providing that letter order is preserved. For instance, "grdn" primes "garden," but "gdrn" does not (Humphreys et al., 1990; Peressotti & Grainger, 1999). Most consecutive letter pairs such as "GA" or "AR" are destroyed by this manipulation, but open bigrams such as

"G–R" are preserved, and can explain why "grdn" is sufficiently similar to "garden" as to prime it.

Grainger and colleagues merely stipulated the existence of "open bigrams." However, physiological constraints on the receptive field structure of local bigram detectors can explain why neurons would behave as open bigram detectors. As shown in Figure 5.1, neurons sensitive to letter pairs achieve this sensitivity by pooling activation from several individual letter detectors from the lower level. Yet, in order to achieve partial location invariance, they have to tolerate some imprecision in the location of their component letters. For instance, a neuron tuned to "G–R" might react to the presence of the letter G at retinal locations 1 or 2, and of the letter R at retinal locations 2 or 3. As a result, a few intermediate letters are allowed to slip in, without affecting the bigram response. For instance, the neuron just described would fire to the combination of a G at retinal location 1 and an R at retinal location 3—thus responding to the word "garden" just as well as to "great."

The local combination detector scheme can thus explain *why* open bigrams are used in reading, rather than merely stipulating their existence. Furthermore, most of the desirable properties of the open-bigram scheme are preserved. In particular, strings with missing letters, such as "GRDN," activate neurons that form a subset of the code for the full word "GARDEN," thus explaining that one can prime the other (Humphreys et al., 1990; Peressotti & Grainger, 1999). Likewise, the code is minimally changed when two letters are transposed, thus explaining that "JUGDE" may prime "judge" (Perea & Lupker, 2003; Schoonbaert & Grainger, 2004).

After the bigram level, the natural next step is ordered combinations of bigrams. Here, we expect neurons to begin to react to recurring multiletter strings, including morphemes or small words (Fig. 5.1). Note, however, that at any stage, words are never encoded by a single neuron or column, but by a sparsely distributed population of partially redundant neurons.

The corticocortical connections needed to establish this hierarchical receptive field structure include intrahemispheric short-range connections, but also, for receptive fields straddling the midline, some longer callosal connections. It has been proposed that "foveal splitting," whereby the left and right halves of a centrally fixated word are initially sent to distinct hemispheres, has important functional consequences for reading (Shillcock, Ellison, & Monaghan, 2000). However, beyond V1, callosal projections have the precise structure required to guarantee the continuity of receptive fields across the midline (Houzel, Carvalho, & Lent, 2002; Hubel & Wiesel, 1967) and allow convergence to common visual representations (Cohen et al., 2000). We believe that these connections minimize the functional impact of the initial foveal split.

For simplicity, we only included feedforward connections in the model. However, feedback and lateral connections are numerous in the visual system. They probably contribute to shaping the neurons' receptive field, for instance by defining probabilistic relations among consecutive letters, or by disambiguating letters and bigrams within words. These connections might be particularly important to explain the word superiority effect (Reicher, 1969).

The Role of Perceptual Learning in Reading

It might be feared that the proposed model leads to a combinatorial explosion, because of the increasing number of letter combinations that are encoded as one moves up the cortical hierarchy. However, this increase is compensated for by a progressive decrease in the number of encoded locations as receptive field size increases. Furthermore, it is likely that, in the course of learning to reading, perceptual learning mechanisms ensure that only frequent, informative letters and combinations are selected to be represented by dedicated neurons (Mozer, 1987; Riesenhuber & Poggio, 1999; Sigman & Gilbert, 2000). At the bigram level, for instance, we might expect detectors for EN, which is useful for recognizing many words, but not for ZH, which is almost never used in English. Indeed, the left inferotemporal VWFA, where letter, bigram, and string detectors are presumably located, responds much more to real words and pseudowords than to random consonant strings (Cohen et al., 2002), suggesting that its neurons have become attuned to the orthographic regularities of writing.

Perceptual learning mechanisms would be expected to shape the tuning of local detectors only at retinal locations where words frequently appear during reading. Due to eye movement patterns, in English readers, this corresponds to a restricted horizontal region close to the fovea and mostly within the right hemifield. The hypothesis that perceptual learning privileges those locations provides a natural explanation for the ubiquitous RVF advantage in reading (Nazir, Ben-Boutayab, Decoppet, Deutsch, & Frost, 2004).

Although letters and bigrams are the relevant units in alphabetic scripts, the same model should ultimately be able to simulate the acquisition of reading in any script. Indeed, perceptual learning should select local detectors for any useful recurrent combination of curves within the cell's receptive field. Thus, in readers of Chinese, neurons might become attuned to recurrent combinations within the characters, perhaps including semantic and phonetic radicals (Ding, Peng, & Taft, 2004), as well as to entire characters. More generally, *orthographic transparency*—the regularity of grapheme–phoneme conversion rules—may be reflected in the size of the units encoded by occipitotemporal neurons. In "transparent" writing systems such as Italian or the Japanese Kana script, the letter and bigram levels suffice for grapheme–phoneme conversion. In an "opaque" script, however, such as English or Kanji, a larger-size visual unit, more anterior along the visual hierarchy, must be used. Compatible with this idea, stronger and more anterior activation is observed in the left occipitotemporal region in English than in Italian readers (Paulesu et al., 2000), and, at a slightly more mesial location, during Kanji than during Kana reading in Japanese readers (Ha Duy Thuy et al., 2004; Nakamura, Dehaene, Jobert, Le Bihan, & Kouider, 2005).

It remains to be explained why perceptual learning mechanisms would, in most individuals, always use the same small patch of left occipitotemporal cortex to acquire reading. The reproducible localization of the VWFA suggests that reading acquisition results from an interaction of perceptual learning mechanisms with strong intrinsic anatomical and functional cortical biases. Indeed, the patch of cortex that responds to visual words is known to be endowed with several properties. Those include its bias for foveal versus peripheral images (Hasson et al., 2002), its location at an intermediate level of the hierarchy of visual areas appropriate for object-level processing (Grill-Spector et al., 1998; Tarkiainen, Cornelissen, & Salmelin, 2002), and its sensitivity to local features rather than to global configural information (Gauthier et al., 2000; Lerner, Hendler, Ben-Bashat, Harel, & Malach, 2001). As to its left lateralization, it may result from hemispheric differences in the processing of spatial frequencies (Kitterle & Selig, 1991), the categorical or token-specific coding of visual objects (Burgund & Marsolek, 1997), or the efficiency of projections to left-hemispheric language areas. The conjunction of these factors may collectively conspire to define a cortical region optimally apt at hosting the functional processes of visual word recognition.

Finally, it should be remembered that it takes years for children to develop expert word recognition (Aghababian & Nazir, 2000), and that the emergence of this expertise correlates with the amount of activation of the VWFA by letter strings in normal and dyslexic children (McCandliss et al., 2003; Shaywitz et al., 2002; Temple, 2002). There is thus no ready-made "module" for visual word recognition, but rather a progressive specialization process that capitalizes on the plasticity of the human ventral inferotemporal cortex to build the VWFA.

Is the LCD Model Testable?

Is a single-neuron model of reading testable? We believe that it is. Not only is it becoming possible to record intracranially from local groups or even single cells in some human patients (Kreiman et al., 2000), but it is also possible to design indirect but sensitive tests using neuroimaging or behavioral techniques.

The main predictions of the LCD coding scheme can be summarized in three statements:

1. In literate participants, occipitotemporal neurons should exhibit a learned preference for fragments of visual words.
2. The size of the preferred elements—letters, bigrams, small strings— should increase progressively along a posterior-to-anterior axis in the occipitotemporal pathway.
3. There should be a concomitant progressive increase in the size of the receptive field, over which this preference should be invariant.

These predictions have begun to be tested with fMRI (Dehaene, 2005; Dehaene et al., 2001; Devlin, Jamison, Matthews, & Gonnerman, 2004). Although the receptive fields of single neurons are beyond the present resolution of fMRI machines, they can be tentatively measured indirectly through fMRI adaptation (Grill-Spector & Malach, 2001), also called *the priming method* (Naccache & Dehaene, 2001). This technique examines whether the fMRI signal diminishes upon repetition of the same object, possibly with changes in size, location, or shape. The object transformations that yield fMRI adaptation are thought to characterize the average receptive field and invariance structure of neurons in each voxel.

Using fMRI priming, an extended strip of left occipitotemporal cortex, lateral to the fusiform gyrus, has been shown to adapt when a word is repeated, even in a different case (e.g., RANGE–range) (Dehaene et al., 2001; Devlin et al., 2004). This fits with the model's suggestion that case invariance is achieved early on. Furthermore, this region is itself hierarchically organized (Dehaene, 2005). In the posterior occipitotemporal cortex ($y = -68$), priming depends on the presence of single letters at a specific location and breaks down if the repeated word is offset by one letter. Thus, this area might thus contain the postulated bank of location-specific letter detectors. More anteriorily ($y = -56$), priming resists a letter shift, but does not differentiate words and their anagrams (e.g., RANGE–anger). This area might therefore be dominated by local bigram detectors. Finally, still more anteriorily ($y = -48$), priming begins to be stronger for words than for anagrams. At this level, therefore, small strings or even entire words might begin to be coded.

By presenting strings of symbols containing a hierarchy of stimuli designed to progressively stimulate increasingly higher levels of the proposed cortical hierarchy (falsefont stimuli, infrequent letters, frequent letters, frequent bigrams, frequent quadrigrams, and real words), we recently demonstrated a systematic progression of activation from posterior occipital to anterior fusiform, as predicted by the LCD model (Vinckier et al., 2007). Bigram frequency has also been found to modulate the VWFA activation (Binder et al., 2006).

Behaviorally, the LCD model impacts on how one should measure the similarity between words, and in particular how to define lexical "neighbors." Currently, lexical neighbors are defined as words of the same length that differ by one letter. We predict that a composite measure, taking into account the proportion of shared letters and bigrams, as well as their retinal distances, should provide a better predictor of priming and of lexical confusions. Measuring the influence of letter distance on priming (Peressotti & Grainger, 1995), migration (Davis & Bowers, 2004), and letter transposition effects (Perea & Lupker, 2003, 2004; Schoonbaert & Grainger, 2004) may provide a quantitative test of the proposed receptive structure for letter and bigram detectors.

The model also predicts conditions under which fast word recognition should be severely disrupted. Letter detectors should be disrupted by rotation (>40 degrees according to monkey electrophysiological data [Logothetis & Pauls, 1995]). Bigram detectors should be disrupted by spacing of the component letters (e.g., H O U S E), with a sudden reading difficulty once the blank space exceeds approximately two letter widths.

Symmetry Generalization: The "Panda's Thumb" of Reading?

There is a final prediction which, in fact, constitutes a broader test of our framework. According to our "neuronal recycling" view, in the course of learning to read, part of the ventral visual system progressively adapts its function to the specific problems raised by the recognition of letters, bigrams, and words. Up to now, we have only considered properties of macaque inferotemporal cortex that are useful for reading, such as size and location invariance. However, are there prior properties of the visual system that are actually detrimental to reading acquisition? Such "vestigial features" might play, for theories of learning to read, a role similar to the one that the "panda's thumb" and other evidence for imperfect design play for evolutionary theory (Dawkins, 1996; Gould, 1992; Gould & Lewontin, 1979). As already noted by Darwin, features of perfect design are ambiguous: they might arise from evolution or from an omnipotent designer—or in the present case, from a universal learning algorithm. Only imperfect features betray the "tinkering" or "recycling" that goes on during the evolutionary process.

In the case of learning to read, mirror image generalization might be such an imperfection. A principle of mirror generalization seems to have been deeply entrenched by evolution into our visual system, presumably because the identity of most objects in the natural world remains the same under a mirror-image transformation. After exposure to a single image in a fixed orientation, humans and many animals spontaneously treat the mirror-symmetrical version as identical to the original (Biederman & Cooper, 1991; Logothetis & Pauls, 1995).

Furthermore, inferotemporal neurons frequently respond identically to mirror-image pairs of objects (Rollenhagen & Olson, 2000), even if they have been trained for months with only one view (Logothetis & Pauls, 1995).

Mirror symmetry was present in some ancient writing systems such as Egyptian and Greek, which could be read in both directions. Our alphabet no longer makes use of this feature: Not only is it always read from left to right, but several letters are distinguished by their left–right orientation (e.g., p, q; d, b). Strikingly, early on in reading acquisition, many children undergo a "mirror stage" during which they spontaneously read and write indifferently in both directions (Cornell, 1985; McMonnies, 1992). As a consequence, they experience confusions between mirror-image letters, which can persist up to adolescence in children with dyslexia (McMonnies, 1992; Terepocki, Kruk, & Willows, 2002).

We propose that mirror generalization is an intrinsic property of the primate visual system, which must be unlearned when learning to read. The finding that young children, without any training, exhibit a superior ability in mirror reading and writing, is illuminating for theories of reading acquisition. It is incompatible with a constructivist or "blank slate" view (e.g., Quartz & Sejnowski, 1997), according to which exposure to print would create, in a purely bottom-up fashion, neurons tuned to letters and words. It fits, however, with a selectionist hypothesis (e.g., Changeux, 1983), according to which learning to read proceeds by minimal reconfiguration of a preexisting architecture evolved for object recognition, and which initially incorporates a principle of mirror-image generalization.

Those ideas were recently tested with fMRI in literate adults, where it was confirmed that the VWFA indeed is sensitive to repetition of pictures in both normal and mirror image form, but is sensitive to word repetition in normal formal only (Dehaene et al., 2009). These results are compatible with the postulated "unlearning" of mirror symmetry in the VWFA during reading acquisition.

Conclusion

Let us summarize the main arguments of this chapter. We argue that the psychology of reading has much to gain from a closer examination of the constraints that reading places on cerebral pathways for visual object recognition. Current evidence indicates that the invariant recognition of letters and words is accomplished by a specialized subpart of the left occipitotemporal cortex. Neuroimaging and neuropsychological methods indicate that this region, collectively termed the VWFA, occupies a highly reproducible location and shows some degree of regional selectivity. Most probably, it must contain subpopulations of neurons specialized for reading, and intermixed with others involved in the recognition of other visual objects and scenes. We have tentatively proposed a rather precise model of how those neuronal assemblies might achieve invariant letter and word recognition, based on a hierarchy of increasingly abstract LCDs.

From a neurophysiological perspective, the internal code for visual words is unlikely to be of the rational and minimal type postulated in cognitive psychology. Rather, we expect a diverse, redundant repertoire of reading-related neurons, resulting from small modifications of the preexisting primate visual system. This model thus opens up the exciting possibility of using the considerable neurophysiological information available on the primate visual cortex to inform models of reading and its acquisition.

Notes

1. Note that this applies only to the peak coordinates: The activation typically occupies an extended anteroposterior strip of cortex that may span some subregions with partially distinct functions in the cortical hierarchy. Furthermore, the standard deviation of about 5 mm is true across multiple subjects within a given fMRI study. Across studies, the variability can be somewhat higher, most likely due to differences in methods used for normalizing brain anatomies.

2. This holds quite generally, at least in passive viewing conditions or with tasks that require equal attention to words and to consonant strings. However, no difference, or even a reversal, can be observed if the task is more difficult to perform with consonant strings than with words. Such a reversal is to be expected if the duration of activation and the amount of top-down attention are greater for consonant strings, thus obscuring an opposite difference in bottom-up responsivity.

References

Aghababian, V., & Nazir, T. A. (2000). Developing normal reading skills: aspects of the visual processes underlying word recognition. *Journal of Experimental Child Psychology, 76*,2, 123–150.

Albert, M. L., Reches, A., & Silverberg, R. (1975). Associative visual agnosia without alexia. *Neurology, 25*, 4, 322–326.

Allison, T., McCarthy, G., Nobre, A. C., Puce, A., & Belger, A. (1994). Human extrastriate visual cortex and the perception of faces, words, numbers and colors. *Cerebral Cortex, 5*, 544–554.

Allison, T., Puce, A., Spencer, D. D., & McCarthy, G. (1999). Electrophysiological studies of human face perception. I: Potentials generated in occipitotemporal cortex by face and non-face stimuli. *Cerebral Cortex, 9*, 5, 415–430.

Ans, B., Carbonnel, S., & Valdois, S. (1998). A connectionist multiple-trace memory model for polysyllabic word reading. *Psychology Review, 105*, 4, 678–723.

Beauregard, M., Chertkow, H., Bub, D., Murtha, S., Dixon, R., & Evans, A. (1997). The neural substrate for concrete, abstract, and emotional word lexica: A positron emission tomography study. *Journal of Cognitive Neuroscience, 9*, 441–461.

Behrmann, M., Nelson, J., & Sekuler, E. B. (1998). Visual complexity in letter-by-letter reading: "pure" alexia is not pure. *Neuropsychologia, 36*, 11, 1115–1132.

Besner, D. (1989). On the role of outline shape and word-specific visual pattern in the identification of function words: NONE. *Quarterly Journal of Experimental Psychology A, 41*, 91–105.

Besner, D., Coltheart, M., & Davelaar, E. (1984). Basic processes in reading: Computation of abstract letter identities. *Canadian Journal of Psychology, 38,* 126–134.

Beversdorf, D. Q., Ratcliffe, N. R., Rhodes, C. H., & Reeves, A. G. (1997). Pure alexia: clinical -pathologic evidence for a lateralized visual language association cortex. *Clinical Neuropathology, 16*, 328–331.

Biederman, I., & Cooper, E. E. (1991). Evidence for complete translational and reflectional invariance in visual object priming. *Perception, 20*, 5, 585–593.

Binder, J. R., & Mohr, J. P. (1992). The topography of callosal reading pathways. A case-control analysis. *Brain, 115*, 1807–1826.

Binder, J. R., Medler, D. A., Westbury, C. F., Liebenthal, E., & Buchanan, L. (2006). Tuning of the human left fusiform gyrus to sublexical orthographic structure. *Neuroimage, 33*(2), 739–748.

Booth, J. R., Burman, D. D., Meyer, J. R., Gitelman, D. R., Parrish, T. B., & Mesulam, M. M. (2002). Functional anatomy of intra- and cross-modal lexical tasks. *Neuroimage, 16*, 1, 7–22.

Booth, J. R., Burman, D. D., Meyer, J. R., Gitelman, D. R., Parrish, T. B., & Mesulam, M. M. (2003). Relation between brain activation and lexical performance. *Human Brain Mapping, 19*, 3, 155–169.

Bowers, J. S., Vigliocco, G., & Haan, R. (1998). Orthographic, phonological, and articulatory contributions to masked letter and word priming. *Journal of Experimental Psychology and Human Perception Performance, 24*, 6, 1705–1719.

Brincat, S. L., & Connor, C. E. (2004). Underlying principles of visual shape selectivity in posterior inferotemporal cortex. *Nature and Neuroscience, 7*, 8, 880–886.

Brunswick, N., McCrory, E., Price, C. J., Frith, C. D., & Frith, U. (1999). Explicit and implicit processing of words and pseudowords by adult developmental dyslexics: A search for Wernicke's Wortschatz? *Brain, 122*, 1901–1917.

Büchel, C., Price, C. J., & Friston, K. (1998). A multimodal language region in the ventral visual pathway. *Nature, 394*, 6690, 274–277.

Burgund, E. D., & Marsolek, C. J. (1997). Letter-case-specific priming in the right cerebral hemisphere with a form-specific perceptual identification task. *Brain and Cognition, 35*, 239–258.

Campbell, J. I. D. (1998). Linguistic influences in cognitive arithmetic: comment on Noel, Fias and Brysbaert (1997). *Cognition, 67*, 353–364.

Castro-Caldas, A., Petersson, K. M., Reis, A., Stone-Elander, S., & Ingvar, M. (1998). The illiterate brain. Learning to read and write during childhood influences the functional organization of the adult brain. *Brain, 121*, Pt. 6, 1053–1063.

Changeux, J. P. (1983). L'homme neuronal. Paris: Fayard.

Chanoine, V., Teixeira Ferreira, C., Demonet, J. F., Nespoulous, J. L., & Poncet, M. (1998). Optic aphasia with pure alexia: a mild form of visual associative agnosia? A case study. *Cortex, 34*, 437–448.

Chee, M. W. L., O'Craven, K. M., Bergida, R., Rosen, B. R., & Savoy, R. L. (1999). Auditory and visual word processing studied with fMRI. *Human Brain Mapping, 7*, 15–28.

Cohen, L., & Dehaene, S. (1995). Number processing in pure alexia: the effect of hemispheric asymmetries and task demands. *NeuroCase, 1*, 121–137.

Cohen, L., & Dehaene, S. (2000). Calculating without reading: unsuspected residual abilities in pure alexia. *Cognitive Neuropsychology, 17*, 6, 563–583.

Cohen, L., & Dehaene, S. (2004). Specialization within the ventral stream: the case for the visual word form area. *Neuroimage, 22,* 1, 466–476.

Cohen, L., Dehaene, S., Naccache, L., Lehéricy, S., Dehaene-Lambertz, G., Hénaff, M. A., et al. (2000). The visual word form area: Spatial and temporal characterization of an initial stage of reading in normal subjects and posterior split-brain patients. *Brain, 123*, 291–307.

Cohen, L., Henry, C., Dehaene, S., Martinaud, O., Lehericy, S., Lemer, C., et al. (2004). The pathophysiology of letter-by-letter reading. *Neuropsychologia, 42,* 13, 1768–1780.

Cohen, L., Jobert, A., Le Bihan, D., & Dehaene, S. (2004). Distinct unimodal and multimodal regions for word processing in the left temporal cortex. *Neuroimage, 23,* 4, 1256–1270.

Cohen, L., Lehericy, S., Chochon, F., Lemer, C., Rivaud, S., & Dehaene, S. (2002). Language-specific tuning of visual cortex? Functional properties of the Visual Word Form Area. *Brain, 125,* Pt 5, 1054–1069.

Cohen, L., Martinaud, O., Lemer, C., Lehéricy, S., Samson, Y., Obadia, M., et al. (2003). Visual word recognition in the left and right hemispheres: Anatomical and functional correlates of peripheral alexias. *Cerebral Cortex,13,* 1313–1333.

Coltheart, M., Rastle, K., Perry, C., Langdon, R., & Ziegler, J. (2001). DRC: a dual route cascaded model of visual word recognition and reading aloud. *Psychology Review 108,* 1, 204–256.

Cornell. (1985). Spontaneous mirror-writing in children. *Canadian Journal of Experimental Psychology39, ,*174–179.

Damasio, A. R., & Damasio, H. (1983). The anatomic basis of pure alexia. *Neurology, 33,* 1573–1583.

Davis, C. J., & Bowers, J. S. (2004). What do letter migration errors reveal about letter position coding in visual word recognition? *Journal of Experimental Psychology and Human Perception Performance, 30,* 5, 923–941.

Dawkins, R. (1996). *The blind watchmaker: why the evidence of evolution reveals a universe without design.* New York: W.W. Norton & Co.

Dehaene, S. (2005). Pre-emption of human cortical circuits by numbers and language: The "neuronal recycling" hypothesis. In S. Dehaene, J. R. Duhamel, M. Hauser & G. Rizzolatti (Eds.), *From monkey brain to human brain* (Vol. in press). Cambridge, Massachusetts: MIT Press.

Dehaene, S., Cohen, L., Sigman, M., & Vinckier, F. (2005). The neural code for written words: a proposal. *Trends in Cognitive Science,* submitted.

Dehaene, S., Jobert, A., Naccache, L., Ciuciu, P., Poline, J. B., Le Bihan, D., et al. (2004). Letter binding and invariant recognition of masked words: behavioral and neuroimaging evidence. *Psychology Science,* 15, 5, 307–313.

Dehaene, S., Le Clec'H, G., Poline, J. B., Le Bihan, D., & Cohen, L. (2002). The visual word form area: a prelexical representation of visual words in the fusiform gyrus. *Neuroreport, 13,* 3, 321–325.

Dehaene, S., Naccache, L., Cohen, L., Bihan, D. L., Mangin, J. F., Poline, J. B., et al. (2001). Cerebral mechanisms of word masking and unconscious repetition priming. *Nature and Neuroscience, 4,* 7, 752–758.

Dehaene, S., Nakamura, K., Jobert, A., Kuroki, C., Ogawa, S., & Cohen, L. (2009). Why do children make mirror errors in reading? Neural correlates of mirror invariance in the visual word form area. *Neuroimage, 49,* 1837–1848.

Dejerine, J. (1892). Contribution à l'étude anatomo-pathologique et clinique des différentes variétés de cécité verbale. *Mémoires de la Société de Biologie, 4*, 61–90.

Devlin, J. T., Jamison, H. L., Matthews, P. M., & Gonnerman, L. M. (2004). Morphology and the internal structure of words. *Proceedings of the National Academy of Science, USA, 101*, 41, 14984–14988.

Ding, G., Peng, D., & Taft, M. (2004). The nature of the mental representation of radicals in Chinese: a priming study. *Journal of Experimental Psychology, Learning, Memory, and Cognition, 30*, 2, 530–539.

Donnenwerth-Nolan, S., Tanenhaus, M. K., & Seidenberg, M. S. (1981). Multiple code activation in word recognition: evidence from rhyme monitoring. *Journal of Experimental Psychology [Human Learning], 7*, 3, 170–180.

Downing, P. E., Jiang, Y., Shuman, M., & Kanwisher, N. (2001). A cortical area selective for visual processing of the human body. *Science, 293*, 5539, 2470–2473.

Farah, M. J., & Wallace, M. A. (1991). Pure alexia as a visual impairment: A reconsideration. *Cognitive Neuropsychology, 8*, 313–334.

Fiez, J. A., Balota, D. A., Raichle, M. E., & Petersen, S. E. (1999). Effects of lexicality, frequency, and spelling-to-sound consistency on the functional anatomy of reading. *Neuron, 24*, 1, 205–218.

Gauthier, I. (2000). What constrains the organization of the ventral temporal cortex? *Trends in Cognitive Science, 4*, 1, 1–2.

Gauthier, I., Tarr, M. J., Moylan, J., Skudlarski, P., Gore, J. C., & Anderson, A. W. (2000). The fusiform "face area" is part of a network that processes faces at the individual level. *Journal of Cognitive Neuroscience, 12*, 3, 495–504.

Giraud, A. L., & Price, C. J. (2001). The constraints functional neuroanatomy places on classical models of auditory word processing. *Journal of Cognitive Neuroscience, 13*, 754–765.

Gomori, A. J., & Hawryluk, G. A. (1984). Visual agnosia without alexia. *Neurology, 34*, 7, 947–950.

Gould, S. J. (1992). *The panda's thumb: more reflections in natural history*. New York: W.W. Norton & Co.

Gould, S. J., & Lewontin, R. C. (1979). The spandrels of San Marco and the Panglossian paradigm: a critique of the adaptationist programme. *Proceedings of the Royal Society of London, B, Biological Science, 205*, 1161, 581–598.

Gould, S. J., & Vrba, E. S. (1982). Exaptation: A missing term in the science of form. *Paleobiology, 8*, 4–15.

Grainger, J., & Jacobs, A. M. (1996). Orthographic processing in visual word recognition: a multiple read-out model. *Psychology Review, 103*, 3, 518–565.

Grainger, J., & Whitney, C. (2004). Does the huamn mnid raed wrods as a wlohe? *Trends in Cognitive Sciencei, 8*, 2, 58–59.

Greenblatt, S. H. (1976). Subangular alexia without agraphia or hemianopsia. *Brain and Language, 3*, 2, 229–245.

Grill-Spector, K., Kushnir, T., Hendler, T., Edelman, S., Itzchak, Y., & Malach, R. (1998). A sequence of object-processing stages revealed by fMRI in the human occipital lobe. *Human Brain Mapping,6*, 4, 316–328.

Grill-Spector, K., & Malach, R. (2001). fMR-adaptation: a tool for studying the functional properties of human cortical neurons. *Acta Psychologia (Amsterdam), 107*, 1–3, 293–321.

Ha Duy Thuy, D., Matsuo, K., Nakamura, K., Toma, K., Oga, T., Nakai, T., et al. (2004). Implicit and explicit processing of kanji and kana words and non-words studied with fMRI. *Neuroimage, 23*, 3, 878–889.

Hallé, P. A., Chéreau, C., & Segui, J. (2000). Where is the /b/ in "absurde" [apsyrd]? It is in French listeners' minds. *Journal of Memory and Language, 43*, 618–639.

Hanley, J. R., & Kay, J. (1996). Reading speed in pure alexia. *Neuropsychologia, 34*, 12, 1165–1174.

Harm, M. W., & Seidenberg, M. S. (1999). Phonology, reading acquisition, and dyslexia: insights from connectionist models. *Psychology Review, 106*, 3, 491–528.

Hasson, U., Harel, M., Levy, I., & Malach, R. (2003). Large-scale mirror-symmetry organization of human occipito-temporal object areas. *Neuron, 37*, 6, 1027–1041.

Hasson, U., Levy, I., Behrmann, M., Hendler, T., & Malach, R. (2002). Eccentricity bias as an organizing principle for human high-order object areas. *Neuron, 34*, 3, 479–490.

Haxby, J. V., Gobbini, M. I., Furey, M. L., Ishai, A., Schouten, J. L., & Pietrini, P. (2001). Distributed and overlapping representations of faces and objects in ventral temporal cortex. *Science, 293*, 5539, 2425–2430.

Haxby, J. V., Ishai, I. I., Chao, L. L., Ungerleider, L. G., & Martin, I. I. (2000). Object-form topology in the ventral temporal lobe. Response to I. Gauthier (2000). *Trends in Cognitive Science, 4*, 1, 3–4.

Holender, D., & Peereman, R. (1987). Differential processing of phonographic and logographic single-digit numbers by the two hemispheres. In G. Deloche & X. Seron (Eds.). *Mathematical disabilities: A cognitive neuropsychological perspective* (pp. 43–86). Hillsdale New Jersey: Lawrence Erlbaum Associates.

Houzel, J. C., Carvalho, M. L., & Lent, R. (2002). Interhemispheric connections between primary visual areas: beyond the midline rule. *Brazilian Journal of Medical and Biological Research, 35*, 12, 1441–1453.

Hubel, D. H., & Wiesel, T. N. (1967). Cortical and callosal connections concerned with the vertical meridian of visual fields in the cat. *Journal of Neurophysiology, 30*, 6, 1561–1573.

Humphreys, G. W., Evett, L. J., & Quinlan, P. T. (1990). Orthographic processing in visual word identification. *Cognitive Psychology, 22*, 517–560.

Iragui, V. J., & Kritchevsky, M. (1991). Alexia without agraphia or hemianopia in parietal infarction. *Journal of Neurology, Neurosurgery, and Psychiatry, 54*, 9, 841–842.

Jacob, F. (1977). Evolution and tinkering. *Science, 196*, 4295, 1161–1166.

Johnson, N. F., & Pugh, K. R. (1994). A cohort model of visual word recognition. *Cognitive Psychology, 26*, 3, 240–346.

Kanwisher, N., McDermott, J., & Chun, M. M. (1997). The fusiform face area: a module in human extrastriate cortex specialized for face perception. *Journal of Neuroscience, 17*, 4302–4311.

Kitterle, F. L., & Selig, L. M. (1991). Visual field effects in the discrimination of sine-wave gratings. *Perceptions and Psychophysiology, 50*, 1, 15–18.

Kreiman, G., Koch, C., & Fried, I. (2000). Category-specific visual responses of single neurons in the human medial temporal lobe. *Nature and Neuroscience, 3*, 9, 946–953.

Lavidor, M., Babkoff, H., & Faust, M. (2001). Analysis of standard and non-standard visual word format in the two hemispheres. *Neuropsychologia, 39*, 4, 430–439.

Lavidor, M., & Ellis, A. W. (2002). Word length and orthographic neighborhood size effects in the left and right cerebral hemispheres. *Brain & Language, 80*, 45–62.

Lerner, Y., Hendler, T., Ben-Bashat, D., Harel, M., & Malach, R. (2001). A hierarchical axis of object processing stages in the human visual cortex. *Cerebral Cortex, 11*, 4, 287–297.

Logothetis, N. K., & Pauls, J. (1995). Psychophysical and physiological evidence for viewer-centered object representations in the primate. *Cerebral Cortex, 5*, 3, 270–288.

Logothetis, N. K., Pauls, J., Bulthoff, H. H., & Poggio, T. (1994). View-dependent object recognition by monkeys. *Current Biology,4*, 5, 401–414.

Malach, R., Levy, I., & Hasson, U. (2002). The topography of high-order human object areas. *Trends in Cognitive Science, 6*, 4, 176–184.

Marinkovic, K., Dhond, R. P., Dale, A. M., Glessner, M., Carr, V., & Halgren, E. (2003). Spatiotemporal dynamics of modality-specific and supramodal word processing. *Neuron, 38*, 3, 487–497.

Mayall, K., Humphreys, G. W., & Olson, A. (1997). Disruption to word or letter processing? The origins of case-mixing effects. *Journal of Experimental Psychology, Learning, Memory, and Cognition, 23*, 5, 1275–1286.

McCandliss, B. D., Cohen, L., & Dehaene, S. (2003). The visual word form area: expertise for reading in the fusiform gyrus. *Trends in Cognitive Science*, 7, 293–299.

McClelland, J. L., & Rumelhart, D. E. (1981). An interactive activation model of context effects in letter perception: I. An account of basic findings. *Psychological Review, 88*, 375–407.

McMonnies, C. W. (1992). Visuo-spatial discrimination and mirror image letter reversals in reading. *Journal of the American Optometry Association, 63*, 10, 698–704.

McNeil, J. E., & Warrington, E. K. (1993). Prosopagnosia: a face-specific disorder. *Quarterly Journal of Experimental Psychology A, 46*, 1, 1–10.

Miyashita, Y. (1988). Neuronal correlate of visual associative long-term memory in the primate temporal cortex. *Nature, 335*, 6193, 817–820.

Molko, N., Cohen, L., Mangin, J. F., Chochon, F., Lehéricy, S., Le Bihan, D., et al. (2002). Visualizing the neural bases of a disconnection syndrome with diffusion tensor imaging. *Journal of Cognitive Neuroscience, 14*, 629–636.

Montant, M., & Behrmann, M. (2000). Pure alexia. *Neurocase, 6*, 265–294.

Mozer, M. C. (1987). Early parallel processing in reading: a connectionist approach. In M. Coltheart (Ed.), Attention and performance XII: the psychology of reading. (pp. 83–104). Hillsdale, NJ: Lawrence Erlbaum Associates.

Naccache, L., & Dehaene, S. (2001). The priming method: imaging unconscious repetition priming reveals an abstract representation of number in the parietal lobes. *Cerebral Cortex, 11*, 10, 966–974.

Nakamura, K., Dehaene, S., Jobert, A., Le Bihan, D., & Kouider, S. (2005). Subliminal convergence of Kanji and Kana words: Further evidence for functional parcellation of the posterior temporal cortex in visual word perception. *Journal of Cognitive Neuroscience*, in press.

Nazir, T. A. (2000). Traces of print along the visual pathway. In A. Kennedy, R. Radach, D. Heller & J. Pynte (Eds.). *Reading as a perceptual process* (pp. 3–22). Amsterdam: Elsevier.

Nazir, T. A., Ben-Boutayab, N., Decoppet, N., Deutsch, A., & Frost, R. (2004). Reading habits, perceptual learning, and recognition of printed words. *Brain & Language, 88*, 3, 294–311.

Nobre, A. C., Allison, T., & McCarthy, G. (1994). Word recognition in the human inferior temporal lobe. *Nature, 372*, 6503, 260–263.

Nobre, A. C., Allison, T., & McCarthy, G. (1998). Modulation of human extrastriate visual processing by selective attention to colours and words. *Brain, 121*, 1357–1368.

Paap, K. R., Newsome, S. L., & Noel, R. W. (1984). Word shape's in poor shape for the race to the lexicon. *Journal of Experimental Psychology: Human Perception and Performance, 10*, 3, 413–428.

Pammer, K., Hansen, P. C., Kringelbach, M. L., Holliday, I., Barnes, G., Hillebrand, A., et al. (2004). Visual word recognition: the first half second. *Neuroimage, 22*, 4, 1819–1825.

Patterson, K., & Kay, J. (1982). Letter-by-letter reading: Psychological descriptions of a neurological syndrome. *The Quarterly Journal of Experimental Psychology, 34A*, 411–441.

Paulesu, E., McCrory, E., Fazio, F., Menoncello, L., Brunswick, N., Cappa, S. F., et al. (2000). A cultural effect on brain function. *Nature and Neuroscienc 3*, 1, 91–96.

Perea, M., & Lupker, S. J. (2003). Does jugde activate COURT? Transposed-letter similarity effects in masked associative priming. *Memory and Cognition, 31*, 6, 829–841.

Perea, M., & Lupker, S. J. (2004). Can Caniso activate Casino? Transposed-letter similarity effect with nonadjacent letter positions. *Journal of Memory and Language, 51*, 231–246.

Peressotti, F., & Grainger, J. (1995). Letter-position coding in random constant arrays. *Perception and Psychophysiology, 57*, 6, 875–890.

Peressotti, F., & Grainger, J. (1999). The role of letter identity and letter position in orthographic priming. *Perception and Psychophysiology, 61,4*, 691–706.

Petersen, S. E., Fox, P. T., Snyder, A. Z., & Raichle, M. E. (1990). Activation of extrastriate and frontal cortical areas by visual words and word-like stimuli. *Science, 249*, 1041–1044.

Pinel, P., Dehaene, S., Riviere, D., & LeBihan, D. (2001). Modulation of parietal activation by semantic distance in a number comparison task. *Neuroimage, 14*, 5, 1013–1026.

Pirozzolo, F. J., Kerr, K. L., Obrzut, J. E., Morley, G. K., Haxby, J. V., & Lundgren, S. (1981). Neurolinguistic analysis of the language abilities of a patient with a "double disconnection syndrome": a case of subangular alexia in the presence of mixed transcortical aphasia. *Journal of Neurology, Neurosurgery, and Psychiatry, 44*, 2, 152–155.

Plaut, D. C., McClelland, J. L., Seidenberg, M. S., & Patterson, K. (1996). Understanding normal and impaired word reading: computational principles in quasi-regular domains. *Psychology Review, 103*, 1, 56–115.

Polk, T. A., & Farah, M. J. (2002). Functional MRI evidence for an abstract, not perceptual, word-form area. *Journal of Experimental Psychology, Gen, 131*, 1, 65–72.

Polk, T. A., Stallcup, M., Aguirre, G. K., Alsop, D. C., D'Esposito, M., Detre, J. A., et al. (2002). Neural specialization for letter recognition. *Journal of Cognitive Neuroscience, 14*, 2, 145–159.

Price, C. J., & Devlin, J. T. (2003). The myth of the visual word form area. *Neuroimage, 19*, 473–481.

Price, C. J., Winterburn, D., Giraud, A. L., Moore, C. J., & Noppeney, U. (2003). Cortical localisation of the visual and auditory word form areas: A reconsideration of the evidence. *Brain & Language, 86*, 2, 272–286.

Price, C. J., Wise, R. J. S., & Frackowiak, R. S. J. (1996). Demonstrating the implicit processing of visually presented words and pseudowords. *Cerebral Cortex, 6*, 62–70.

Puce, A., Allison, T., Asgari, M., Gore, J. C., & McCarthy, G. (1996). Differential sensitivity of human visual cortex to faces, letterstrings, and textures: a functional magnetic resonance imaging study. *Journal of Neuroscience, 16*, 5205–5215.

Puce, A., Allison, T., & McCarthy, G. (1999). Electrophysiological studies of human face perception. III: Effects of top-down processing on face-specific potentials. *Cerebral Cortex, 9*, 5, 445–458.

Quartz, S. R., & Sejnowski, T. J. (1997). The neural basis of cognitive development: a constructivist manifesto. *Behavior Brain Science, 20*, 4, 537–556; discussion 556–596.

Rees, G., Russell, C., Frith, C. D., & Driver, J. (1999). Inattentional blindness versus inattentional amnesia for fixated but ignored words. *Science, 286*, 2504–2507.

Reicher, G. M. (1969). Perceptual recognition as a function of meaningfulness of stimulus material. *Journal of Experimental Psychology, 81*, 274–280.

Riesenhuber, M., & Poggio, T. (1999). Hierarchical models of object recognition in cortex. *Nature Neuroscience, 2*, 1019–1025.

Rollenhagen, J. E., & Olson, C. R. (2000). Mirror-image confusion in single neurons of the macaque inferotemporal cortex. *Science, 287*, 5457, 1506–1508.

Rolls, E. T. (2000). Functions of the primate temporal lobe cortical visual areas in invariant visual object and face recognition. *Neuron, 27*, 2, p205–218.

Rumelhart, D. E., & McClelland, J. L. (1982). An interactive activation model of context effects in letter perception: Part 2. The contextual enhancement effect and some tests and extensions of the model. *Psychology Review, 89*, 1, 60–94.

Salmelin, R., Service, E., Kiesilä, P., Uutela, K., & Salonen, O. (1996). Impaired visual word processing in dyslexia revealed with magnetoencephalography. *Annals of Neurology, 40*, 157–162.

Schoonbaert, S., & Grainger, J. (2004). Letter position coding in printed word perception: Effects of repeated and transposed letters. *Language and Cognitive Processes, 19*, 333–367.

Seidenberg, M. S., & McClelland, J. L. (1989). A distributed, developmental model of word recognition and naming. *Psychology Review, 96*, 4, 523–568.

Shallice, T. (1988). *From neuropsychology to mental structure*. Cambridge: Cambridge University Press.

Shaywitz, B. A., Shaywitz, S. E., Pugh, K. R., Mencl, W. E., Fulbright, R. K., Skudlarski, P., et al. (2002). Disruption of posterior brain systems for reading in children with developmental dyslexia. *Biology and Psychiatry, 52*, 2, 101–110.

Shillcock, R., Ellison, T. M., & Monaghan, P. (2000). Eye-fixation behavior, lexical storage, and visual word recognition in a split processing model. *Psychology Review, 107*, 4, 824–851.

Sigman, M., & Gilbert, C. D. (2000). Learning to find a shape. *Nature and Neuroscience, 3*, 3, 264–269.

Simos, P. G., Fletcher, J. M., Foorman, B. R., Francis, D. J., Castillo, E. M., Davis, R. N., et al. (2002). Brain activation profiles during the early stages of reading acquisition. *Journal of Child Neurology, 17*, 3, 159–163.

Sowell, E. R., Thompson, P. M., Rex, D., Kornsand, D., Tessner, K. D., Jernigan, T. L., et al. (2002). Mapping sulcal pattern asymmetry and local cortical surface gray matter distribution in vivo: maturation in perisylvian cortices. *Cerebral Cortex, 12*, 1, 17–26.

Spoehr, K. T., & Smith, E. E. (1975). The role of orthographic and phonotactic rules in perceiving letter patterns. *Journal of Experimental Psychology: Human Perception and Performance, 104*, 1, 21–34.

Stromswold, K., Caplan, D., Alpert, N., & Rauch, S. (1996). Localization of syntactic comprehension by positron emission tomography. *Brain & Language, 52*, 3, 452–473.

Suzuki, K., Yamadori, A., Endo, K., Fujii, T., Ezura, M., & Takahashi, A. (1998). Dissociation of letter and picture naming resulting from callosal disconnection. *Neurology, 51*, 1390–1394.

Taft, M., & Hambly, G. (1985). The influence of orthography on phonological representations in the lexicon. *Journal of Memory and Language, 24*, 320–335.

Tarkiainen, A., Cornelissen, P. L., & Salmelin, R. (2002). Dynamics of visual feature analysis and object-level processing in face versus letter-string perception. *Brain, 125*, Pt 5, 1125–1136.

Tarkiainen, A., Helenius, P., Hansen, P. C., Cornelissen, P. L., & Salmelin, R. (1999). Dynamics of letter string perception in the human occipitotemporal cortex. *Brain, 122*, Pt 11, 2119–2132.

Temple, E. (2002). Brain mechanisms in normal and dyslexic readers. *Current Opinions in Neurobiology, 12*, 2, 178–183.

Terepocki, M., Kruk, R. S., & Willows, D. M. (2002). The incidence and nature of letter orientation errors in reading disability. *Journal of Learning Disabilities, 35*, 3, 214–233.

Thompson, P. M., Schwartz, C., Lin, R. T., Khan, A. A., & Toga, A. W. (1996). Three-dimensional statistical analysis of sulcal variability in the human brain. *Journal of Neurosciences, 16*, 13, 4261–4274.

Tsunoda, K., Yamane, Y., Nishizaki, M., & Tanifuji, M. (2001). Complex objects are represented in macaque inferotemporal cortex by the combination of feature columns. *Nature and Neuroscience, 4*, 8, 832–838.

Vinckier, F., Dehaene, S., Jobert, A., Dubus, J. P., Sigman, M., & Cohen, L. (2007). Hierarchical coding of letter strings in the ventral stream: dissecting the inner organization of the visual word-form system. *Neuron, 55*(1), 143–156.

Wagner, A. D., Schacter, D. L., Rotte, M., Koutstaal, W., Maril, A., Dale, A. M., et al. (1998). Building memories: remembering and forgetting of verbal experiences as predicted by brain activity. *Science, 281*, 5380, 1188–1191.

Wang, G., Tanaka, K., & Tanifuji, M. (1996). Optical imaging of functional organization in the monkey inferotemporal cortex. *Science, 272*, 5268, 1665–1668.

Warrington, E. K., & Shallice, T. (1980). Word-form dyslexia. *Brain, 103*, 99–112.

Weekes, B. (1997). Differential effects of number of letters on word and nonword naming latency. *Quarterly Journal of Experimental Psychology, 50A*, 439–456.

Whitney, C. (2001). How the brain encodes the order of letters in a printed word: the SERIOL model and selective literature review. *Psychology Bulletin Review,8*, 2, 221–243.

Whitney, C., & Lavidor, M. (2004). Why word length only matters in the left visual field. *Neuropsychologia, 42*, 12, 1680–1688.

Xu, B., Grafman, J., Gaillard, W. D., Ishii, K., Vega-Bermudez, F., Pietrini, P., et al. (2001). Conjoint and extended neural networks for the computation of speech codes: the neural basis of selective impairment in reading words and pseudowords. *Cerebral Cortex, 11*, 3, 267–277.

Ziegler, J. C., & Ferrand, L., 1998). Orthography shapes the perception of speech: The consistency effect in auditory word recognition. *Psychonomic Bulletin and Review,5*, 683–689.

Zorzi, M., Houghton, G., & Butterworth, B. (1998). Two routes or one in reading aloud? A connectionist dual-process model. *Journal of Experimental Psychology: Human Perception and Performance, 24*, 1131–1161

6

The Neural Bases of Reading

Universals and Writing System Variations

Charles Perfetti, Jessica Nelson, Ying Liu, Julie Fiez, and Li-Hai Tan

The neural substrate for reading includes highly general subsystems, collectively known as the "reading network." To the extent that these subsystems are universal, they must somehow support the reading of a wide range of languages with a diverse set of written forms and mapping principles. In this chapter, we explore the highly contrastive cases of English and Chinese to examine how the neural basis of reading accommodates variability in the structure of languages. The notion of accommodation, in fact, is central to our analysis. We conclude that the reading network must accommodate variation in writing systems by organizing in a way that reflects the properties of each particular writing system. However, we also suggest that the prior state of the network—the organization of the network when there is a previously learned language—influences how the network adapts to those properties specific to a second language. In particular, to some extent, the prior network may assimilate the second language, using its first-language procedures to the extent possible.

In elaborating this conclusion, we first review the orthographic structure and phonological mapping principles of Chinese and English, with some attention to how these two writing systems are learned by native speakers. We follow with a review of the comparative (across writing system) neuroscience research, and explore what the differences in brain regions used for Chinese and English might tell us about how these writing systems are processed. Finally, we review recent research that asks how the brain accommodates learning to read a second writing system.

Word Reading from a Writing System Perspective

At its core, reading is fundamentally about converting graphic input to linguistic-conceptual objects (words and morphemes). A universal theory of reading must explain how this occurs, considering the form of the graphic input and how it maps to phonological and semantic representations. To the extent that there are differences between writing systems in visual form and mapping principles, we might expect to see differences in the underlying neural subsystems recruited when reading. To provide a framework with which to interpret neuropsychological data, we consider three areas that are known to differ between English and Chinese: the visual properties, the principles of mapping to phonology, and the way in which these writing systems are learned.

Visual Properties

The visual properties of a given orthography include both deeper features of the writing system that they exemplify and more surface-level features of the script in which they are written. *Writing systems* reflect design principles, not appearances. For example, alphabetic writing systems represent words as a sequence of letters that roughly map to phonemes, whereas syllabaries (e.g., Japanese Kana) map graphic symbols to syllables. Chinese (often called a "logographic" language) is an example of a morpho-syllabic writing system, in which characters represent both pronunciation and meaning units. The implementation of a writing system in a specific language is *orthography*. Thus, written English is a distinctive orthography that differs from the orthographies of Italian and Korean. Within the alphabetic writing system, orthographies vary in the transparency of mappings between letters and phonemes; Italian and Finnish are very transparent; English is relatively nontransparent. Danish is in-between. (See Perfetti & Dunlap, 2008, for how this matters for reading.)

Additionally, orthographies can appear in various scripts. For example, the Roman alphabet can be written in a wide range of cursive and typeface fonts and all of these are different from the forms in the Greek or Cyrillic alphabet. These superficial appearances, the forms of the graphs, are visually salient and might be relevant for how the brain handles written language variability. For example, although Korean Hangŭl is an alphabetic orthography, the arrangement of its letters into square syllables that visually resemble Chinese characters presents a contrast to the linear alphabets of European writing (see Figure 6.1 for examples of the range of writing systems and scripts).

The Chinese-alphabetic contrast in visual appearance could matter for reading, even beyond a contrast in design principles. Whereas English words are formed by stringing together the letters that represent the sounds of the words, Chinese characters are formed by arranging component radicals into a

Writing System Category		Script Example	Spoken Language
Alphabetic	Cyrillic	Кириллица	Russian
	Hangŭl	한글	Korean
	Manchu	ᠵᡳ᠂	Manchu
Syllabic	Hiragana	ひらがな	Japanese
	Inukitut	ᐁᐯᕆ ᓄᑕᐃ	Inukitut
Morphosyllabic	Simplified Chinese	简化字	Mandarin

Figure 6.1 Illustration of writing variety across the three world's major writing systems: alphabetic, syllabic, and morpho-syllabic. Scripts vary both within and across writing systems.

square shape. The configuration of radicals within that square can be left-right, top-bottom, or inside-outside. For example, the same two radicals, 口 and 木 can be combined to make the single-character words 杏 (apricot), 呆 (stupid), and 困 (sleepy), and the component radical 木 can also stand alone as the character for tree. Even more complex characters can be formed by vertically or horizontally inserting a radical between two others. For example, 鼻 (nose) is formed by combining the component radicals 自, 田, and 廾 vertically. Component radicals often have their own meaning and pronunciation, and can provide cues for the meaning and pronunciation of the whole character. However, the low cue reliability of these radicals limit their general usefulness for character identification, making it important that whole character recognition processes are acquired. These whole character processes may include configural visual processing similar to that used in recognizing faces. Whereas stroke sequences contain high spatial frequency information, the relations among the radicals is encoded by low spatial frequency information. Accordingly, visual processes tuned to low spatial frequencies could be especially useful for Chinese.

Phonological Properties

Chinese is a morpho-syllabic system: A character corresponds to a spoken syllable that is usually a morpheme, and often a word. Given its mapping to morphemes and words, Chinese has often been viewed as a system that takes the reader directly to meaning, with phonology not playing an important role. However, the fact that the meaning units are spoken syllables allows the possibility that spoken language units are involved. As we noted earlier, compound characters contain components that can provide information about meaning (semantic radicals) and pronunciation (phonetic radicals), although not with high reliability.

For comparative purposes, the most important fact about a character is that it maps onto a syllable, not a phoneme. Whereas the _b_ in _bike_ maps to the initial segment (/b/) of the spoken word, a phonetic radical does not map to any segment of the syllable-morpheme represented by the character. Instead, it maps to a whole syllable that may (or may not) be the syllable-morpheme represented by the character. Thus, the critical departure from alphabetic writing is that Chinese writing does not reflect the segmental structure fundamental to alphabetic systems (Leong, 1997; Mattingly, 1987).

This analysis of Chinese writing leads to an important conclusion about reading: Phonological assembly, the activation of phonemes by graphemes and their "assembly" into syllables and words, is not possible for a single Chinese character. Syllable-level phonological assembly is possible for two- and three-character words, and there is some evidence that this is how two-character words are identified (Tan & Perfetti, 1999.)

Not allowing phonological assembly, however, is not the same as not allowing phonology. Like alphabetic readers, Chinese readers engage phonology when they read, from the sentence level (Hung, Tzeng, & Tzeng, 1992; Zhang & Perfetti, 1993), where phonology supports memory and comprehension, down to the single-character level (Chua, 1999; Perfetti & Zhang, 1991; Perfetti & Zhang, 1995; Xu, Pollatsek & Potter, 1999). At the character level, the evidence is consistent with the _identification-with-phonology_ hypothesis (Perfetti & Tan, 1998; Perfetti & Zhang, 1995; Tan & Perfetti, 1997): phonology as a _constituent_ of word identification, rather than either a prelexical mediator or a postlexical by-product. This characterization applies to alphabetic writing as well at the whole-word phonology level (Perfetti, Liu, & Tan, 2005).

In the lexical constituency model (Perfetti et al., 2005), which builds on the identification-with-phonology hypothesis, phonology is activated at the moment of orthographic recognition—the point at which the identification system distinguishes a given graphic representation from other (similar and partly activated) representations. Phonological activation is part of a psychological moment of identification that is observable across writing systems. The difference among writing systems is that, in an alphabetic system, the graphic units that initiate phonology correspond to phonemes, whereas in Chinese, these units correspond to a syllable.

The lexical constituency model (Perfetti & Tan, 1998; Perfetti et al., 2005) is an expression of these ideas that includes computational assumptions about identifying characters. The model has implications for how the brain's reading network might respond to variations in writing systems. It assumes that orthographic, phonological, and semantic constituents specify word identity. It further assumes that form form relationships are available rapidly, so that phonological information is quickly retrieved given a graphic input. The most important feature of the model's application to Chinese is that it captures an asynchrony between orthographic and phonological processing that is absent in alphabetic reading. In reading an alphabetic word, the individual graphemes can activate phonemes, and the process of word identification can proceed with the assembly of these phonemes toward a match with a word representation. (Identification also can proceed along a direct path to the stored representation, the addressed route of dual-route models) (Coltheart, Rastle, Perry, Langdon, & Ziegler, 2001).

The fact that Chinese does not allow an assembled route for a single character is a writing system factor that is expressed in behavioral data; for example, Chinese shows an asynchrony in the time course of graphic and phonological priming (Perfetti & Tan, 1998). Phonological priming, a reduction in naming time when a character is preceded by a graphically nonoverlapping homophone, began at the same time point when facilitation by graphic priming became inhibitory. (When a prime preceded the target by 43 ms (43 ms SOA), the graphic prime was facilitative, and there was no phonological or semantic priming; at 57 ms SOA, phonological priming appeared, and graphic facilitation turned to inhibition.) In alphabetic reading, this pattern has not been observed. Instead, in comparable time windows, one observes graphic facilitation followed quickly by phonological facilitation (e.g., Perfetti & Bell, 1991). Perfetti and colleagues (2005) interpret these differences this way: Reading alphabetic writing involves a cascaded process of phonology, in which phonological processes can begin prior to the completion of orthographic processes (Coltheart, Curtis, Atkins, & Haller, 1993). Reading Chinese involves a threshold process of phonology, in which phonology awaits the completion of orthographic processes.

Finally, an important factor for reading is that Chinese contains many homophones, an average of 11 per single-syllable words not counting tone (and about four counting tone; Language and Teaching Institute of Beijing Linguistic College, 1986), making the use of phonology to mediate access to meaning difficult. Only a process that uses the character in meaning access can be reliably successful. That fact, coupled with the evidence that character-level phonology is always activated in reading Chinese, implies the following: The character's orthographic form has connections to both meaning and phonology (syllable level). In reading an alphabetic word, the corresponding connections are also functional. The difference is that the Chinese reader may need to retain the orthography (the character) rather than relying on phonology while meaning is retrieved. This possible difference may have an effect in how the brain reads the two different systems.

Thus, the picture is one that shows a Universal Phonological Principle in reading (Perfetti, Zhang, & Berent, 1992) that derives from the dependence of reading on spoken language. However, the simple picture of a universal phonology at this level does not mean that there is a universal implementation of phonology, either as observed in behavior, which we have just shown may be different, or in the brain.

Elements of Learning

In addition to structural differences, and largely because of them, English and Chinese are taught and learned differently. These differences in learning strategies may have their own role in shaping the reading networks. The covariant learning hypothesis, an extension of Hebbian learning, suggests that brain networks are tuned by learning strategies because of correlated brain activity arising from the learning process and, in the case of reading, viewing the written form of the words being learned. This follows general proposals that the procedures for learning to read tune the brain systems that support skilled reading (Booth, Burman, Meyer, Gitelman, Parrish, & Mesulam, 2004; Booth, Burman, Van Santen, Harasaki, Gitelman, & Parrish, 2001; Kochunov, Fox, Lancaster, Tan, Amunts, & Zilles, 2003; McCandliss, Cohen, & Dehaene, 2003). Tan and colleagues (2005) apply this principle to understanding differences in how the brain becomes tuned through experience for specific procedures for Chinese or alphabetic reading. Children learning to read an alphabetic writing system either explicitly or implicitly learn to take account of the phonemic structure of speech. This supports the learning of grapheme–phoneme connections and accounts for the high correlations between phonemic awareness and learning to read. This learning procedure forges connections between speech and print, and leads to the tuning of a brain system that links the auditory mechanisms used in speech to the visual mechanisms used for print.

The speech–print connection is important in Chinese, as well, but with significant differences. First, because Chinese connects its written characters to speech at the syllable level, the phoneme level of speech is less accessible to Chinese children during character reading (Leong, Tan, Cheng, & Hau, 2005). This difference in phonological grain size (Ziegler & Goswami, 2005) reduces the role of analytic phonology for Chinese learners compared with alphabetic learners. Second, because of the many homophones in Chinese, the syllable pronunciation of the character is not sufficient for meaning access, for which the character itself is essential. Indeed, Cao and colleagues (2009) concluded that Chinese children show an increasing sensitivity to orthography and decreasing reliance on phonology as they become more skilled, perhaps stemming from an increased ability to visually chunk the component strokes of characters into larger units (Pak, Cheng-Lai, Tso, Shu, Li, & Anderson, 2005). Third, Chinese children, unlike alphabetic learners, spend a great deal of time copying single characters. Tan, Spinks, Eden, Perfetti, and Siok (2005), found that children's reading ability in Chinese is more strongly related to character copying skills than to phonological awareness. These three facts suggest that in learning to read Chinese, character forms—the visual-spatial layout of the strokes and the radicals—play a critical role.

Comparative Functional Neuroimaging of Reading Networks

A comparative look at the underlying neural networks revealed through the functional neuroimaging of English and Chinese readers demonstrates that differences between the two languages extend to the brain regions used to support reading.

The Neural System for Alphabetic Reading

In general terms (with ample uncertainty about details), a consensus has emerged on how the brain supports alphabetic reading. Several meta-analyses (Bolger, Perfetti, & Schneider, 2005; Fiez & Petersen, 1998; Jobard, Crivello, & Tzourio-Mazoyer, 2003; Mechelli, Gorno-Tempini, & Price, 2003; Price, 2000; Turkeltaub, Eden, Jones, & Zeffiro, 2002) point to a neural network whose components share responsibility for the orthographic, phonological, and semantic processes of word reading.

The alphabetic reading network includes posterior visual regions (occipital areas and the left mid-fusiform gyrus) for orthographic processes, temporal/parietal and anterior areas (superior temporal sulcus and inferior frontal sulcus/insula) for phonology, and both posterior (anterior fusiform) and anterior regions (inferior frontal gyrus) for meaning. A differentiation of the alphabetic reading network into five or six components is required for more precise functional descriptions (Pugh, Shaywitz, Shaywitz, Constable, Skudlarski, & Fulbright, 1996), but to provide a point of departure for Chinese, a more coarse-grain three-part network—(1) occipital-temporal areas that include the left fusiform gyrus, (2) temporal-parietal areas, and (3) the inferior frontal gyrus—is sufficient.

The network identified for alphabetic reading has wide applicability to both alphabetic and nonalphabetic writing systems. However, even comparisons within alphabetic systems suggest differences (Paulesu et al., 2000). Imaging studies in Asian languages, including Japanese (Nakada, Fugii, & Kwee, 2001; Nakamura, Dehaene, Jobert, Bihan, & Kouider, 2005; Sakurai, Momose, Iwata, Sudo, Ohtomo, & Kanazawa 2000) and Korean (Lee, 2004; Yoon, Cho, Chung, & Park, 2005; Yoon, Cho, & Park, 2005), as well as Chinese (Chee, Tan, & Thiel, 1999; Chee, Weekes, Lee, Soon, Schreiber, & Hoon, 2000), now provide richer alphabetic and nonalphabetic comparisons.

The Neural System for Chinese Reading

The first studies of Chinese showed a convergence with alphabetic research in key respects. Chee, Tan, and Thiel (1999) found generally similar patterns of activation in Chinese and English, including in the left fusiform gyrus. Tan, Spinks, Gao, Liu, Perfetti, and Fox (2000) also reported overlap with English, especially emphasizing that left hemisphere (LH) areas, both posterior and anterior, were activated more than right hemisphere (RH) areas by Chinese. Tan and colleagues (2000) emphasized the left lateralization of Chinese reading to counter a widespread belief that Chinese is read by the RH. However, differences were also present in these studies, although not emphasized in the papers. Although Tan and colleagues (2000) correctly emphasized a general LH lateralization, their results for the occipital and occipital-temporal regions showed bilateral activation. There was no explicit comparison with alphabetic results, but Chinese reading did seem to show more RH activation than studies in alphabetic reading had reported.

As other studies were carried out (Tan, Liu, Perfetti, Spinks, Fox, & Gao, 2001; Tan, Spinks, Feng, Siok, Perfetti, Xiong, Fox, & Gao, 2003), the differences between Chinese and alphabetic reading became impossible to ignore. Not only did results show more bilateral activation for Chinese in occipital and fusiform regions, they showed more activation in a frontal area, the left middle frontal gyrus (LMFG). Siok, Perfetti, Jin, and Tan (2004) added the finding that Chinese children who were poor in reading showed underactivation of the LMFG, compared with children who were skilled readers. Activation of the LMFG has been found consistently enough in research to warrant the conclusion that it has a specific role in reading Chinese. The function of the LMFG remains to be clarified, but its importance is not in doubt. At the same time, studies of Chinese typically were not finding the same levels of activation of the temporal-parietal region nor the inferior frontal gyrus as found in alphabetic reading, where both are assumed to support phonological processes.

Two meta-analyses that include Chinese tend to confirm these differences, although the use of different task selection criteria seems to have produced less than complete agreement. Bolger, Perfetti, and Schneider (2005) reviewed nine studies of Chinese and five of Japanese, along with 35 studies of alphabetic languages, across a wide range of single-word reading tasks. They observed overlapping areas of activation across languages in the left ventral visual cortex, including the fusiform area seen in English reading, but also observed that Chinese showed greater bilateral activation.

Tan, Laird, Li, and Fox (2005) reviewed six studies of Chinese reading and 13 studies of alphabetic reading that used a more restricted set of explicit phonology tasks. Tan and colleagues (2005) concluded that alphabetic word and character phonological processing shared a network of three areas, the same three areas identified for alphabetic reading: (1) ventral prefrontal areas involving superior portions of the left inferior frontal gyrus; (2) a left dorsal temporoparietal system, including mid-superior temporal gyri and the ventral aspect of inferior parietal cortex (supramarginal region); and (3) left ventral occipitotemporal areas. However, corresponding to these three general regions (frontal, temporal-parietal, and occipital-temporal), there were also three points of departure in the Chinese data: (1) the left dorsal lateral frontal area at BA 9 showed distinctly more activation for Chinese than for English, whereas the inferior frontal gyrus was not as active in Chinese; (2) a dorsal left inferior parietal area was more active for Chinese than English, whereas the superior temporal area was less active for Chinese; and (3) bilateral instead of left-lateralized occipital-temporal regions along the fusiform gyrus were found. See Figure 6.2 for a comparison of regions recruited in reading Chinese and regions recruited in reading English.

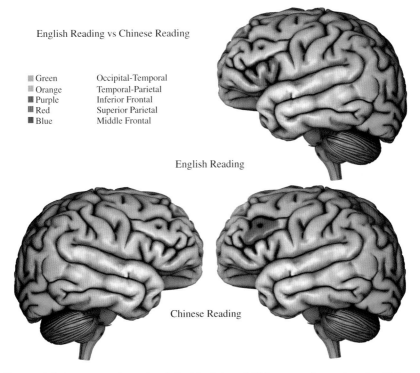

Figure 6.2 A coarse schematic of the English and Chinese reading networks. Chinese reading involves reduced activation of the superior temporal gyrus/supramarginal region and the inferior frontal region across studies. Each subsystem contains additional subsystems that could be functionally distinct.

To understand the source of these differences, we need to consider the reading networks in light of the different demands placed by Chinese and alphabetic reading.

Occipital-Temporal Regions

The occipital-temporal cortex, especially the fusiform gyrus, is part of the ventral visual processing stream and is often associated with tasks involving object recognition, including the recognition of words. The region is sometimes referred to as the "visual word form area (VWFA)" because of its important role in identifying words and word-like letter strings, although it is equally involved in other perceptual tasks (Price & Devlin, 2003). Its role in reading is assumed to have developed through experience with word forms (McCandliss, Cohen, & Dehaene, 2003). Experienced, skilled readers have become experts at the visual processing of written words. Pugh and colleagues (Pugh et al., 2001) have called the left fusiform area the "reading skill area," because it seems to be less active for dyslexics (Pugh et al., 2001) and because it shows the effects of orthographic–phonological training (Sandak et al., 2004).

The difference between processing English and Chinese in this area is primarily hemispheric: English and other alphabetic languages localize word recognition to a region of the left fusiform (Bolger, Perfetti, & Schneider, 2005; Cohen, Dehaene, Naccache, Lehericy, Dehaene-Lambertz, Henaff, & Michel, 2000), whereas Chinese activates the bilateral fusiform gyri (Bolger, Perfetti, & Schneider, 2005).

Theories about the hemispheric organization of the ventral visual processing stream suggest hemispheric organization based on the hierarchical nature of the visual input (Delis, Robertson, & Efron, 1986) or the spatial frequencies of its elements (Christman, Kitterle, & Hellige, 1991; Kitterle, Hellige, & Christman, 1992; Sergent, 1982). Specifically, the LH occipital-temporal region supports the component details (high spatial frequency information) of a larger form, whereas the RH occipital regions process more global forms—low spatial frequency information. There may be an attentional component to recruitment of these regions as well, with the RH responding to directed global attention and the LH to directed local attention (Fink, Marshall, Halligan, & Dolan, 1999).

The spatial frequency explanation rests on the differential use of low spatial frequency. Although both Chinese and English require the processing of high spatial frequency information (contained in letter features and strokes), Chinese has additional low-frequency relational demands. It requires distinguishing relational patterns between larger chunks—radicals—within a square character. As we noted in describing the visual layout of characters, two radicals can combine in as many as five ways, each a different character.

Visual processing needs to distinguish 杏 from 呆, two different characters using the same two radicals. It might be this processing that recruits the RH occipital-temporal area. The bilateral Chinese pattern reflects, we hypothesize, the simultaneous processing of fine grain stroke information in LH and coarser spatial relations in the RH.

Temporal-Parietal Region

Some uncertainty remains about the role of temporal and parietal areas that support word-level phonology. The left superior temporal gyrus is important in alphabetic reading and, according to Bolger and colleagues' meta-analysis, it is also functional in Chinese reading; however, Tan and colleagues (2005) concluded that, instead of the left superior temporal gyrus, the dorsal left inferior parietal area is more important for Chinese phonology. The Tan et al. conclusion accords with the distinction between assembled phonology (grapheme–phoneme conversion supported by the left superior temporal gyrus) and retrieved phonology (based on syllables or whole words supported by the dorsal left inferior parietal).

The assembly of phonology has been attributed to the left superior temporal gyrus (e.g., Booth, Burman, Meyer, Gitelman, Parrish, & Mesulam, 2003; Eden et al., 2004; Poldrack, Temple, Protopapas, Nagarajan, Tallal, Merzenich, & Gabriel, 2001; Shaywitz, et al., 1998) and the temporal-parietal region including the angular and supramarginal gyri (Sandak et al., 2004). The dorsal left inferior parietal area, on the other hand, has been connected to phonological memory (Ravizza, Delgado, Chein, Becker, & Fiez, 2004; Smith & Jonides, 1999), a function that would be required by syllable-level comparisons involved in the studies reviewed by Tan and colleagues.

Frontal Region

Reading in alphabetic languages consistently activates the inferior frontal gyrus. The activity in this region is closely associated with activity in the temporal-parietal area and is thus also generally thought to be involved in the recoding of visual information into phonological information (Sandak et al., 2004). This area is also found in some studies of Chinese, but generally to a lesser extent than in English. The Bolger group's (2005) meta-analysis concluded that Chinese reading, in comparison to English reading, activates a broader extent of the inferior frontal gyrus moving anterior along the lateral surface of the frontal cortex from the location reported in English. Tan and colleagues (2005) confirm the finding that Chinese activates the inferior frontal gyrus, but additionally find LMFG activity at Brodmann area 9, at least in tasks that require phonology.

If the LMFG has a role in reading that is distinctive for Chinese, the question is, why? Although the answer is far from clear, there are some plausible conjectures. One hypothesis, proposed by Tan and colleagues (2005), is that activity in the region stems from the process of learning Chinese. Since there is more of a focus on writing in learning to read Chinese, it is possible that the LMFG, which is close to the premotor cortex, has become integrated into the reading network through repeated concurrent reading and writing. The fact that writing plays a role in establishing orthographic representations may not mean that skilled reading depends on continued practice in writing. Bi, Han, and Zhang (2009) present a case study of a brain-damaged Chinese individual who has lost all ability to write despite having completely preserved reading ability.

Two related possibilities for the role of the LMFG derive from the highly homophonic nature of Chinese. The first of these is that homophony forces a need to remember the visual form of the character during access to meaning or phonology. By retaining the orthographic form, the reader can avoid the effect of a phonology that does not pick out a single word but a large number of them. This would be especially useful if phonology is automatically activated with the character, as the behavioral evidence suggests (Perfetti et al., 2005). Thus, the LMFG may support an orthographic memory of the character allowing the integration of character form with meaning. The second, related possibility is that the LMFG, even without retaining orthographic form, is involved in a phonology inhibition process to allow access to meaning. Either of these, alone or in combination, would support the selection of meaning and both are at least plausible in the context of other research that has examined the LMFG. The LMFG has been implicated in spatial working memory and face working memory (Courtney, Petit, Maisog, Ungerleider, & Haxby, 1998), verbal working memory (Petrides, Alivisatos, Meyer, & Evans, 1993), and central executive functions (D'Esposito, Detre, Alsop, Shin, Atlas, & Grossman, 1995). These rather different characterizations are consistent with either a visual or phonological memory initiated by character recognition or a control function that can suppress phonology or otherwise support a selection of specific character meaning.

Learning a Second Writing System

The Chinese–English comparison provides a valuable example of two languages whose differences in writing occur in both design principles and visual forms. These differences affect reading processes that are expressed in the underlying neural circuitry for reading. It is interesting then to wonder about the neural circuitry when a reader learns a second writing system. Are the procedures for reading the new writing system assimilated into the procedures of the existing reading network? Or, does learning the new writing system force an accommodation to new procedures? It is probably more realistic to think of adaptation to a second written language as a mix of these options, with assimilation and accommodation at endpoints of a continuum.

Our hypothesis is that assimilation is the default option, the path of least resistance. For a Chinese reader, assimilation says, "try to read English as if it were Chinese"; for an English reader, "try to read Chinese as if it were English." Put this way, one can see immediately that total assimilation is unlikely to work, unless what seem to be dramatic differences between the systems do not require corresponding differences in the brain. The accommodation hypothesis (Perfetti & Liu, 2005), that the brain acquires new procedures (and corresponding neural resources) when learning a second written language, applies to those circumstances in which what is required by the new writing system exceeds what can be assimilated by the old.

Functional Magnetic Resonance Imaging Studies of Second Writing System Learning

In one functional magnetic resonance imaging (fMRI) study that bears on the question of assimilation versus accommodation, Nelson, Liu, Fiez, and Perfetti (2009) examined neural activation patterns, focusing on posterior visual area brain structures, in Chinese-English bilinguals and English-language learners of Chinese. The main question was whether learners show evidence that they recruit new brain regions for visual processing of the second language (accommodation), or whether they are able to use their native language networks to read in the new writing system (assimilation).

The critical results for word perception areas showed an interesting asymmetry. English speakers learning Chinese showed only left fusiform activation when viewing English, but bilateral fusiform activation when viewing Chinese—a pattern of accommodation. In contrast, Chinese native speakers for whom English was a second language did not show the LH-dominant alphabetic arrangement for English, but showed instead bilateral activation mimicking the native Chinese arrangement—a pattern of assimilation (consistent with Tan et al., 2003; see Figure 6.3).

Thus, for English learners of Chinese, we find evidence for the system accommodation hypothesis: The system for graphic processing depends on the writing system, even when a network is already in place for reading. In this particular case, the reading network that has worked for English is supplemented by areas that are specifically adaptive for the properties of Chinese writing.

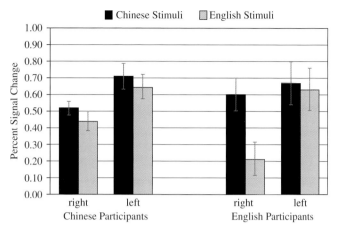

Figure 6.3 Activity in the left and right fusiform areas for Chinese-English bilinguals and English speakers who have had a year of Chinese instruction. Although Chinese-English bilinguals activate both hemispheres equally for each language, English speakers recruit the right hemisphere significantly more for Chinese than for English.

In contrast, Chinese native speakers for whom English was a second language showed the Chinese pattern of bilateral occipital and occipital-temporal activation for both Chinese and English, as shown in Figure 6.3. Thus, whereas alphabetic readers showed the accommodation pattern, Chinese readers showed the assimilation pattern, with their native language reading network supporting their second language reading.

Although the visual occipital-temporal regions provided the clearest example of assimilation and accommodation, this pattern also held for the LMFG. Nelson et al. (2009) found LMFG activity for native English speakers primarily when they read in Chinese. Chinese readers instead activated the LMFG for both Chinese and English.

A similar pattern of accommodation for English speakers learning Chinese was found in a laboratory learning study by Liu, Dunlap, Fiez, and Perfetti (2007). In this study, Chinese characters were taught to English speakers in a more controlled laboratory setting. Across three different training conditions, a printed character was presented to the subject, who learned its phonology and/or meaning: (1) meaning only (English translation), (2) phonology only (the spoken Chinese syllable), and (3) phonology + meaning (English translation plus Chinese syllable). All conditions included visual training on character form, and accommodation in the occipital-temporal region (recruitment of the bilateral fusiform gyri) was seen in all conditions. Thus, whether the character was associated with phonology, meaning, or both, the bilateral activation pattern typical for native Chinese readers was present for English speakers after only a few hours of laboratory instruction.

Interestingly, Liu and colleagues also found activation in both the left and right middle frontal gyrus, near the junction of the inferior frontal and precentral sulci (BA 6, 9, 44), for all conditions. Because orthography was the only constituent learned in all of the training conditions, and no writing was involved in learning, this may suggest a more orthographic function for the LMFG, consistent with the idea that this allows a visual memory for the character during the retrieval of associations. Liu and colleagues also found a more superior medial area of the LMFG that responded more to words trained in both phonology and meaning than in either one alone. This might reflect the integration demands across all three word constituents (orthography, phonology, and meaning), or perhaps the general difficulty of multiple associations to a single stimulus. Generalization from results based on a few hours of learning in a laboratory setting to Chinese reading or even English-Chinese bilingualism is unwarranted, of course. However, the larger point is that the LMFG is a large stretch of cortex, and general references to the functions of LMFG in reading may need to be replaced by more precise anatomical designations.

The data from these two studies are consistent with the hypothesis that assimilation is the path of least resistance and takes place when possible. When the system cannot assimilate the second writing system due to its unique demands, new brain regions appropriate for its demands are recruited into the developing reading network. It may be possible to successfully learn to read English in a "Chinese-like way," an assimilation process. In contrast, it is not possible to read Chinese in an "English-like way," so accommodation occurs, with manifest changes in both reading processes and in the brain areas required. This makes sense, agreeing with what we know about the requirements of these two languages. Whereas it is possible to recognize whole English words as if they were Chinese characters, it is impossible to apply the alphabetic principle to reading Chinese.

If it is true that native Chinese speakers use a Chinese-like strategy for reading English, and if it is true that a Chinese-like strategy involves more holistic, configural visual processing, then there should be behavioral evidence that Chinese readers visually recognize English words in a more holistic, shape-dependent manner than do native English speakers. In fact, we do see such evidence. Wang, Koda, and Perfetti (2003) found that Chinese-English bilinguals showed less phonological coding in reading English compared with comparably skilled Korean-English bilinguals, who could be expected to transfer an alphabetic strategy from their first language to English. In addition, native Chinese speakers suffered a greater deficit than native English speakers in naming words written in alternating case, a manipulation that primarily changes the shape of a word, but not its decodability (Akamatsu, 1999). English-as-second-language (ESL) students with Chinese as their native language also show a particular deficit in spelling nonwords when compared to real words (Wang & Geva, 2003), and show a pattern of comparatively more confusion from graphic similarity along with less homophone confusion (Wang, Perfetti, & Liu, 2003), consistent with greater attention to visual word form than decoding.

Event-related Potentials Studies of Second Writing System Learning

Although it may be tempting to interpret fMRI patterns of assimilation as meaning that the underlying brain processes are the same in those cases, event-related potentials (ERP) studies providing a finer-grained analysis of timing and amplitude of activity show that such an interpretation would be an oversimplification. Results from two ERP studies sampling from the same subject populations as the fMRI studies described earlier (English speakers learning Chinese and bilinguals with Chinese as their first language) reveal that even when brain regions overlap, there is no evidence for complete assimilation.

Chinese-English Bilinguals

The clearest case of an assimilation pattern in the fMRI data was in the occipital-temporal region for Chinese-English bilinguals. Both languages activated bilateral fusiform areas, a clearly different pattern from the left-lateralized one observed when native English speakers read English. Event-related potentials evidence from a naming study of Chinese-English bilinguals (Liu & Perfetti, 2003) found, however, that the timing and pattern of activity differed in these visual regions depending on whether the bilinguals were reading English or Chinese. English was 50–100 ms slower to activate occipital regions at all, suggesting that orthographic processing for the second language takes longer.

More interestingly, there was also a qualitative difference when each hemisphere of the occipital region came online. Both high- and low-frequency Chinese characters first showed effects in the left occipital region (150 ms), then showed a rapid shift to the right occipital region (by 200 ms). Then, after another shift in processing to the frontal area, the left occipital region was reactivated at around 450 ms. High-frequency English words actually showed only a left occipital source, both before and after frontal activation. However, low-frequency English words activated both left and right occipital regions simultaneously before a late frontal activation, and then a reactivation of both right and then left occipital regions at 450 ms. This pattern might imply that Chinese-English bilingual readers process component radicals (LH; high spatial frequency stroke information) before analyzing their radical configuration (RH; low spatial frequency spatial relations) when reading character; in English, there is more "cross-talk" in their analysis of high and low spatial frequency elements of English words, especially those that are less familiar. For more familiar words, Chinese bilinguals may be able to apply a more letter-based (LH) process, with less need for RH shape processing support.

This study also found that the timing of frontal region activity varied with familiarity: high-frequency Chinese characters as early as 100 ms, followed by low-frequency characters, and finally English words, with low-frequency English words not activating a frontal region until as late as 400 ms. The posterior-to-frontal time difference may reflect proficiency differences between the languages or simply differences in the amount of experience with the various stimuli.

English Learners of Chinese

Recall that the fMRI data showed a pattern of accommodation for English learners of Chinese in which left middle frontal and right occipital-temporal areas were recruited to read characters. An ERP study by Liu, Perfetti, and Wang (2006) examining a similar population of learners showed how patterns of activity might change over the course of learning. The study compared ERPs during delayed naming by students with one term of Chinese study and students with two terms. Differences emerged at 200 ms (a P200/N200; positive in the frontal area, negative in the occipital area) and the N400 in central electrodes. The P200/N200 reflects Chinese orthographic processing in native Chinese readers (Liu, Perfetti, & Hart, 2003).

In the first term, the P200/N200 component scores were larger for Chinese than English materials at both frontal and occipital electrodes, suggesting that a higher level of processing was required for the second language. Consistent with the imaging data, source analysis for the P200/N200 showed that right occipital and left middle frontal areas were stronger generators of voltage shifts for Chinese than for English.

At the end of the second term, the larger P200 for Chinese was observed at frontal but not occipital electrodes (see Fig. 6.4). For curriculum-defined frequency, the N200 was larger for high-frequency than low-frequency Chinese characters only at the first term. The reduction in occipital differences across one term of learning may be a reflection of the rapid learning of character forms, which was observed also in learners' behavioral results on lexical decisions (Wang, Perfetti, & Liu, 2003).

A second ERP learning result concerns the N400, widely taken as an indicator of semantic and phonological processing (Kutas & Hillyard, 1980;

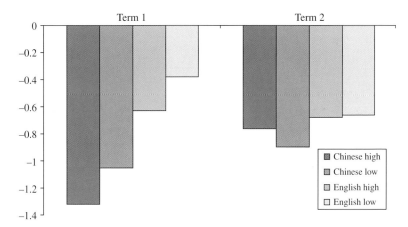

Figure 6.4 The occipital region N200 event-related potential (ERP) response in native English speakers learning Chinese. After one term of instruction, there is a larger visual response to the less familiar Chinese than to English. After two terms of instruction, the visual response to Chinese approximates the native language level.

Rugg, 1984). Liu and colleagues (2006) observed the N400 effect in priming with English materials, but not with Chinese (in either first or second term), perhaps implying that the learners' semantic processing of Chinese characters was too slow or too variable to be observed within the 1,000 ms measuring range of the ERP experiments.

The results indicate that more visual processing (occipital) and lexical processing (frontal and central) was needed for Chinese for these first-term learners. By the second term, visual processing differences (occipital electrodes N200) had been reduced, while lexical processing differences (frontal electrodes P200) persisted. This separation of visual learning from character identification links to the lexical constituency model (Perfetti et al., 2005) through the threshold mechanism the model assumes for character identification. Learning over two terms of study brought about gains in character familiarity that reduced the amount of visual processing required to reach a threshold of character identification. This interpretation is further supported by a separate behavioral finding of first-term orthographic priming followed by no orthographic priming in the second term (Liu, Wang, & Perfetti, 2007). Only when a character's orthographic representation reaches threshold is there activation along links to phonology and semantics. Beyond the threshold, character-level orthographic inhibition and phonological and semantic facilitation occur.

In summary, ERP studies show differences in processing English and Chinese, both when the readers are Chinese-English bilinguals and when they are English speakers learning Chinese. Even for a skilled bilingual,

Chinese and English reading produce different temporal patterns across different posterior and frontal sources, including the familiar pattern of RH activation in visual areas. For learners, we can see changes over two terms of learning, including a reduction in the RH visual activation areas as Chinese characters become more familiar. The ERP results are consistent with the system accommodation hypothesis in showing language differences in temporal patterns and coarse-grain localizations for both skilled readers and learners.

Conclusion

Reading universally involves the mapping of written graphs to units of language. Thus, we find manifestations of this universality in behavioral studies of reading and in studies of the neural correlates of reading. When we compare alphabetic reading with Chinese, a writing system of maximal contrast for alphabetic comparisons, the results of cognitive-behavioral research show a highly general role for phonology across writing systems; and the results of imaging studies show networks of brain areas that partially overlap across writing systems. However, along with the universals come variations that are imposed by all three dimensions of writing variation—script, orthography, and writing system. These variations produce corresponding differences in the critical details of reading procedures that respond to the visual–spatial properties of the script, the consistency of grapheme–phoneme mappings within the family of alphabetic systems, and the deep mapping features that distinguish one writing system from another. Each of these differences is accompanied by corresponding differences in the neural basis of reading.

Our focus here has been on how the brain's reading network compares across English and Chinese. Cognitive-behavioral studies have suggested that phonology, although important in both systems, is implemented in different ways. Comparative ERP and fMRI studies converge with this conclusion in general terms, and suggest some specific possibilities for how the brain's reading network accommodates these differences. Chinese brain imaging studies and meta-analyses of these studies point to several departures from the results of alphabetic studies. One is the bilateral activation of occipital and fusiform regions that support the initial perceptual process of word identification, as opposed to the left-dominant pattern for alphabetic reading. This difference appears to reflect specific spatial demands of Chinese characters, perhaps associated with spatial relations among component radicals.

A second point of departure is the distinctive role of the LMFG in Chinese, a role that has been revealed in nearly every imaging study. Although the exact role of the mid-frontal gyrus remains to be determined, our suggestion is that this part of the Chinese reading network supports a brief sustained memory for the orthographic form of the character during the retrieval of its associated phonological and semantic constituents. Other differences include reduced roles for both the left inferior frontal gyrus and the left superior temporal-parietal regions for Chinese, compared with alphabetic reading.

Studies of learning Chinese using both ERP and fMRI add to this picture. Event-related potentials evidence shows that characters require more visual processing at the beginning of learning, as one would expect. However, significant gains in experience with Chinese characters appear within two terms of classroom learning, with results showing reduced differences between English and Chinese and between high- and low-frequency characters. Event-related potentials evidence also suggests that semantic processing of characters continues to be slow or weak, even after two terms. These results help support the interpretation of changes with learning of orthographic priming effects and are consistent with the lexical constituency model of reading (Perfetti et al., 2005).

Functional MRI studies of Chinese learners converge to show activation in two areas that are found in studies of native Chinese speakers: Learners show (1) bilateral occipital and fusiform activation and (2) activation of the LMFG near to that observed in studies of native speakers. For learners who acquired both phonology and meaning links for the characters, we find an additional LMFG area, slightly superior to that observed for native speakers, that may be involved when both pronunciation and meaning are connected to orthography.

Our learning results for Chinese are consistent with the accommodation hypothesis, which assumes that the brain's reading network must adapt to features of a new writing system when those features require different reading procedures. In learning Chinese, the brain's reading network accommodates the script demands of characters by recruiting RH visual areas that are suited for the global spatial analysis required by the characters. And it responds to the distinctive mapping demands of Chinese, which requires nonmediated, syllable-level phonology and meaning to be to be retrieved by recruiting the LMFG, which is suited for retaining the character form during lexical processing.

The accommodation process may apply more to an alphabetic learner of Chinese than to a Chinese learner of English. Chinese readers may be able to assimilate English to some extent into their Chinese reading procedures. In fact, Chinese-English bilinguals tend to show the same bilateral activation of visual areas, including the fusiform, when they read English, as when they read Chinese. The generalization is that Chinese reading procedures can be applied to English and other alphabetic writing in a way that alphabetic reading procedures cannot be applied to Chinese.

We caution, however, against drawing too strong an inference from this assimilation conclusion. Event-related potentials data showed that, although the regions activated were similar, there were timing differences in when the regions came online, beyond just latency differences between the two languages. In addition, the success of Chinese reading procedures in assimilating alphabetic reading may be limited. Higher levels of second-language skill show brain-related as well as behavioral differences from lower levels of skill (Abutalebi, Cappa, & Perani, 2001). A similar conclusion may apply to reading alphabetic writing for Chinese readers. Higher levels of ESL reading may being accomplished through supplementary reading procedures and associated brain areas that are specifically supportive of alphabetic reading.

Acknowledgments

Some of the research reported in this chapter was supported by grants from the National Science Foundation and from the James S. McDonnell foundation. Some of the material in this chapter draws on Perfetti, Liu, Fiez, Nelson, Bolger, & Tan (2007).

References

Akamatsu, N. (1999). The effects of first language orthographic features on word recognition processing in English as a second language. *Reading and Writing, 11,*4, 381–403.

Abutalebi, J., Cappa, S. F., & Perani, D. (2001). The bilingual brain as revealed by functional neuroimaging. *Bilingualism: Language and Cognition, 4,* 179–190.

Bi, Y., Han, Z., & Zhang (2009). Reading does not depend on writing, even in Chinese. *Neuropsychologia, 47,* 4, 1193–1199.

Bolger, D. J., Perfetti, C. A., & Schneider, W. (2005). A cross-cultural effect on the brain revisited: Universal structures plus writing system variation. *Journal of Human Brain Mapping, 25,*1, 83–91.

Booth, J. R., Burman, D. D., Meyer, J. R., Trommer, B. L., Davenport, N. D., & Parrish, T. B. (2004). Brain-behavior correlation in children depends on the neurocognitive network. *Human Brain Mapping. 23,* 2, 99–108.

Booth, J. R., Burman, D. D., Van Santen, F. W., Harasaki, Y., Gitelman, D. R., & Parrish, T. B. (2001). The development of specialized brain systems in reading and oral-language. *Child Neuropsychology, 7,* 3, 119–141.

Cao, F., Lee, R., Shu, H., Yang, Y., Xu, G., Li, K., & Booth, J. (2009). Cultural constraints on brain development: Evidence from a developmental study of visual word processing in Mandarin Chinese. *Cerebral Cortex* doi:10.1093/cercor/bhp186. Advance access published online, September 22, 2009.

Chee, M. W., Tan, E. W., & Thiel, T. (1999). Mandarin and English single word processing studied with functional magnetic resonance imaging. *Journal of Neuroscience, 19,* 3050–3056.

Chee, M. W., Weekes, B., Lee, K. M., Soon, C. S., Schreiber, A., & Hoon, J. J. (2000). Overlap and dissociation of semantic processing of Chinese characters, English words, and pictures: Evidence from fMRI [in process citation]. *Neuroimage, 12*, 4, 392–403.

Christman, S., Kitterle, F. L., & Hellige, J. (1991). Hemispheric asymmetry in the processing of absolute versus relative spatial frequency. *Brain & Cognition, 16*, 1, 62–73.

Chua, F. K. (1999). Phonological recoding in Chinese logograph recognition. *Journal of Experimental Psychology: Learning, Memory, and Cognition, 25*, 4, 876–891.

Cohen, L., Dehaene, S., Naccache, L., Lehericy, S., Dehaene-Lambertz, G., Henaff, M., & Michel, F. (2000). The visual word form area: Spatial and temporal characterization of an initial stage of reading in normal subjects and posterior split-brain patients. *Brain, 123*, 291–307.

Coltheart, M., Curtis, B., Atkins, P., & Haller, M. (1993). Models of reading aloud: Dual-route and parallel-distributed-processing approaches. *Psychological Review, 100*, 4, 589–608.

Coltheart, M., Rastle, K., Perry, C., Langdon, R., & Ziegler, J. (2001). The DRC model: A model of visual word recognition and reading aloud. *Psychological Review, 108*, 204–258.

Courtney, S. M., Petit, L., Maisog, J. M., Ungerleider, L. G., & Haxby, J. V. (1998). An area specialized for spatial working memory in human frontal cortex. *Science, 279*, 5355, 1347–1352.

D'Esposito, M., Detre, J. A., Alsop, D. C., Shin, R. K., Atlas, S., & Grossman, M. (1995). The neural basis of the central executive system of working memory. *Nature, 378*, 6554, 279–281.

Delis, D. C., Robertson, L.C., & Efron, R. (1986). Hemispheric specialization of memory for visual hierarchical stimuli, *Neuropsychologia, 24*, 2, 205–214.

Eden, G. F., Jones, K. M., Cappell, K., Gareau, L., Wood, F. B., Zeffiro, T. A., et al. (2004). Neural changes following remediation in adult developmental dyslexia. *Neuron, 44*, 411–422.

Fiez, J. A., & Petersen, S. E. (1998). Neuroimaging studies of word reading. *Proceedings of the National Academy of Science, USA, 95*, 914–921.

Fink, F., Marshall, J., Halligan, P., & Dolan, R. (1999). Hemispheric asymmetries in global/local processing are modulated by perceptual salience. *Neuropsychologia, 37*, 1, 31–40.

Hung, D. L., Tzeng, O. J. L., & Tzeng, A. K. Y. (1992). Automatic activation of linguistic information in Chinese character recognition. In R. Frost (Ed.), *Orthography, phonology, morphology, and meaning* (pp. 119–130). Amsterdam, Netherlands: North-Holland.

Jobard, G., Crivello, F., & Tzourio-Magoyer, N. (2003). Evaluation of the dual route theory of reading: A metaanalysis of 35 neuroimaging studies. *Neuroimage, 20*, 2, 693–712.

Kitterle, F.L., Hellige, J.B., & Christman, S. (1992). Visual hemispheric asymmetries depend on which spatial frequencies are task relevant. *Brain and Cognition, 20*, 2, 308–314.

Kochunov, P., Fox, P., Lancaster, J., Tan, L. H., Amunts, K., & Zilles, K. (2003). Localized morphological brain differences between English-speaking Caucasians and Chinese-speaking Asians: New evidence of anatomical plasticity. *Neuroreport, 14*, 7, 961–964.

Kutas, M., & Hillyard, S. A. (1980). Reading senseless sentences: Brain potentials reflect semantic incongruity. *Science, 207,* 4427, 203–205.

Language and Teaching Institute of Beijing Linguistic College. (1986). *Modern Chinese frequency dictionary [Xiandai Hanyu Pinlu Cidian].* Beijing, China: Beijing Language Institute Press.

Lee, K.-M. (2004). Functional MRI comparison between reading ideographic and phonographic scripts of one language. *Brain and Language, 91,* 245–251.

Leong, C. K. (1997). Paradigmatic analysis of Chinese word reading: Research findings and classroom practices. In C. K. Leong & R. M. Joshi (Eds.), *Cross-language studies of learning to reading and spell: Phonological and orthographic processing* (pp. 379–417). Netherlands: Kluwer Academic.

Leong, C.K., Tan, L.H., Cheng, P., & Hau, K.T. (2005). Learning to read and spell English words by Chinese students. *Scientific Studies of Reading, 9,* 63–84.

Liu, Y., Dunlap, S., Fiez, J., & Perfetti, C. A. (2007). Evidence for neural accommodation to a new writing system following learning. *Human Brain Mapping, 28,* 1223–1234.

Liu, Y., & Perfetti, C. A. (2003). The time course of brain activity in reading English and Chinese: An ERP study of Chinese bilinguals. *Human Brain Mapping, 18,* 3, 167–175.

Liu, Y., Perfetti, C. A., & Hart, L. (2003). ERP evidence for the time course of graphic, phonological and semantic information in Chinese meaning and pronunciation decisions. *Journal of Experimental Psychology: Learning, Memory, and Cognition, 29,* 6, 1231–1247.

Liu, Y., Perfetti, C. A., & Wang, M. (2006). Visual analysis and lexical access of Chinese characters by Chinese as second language readers. *Linguistics and Language, 7,* 3, 637–657.

Liu, Y., Wang, M., Perfetti, C. A. (2007) Threshold-style processing of Chinese characters for adult second language learners. *Memory and Cognition, 35,* 3, 471–480.

Mattingly, I. G. (1987). Morphological structure and segmental awareness. *Cahiers de Psychologie Cognitive/Current Psychology of Cognition, 7,* 5, 488–493.

McCandliss, B. D., Cohen, L., & Dehaene, S. (2003). The visual word form area: Expertise for reading in the fusiform gyrus. *Trends in Cognitive Science, 7,* 293–299.

Mechelli, A., Gorno-Tempini, M.L., & Price, C.J. (2003). Neuroimaging studies of word and pseudoword reading: Consistencies, inconsistencies, and limitations. *Journal of Cognitive Neuroscience, 15,* 260.

Nakada, T., Fugii, Y., & Kwee, I. L. (2001). Brain strategies for reading in the second language are determined by the first language. *Neuroscience Research, 40,* 4, 351–358.

Nakamura K., Dehaene S., Jobert A., Bihan D. L., & Kouider S. (2005). Subliminal convergence of Kanji and Kana words: further evidence for functional parcellation of the posterior temporal cortex in visual word perception. *Journal of Cognitive Neuroscience, 17,* 6, 954–968.

Nelson, J. R., Liu, Y., Fiez, J., & Perfetti, C. A. (2009). Assimilation and accommodation patters in ventral occipitotemporal cortex in learning a second writing system. *Human Brain Mapping, 30,* 810–820.

Pak, A.K.H., Cheng-Lai, A., Tso, I.F., Shu, H., Li, W., & Anderson, R.C. (2005). Visual chunking skills of Hong Kong children. *Reading and Writing, 18,* 5, 437–454.

Paulesu, E., McCrory, E., Fazio, F., Menoncello, L., Brunswick, N., Cappa, S. F., et al. (2000). A cultural effect on brain function. *Nature Neuroscience, 3,* 91–96.

Perfetti, C.A., & Bell, L. (1991). Phonemic activation during the first 40 ms of word identification: Evidence from backward masking and masked priming. *Journal of Memory and Language, 30,* 473–485.

Perfetti, C. A., & Dunlap, S. (2008). Universal principles and writing system variations in learning to read. In K. Koda & A. Zehler (Eds.), *Learning to read across languages* (pp. 13–38). Mahwah, NJ: Erlbaum.

Perfetti, C. A., & Liu, Y. (2005). Orthography to phonology and meaning: Comparisons across and within writing systems. *Reading and Writing, 18,* 193–210.

Perfetti, C.A., Liu, Y., & Tan, L.H. (2005). The lexical constituency model: Some implications of research on Chinese for general theories of reading. *Psychological Review, 12,* 11, 43–59.

Perfetti, C.A., Liu, Y., Fiez, J., Nelson, J., Bolger, D.J., & Tan, L-H. (2007). Reading in two writing systems: Accommodation and assimilation in the brain's reading network. *Bilingualism: Language and Cognition, 10,* 2, 131–146. Special Issue on "Neurocognitive approaches to bilingualism: Asian languages", P. Li (Ed.).

Perfetti, C.A., & Tan, L.H. (1998). The time course of graphic, phonological, and semantic activation in Chinese character identification. *Journal of Experimental Psychology: Learning, Memory, and Cognition, 24,* 101–118.

Perfetti, C. A., & Zhang, S. (1991). Phonological processes in reading Chinese characters. *Journal of Experimental Psychology: Learning, Memory, and Cognition, 17,* 633–643.

Perfetti, C.A., & Zhang, S. (1995). Very early phonological activation in Chinese reading. *Journal of Experimental Psychology: Learning, Memory, and Cognition, 21,* 24–33.

Perfetti, C. A., Zhang, S., & Berent, I. (1992). Reading in English and Chinese: Evidence for a "universal" phonological principle. In R. Frost & L Katz (Eds.), *Orthography, phonology, morphology, and meaning* (pp. 227–248). Amsterdam: North-Holland.

Petrides, M., Alivisatos, B., Meyer, E., & Evans, A. C. (1993). Functional activation of the human frontal cortex during the performance of verbal working memory tasks. *Proceedings of the National Academy of Sciences of the United States of America, 90,* 3, 873–877.

Poldrack, R.A., Temple, E., Protopapas, A., Nagarajan, S., Tallal, P., Merzenich, M.M., & Gabrieli, J.D.E. (2001). Relations between the neural bases of dynamic auditory processing and phonological processing: Evidence from fMRI. *Journal of Cognitive Neuroscience, 13,* 687–697.

Price, C. J. (2000). The anatomy of language: Contributions from functional neuroimaging. *Journal of Anatomy, 197,* 335–359.

Price, C. J., & Devlin, J. T. (2003). The myth of the visual word form area. *Neuroimage, 19,* 3, 473–481.

Pugh, K. R., Mencl, W. E., Jenner, A. R., Katz, L., Frost, S. J., Lee, J. R., et al. (2001). Neurobiological studies of reading and reading disability. *Journal of Communication Disorders, 39,* 479–492.

Pugh, K. R., Shaywitz, B. A., Shaywitz, S. E., Constable, R., Skudlarski, P., & Fulbright, R. K. (1996). Cerebral organization of component processes in reading. *Brain, 119,* 4, 1221–1238.

Ravizza, S. M., Delgado, M. R., Chein, J. M., Becker, J. T., & Fiez, J. A. (2004). Functional dissociations within the inferior parietal cortex in verbal working memory. *Neuroimage, 22,* 562–573.

Rugg, M. D. (1984). Event-related potentials in phonological matching tasks. *Brain and Language, 23,* 2, 225–240.

Sakurai Y., Momose T., Iwata M., Sudo Y., Ohtomo K., & Kanazawa I. (2000). Different cortical activity in reading of Kanji words, Kana words and Kana nonwords. *Cognitive Brain Research, 9,* 111–115.

Sandak, R., Mencl, W. E., Frost, S. J., Rueckl, J. G., Katz, L., Moore, D., et al. (2004). The neurobiology of adaptive learning in reading: A contrast of different training conditions. *Cognitive, Affective, & Behavioral Neuroscience, 4*, 67–88.

Sergent J. (1982). The cerebral balance of power: Confrontation or cooperation? *Journal of Experimental Psychology: Human Perception and Performance, 8*, 253–272.

Shaywitz, S. E., Shaywitz, B. A., Pugh, K. R., Fulbright, R. K., Constable, R. T., Mencel, W. E., et al. (1998). Functional disruption in the organization of the brain for reading in dyslexia. *Proceedings of the National Academy of Science, USA, 95*, 5, 2636–2641.

Siok, W. T., Perfetti, C. A., Jin, Z., & Tan, L. H. (2004). Biological abnormality of impaired reading constrained by culture: Evidence from Chinese. *Nature*, September 1, 71–76.

Smith, E. E., & Jonides, J. (1999). Storage and executive processes in the frontal lobes. *Science, 283*, 1657–1661.

Tan, L. H., Laird, A., Li, K., & Fox, P.T. (2005). Neuroanatomical correlates of phonological processing of Chinese characters and alphabetic words: A meta-analysis. *Human Brain Mapping, 25*, 83–91.

Tan, L. H., Liu, H. L., Perfetti, C. A., Spinks, J. A., Fox, P. T., & Gao, J. H. (2001). The neural system underlying Chinese logograph reading. *NeuroImage, 13*, 836–846.

Tan, L. H., & Perfetti, C. A. (1999). Phonological activation in visual identification of Chinese two-character words. *Journal of Experimental Psychology: Learning, Memory, and Cognition, 25*, 382–393.

Tan, L. H., & Perfetti, C. A. (1997). Visual Chinese character recognition: Does phonological information mediate access to meaning? *Journal of Memory and Language, 37*, 41–57.

Tan, L. H., Spinks, J. A., Eden, G. F., Perfetti, C. A., & Siok, W. T. (2005). Reading depends on writing, in Chinese. *Proceedings of the National Academy of Sciences, USA, 102*, 24, 8781–8785.

Tan, L. H., Spinks, J. A., Feng, C. M., Siok, W. T., Perfetti, C. A., Xiong, J., et al. (2003). Neural systems of second language reading are shaped by native language. *Human Brain Mapping, 18*, 158–166.

Tan L. H., Spinks J. A., Gao, J. H., Liu H. L., Perfetti, C. A., & Fox, P. T. (2000). Brain activation in the processing of Chinese characters and words: A functional MRI study. *Human Brain Mapping, 10*, 1, 16–27.

Turkeltaub, P. E., Eden, G. F., Jones, K. M., & Zeffiro, T. A. (2002). Meta-analysis of the functional neuroanatomy of single-word reading: method and validation. *Neuroimage, 16*, 3 Pt 1, 765–780.

Wang, M. & Geva, E. (2003). Spelling performance of Chinese children using English as a second language: Lexical and visual-orthographic processes. *Applied Psycholinguistics, 24*, 1–25.

Wang, M., Koda, K., & Perfetti, C. A. (2003). Alphabetic and nonalphabetic L1 effects in English word identification: A comparison of Korean and Chinese English L2 learners. *Cognition, 87*, 129–149.

Wang, M., Perfetti, C. A., & Liu, Y. (2003). Alphabetic readers quickly acquire orthographic structure in learning to read Chinese. *Scientific Studies of Reading, 7*, 2, 183–208.

Xu, Y., Pollatsek, A., & Potter, M. C. (1999). The activation of phonology during silent Chinese word reading. *Journal of Experimental Psychology: Learning, Memory, and Cognition, 25*, 4, 838–857.

Yoon, H. W., Cho, K.-D., Chung, J.-Y., & Park, H. W. (2005). Neural mechanisms of Korean word reading: A functional magnetic resonance imaging study. *Neuroscience Letters, 373*, 206–211.

Yoon, H. W., Cho, K.-D., & Park, H. W. (2005). Brain activation of reading Korean words and recognizing pictures by Korean native speakers: A functional magnetic resonance imaging study. *International Journal of Neuroscience, 115*, 757–768.

Zhang, S., & Perfetti, C. A. (1993). The tongue twister effect in reading Chinese. *Journal of Experimental Psychology: Learning, Memory, and Cognition, 19*, 1082–1093.

Ziegler, J., & Goswami, U. (2005). Reading acquisition, developmental dyslexia, and skilled reading across languages: A psycholinguistic grain size theory. *Psychological Bulletin, 131*, 1, 3–29.

7

Functional Neuroanatomy of Reading in Japanese

Language-specific Exploitation of the Visual Word Form System in the Left Occipitotemporal Cortex

Kimihiro Nakamura

The use of verbal symbols is generally thought to be a culture-specific skill acquired only through a conscious effort to learn the arbitrary association between sound and print in any given language. As such, the degree to which such language codes are linked with sound and meaning varies across different writing systems and may exert a varying impact on the ultimate achievement of literacy learning. Notably, behavioral evidence from dyslexic people suggests that literacy development is sensitive to the specific processing demands of writing systems used, such as print-to-sound translation (Paulesu et al., 2001; Wydell & Butterworth, 1999) and visuospatial analysis of written words (Siok, Spinks, Jin, & Tan, 2008).

Traditionally, neuropsychological data from brain-damaged Japanese patients have provided a unique resource for testing such language-specificity in the cerebral organization for reading. This is because focal brain damage often affects reading ability differently between two writing systems in Japanese, kanji (logographic) and kana (syllabic). However, the relationship between the patterns of reading deficit and their lesion sites is often hard to determine in a straightforward way because of the apparent lack of reproducibility—damage to a particular brain region may not cause a consistent pattern of reading impairment across individuals (Sugishita, Otomo, Kabe, & Yunoki, 1992). The question of lesion–phenomenon correlation is still unresolved, and is complicated by some additional factors; for example, (a) clinically detectable lesions occupy a rather extensive brain volume, often without clear boundaries with surrounding normal tissue; (b) the observed pattern of alexia in itself may change with the passage of time to a varied extent, especially for cerebrovascular lesions, and (c) there is large across-study variability of the materials and methods used for testing reading performance.

In this chapter, we examine past neuropsychological and brain imaging data of the Japanese language to shed light on the universal and language-specific aspects of the cerebral reading system. First, we discuss several types of script-specific alexia under the current framework of the functional architecture of the ventral visual system (Martin & Chao, 2001). We will then look at previous functional brain imaging evidence for possible intra- and interhemispheric differences between two scripts. Last, we present our functional magnetic resonance imaging (fMRI) studies on cross-script convergence of kanji and kana, rather than between-script difference, and argue for a possible language-specific exploitation of the visual word recognition system in the occipitotemporal cortex.

Neuropsychological Studies of the Japanese Language

The Japanese Writing Systems and Their Reading Disorders

Logographic kanji characters were originally imported from China in the fifth century and are used mainly for nouns and for the roots of verbs, adjectives, and adverbs. Most of them have rather complex graphic forms and several different readings (Fig.7.1). It is generally thought that normal Japanese adults

Kanji

神	/ka-mi/	*God*
神社	/ji-N-ja/	*Temple*
神経	/shi-N-kei/	*Nerve*
精神	/se-i-shi-N/	*Mind*
神主	/ka-N-nu-shi/	*Priest (Shintoist)*
神戸	/ko-u-be/	*Kobe (city)*

Kana

	hiragana	*katakana*	
/ka-mo-me/	かもめ	カモメ	*seagull*
/sa-ka-na/	さかな	サカナ	*fish*
/i-ru-ka/	いるか	イルカ	*dolphin*

Figure 7.1 Examples of logographic kanji and syllabic kana in Japanese. Typically, each kanji character has several different readings, which are specified by the lexical or morphological context of words. For example, a kanji character "神" represents a morphemic unit for "god" and "spirit" and have different pronunciations when combined with other characters. In contrast, kana is a syllabary script and consists of two parallel systems, hiragana and katakana. Kana characters each have a one-to-one correspondence with sound, which is constant regardless of lexical context and positions in a word.

need more than 3,000 kanji characters for everyday communication. On the other hand, kana writing systems, developed by simplifying the graphic forms of kanji, consist of two parallel phonetic syllabaries, hiragana and katakana, each composed of 46 basic characters. Kana characters are mainly used for loan words, inflections, and conjunctions.

A number of behavioral studies with healthy and brain-damaged subjects have suggested that different neurocognitive systems are involved in the skilled reading of kanji and kana. For instance, normal adults read aloud words printed in kana more rapidly than those in kanji but can recognize word meaning more rapidly when written in kanji than in kana (Feldman & Turvey, 1980; Nomura, 1981; Saito, 1981), whereas the script-specific behavioral advantage could be greatly influenced by external factors, such as script frequency, familiarity, word length, and lexicality of stimuli (Besner & Hildebrandt, 1987; Hirose, 1984; Nomura, 1981; Sasanuma, Sakuma, & Tatsumi, 1988; Tanaka & Konishi, 1990; Yamada, Imai, & Ikebe, 1990). Several tachistoscopic studies have shown that hemispheric asymmetry is also different, with the right hemisphere partially involved in processing of kanji (Sasanuma, Itoh, Mori, & Kobayashi, 1977; Sasanuma, Itoh, Kobayashi, & Mori, 1980; Sugishita, Yoshioka, & Kawamura, 1986). Therefore, these behavioral data support that neural processing of kanji and kana differs both at the intra- and interhemispheric levels.

The fact that focal brain damage can produce a differential impact on reading skill between the two scripts has been known as "kanji–kana dissociation" in the neurological literature of Japanese. Notably, the neuroanatomical correlates of such language-specific manifestations were first illustrated by Iwata's dual-route model (1986), whereby dorsal lesions involving the left parieto-occipital cortex affect the reading of kana more severely, whereas those involving the ventral occipitotemporal area affect that of kanji selectively. This early neurocognitive model, which linked scripts, or a mere cultural invention, with particular cerebral structures, has long been accepted with reservation and even challenged by a later study showing that brain damage yields no consistent pattern of dissociation in reading performance between two scripts (Sugishita, Otomo, Kabe, & Yunoki, et al., 1992). Nevertheless, as discussed in this chapter, recent evidence from neuropsychological and functional brain imaging data may provide some supporting evidence for the basic framework proposed by Iwata.

Kanji Alexia Associated with Left Temporal Damage

At least two distinct forms of kanji-selective reading disorders are associated with left temporal lobe damage (Fig. 7.2). First, left posterior temporal damage is known to affect the visual recognition and writing of kanji, *alexia*

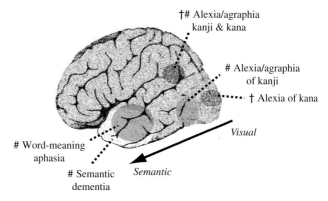

Figure 7.2 Neuroanatomical correlates of script-specific alexia in Japanese. Focal damage to the left occipitotemporal cortex is known to affect the visual recognition of kanji[#] selectively ("alexia and agraphia of kanji"). Alexia of kanji is also known to occur with semantic dysfunction in left anterior temporal pathology, including focal lesions ("word-meaning aphasia") and more diffuse degenerative changes ("semantic dementia"). Other types of kanji alexia have been reported in patients with left mid-lateral temporal damage (see text). Thus, cerebral lesions associated with kanji alexia are overall distributed along the ventral processing stream, which is organized from posterior to anterior with progressively abstract representations, ranging from visual word form to abstract concept. Reading disorder of kana[†] seems to occur rarely but has been reported in patients with left lateral occipital damage ("pure alexia of kana"). Finally, left inferior parietal lesions generally affect the reading of both scripts, but reading comprehension, rather than reading aloud, might be affected more greatly for kana (see text).

with agraphia of kanji (Kawahata, Nagata, & Shishido, 1988; Mochizuki & Ohtomo, 1988; Sakurai, Sakai, Sakuta, & Iwata, 1994). The reading disorder is highly selective for kanji almost without exception, but seems rather transient and may disappear gradually in the course of a few weeks (Soma, Sugishita, Kitamura, Maruyama, & Imanaga, 1989). Second, *word-meaning aphasia*, a variant form of transcortical sensory aphasia in Japanese, has been known to present kanji-specific pronunciation errors (Sasanuma & Monoi, 1975). This latter condition is typically associated with left anteriormost temporal damage and thought to reflect a breakdown of higher-order verbal knowledge. This is because kanji characters each have several different readings, such that the selection of appropriate pronunciation should heavily depend on the lexical-semantic knowledge of words (see Fig. 7.1). Indeed, a similar pattern of reading deficit has been known for patients with semantic dementia, a degenerative neurological disorder associated with anterior temporal atrophy and characterized by a global dysfunction of the semantic system (e.g., Fushimi, Komoir, Ikeda, Lambon-Ralph, & Patterson, 2009).

By and large, the two types of kanji alexia seem to occur as a function of lesion sites along the ventral visual stream, with the visual type associated with posterior temporal damage and the semantic type associated with anterior temporal damage. In other words, both types of alexia can be explained as reflecting the known functional gradient of the occipitotemporal cortex. That is, functional brain imaging (Martin & Chao, 2001; Price, Moore, Humphreys, & Wise, 1997) and neuropsychological (Mummery, Patterson, Wise, Vandenbergh, Price, & Hodges, 1999) studies propose that the ventral visual area is organized with progressively abstract representations, from posterior to anterior, in which the left anterior temporal cortex is associated with semantic level of representations (Fig. 7.2). Interestingly, left temporal lobe damage may produce various "intermediate" forms of reading disorders between the visual and semantic types of kanji alexia. For instance, two alexic patients reported by Jibiki and Yamaguchi (1993) had anterior temporal damage typically associated with word-meaning aphasia but presented visual recognition errors typically associated with posterior temporal damage. Another patient described by Yamawaki and colleagues (2005) had kanji-selective alexia with anomia after left lateral temporal damage, but his reading performance was superior for reading comprehension relative to reading aloud. Since kanji alexia associated with left posteroinferior temporal lesions typically affects the reading skill more globally, both for comprehension and oral reading, the observed dissociation was interpreted as suggesting a distinct neurocognitive focus, that is, a meaning-mediated speech production process, which is functionally more downstream of the visual word recognition mediated by the occipitotemporal junction area. Taken together, these atypical forms of kanji alexia are likely to represent a functional disruption of the ventral processing stream at different representational levels, ranging from visual word form to abstract concept.

Kana-predominant Alexia

For alphabetical languages, it is well established that damage to the left inferior parietal lobe surrounding the angular gyrus causes alexia with agraphia (Roeltgen, 1993). For the Japanese language, focal damage to this brain region has been thought to affect the reading ability of phonographic kana more severely than that of logographic kanji (Yamadori, 1975; Iwata, 1986). A few other studies also suggested that more anterior lesions involving Broca's area may selectively affect the reading of phonographic kana (Sasanuma & Fujimura, 1971; Yamadori, 1985). As mentioned, these observations have led to the idea that a more dorsal neural pathway linking the occipital and perisylvian areas via the inferior parietal lobe is especially important for the phonological translation of kana words (Iwata, 1986). A major weakness of the hypothesized neural model was that it was seemingly unable to account for the fact that left inferior parietal damage affects reading of logographic kanji to a varied extent (Sugishita et al., 1992).

Importantly, however, more recent behavioral work with normal people suggest that phonological activation (i.e., print-to-sound conversion) occurs highly automatically during visual word recognition and plays a more important role than previously believed in the reading of logographic scripts (Hino, Lupker, Ogawa, & Sears, 2003; Sakuma, Sasanumam, Tatsumi, & Masaki, 1998; Wydell, Patterson, & Humphreys, 1993). Therefore, it seems more likely that the inferior parietal cortex is generally involved in reading regardless of the script type of words, since the region is currently thought to mediate cross-modal translation from orthography to pronunciation (Price, 1998). Moreover, our recent work has shown that interregional connection strength increases in the dorsal reading pathway when people are engaged in reading aloud, but not in word comprehension (Nakamura, Hara, Kouider, Takayama, Hanajima, Sakai, & Ugawa, 2006). Thus, the nature of the behavioral task is critical for assessing the reading performance in alexic patients, because reading aloud should recruit the same network for both scripts (perhaps with some between-script difference) and thus should be much less sensitive relative to reading comprehension for detecting the possible neurofunctional dissociation between kanji and kana. This seems indeed the case for the multiple-case study by Sugishita and colleagues, which used a reading aloud task and found no significant neuroanatomical correlation with script types.

On the other hand, Sakurai and colleagues (2001) reported a rare case of pure kana alexia caused by a left lateral occipital lesion. The patient's reading impairment was strictly visual in nature and characterized by letter-by-letter reading and visual recognition errors (i.e., visuoperceptual confusion occurred when two or more kana characters had similar graphic forms). In fact, at least two other cases of similar kana-predominant alexia have been associated with extensive damage of the occipital lobe, including the lateral occipital area (Kawahata et al., 1988; Mochizuki & Ohtomo, 1988). Possibly, the lateral occipital region should play a greater role in the visual recognition of kana than that of kanji, because visual word length tends to increase almost invariably when written in kana script. This in turn places a greater processing demand on the lateral occipital area involved in object recognition since this higher-order visual association area is partially sensitive to the retinal size of the stimuli (see below). Relatedly, the occipital kana alexia might be also attributed to the fact that kana characters overall have simple graphic shapes relative to kanji and thus have only a lower degree of visual distinctiveness from each other (Kaiho & Nomura, 1983; Yokoyama & Yoneda, 1995). That is, the visual recognition of kana should be affected more severely when the high-resolution visual analysis is compromised after lateral occipital damage. To summarize, the existing neuropsychological data suggest that (a) left posterior inferior temporal damage affects the visual recognition of kanji selectively; (b) damage to the left anterior temporal lobe may also interfere with the reading of kanji rather selectively by disrupting the access to lexicosemantic knowledge, or a cognitive component probably more important for kanji during phonological retrieval; (c) damage to the left inferior parietal lobe affects the phonological translation of written words for both scripts, but probably with a greater impact on kana and; (d) a left lateral occipital lesion may cause a more severe visual recognition deficit for kana.

Functional Brain Imaging of Reading in Japanese

Script-specific Activation

A variety of brain imaging techniques have been used to search for script-specific neuroanatomical components of skilled reading as predicted from neuropsychological data (Kamada, Kober, Saguer, Moller, Kaltenhauser, & Vieth, 1998; Sakurai, Momose, Iwata, Sudo, Ohtomo, & Kanazawa, 2000; Yamaguchi, Toyoda, Xu, Kobayashi, & Henik., 2002). Using positron emission tomography, Sakurai and colleagues (2000) showed that kanji words produced strong activation in the left lateral fusiform area, whereas their transcriptions in kana activated the left lateral occipital and temporoparietal areas. Although not compared statistically, these script-specific activations correspond to the lesion sites associated with the script-selective alexia, as discussed earlier.

Furthermore, we previously conducted two fMRI experiment for testing the effect of scripts with direct statistical comparisons (Nakamura, Dehaene, Jobert, Le Bihan, & Kouider, 2005a; 2007). Our results revealed that words in kanji and those in kana activate largely overlapping brain regions, including the frontotemporal junction, inferior parietal, and occipitotemporal cortices, more extensively in the left hemisphere for both scripts. For script-specific effects, kanji words activated a medial part of the bilateral fusiform gyrus more greatly, relative to kana words, whereas this activation was more extensive in the right hemisphere (Fig. 7.3). In contrast, kana words relative to kanji words activated the bilateral occipital pole and left inferior parietal area, including the supramarginal gyrus and inferior parietal lobule. Thus, these results overall are consistent with the neuropsychological and brain imaging evidence mentioned earlier and support that the left fusiform area and lateral occipital area play a differential role in the reading of kanji and kana, respectively. Additionally, the extensive parietal activation for kana may reflect some greater reliance on the print-to-sound translation system, which is thought be more important for kana relative to kanji (Nomura, 1981), but also could be partially attributed to the deployment of visuospatial attentional processes that are needed to assemble the spatially extended series of characters within a word.

Target Kanji > Target Kana   Target Kanji < Target Kana

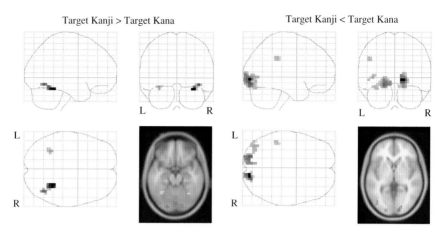

Figure 7.3 Brain regions showing different levels of activation between kanji and kana. Target words in kanji activated the bilateral fusiform region more greatly than those in kana. Conversely, kana targets activated the bilateral occipital pole and left inferior parietal region relative to kanji targets.

Neural Mechanism for Script-specific Activation

We proposed two possible mechanisms for the between-script double disso-ciation observed in the left occipitotemporal cortex. First, the partial specia-lization of kanji and kana might be interpreted within the larger context of specialization for different categories of visual stimuli such as faces, houses, words, or objects within the ventral visual stream. Specifically, Hasson and colleagues (2002) have proposed "retinotopic bias" as an organization prin-ciple of the lateral occipital complex, in which object specialization reflects the requirements placed on foveal processing by each category of visual stimuli, with objects requiring high precision (words, faces) falling within lateral regions biased toward foveal processing, and stimuli requiring more global retinal processing (places) falling within mesial regions biased toward the lateral field. According to this framework, the visual recognition of kanji would require slightly more global processing than alphabetic or kana scripts, whereas its identification might be supported by neurons biased toward the more lateral sectors of the retina, located in a more mesial portion of the fusiform gyrus. This account fits nicely with a recent proposal from neurop-sychological data (Sakurai, 2004), whereby damage to the ventromedial occipitotemporal area causes a disorder of whole-word level recognition which is more important for the reading of kanji, whereas more posterior lesions in the left occipital lobe affect primarily a character (or sublexical) level of visual recognition, which would be more important for the reading of kana. Additionally, it is also possible that the local-versus-global bias in visual recognition is represented at an interhemispheric level, or as a rightward lateralization for kanji, since the right hemisphere has been thought to exhibit advantage for more global visual processing.

A second possible account for the kanji-selective fusiform activation is that reading of kanji would induce the greater activation of regions associated with higher-order, semantic-level knowledge of words. This is indeed plausible because the observed effect in the mesial fusiform gyrus is located outside the retinotopic occipital area and thus probably cannot be explained only by visuospatial features of stimuli. Moreover, a meta-analysis of neuroimaging data by Cohen and colleagues (2002) suggests that the anterior portion of the left fusiform region ($y = -43$ on average) is sensitive to increased task demand during semantic processing of visual or auditory words. The close linkage of kanji and semantics is indeed supported by the neuropsychological studies showing that left posterior temporal lesions affect kanji reading and object naming simultaneously (Kawahata et al., 1988; Soma et al., 1989; Sakurai et al., 1994; Yokota, Ishiai, Furukawa, & Ksukagoshi, 1990). Therefore, the observed specialization in occipitotemporal cortex might be contributed to by both visual-based segregation and rapid semantic activation.

Hemispheric Asymmetry

The logographic nature of kanji is generally believed to allow readers to extract meaning directly from written forms without the mediation of phonology. This faster and more direct semantic access might be partially mediated by the right hemisphere, because the right hemisphere word recognition system is thought to have relative advantage in coarse semantic encoding over the left hemisphere (e.g., Beeman, Friedman, Grafman, Perez, Diamond, & Lindsay, 1994) and because the reading of kanji requires more global visuoperceptual processing, as mentioned earlier, which is generally more biased to the right hemisphere (e.g., Fink, Halligan, Marshall, Frith, Frackowiak, & Dolan, 1996). Indeed, right-hemisphere advantage in the recognition of kanji has been shown by several different lines of evidence, including behavioral (Hatta, 1977; Nakagawa, 1994; Sasanuma et al., 1977), neuropsychological (Sugishita et al., 1986; Sugishita & Yoshioka, 1987), electrophysiological (Hatta, Honjoh, & Mito, 1983; Yamaguchi et al., 2002), and magnetoencephalographic (MEG; Kamada et al., 1998). However, the neural source of such hemispheric asymmetry seems to vary across studies. For instance, an event-related potential study by Yamaguchi and colleagues (2002) compared the patterns of interhemispheric difference between two scripts and found that the right and left hemisphere each has the behavioral advantage in processing of kanji and kana and that this hemispheric specialization was mirrored by lateralized brain response peaking at the frontocentral area. On the other hand, a MEG study by Kamada and colleagues (1998) showed that kanji characters elicited greater response from the right occipitotemporal cortices relative to visual control stimuli, not only for native Japanese (peak latency of ~273 ms) but also for German speakers (~245 ms) who have never learned the Japanese language. Left-lateralized response appeared much later (~600 ms) in the superior temporal and supramarginal gyri only for the Japanese group.

Our fMRI results further revealed that kanji-specific activation of the fusiform area is more extensive in the right hemisphere (Nakamura et al., 2005b). In another fMRI study, we showed that this rightward asymmetry for the visual recognition of kanji is significant in the medial fusiform cortex, whereas phonographic kana exhibits a leftward lateralization in the occipito-temporal junction area (Nakamura et al., 2005b). This rightward asymmetry for kanji in the fusiform cortex is consistent with the MEG data presented by Kamada and colleagues (2002) and may suggest that the right hemisphere advantage for kanji appears early in the ventral visual pathway and represents a neuroanatomical substrate of the right hemisphere advantage in processing of logographic relative to phonographic scripts.

Cross-script Convergence of Kanji and Kana: An fMRI Study

Cerebral Correlate of Cross-script Priming in Japanese

For alphabetical languages, visual recognition of a target word is known to be facilitated when preceded by the same word, irrespective of whether this prime-target pair is written in the same or different case (e.g., radio–radio vs. radio–RADIO). This is the case even when the prime word is masked, such that participants are unaware of its presence. This subliminal cross-case priming has been taken as the behavioral evidence for the existence of an abstract-level orthographic representation of printed words, independent of the physical features of visual stimuli (Forster, Mohan, & Hector, 2003; Humphreys, Evett, & Quinlan, 1990). Using fMRI, Dehaene and colleagues (2001) demonstrated that, at the neural level, this subliminal priming is visualized as an attenuated response, or repetition suppression, of the left middle fusiform area, a region termed the *visual word form area* (VWFA).

A few behavioral studies have shown that similar response facilitation occurs between two different scripts having no one-to-one correspondence at the sublexical level, such as kanji and kana (see Fig. 7.4A) (Hino et al., 2003) and even between different languages, such as English and Chinese (Jiang, 1999). This behavioral phenomenon, or *cross-script priming*, is attributable only to phonological, lexical, or semantic activations beyond the orthographic

A

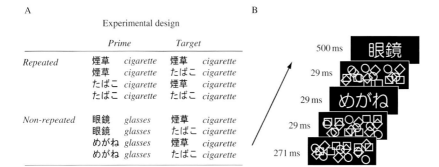

Experimental design

	Prime		Target	
Repeated	煙草	*cigarette*	煙草	*cigarette*
	煙草	*cigarette*	たばこ	*cigarette*
	たばこ	*cigarette*	煙草	*cigarette*
	たばこ	*cigarette*	たばこ	*cigarette*
Non-repeated	眼鏡	*glasses*	煙草	*cigarette*
	眼鏡	*glasses*	たばこ	*cigarette*
	めがね	*glasses*	煙草	*cigarette*
	めがね	*glasses*	たばこ	*cigarette*

B

500 ms — 眼鏡

29 ms

29 ms — めがね

29 ms

271 ms

C

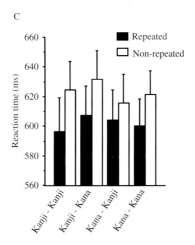

Reaction time (ms)

Repeated / Non-repeated

Kanji - Kanji / Kanji - Kana / Kana - Kanji / Kana - Kana

Figure 7.4 Experimental design and behavioral priming effects. **A.** The prime-target relation was varied by manipulating repetition (repeated or nonrepeated), prime-script (kanji or kana), and target-script (kanji or kana). For instance, a target word (/ta-ba-ko/, or "cigarette") was presented in kanji (煙草) or in kana (たばこ) and preceded by the same word or a different word (/me-ga-ne/, or "glasses", 眼鏡/めがね), written in either kanji or in kana. Note that kanji words generally have no one-to-one correspondence with their transcriptions in kana at letter-level, as is the case between the upper- and lower-case words in English (e.g., apple-APPLE). Since normal Japanese readers can quickly recognize a same word written in either kanji or kana, the cognitive convergence between two scripts should occur not at the orthographic level but at lexical or even higher levels of word processing. **B.** Sequence of events used for the behavioral task. Each trial consisted of a timed sequence of a masked (and thus invisible) prime and a visible target. Participants made natural/artificial judgment about visible targets. **C.** Mean reaction times (±SEM) during semantic categorization. Participants responded more quickly on repeated trials than on nonrepeated trials, not only when subliminal primes and visible targets were written in a same script ("within-script priming") but also when they were written in different scripts ("cross-script priming").

representations of words, and thus is distinct from the cross-case priming observed in alphabetical languages. As such, it will be expected that this form of behavioral priming should be mediated by a cerebral substrate distinct from the VWFA.

Our fMRI study used the cross-script priming paradigm with 16 native Japanese speakers (Nakamura et al., 2005a). As illustrated in Figure 7.4A, the experiment was arranged in a $2 \times 2 \times 2$ factorial design in which the main effects of interest were prime-target repetition (same or different word), prime script (kanji or kana), and target script (kanji or kana). Each trial consisted of a precisely timed sequence of a masked prime and a visible target (Fig. 7.4B). Behaviorally, we confirmed that the cross-script priming indeed occurs between words in kanji and their transcriptions in kana (Fig. 7.4C). These results suggest that subliminal word processing goes beyond the orthographic level and taps higher-order representations, such as phonological, lexical, or semantic systems.

At the neural level, repetition of kanji produced two distinct clusters in the left posterior temporal area, one in the anterior superior/middle temporal gyri and the other in the middle fusiform gyrus (Fig. 7.5). By contrast, only the anterior portion of the middle temporal gyrus (MTG) exhibited repetition suppression when words were repeated in different scripts ($x = -48$, $y = -43$, $z = 2$). We additionally searched for a left occipitotemporal peak showing repetition suppression for kana with a more lenient statistical threshold (voxel-level $p < 0.01$). A weaker trend of activation reduction was detected in a more posterior part of the MTG (peak coordinate $x = -63$, $y = -54$, $z = 3$; $Z = 2.39$, see Fig. 7.5).

These lateral temporal regions showing priming effect for the Japanese scripts are spatially distinct and located more anterolateral relative to the VWFA identified for alphabetical languages (Fig. 7.5). That is, the VWFA associated with orthographic codes is located at $x = -43$, $y = -54$, $z = -12$ in the left fusiform gyrus (Cohen et al., 2000), whereas the left MTG showing cross-script priming is approximately 18 mm downstream along the posterior temporal cortex. Since the cross-script convergence of kanji and kana is assumed to occur at later stages of word recognition (i.e., lexicosemantic or phonological), these results overall fit with the hierarchical architecture of the ventral visual stream for word processing, whereby raw visual features of stimuli are transformed progressively from perceptual to conceptual (Vinckier, Dehaene, Jobert, Dubus, Sigman, & Cohen, 2007).

Nature of Representations Associated with the Neural Priming Effects

Our fMRI results identified two subregions of the left occipitotemporal cortex associated with the repetition priming in Japanese, one in the medial part of the left fusiform gyrus for kanji and the other in the left MTG for the

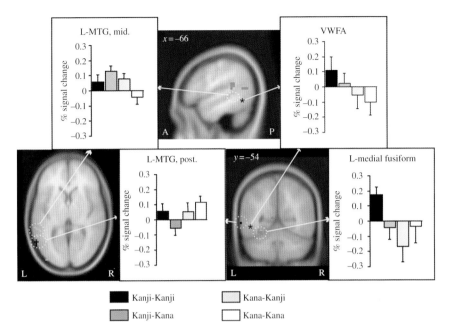

Figure 7.5 Magnitude of repetition suppression (±SEM) in the left occipitotemporal cortex. A medial part of the left fusiform gyrus exhibited repetition suppression when primes and targets were written in kanji. The VWFA showed only a nonsignificant trend of within-script priming for kanji. In contrast, a posterior part of the left middle temporal gyrus (MTG) showed a trend of repetition suppression when primes and targets were written in kana. In further downstream, a middle part of the left MTG exhibited repetition suppression when primes and targets were presented in different scripts. This same region showed within-script priming for kanji but not for kana.

cross-script convergence of kanji and kana. In addition, we also found that a lateral part of the left posterior temporal cortex is involved in the repetition priming of kana words.

First, within-script priming was detected in the left posterior temporal cortex, with its medial sector for kanji and a more lateral sector for kana, mirroring the medial-to-lateral gradient for kanji and kana found in the same region (see Fig. 7.3). Since the observed within-script priming should comprise repetition suppression at multiple neurocognitive levels (i.e., ranging from visuoperceptual to lexicosemantic), this script-specific specialization in the occipitotemporal cortex might be partially attributed to some between-script difference, either in the eccentricity bias or in the depth of automatic lexicosemantic activation, as mentioned earlier.

Second, cross-script priming was found at a lateral part of the left MTG. We proposed that this neural effect reflects lexicosemantic activation during reading, because masked priming effect is thought to be generated at the lexical level (Forster, Mohan, & Hector, 2003), whereas phonological activation for subliminal words may occur only to a limited extent (Kouider & Dupoux, 2001). Moreover, functional brain imaging (Chao, Haxby, & Martin et al., 1999; Devlin, J. T., Jamison, H. L., Matthews, P. M., & Gonnerman, 2004; Thompson-Schill, D'Esposito, & Kan, et al., 1999; Tyler et al., 2003) and neuropsychological data (Chertkow, Bub, Dcaudon, & Whitehead, et al., 1997; Yamawaki et al., 2005) converge to suggest that the mid-lateral MTG is associated with semantic/conceptual representation.

The Visual Word Form Area in Japanese Readers

Our fMRI results revealed that the left middle fusiform region corresponding to the VWFA was active while Japanese readers are engaged in word reading, both for kanji and kana, but that this same region exhibited no repetition suppression, irrespective of the script changes between prime and target. The absence of cross-script priming in the VWFA is at least consistent with the notion that the canonical coordinate of the region is associated with abstract orthographic representation of letter strings, whereas the convergence between kanji and kana should occur at some later stages of word recognition. More generally, these findings are in accord with the proposal that the size of "granular units" encoded by occipitotemporal neurons is essentially different between alphabet letters, kana, and kanji (Dehaene, Cohen, Sigman, & Vinckier, 2005; Wydell & Butterworth, 1999).

On the other hand, it is possible to assume the existence of an amodal-level orthographic representation of words between the two parallel script systems of kana (hiragana and katakana), which may be comparable to the upper- and lowercase letters in English. In fact, some behavioral studies have shown that repetition priming does occur between hiragana and katakana (Hatta & Ogawa, 1983; Hayashi, 2005; Komatsu & Naito, 1992). These results may support the possible existence of a common orthographic representation shared by two systems of kana. If this is the case, the cross-script neural priming between two types of kana would be expected to fall in or around the left posterolateral temporal region showing within-script priming for kana ($x = -63$, $y = -54$, $z = 3$; see above). Possibly, such cross-script alteration might induce repetition enhancement, rather than repetition suppression, because the relative frequency of usage is often asymmetric between hiragana and katakana, and because the neural priming direction in the ventral visual region is shown to change with the visual familiarity of the stimuli used (Henson and & Rugg, 2003).

Finally, several other questions are still left open about the potential or "dormant" role of the VWFA in nonalphabetical readers. For instance, it is unknown whether the canonical VWFA, or the occipitotemporal subregion associated with orthographic codes of alphabetic words, operates similarly in Chinese or Japanese readers when those people are engaged in reading

English. This is an interesting question, since a majority of skilled readers in the world are estimated to understand written texts in nonnative languages (e.g., De Bot & Kroll, 2002). Presumably, the basic functional organization of the ventral visual stream is predetermined and structured similarly across users of different languages, despite the notorious diversity of writing systems in the world. However, the cultural impact of a writing system may reshape the large-scale functional organization of the occipitotemporal cortex at least to some extent, since the large-scale functional organization of the occipitotemporal cortex seems indeed sensitive to external, experience-dependent modifications (Gauthier et al., 2000; Henson, Shallice, & Dolan, 2000).

More generally, given that the large stretch of occipitotemporal cortex is involved in visual word recognition from perceptual to lexicosemantic levels, the degree of experience-dependent plasticity in the region is important for predicting the behavioral learning effects produced by late language training. That is, understanding the extent and possible constraints of bottom-up neural processing for late-learned orthographies would have some practical impact on language teaching and remediation. Clearly, further study will be needed for testing the functional property and plasticity of the occipitotemporal visual word-form system across readers of different languages.

Conclusion

It has long been known that brain damage affects the reading ability of Japanese adults to varying degrees between logographic and syllabic scripts. Such reading disorders have been taken as supporting the notion that different neural components are involved in reading as a function of the cognitive processing demands of writing systems used. Guided by the current neurocognitive model of visual word recognition, this chapter reexamined the brain imaging and neuropsychological studies of the Japanese language to propose a clearer view of a language-specific exploitation of the left occipitotemporal cortex as a neural basis of the universal visual word recognition system. A review of the existing evidence suggests that the two types of Japanese scripts recruit the left occipitotemporal cortex similarly to alphabet letters, but with more mesial and rightward bias for kanji and with greater occipitoparietal involvement for kana. In contrast, visual words written in the two different formats converge in the left MTG anterolateral to the VWFA, probably reflecting lexicosemantic activation during reading. It is proposed that the ventral visual stream for word recognition is structured similarly across readers of different writing systems but is exploited with slightly different intra- and interhemispheric bias according to specific processing demands placed by writing systems.

Acknowledgment

This work was supported by Nakayama Foundation for Human Sciences.

References

Beeman, M., Friedman, R. B., Grafman, J., Perez, E., Diamond, S., & Lindsay, M. B. (1994). Summation Priming and Coarse Semantic Coding in the Right Hemisphere. *Journal of Cognitive Neuroscience, 6,* 26–45.

Besner, D., & Hildebrandt, N. (1987). Orthographic and phonological codes in the oral reading of Japanese Kana. *Journal of Experimental Psychology: Learning, Memory, and Cognition, 13,* 335–343.

Chao, L.L., Haxby, J.V., & Martin, A. (1999). Attribute-based neural substrates in temporal cortex for perceiving and knowing about objects. *Nature and Neuroscience, 2,* 913–919.

Chertkow, H., Bub, D., Deaudon, C., & Whitehead, V. (1997). On the status of object concepts in aphasia. *Brain & Language 58,* 203–232.

Cohen, L., Dehaene, S., Naccache, L., Lehericy, S., Dehaene-Lambertz, G., Henaff, M.A., et al. (2000). The visual word form area: spatial and temporal characterization of an initial stage of reading in normal subjects and posterior split-brain patients. *Brain, 123,* 291–307.

Cohen, L., Lehericy, S., Chochon, F., Lemer, C., Rivaud, S., & Dehaene, S. (2002). Language-specific tuning of visual cortex? Functional properties of the visual word form area. *Brain, 125,* 1054–1069.

De Bot, K., & Kroll, J. F. (2002). Psycholinguistics. In N. Schmitt (Ed.), *An Introduction to Applied Linguistics.* (pp. 133–149). London: Oxford University Press.

Dehaene, S., Cohen, L., Sigman, M., & Vinckier, F. (2005). The neural code for written words: a proposal. *Trends in Cognitive Science, 9,* 335–341.

Dehaene, S., Naccache, L., Cohen, L., Bihan, D.L., Mangin, J.F., Poline, J.B., et al. (2001). Cerebral mechanisms of word masking and unconscious repetition priming. *Nature Neuroscience, 4,* 752–758.

Devlin, J. T., Jamison, H. L., Matthews, P. M., & Gonnerman, L. M. (2004). Morphology and the internal structure of words. *Proceedings of the National Academy of Sciences of the United States of America,* 101, 14984–14988.

Feldman, L.B., & Turvey, M.T. (1980). Words written in Kana are named faster than the same words written in Kanji. *Language and Speech, 23,* 141–147.

Fink, G. R., Halligan, P. W., Marshall, J. C., Frith, C. D., Frackowiak, R. S., & Dolan, R. J. (1996). Where in the brain does visual attention select the forest and the trees? *Nature, 382,* 626–628.

Forster, K. I., Mohan, K., & Hector, J. (2003). The mechanics of masked priming. In K. Kinoshita & S. J. Lupker (Eds.), *Masked priming: State of the art.* (pp. 3–37). Hove, UK: Psychology Press.

Fushimi, T., Komori, K., Ikeda, M., Lambon Ralph, M. A., & Patterson, K. (2009). The association between semantic dementia and surface dyslexia in Japanese. *Neuropsychologia 47,* 1061–1068.

Gauthier, I., Skudlarski, P., Gore, J. C., & Anderson, A. W. (2000). Expertise for cars and birds recruits brain areas involved in face recognition. *Nature Neuroscience, 3,* 191–197.

Hasson, U., Levy, I., Behrmann, M., Hendler, T., & Malach, R. (2002). Eccentricity bias as an organizing principle for human high-order object areas. *Neuron, 34,* 479–490.

Hatta, T. (1977). Recognition of Japanese kanji in the left and right visual fields. *Europsychologia, 15,* 685–688.

Hatta, T., Honjoh, Y., & Mito, H. (1983). Event-related potentials and reaction times as measures of hemispheric differences for physical and semantic Kanji matching. *Cortex, 19,* 517–528.

Hatta, T., & Ogawa, T. (1983). Hiragana and Katakana in Japanese orthography and lexical representation. *Language Sciences, 5,* 185–196.

Hayashi, C. (2005). Effects of script types of Japanese loan words on priming performance. *Perception and Motor Skills, 100,* 403–408.

Henson, R.N., & Rugg, M.D. (2003). Neural response suppression, haemodynamic repetition effects, and behavioural priming. *Neuropsychologia, 41,* 263–270.

Henson, R.N., Shallice, T., & Dolan, R. (2000). Neuroimaging evidence for dissociable forms of repetition priming. *Science, 287,* 1269–1272.

Hino, Y., Lupker, S.J., Ogawa, T., & Sears, C.R. (2003). Masked repetition priming and word frequency effects across different types of Japanese scripts: An examination of the lexical activation account. *Journal of Memory and Language, 48,* 33–66.

Hirose, T. (1984). [The effect of script frequency on semantic processing of Kanji and Kana words]. *Shinrigaku Kenkyu, 55,* 173–176.

Humphreys, G. W., Evett, L. J., & Quinlan, P. T. (1990). Orthographic processing in visual word identification. *Cognitive Psychology, 22,* 517–560.

Iwata, M. (1986). Neural mechanism of reading and writing in the Japanese language. *Functional Neurology, 1,* 43–52.

Jiang, N. (1999). Testing explanations for asymmetry in cross-language priming. Bilingualism: *Language and Cognition, 2,* 59–75.

Jibiki, I., &Yamaguchi, N. (1993). The Gogi (word-meaning) syndrome with impaired kanji processing: alexia with agraphia. *Brain & Language, 45,* 61–69.

Kaiho, H., & Nomura, Y. (1983). *Kanji jouhou shori no shinrigaku. [Psychology of information processing of kanji.]* Tokyo: Kyoiku-Shuppan.

Kamada, K., Kober, H., Saguer, M., Moller, M., Kaltenhauser, M., & Vieth, J. (1998). Responses to silent Kanji reading of the native Japanese and German in task subtraction magnetoencephalography. *Brain Research Cognitive Brain Research, 7,* 89–98.

Kawahata, N., Nagata, K., & Shishido, F. (1988). Alexia with agraphia due to the left posterior inferior temporal lobe lesion–neuropsychological analysis and its pathogenetic mechanisms. *Brain & Language, 33,* 296–310.

Komatsu, S., & Naito, M. (1992). Repetition priming with Japanese Kana scripts in word-fragment completion. *Memory and Cognition, 20,* 160–170.

Kouider, S., & Dupoux, E. (2001). A functional disconnection between spoken and visual word recognition: evidence from unconscious priming. *Cognition, 82,* B35–49.

Martin, A., & Chao, L.L. (2001). Semantic memory and the brain: structure and processes. *Current Opinions in Neurobiology, 11,* 194–201.

Mochizuki, H., & Ohtomo, R. (1988). Pure alexia in Japanese and agraphia without alexia in kanji. The ability dissociation between reading and writing in kanji vs kana. *Archives of Neurology, 45,* 1157–1159.

Mummery, C.J., Patterson, K., Wise, R.J., Vandenbergh, R., Price, C.J., & Hodges, J.R. (1999). Disrupted temporal lobe connections in semantic dementia. *Brain, 122,* 61–73.

Nakagawa, A. (1994). Visual and semantic processing in reading Kanji. *Journal of Experimental Psychology and Human Perceptual Performance, 20,* 864–875.

Nakamura, K., Dehaene, S., Jobert, A., Le Bihan, D., & Kouider, S. (2007). Task-specific change of unconscious neural priming in the cerebral language network. *Proceedings of the National Academy of Sciences of the United States of America, 104,* 19643–19648.

Nakamura, K., Dehaene, S., Jobert, A., Le Bihan, D., & Kouider, S. (2005a). Subliminal convergence of Kanji and Kana words: further evidence for functional parcellation of the posterior temporal cortex in visual word perception. *Journal of Cognitive Neuroscience, 17,* 954–68.

Nakamura, K., Hara, N., Kouider, S., Takayama, Y., Hanajima, R., Sakai, K., & Ugawa, Y. (2006). Task-guided selection of the dual neural pathways for reading. *Neuron, 52,* 557–564.

Nakamura, K., Oga, T., Okada, T., Sadato, N., Takayama, Y., Wydell, T., et al. (2005b). Hemispheric asymmetry emerges at distinct parts of the occipitotemporal cortex for objects, logograms and phonograms: A functional MRI study. *Neuroimage 28,* 3, 521–528.

Nomura, Y. (1981). The information processing of kanji, kana script: The effects of data-driven and conceptually-driven processing on reading. *The Japanese Journal of Psychology 51,* 327–334.

Paulesu, E., Demonet, J.F., Fazio, F., McCrory, E., Chanoine, V., Brunswick, N., et al. (2001). Dyslexia: cultural diversity and biological unity. *Science, 291,* 2165–2167.

Price, C.J. (1998). The functional anatomy of word comprehension and production. *Trends in Cognitive Sciences, 2,* 281–288.

Price, C.J., Moore, C.J., Humphreys, G.W., & Wise, R.J.S. (1997). Segregating semantic from phonological processes during reading. *Journal of Cognitive Neuroscience, 9,* 727–733.

Roeltgen, D.P. (1993). Agraphia. In K.M. Heilman & E. Valenstein E. (Eds.). *Clinical Neuropsychology.* New York: Oxford University Press, 63–89.

Saito, H. (1981). Use of graphemic and phonemic encoding in reading kanji and kana. *The Japanese Journal of Psychology, 52,* 266–273.

Sakuma, N., Sasanumam S., Tatsumi, I.F., & Masaki, S. (1998). Orthography and phonology in reading Japanese kanji words, evidence from the semantic decision task with homophones. *Memory and Cognition, 26,* 75–87.

Sakurai, Y. (2004). Varieties of alexia from fusiform, posterior inferior temporal and posterior occipital gyrus lesions. *Behavioral Neurology, 15,* 35–50.

Sakurai, Y., Ichikawa, Y., & Mannen, T. (2001). Pure alexia from a posterior occipital lesion. *Neurology, 56,* 778–781.

Sakurai, Y., Momose, T., Iwata, M., Sudo, Y., Ohtomo, K., & Kanazawa, I. (2000). Different cortical activity in reading of Kanji words, Kana words and Kana nonwords. *Brain Research and Cognitive Brain Research, 9,* 111–115.

Sakurai, Y., Sakai, K., Sakuta, M., & Iwata, M. (1994). Naming difficulties in alexia with agraphia for kanji after a left posterior inferior temporal lesion. *Journal of Neurology, Neurosugery and Psychiatry, 57,* 609–13.

Sasanuma, S., & Fujimura, O. (1971). Selective impairment of phonetic and non-phonetic transcription of words in Japanese aphasic patients: kana vs. kanji in visual recognition and writing. *Cortex, 7,* 1–18.

Sasanuma, S., Itoh, M., Kobayashi, Y., & Mori, K. (1980). The nature of the task-stimulus interaction in the tachistoscopic recognition of kana and kanji words. *Brain & Language 9,* 298–306.

Sasanuma, S., Itoh, M., Mori, K., & Kobayashi, Y. (1977). Tachistoscopic recognition of kana and kanji words. *Neuropsychologia, 15,* 547–553.

Sasanuma, S., & Monoi, H. (1975). The syndrome of Gogi (word meaning) aphasia. Selective impairment of kanji processing. *Neurology, 25,* 627–632.

Sasanuma, S., Sakuma, N., & Tatsumi, I. (1988). Lexical access of kana words and words in kana. *Annual Bulletin Research Institute of Logopedics and Phoniatrics, 22,* 117–123.

Siok, W. T., Spinks, J. A., Jin, Z., & Tan, L. H. (2009). Developmental dyslexia is characterized by the co-existence of visuospatial and phonological disorders in Chinese children. *Current Biology, 19,* R890–892.

Soma, Y., Sugishita, M., Kitamura, K., Maruyama, S., & Imanaga, H. (1989). Lexical agraphia in the Japanese language: Pure agraphia for Kanji due to left posteroinferior temporal lesions. *Brain, 112,* 1549–1561.

Sugishita, M., Otomo, K., Kabe, S., & Yunoki, K. (1992). A critical appraisal of neuropsychological correlates of Japanese ideogram (kanji) and phonogram (kana) reading. *Brain, 115* (Pt 5), 1563–1585.

Sugishita, M., & Yoshioka, M. (1987). Visual processes in a hemialexic patient with posterior callosal section. *Neuropsychologia, 25,* 329–339.

Sugishita, M., Yoshioka, M., & Kawamura, M. (1986). Recovery from hemialexia. *Brain & Language, 29,* 106–18.

Tanaka, H., & Konishi, K. (1990). Katakana hyoki tango no shori katei hyoki hindo no eikyo. [Semantic processing of katakana words effects of script frequency.] *Shinkei Shinrigaku, 6,* 231–239.

Thompson-Schill, S.L., D'Esposito, M., & Kan I.P. (1999). Effects of repetition and competition on activity in left prefrontal cortex during word generation. *Neuron, 23,* 513–522.

Tyler, L.K., Bright, P., Dick, E., Tavares, P., Pilgrim, L., Fletcher, P., et al. (2003). Do semantic categories activate distinct cortical regions? Evidence for a distributed neural semantic system. *Cognitive Neuropsychology, 20,* 541–559.

Vinckier, F., Dehaene, S., Jobert, A., Dubus, J.P., Sigman, M., & Cohen, L. (2007). Hierarchical coding of letter strings in the ventral stream: dissecting the inner organization of the visual word-form system. *Neuron, 55,* 143–156.

Wydell, T.N., & Butterworth B. (1999). A case study of an English-Japanese bilingual with monolingual dyslexia. *Cognition, 70,* 273–305.

Wydell, T.N., Patterson, K., & Humphreys, G.W. (1993). Phonologically mediated access to meaning for kanji: Is a ROWS still a ROSE in Japanese Kanji? *Journal of Experimental Psychology: Learning, Memory and Cognition, 19,* 491–514.

Yamada, J., Imai, H., & Ikebe, Y. (1990). The use of the orthographic lexicon in reading kana words. *Journal of General Psychology, 117,* 311–23.

Yamadori, A. (1975). Ideogram reading in alexia. *Brain, 98,* 231–8.

Yamadori, A. (1985). *Shinkei-Shinrgaku-Nyumon.* Tokyo: Igaku-Shoin.

Yamaguchi, S., Toyoda, G., Xu, J., Kobayashi, S., & Henik, A. (2002). Electroencephalographic activity in a flanker interference task using Japanese orthography. *Journal of Cognition and Neuroscience, 14,* 971–979.

Yamawaki, R., Suzuki, K., Tanji, K., Fujii, T., Endo, K., Meguro, K., et al. (2005). Anomic alexia of kanji in a patient with anomic aphasia. *Cortex, 41,* 555–559.

Yokota, T., Ishiai, S., Furukawa, T., & Tsukagoshi, H. (1990). Pure agraphia of kanji due to thrombosis of the Labbe vein. *Journal of Neurology, Neurosurgery and Psychiatry, 53,* 335–338.

Yokoyama, S., & Yoneda, J. (1995). Noizu ni uzumoreta kanji to kana no ninchi. [Recognition of kan ji and kana with additive noise.] *Kokuritsu Kokugo Kenkyusho Hokoku 110,* 99–119.

8

Visual Word Recognition: The First 500 Milliseconds

Recent Insights from Magnetoencephalography

*Piers L. Cornelissen, Morten L. Kringelbach, and
Peter C. Hansen*

The ability to fluently and, seemingly effortlessly, read words is one of few uniquely special human attributes, but one which has assumed inordinate significance because of the role that this activity has come to have in modern society. A disadvantage in reading ability not only has profound personal impact for the individuals concerned, but in terms of economic and social problems also has a wider negative influence on society at large. According to current government figures in the United Kingdom, 22% of 11-year-olds do not reach the minimum standard required in English national curriculum tests. Despite its importance, however, the scientific under-standing of the neural basis of reading, and more particularly the visual aspect of visual word recognition, is relatively poorly understood. Thus far, a coherent overarching model that spans the various conceptual levels, from behavior through functional description to neuroanatomy, has proven extra-ordinarily challenging to elucidate. A fuller understanding of the computa-tional processing and neurophysiological basis of how the reading system functions would therefore represent significant progress.

As with most complex behaviors, visual word recognition is thought to result from the dynamic interplay between the elements of a distributed cortical and subcortical network. To fully understand how visual word recog-nition is achieved therefore, and how it may fail in developmental dyslexia, we need to identify not only the necessary and sufficient complement of nodes that comprise this network—its functional anatomy—but we also need to understand how information flows through this network with time, and indeed how the structure of the network itself may adapt in both the short and long term. In this chapter we take a historical approach to reviewing recent magnetoencephalography (MEG) research that elucidates these temporal dynamics, focusing particularly on events with the first 300 ms of a visually presented word, and which we believe should set crucial constraints on models of visual word recognition and reading.

Equivalent Current Dipole Modeling

In our first attempts to explore the temporal sequence of cortical activation for visually presented words we used equivalent current dipole (ECD) modeling of MEG data. This technique is based on source modeling of evoked averaged data, and can therefore only reveal current sources in the brain that show a high degree of phase synchrony across trials. Unlike minimum current estimation (MCE) (Uutela, Hämäläinen, & Somersalo, 1999) and minimum norm estimation (MNE) (Hämäläinen & Ilmoniemi, 1984), whose solutions give a spatially distributed estimation of current spread, multi-dipole ECD models render a set of tightly focused point sources for each subject for each experimental condition. At the individual subject level, this can give the impression that activity is well localized in the brain with ECDs. While this may be true for auditory and somatesthetic cortex, where very clear dipolar field patterns are reliably seen, this is rarely the situation for experimental tasks that involve a widely distributed cortical network, such as reading and visual word recognition. As a result, we tend to see considerable variability in terms of anatomical localization across different subjects. Therefore, we suggest that the best way to interpret the data from multi-dipole models is in terms of robust, but rather simplified views of brain activation, in which the temporal sequence and response characteristics of a set of coarsely defined regions of interest (ROIs) can be described.

In a series of four studies of word reading and visual word recognition (Cornelissen, Tarkiainen, Helenius, & Salmelin, 2003; Helenius, Tarkiainen, Cornelissen, Hansen, & Salmelin, 1999; Tarkiainen, Helenius, Hansen, Cornelissen, & Salmelin, 1999; Tarkiainen, Cornelissen, & Salmelin, 2002), we applied the following logic to stimulus design. As Figure 8.1A shows, we presented dark gray stimuli, such as letter strings, symbol strings, objects, and faces on a light gray background. We then systematically varied the visibility of such stimuli by adding increasing amounts of pixel noise. This manipulation has two useful properties that allow us to look for dissociations in the patterns of evoked response. First, as noise increases, stimulus visibility reduces. This means that those cortical areas that are sensitive to higher-order

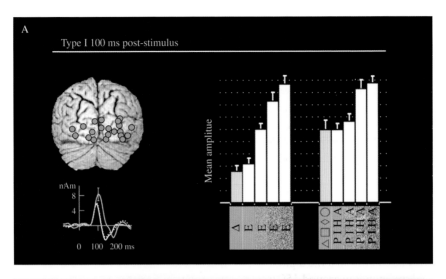

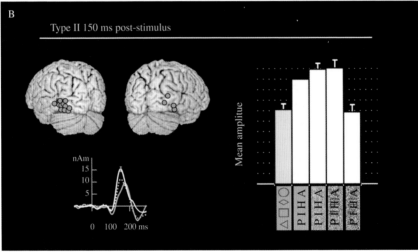

Figure 8.1 A: Type I equivalent current dipoles (ECDs) and mean amplitude of response to one- and four-element symbol and letter strings. B: Type II ECDs and mean amplitude of response to one- and four-element symbol and letter strings.

stimulus properties should show increasingly weaker responses as a function of increasing stimulus noise. Second, as pixel noise increases so does the number of contrasty edges in the image. Therefore, any neurons that are primarily tuned to low-level image properties, such as contrast borders, should show an increase in the amplitude of their responses as a function of stimulus noise. By using these manipulations we identified two main response patterns, and these are illustrated in Figure 8.1A,B.

The first of these, which we called Type I, took place around 100 ms after stimulus onset. It originated in the midline-occipital region the vicinity of V1/ V2/V3 and was distributed along the ventral visual stream. This response was systematically and monotonically modulated by noise but was insensitive to the stimulus content, suggesting involvement in low-level analysis of visual features. The second pattern, which we call Type II, took place around 150 ms after stimulus onset and was concentrated in the inferior occipitotemporal region with left-hemisphere dominance. This activation was greater for letter strings than for symbol strings. The response to noise masking was nonlinear: response amplitude increased moderately with increasing pixel noise, and then as stimulus visibility became severely impaired at even higher noise levels, response amplitude reduced back toward baseline. We argue that this very different pattern of responses is therefore likely to reflect an object-level processing stage that acts as a gateway to higher processing areas. In addition, we also identified a third pattern of response (Type III). This also occurred in the time window around 150 ms after stimulus onset, but originated mainly in the right occipital area. Like Type II responses, it was modulated by string length, but showed no preference for letters as compared with symbols.

These data suggest an important role for the inferior occipitotemporal cortex in reading within 200 ms after stimulus onset and are consistent with findings from intracranial recordings (Nobre, Allison, & McCarthy, 1994) and earlier MEG results (Salmelin, Service, Kiesilä, Uutela, & Salonen, 1996). Nobre and colleagues (1994) demonstrated letter string–specific responses bilaterally in posterior fusiform gyrus about 200 ms after stimulus onset. MEG recordings by Salmelin and colleagues (1996) showed strong transient responses to words and nonwords in the bilateral inferior occipitotemporal cortex in fluent readers at 150–200 ms. However, in dyslexic subjects, the left- but not right-hemisphere response was missing, suggesting a special role for the left inferior occipitotemporal cortex in fluent reading within the first 200 ms after seeing a letter string (Helenius, Tarkiainen, Cornelissen, Hansen, & Salmelin, 1999).

The fact that the Type II occipitotemporal response at approximately 150 ms is stronger for letter than symbol strings in a silent reading task suggests a degree of orthographic selectivity. This raises the question whether it may also be sensitive to the lexical status of the letter string. However, other data suggest that the Type II response is prelexical. The strength of this response, as well as its latency, are very similar for words, nonwords, and consonant strings (Cornelissen, Tarkiainen, Helenius, & Salmelin, 2003; Salmelin et al., 1996). Moreover, in these studies, the effect of lexicality (i.e., words > nonwords or words > consonant strings) only starts to appear at about 200 to 300 ms after stimulus onset (Fig. 8.2), in perisylvian cortex including the left superior temporal and inferior parietal areas (Marinkovic et al., 2003;

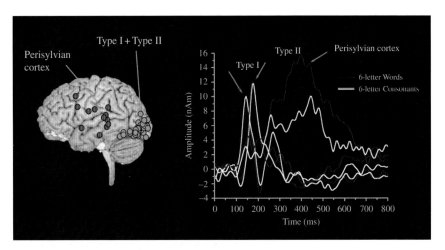

Figure 8.2 Type I and II equivalent current dipoles (ECDs) together with ECDs showing significantly stronger responses to six-letter Finnish words than six-letter consonant strings. Plot showing grand average waveforms for each of the three ECD types, separately for words and consonant strings.

Cornelissen et al., 2003; Helenius, Salmelin, Service, & Connolly, 1998) and at the base of the left anterior temporal lobe (Nobre & McCarthy, 1995).

Source Reconstruction with Synthetic Aperture Magnetometry

Synthetic aperture magnetometry (SAM) is an adaptive beam-forming technique for the analysis of electroencephalographic (EEG) and MEG data (Robinson & Vrba, 1999; Van Veen et al., 1997; Vrba & Robinson, 2001). It uses a linear weighting of the sensor channels to focus the array on a given target location or set of locations—in this case a regular array of virtual electrodes (or voxels) in the brain placed 5 mm apart from each other. The result is a reconstruction of the time series for every voxel or virtual electrode in the brain. Thereafter, for a nominated frequency range, it is possible to compare the power in the Fourier domain between a passive or baseline time window and a sequence of active time windows of interest, as well as to compute time–frequency plots for particular virtual electrodes of interest. As a result, it is possible to image changes in spectral power for both event-related synchronization (ERS) (i.e., in which power in the active window > passive window) and event-related resynchronization (ERD) (i.e., in which power in the active window < passive window).

The main advantages of source reconstruction techniques like SAM are twofold. First, unlike ECDs, it is possible to localize sources in the brain with SAM based on both evoked and induced activity, be they ERSs or ERDs.

Epochs of evoked activity are those which are tightly phase-locked to the stimulus across successive trials, whereas induced activity is not (see Hillibrand & Barnes, 2005). In the time domain, simple averaging across trials is sufficient to reveal an evoked signal component that will also be reflected in the frequency domain. In comparison, simple averaging in the time domain will not reveal sources of induced activity because of phase jitter from one trial to the next, but they will still be revealed in the frequency domain. The second advantage is that using the appropriate anatomical information from an individual enables individual SAM statistical maps to be transformed to a standard Montreal Neurological Institute (MNI) space and used to make group statistical inferences. The main limitation of adaptive beam-former techniques is dealing with sources that are perfectly temporally correlated. However, perfect neural synchrony between two sources in the brain over the entire course of the experiment is exceedingly unlikely, and it has been shown that two sources can be resolved even at relatively large temporal correlation levels (Sekihara et al., 2002; Van Veen et al., 1997).

Lexical Decision

We recently used SAM analysis of MEG data from a visual lexical decision task to map the spatio-temporal evolution of cortical events during visual word recognition (Pammer et al., 2004). As Figure 8.3 shows, during approximately the first 150 ms following the central presentation of five-letter words, we saw ERS in primary visual areas in the lingual gyrus, cuneus (BA 17).

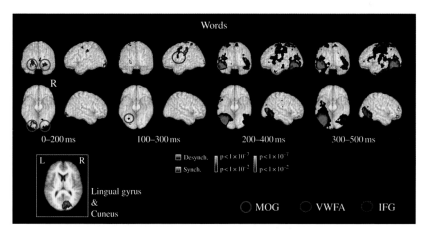

Figure 8.3 Group synthetic aperture magnetometry (SAM) maps of responses in the β-frequency band (10.20 Hz) to five-letter words. MOG, middle occipital gyrus; VWFA, visual word form area; IFG, inferior frontal gyrus.

In the same time frame, we also saw bilateral ERS in the inferior and middle occipital gyri (BA 18/19), with the responses being stronger in the left (LH) than the right hemisphere (RH). These findings are entirely consistent with other MEG studies of visual word recognition and reading using equivalent current dipole modeling (Tarkiainen et al., 1999; Salmelin et al., 2000; Cornelissen et al., 2003), minimum norm current estimation (Dhond et al., 2001), and dynamic imaging of coherent sources (DICS) (Kujala et al., 2007). After approximately 150 ms, we saw ERD in the left and right fusiform gyri (LH > RH) that expanded systematically in both the posterior–anterior and medial–lateral directions over the course of the next 500 ms. In the LH, that part of the mid-fusiform region that has recently been dubbed the visual word form area (VWFA) was activated around 200 ms post-stimulus, and this is in good agreement with the timing of word-specific responses from other neurophysiological recordings (Cohen et al., 2000; Nobre et al., 1994).

Comparing SAM with ECDs and Functional MRI

On the basis of anatomical location and timing, there appears to be good correspondence between the ERS in lingual gyrus and cuneus identified with SAM and the Type I sources defined with equivalent current dipole modeling. Similarly, the ERS in the left and right middle occipital gyrus (MOG) defined by SAM would appear to correspond reasonably with the Type II ECD response. Nevertheless, despite the fact that both sets of results are based on MEG data recorded during visual word recognition tasks, the SAM maps in Figure 8.3 show a much finer anatomical parcellation of functional activation than is the case with ECDs. For example, the SAM maps show activations in the MOG that are distinctly separate from those in the fusiform gyri, whereas the published ECD results have never convincingly separated two such components. One explanation for this difference could be that the activation in MOG is largely phase-locked, whereas that in the fusiform is not. If so, ECD algorithms would likely fail to "see" the fusiform activation. Alternatively, it may be the case that fixed location, fixed orientation dipoles (as were used in Tarkiainen et al 1999) are not sensitive enough to separate out two sources that are both close to each other and active within a similar time frame. Fortunately, the application of a third analysis technique to these kinds of MEG data, minimum norm estimation (see Marincovic et al., 2003), does help us to resolve this apparent discrepancy because it also suggests that there is a systematic spread of activation along the ventral stream, from V1 toward the lateral occipital complex and the fusiform gyrus, during visual word recognition.

The comparison between functional magnetic resonance imaging (fMRI) and SAM data throws up another striking difference between the results from

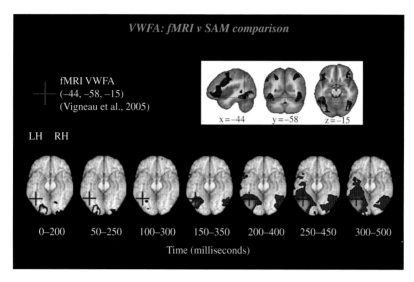

Figure 8.4 Group synthetic aperture magnetometry (SAM) maps of responses in the β-frequency band to centrally presented words. Left and right middle occipital gyrus (MOG) activations appear as red event-related synchronization (ERS). Left and right fusiform gyrus activations appear as blue event-related resynchronization (ERD).

different imaging modalities. As Figure 8.4 shows, based on the meta-analysis of fMRI studies of reading by Vigneau and colleagues (2005), there is a restricted patch of left-hemispheric fusiform cortex (average Talairach coordinates: x = –43, y = –54, z = 12), which is reproducibly activated during reading. Among many others, Cohen and colleagues (2000) showed that this so-called VWFA responds more strongly to alphabetic letter strings than to checkerboard stimuli, more strongly to words than to consonant strings, and demonstrates invariance with respect to retinal position. In addition, VWFA shows font-type invariance (Dehaene et al., 2002). At issue here is not the validity of the interpretation as far as the role of this neuronal population is concerned. Instead, it is the very different impressions of what might be going on depending on whether information about timing (in the millisecond range) is available or not. On the one hand, the fMRI results give the strong impression that a relatively fixed population of neurons is doing something that contributes en masse to letter-string processing—whatever that is. On the other hand, it is very tempting to interpret the SAM and minimum norm estimates as evidence of a progressive sweep of corticocortical activation along the fusiform gyrus. Consistent with recent computational and conceptual models of visual word recognition (see for example, Whitney, 2001; Dehaene, Cohen, Sigman, & Vinckier, 2005), this suggests the idea of a sequence along the fusiform in which progressively complex attributes of letter strings are extracted: from simple lines and edges in a retinotopic spatial framework, through to font and case-invariant letters, letter clusters, and ultimately whole words.

Retinotopicity and Hemifield Presentations

In languages in which the orthography is read from left to right, we tend to fixate letters situated somewhere between the beginning and the middle of a word. According to recent research (Lavidor & Walsh, 2004; Lavidor, Ellis, Shillcock, & Bland, 2001; Monaghan, Shillcock, & McDonald, 2004), this means that the letters falling to the left of fixation project initially *only* to the visual cortex in the right cerebral hemisphere, whereas letters to the right of fixation project initially *only* to the visual cortex in the left cerebral hemisphere. There appears to be *no* overlap between the two. Consistent with this split fovea model, Cohen and colleagues (2000) recorded fMRI activations during the presentation of words, consonant strings, and checkerboards to the left and right halves of the visual field. As expected, they found position-invariant activation in the VWFA for words especially. However, this activation was distinction from more posterior hemifield-dependent MOG (BA19) responses that were stronger for contralateral than ipsilateral stimulation, irrespective of whether the participants viewed words, consonant strings, or checkerboards. Therefore, these data are consistent with retinotopic coding at this location in the reading network. Ultimately however, to confirm retinotopicity, it would be necessary to view these posterior activations in individual participants, where not only have the boundaries between visual areas been carefully demarcated by retinotopic mapping (see for example, Dougherty, Koch, Brewer, Fischer, Modersitzki, & Wandell, 2003), but also the word stimuli have been systematically shifted across the visual field relative to a fixation point.

Figure 8.5 shows results from our own MEG data in which five-letter words were presented to the left and right upper and lower quadrants of the visual field. In these analyses, the data are averaged across the upper and lower quadrants, in order to compare the LH and RH responses with each other. They show that, within the first 250 ms after stimulus presentation, the response to words in the region of the MOG is largely contralateral, suggesting processing within a retinotopic spatial framework. However, by around 300 ms, the responses have become lateralized to the left fusiform. Thus, the left and right halves of words appear initially to be processed independently in retinotopic cortical representations in the right and left occipital cortex, respectively. Approximately 50–100 ms later, processing appears to localize, and lateralize to the LH's (nonretinotopic) mid-fusiform cortex.

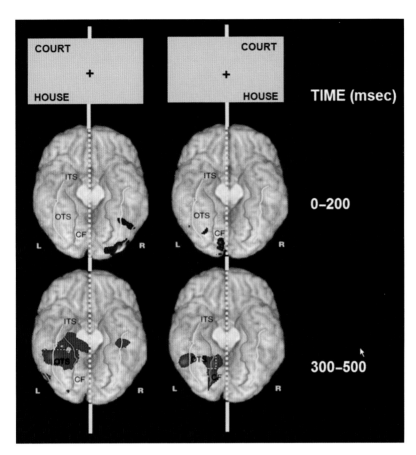

Figure 8.5 Group synthetic aperture magnetometry (SAM) maps of responses in the β-frequency band to five-letter words presented to either the left or the right visual field.

Early Broca's Activation

Surprisingly, Pammer and colleagues (2004) found an ERD in the left pars opercularis of the inferior frontal gyrus (IFG) and the precentral gyrus (BA 44/6) started early, at around 100–200 ms post-stimulus. This early IFG activity followed immediately after the bilateral ERS in the MOG, and overlapped in time with the onset of activation in the LH mid-fusiform. Together, these findings suggest that the interplay between the vision and language domains starts early during visual word recognition.

The early involvement of Broca's area in visual word recognition may at first seem puzzling but in fact a number of other studies have also found indications of this. For example, in their analysis of evoked responses in a reading task, measured with MEG, Salmelin and colleagues (2000) report an early left frontoparietal activation (between 100 and 200 ms post-stimulus) in five of ten stutterers and five of ten controls. Kober and colleagues (2001) used MEG to identify responses in Broca's and Wernicke's areas in subjects who carried out a silent reading task. Although Kober and colleagues' (2001) report focuses attention on the response in Broca's area at 720 ms post-stimulus, nevertheless an earlier peak is clear in their data at around 170 ms post-stimulus. Finally, Julien and associates (2007) measured cortical activity from surface electrodes implanted in epilepsy patients. Subjects were presented two interleaved stories in an Rapid Sequential Visual Presentation (RSVP) format. Words from the story to be attended appeared in one color, while words from the story to be ignored appeared in a different color. Time–frequency analysis based on data averaged in relation to word onset showed clear, early β-frequency band activity for both story lines in left IFG.

The required connectivity between extrastriate visual areas and posterior and superior IFG could be supplied via the superior longitudinal fasciculus (SLF). Recent Diffusion Tensor Imaging (DTI) and histological studies of the SLF in human brains (Makris et al., 2005; Burgel et al. 2006) support Dejerine's (1895) original proposals, and suggest direct connections between Brodmann's areas 18 and 19 and the lateral frontal association areas. Moreover, DiVirgilio and Clarke (1997) used the Nauta technique to demonstrate anterograde axonal degeneration in a postmortem brain that had suffered a right inferior temporal infarction. These authors found crossed monosynaptic connections between extrastriate visual cortex and Wernicke's and Broca's areas. In the current study, we found a difference in latency between the MOG (i.e., BA 18/19) and IFG of around 10–15 ms. Therefore, assuming no additional synaptic delays, this latency difference is consistent with the conduction velocity of a myelinated fibre of about 1 μ diameter over an 8–10 cm distance (Patton, 1982). In summary, there is good reason to suppose that early activation in IFG to visually presented words is both plausible as an empirical phenomenon and supportable by the known anatomical connectivity. Consistent with this, a Granger causality analysis reported in a recent MEG study of continuous reading (Kujala et al., 2007) also suggests that direct functional connections exist between occipitotemporal cortex and LH frontal areas during reading (Fig. 8.6).

The role of IFG in visual word recognition is well established from a number of neuroimaging studies (Bookheimer, 2002). The cortical regions in and around Broca's area in the IFG appear to be associated with fine-grained, speech-gestural, phonological recoding; direct stimulation/recording studies have shown very fast connections between this region in the IFG and motor neurons in the motor strip that drive the speech articulators (Greenlee et al., 2004). This system has been found to function in silent reading and naming (Fiez and

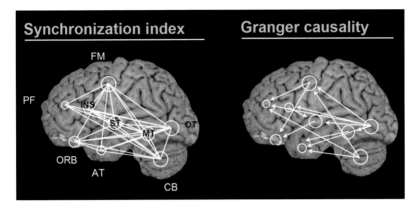

Figure 8.6 Phase synchronization and Granger causality estimates between left hemisphere cortical network nodes during continuous reading. OT, inferior occipitotemporal cortex; MT, medial temporal cortex; ST, superior temporal cortex; AT, anterior part of the inferior temporal cortex; FM, face motor cortex; INS, insula; CB, cerebellum; PF, prefrontal cortex; ORB, orbital cortex.

Petersen, 1998; Pugh et al., 1996; Pugh et al., 1997) and is thought to be more strongly engaged by low-frequency words and pseudowords than by high-frequency words (Fiebach et al., 2002; Fiez & Petersen, 1998; Pugh et al., 1996; Pugh et al., 1997). Moreover, functional connectivity between the left dorsal IFG and occipitotemporal cortex for words, pseudowords, and letter strings, but not false-fonts, has been demonstrated (Bokde et al., 2001; Mechelli et al., 2005). Hemodynamic functional imaging has therefore delimited quite precisely the anatomical extent of left posterior IFG activation during visual word recognition, and elucidated a likely role for it in phonological encoding.

However, while the functional connectivity data imply direct interplay between the vision and language domains, they cannot inform us about the time course of these effects nor how they evolve over time. In contrast, neurophysiological studies using event-related potentials (ERPs) or event-related fields (ERFs) can pinpoint events in time with millisecond precision, but they often face the converse problem that they lack anatomical precision. Nevertheless, a number of such studies have been carried out that indicate that interactions between visual and linguistic factors during visual word recognition do begin early. For example, Assadollahi and Pulvermüller (2003) showed an interaction between word length and frequency in MEG, with short words exhibiting a frequency effect around 150 ms but long words at around 240 ms. Effects of lexicality (i.e., a differential response between words and pseudowords) have been reported as early as 110 ms (Sereno et al., 1998), although more commonly around 200 ms (Cornelissen et al., 2003; Martin-Loeches et al.,

1999). Lexico-semantic variables have been found to influence brain responses as early as 160 ms after visual word onset (Pulvermüller et al., 1995; Pulvermüller et al., 2001) as has semantic coherence, which is a "measure that quantifies the degree to which words sharing a root morpheme, (e.g., gold, golden, goldsmith) are related to each other in meaning" (Hauk et al., 2006). Intriguingly, Figures 5 and 7 in Hauk et al. (2006) suggest early left frontal involvement, particularly for semantic coherence, but unfortunately it is not possible to be more anatomically precise from their data.

Time-Frequency Responses in Broca's Area, VWFA, and MOG

Recently, we sought further evidence for early activation of IFG—specifically in the pars opercularis and precentral gyrus—in response to visually presented words. Based on our previous work and the studies reviewed earlier, we hypothesized that IFG activation should first be detected in a time window between the start of bilateral activation of the MOG (BA 18/19) and the start of activation of the LH mid-fusiform (BA 37). Therefore, we used SAM analysis to identify six ROIs: one in each of the left and right MOG, the left and right mid-fusiform, and the left posterior IFG and its right hemisphere homologue. We tested the specificity of any early IFG activation by comparing responses to centrally presented words, consonant strings, false-font strings, and faces. In addition, we wanted to ensure that the cognitive and attentional demands of the experimental task were held constant across different stimulus types by asking subjects to fixate a central cross continuously, and to simply monitor and respond to any color change of the cross. For each site and for each subject, we then calculated the time course of the MEG signal in order to compare the relative timings and amplitudes of responses to words, faces, false-fonts, and consonants.

Figure 8.7 shows a burst of evoked activity in the 5–20 Hz region from approximately 100–200 ms post-stimulus in the left and right MOG, the left IFG, the left mid-fusiform, and also in the right mid-fusiform, although the latter was restricted to 5–10 Hz. However, no such evoked activity was seen in the right IFG, and this suggests that early evoked responses to written words by the IFG are strongly lateralized to the LH. In contrast, Figure 8.7 shows that both the left and right IFG showed almost continuous non–phase-locked activity at 10–30 Hz, suggesting involvement of the IFG in aspects of task performance unrelated to the precise arrival time of the stimulus. In addition, in the left and right MOG, as well as in the left and right mid-fusiform, the initial increase in power (red) following stimulus presentation was followed by a decrease in power (blue) up to 500 ms post-stimulus. This later reduction in power, particularly in the mid-fusiform, reflecting an event-related resynchronization, is consistent with the findings of Pammer and colleagues (2004).

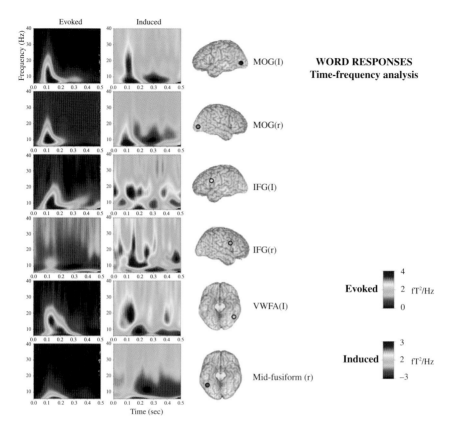

Figure 8.7 Time–frequency plots in response to passively viewed words extracted from six virtual electrodes: left and right middle occipital gyrus (MOG); left and right pars opercularis of the inferior frontal gyrus (IFG); left hemisphere visual word form area (VWFA) and its right hemisphere mid-fusiform homologue.

Time Domain Analysis: ERFs in Broca's Area, VWFA, and MOG

To examine the relative timings of evoked activity in these six ROIs, and also to compare between responses to words, faces, false-fonts, and consonant strings, we carried out further analyses in the time domain, restricted to the time window 0–300 ms post-stimulus. Significant differences between conditions in the resultant difference waveforms were computed using a nonparametric randomization technique, the record orthogonality test by permutations (ROT-p) (Achim, 1995).

Figure 8.8A,B shows the normalized ERFs for centrally presented words in the left IFG ROI, compared with its RH homologue as well as word responses in the VWFA ROI compared to its RH homologue. Consistent with our hypothesis, the left IFG showed a significantly stronger, early response at

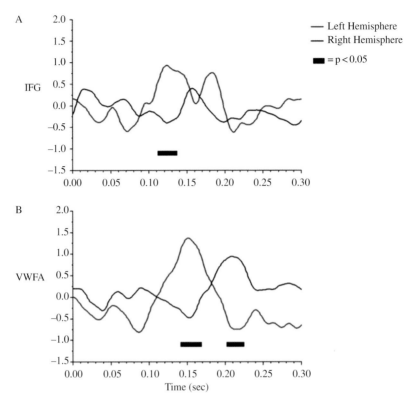

Figure 8.8 A: Normalized event-related fields (ERFs) for centrally presented words in the left inferior frontal gyrus (IFG; *red*), compared with its right hemisphere homologue (*blue*) as well as, B: word responses in the visual word form area (VWFA; *red*) compared to its right hemisphere homologue (*blue*). Black bars illustrate significant differences between each pair of time series (*p* <0.05) as computed with ROT-p.

approximately 125 ms to words than did its RH homologue. Interestingly, we also found a significantly stronger response to words in the VWFA at approximately 150 ms than its RH homologue.

Figure 8.9 shows pair-wise comparisons between words and faces (Fig. 8.9A), words and false-fonts (Fig. 8.9B), and words and consonant-strings (Fig. 8.9C) for all six ROIs. ROT-p analyses showed significantly stronger responses to words than faces in left and right MOG, left IFG, and VWFA at between about 80–150 ms post-stimulus. We also found a significantly stronger response to faces than to words in the right IFG between about 150–200 ms. Moreover, Figure 8.9A shows that the peak response to words in the left IFG ROI occurred approximately 10–15 ms later than the commensurate peaks in left and right MOG, but approximately 20 ms earlier than that in the VWFA. These differences in response timing are confirmed by Figure 8.10, which shows the mean cross-correlation function between the

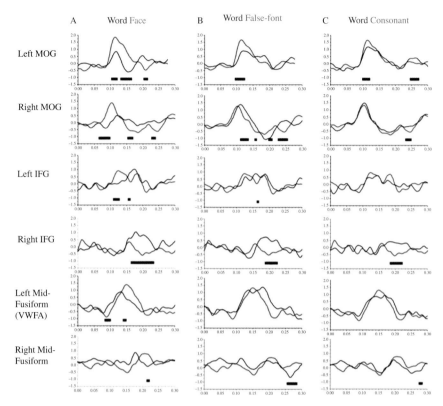

Figure 8.9 (A) Normalized event-related fields (ERFs) for centrally presented words (*red*) and faces (*blue*), (B) words (*red*) and false-fonts (*blue*), (C) words (*red*) and consonants (*blue*) in all six virtual electrodes. Black bars illustrate significant differences between each pair of time series ($p < 0.05$) as computed with ROT-p.

IFG and the other three ROIs for centrally presented words. Over the 200 ms window for which cross-correlations were computed, IFG shows a phase advance of approximately 20 ms compared to VWFA, and a phase lag of approximately 10–15 ms compared to left and right MOG.

Our experimental task arguably minimized differences in attentional demands and cognitive loading between stimulus classes because subjects only had to monitor and respond to color changes in the fixation cross. Therefore, this leaves two main reasons, in principle, for stronger responses to words than faces. Consistent with the electrophysiological findings reviewed earlier (e.g., Hauk et al. 2006; Pulvermuller et al. 1995; Pulvermuller et al. 2001; Sereno et al. 1998), one possibility is that these differences may genuinely reflect word-specific effects related to early interactions between the vision and language domains. However, at least as far as the MOG ROIs are concerned, a second possibility exists. The MOG ROIs were located in retinotopic extrastriate visual cortex (see, e.g., Dougherty et al., 2003; Brewer et al., 2005). Therefore, since the

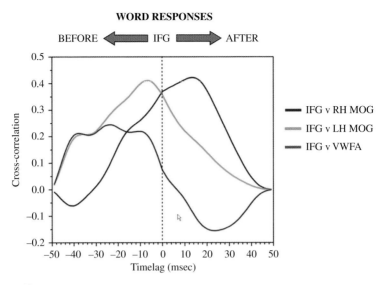

Figure 8.10 The mean cross-correlation between inferior frontal gyrus (IFG) and visual word form area (VWFA) (*blue*), IFG and left mid occipital gyrus (MOG; *green*) and IFG and right MOG (*red*).

horizontal extent of the words on the retina exceeded that of the faces, it is quite possible that the stronger response to words merely reflected activity in more peripheral receptive fields. The word/consonant string and word/false-font string comparisons allow us to disambiguate these possibilities for MOG, because, unlike faces, words, consonants, and false-fonts were the same size. For left MOG, Figures 8.9B and C show that word responses were stronger than both false-font and consonant-string responses at around 100 ms post-stimulus. This differential response is more consistent with word specific than low-level visual effects, for which we would have expected no differences between words, false-fonts, and consonant strings. For the right MOG, responses to words were stronger than those to false-fonts at around 100 ms but not to consonant strings. This suggests that the right MOG activation may be sensitive to strings with real orthographic content, but that this does not extend to the more elaborate word/ morpheme level of processing. Finally, Figures 8.9B and C show that neither the left IFG nor the VWFA showed significantly different responses comparing words with consonant strings or words with false-fonts.

Response Specificity: MOG

The time domain analyses showed stronger responses to words than faces in left and right MOG, where retinotopicity is maintained. The fact that both sites also showed stronger responses to words than false-fonts, and very similar responses to words and consonant strings, suggests that the word-versus-face difference in these two areas cannot be attributed simply to differences in the retinal extent of the stimuli. Instead, the MOG sites appear to demonstrate some degree of selectivity for the letter-likeness of the objects in the visual field. This finding is entirely consistent with previous MEG findings (Cornelissen et al., 2003; Tarkiainen et al., 1999), in which stronger responses at 150 ms post-stimulus were found in occipitotemporal cortex to words, consonant strings, and even rotated letters than to equivalent length symbol strings. One way to interpret these data is in the light of recent models for letter strings encoding along the occipitotemporal complex, which assume that there is a hierarchy of information processing on a continuum from simple features through to increasingly elaborate and abstracted objects (e.g., Dehaene et al., 2005; Whitney, 2001; Davies, 1999). For example, the local combination detector (LCD) model proposed by Dehaene and colleagues (2005) suggests a succession of larger and larger receptive fields, from V1, though V2, V4 and V8 to occipitotemporal sulcus (OTS), which extract letter fragments, then case-specific letter shapes, then abstract letter identities, then letter clusters, and so on. Therefore, in skilled readers in whom the visual word recognition network has been trained over hundreds of thousands of hours on central presentations of words, we ought to expect stimulus-driven, bottom-up responses that reflect this tuning (see, e.g., Nazir et al., 2004; Polk & Farah, 1998).

Response Specificity: VWFA

We placed one ROI in the left hemisphere mid-fusiform gyrus, or VWFA, as defined in fMRI by Vigneau (2005). At this site, we found an evoked response to words that peaked around 150 ms post-stimulus, was stronger at this time point for words than faces, but was not distinguishable from the commensurate responses to consonant strings or false-fonts. This result is in disagreement with some hemodynamic neuroimaging studies that suggest word-specific responses in the VWFA (e.g., Cohen et al., 2000; Dehaene et al., 2002; Ben-Sachar et al., 2006), but is consistent with other studies that demonstrate a lack of word-specific tuning in this region. For example, Price and Devlin (2003) point out that VWFA is engaged: (a) when subjects make manual twist or pour actions in response to pictures of familiar objects relative to perceptual judgments on the same stimuli (Phillips et al., 2002); (b) when they hear, repeat, or think about the meaning of auditory words (Price et al., 2003); and (c) when congenitally blind subjects read tactile words with abstract meanings in Braille (Buechel et al., 1998). None of these acts requires access to a visual word form. One way to resolve the discrepancies in the literature, as well as to reconcile our own data, is suggested by a recent priming study in fMRI (Devlin et al., 2006). These authors found that repetition of pseudowords (solstsolst) did not produce a neural priming effect in left posterior fusiform gyrus. In contrast, orthographically related words, such as "corner-corn," did produce an orthographic priming effect, but this was reduced when prime-target pairs were semantically related (e.g., "teacher – teach"). These findings led to the suggestion that the VWFA may act as an interface between visual form information and higher-order stimulus properties, such as its associated sound and meaning, when overt naming is required by the experimental task—and our task did not require this. This latter point is emphasized by Hillis and colleagues (2005), who administered lexical tasks with spoken and written input and output to 80 patients with acute damage to the VWFA. Damage or dysfunction of the VWFA was not significantly associated with impairment of written-word comprehension or lexical decision, but was significantly associated with impairment of all tasks requiring overt lexical output. Hillis and colleagues (2005) proposed that "the left mid-fusiform gyrus normally has two roles in reading: (1) Computation of location and modality independent grapheme sequences from written word stimuli, and (2), a modality independent stage of lexical processing, that links modality specific input and output representations." They suggested that the VWFA is not necessary for the former function, because the right homologue of the VWFA can immediately assume this role.

A second important reason why we did not see differential responses between words, consonant strings, and false-fonts in the ROI placed in the VWFA (as defined by fMRI) may also be related to intrinsic differences between neuroimaging modalities. Specifically, while the appropriate fMRI contrasts for visually presented words tend to reveal a spatially restricted response in the mid-fusiform gyrus, as discussed earlier, most MEG and direct neurophysiological recordings in this area reveal the appearance of a progression, or sweep of activity along the fusiform gyrus over the course of 200–300 ms and whose spatial extent is considerably larger than that suggested by fMRI (e.g., Dhond et al., 2001; Marinkovic et al., 2003; Pammer et al., 2004; Alison et al., 1994). In part, this may be attributable to the more diffuse nature of the current estimates revealed by the minimum norm estimate as used in the Dhond et al. (2001) and Marincovic (2003) studies (see Auranen et al., 2005). Nevertheless, if true, the placement of a single electrode in the fMRI-defined "VWFA" can only reveal limited information with regard to a local neuronal population and may miss potential differences between stimuli that emerge more anteriorly and later in time.

Response Specificity: IFG

The left IFG gave a stronger response at 125 ms to words than faces, but responded equally strongly to false-fonts and consonant strings. The simplest way to interpret this pattern of results is to assume that the same stereotypical response to any equivalent length string of letter-like objects would always be produced, irrespective of task demands (i.e., whether explicit naming is required or whether stimuli are viewed passively as in the current experiment). If so, this might suggest that for a skilled reader who has had many thousands of hours of experience with print, the very presence of word-like stimuli in the visual field can trigger a response in the IFG, and its role is to prime the rest of the language system to prepare for upcoming cross-modal interactions between the vision and language systems—almost like a stimulus-driven anticipatory response. This proposal is similar to recent claims by Bar and colleagues (2006), who showed that low spatial frequencies can facilitate visual object recognition by initiating top-down processes projected from orbitofrontal to visual cortex; object recognition elicited differential activity that developed in the left orbitofrontal cortex 50 ms earlier than it did in recognition-related areas in the temporal cortex.

An alternative possibility is that early IFG activation in response to visually presented words reflects grapheme-to-phoneme conversion processes, perhaps along a sublexical route for reading (Coltheart et al., 1993; Harm & Seidenberg, 2004). According to this argument, what we would normally expect to see early in the IFG is a stronger response to words than to consonant strings or false-fonts when there is an explicit requirement for naming. The reason that we did not see the expected difference was due to the particular requirements of the current experiment, namely no explicit engagement with the stimuli.

This interpretation, although speculative, is in line with other imaging studies that have implicated this frontal area in phonological processing during visual word recognition (Burton et al., 2005; Joubert et al., 2004), and with priming studies showing early activation of phonological representations (Carreiras et al., 2005; Lee et al., 1999; Lukatela et al., 1998; Lukatela & Turvey, 1994). Moreover, this possibility is in alignment with research on verbal short-term memory. Effects of word length and phonological similarity indicate that visually presented items, such as letters or numerals, are recoded into phonological form prior to storage in short-term memory (Baddeley, 1986; Conrad & Hull, 1964). Articulatory suppression removes the phonological similarity effect, indicating the importance of articulatory processes for such recoding (Baddeley, 1986). Indeed, an fMRI study showed activation of the IFG, inferior parietal cortex, and posterior temporal cortex in response to working memory for letters versus abstract symbols (Henson et al., 2000). Imaging studies have indicated that inferior parietal cortex encodes the phonological information itself, providing the so-called phonological store (Baddeley, 1986), whereas the IFG also controls the rehearsal process via reactivation of information within the phonological store (Awh et al., 1996; Henson et al., 2000; Paulesu et al., 1993). Thus, it appears that visual information is recoded into an articulatory–phonological form in IFG, which activates an auditory–phonological representation in the inferior parietal cortex, which in turn activates lexical forms in the temporal cortex (Henson et al., 2000). We suggest that this same pathway may also comprise the sublexical route in visual word recognition.

However, this interpretation, coupled with our timing data, presents a conundrum. The sublexical route would require an abstract encoding of letter order. The standard interpretation of VWFA functionality is that it provides such an encoding (Dehaene et al., 2004; McCandliss, Cohen, & Dehaene, 2003, Hillis et al., 2005). However, our data indicate that the IFG is activated *prior to* the VWFA. If the VWFA encodes letter order, and such information is required by the IFG to perform grapheme–phoneme conversion, how could IFG activation precede VWFA activation?

The account of visual word recognition presented by Whitney and Cornelissen (2005) may provide an answer to this question. Based on the Sequential Encoding Regulated by Inputs to Oscillations within Letter units (SERIOL) model of letter-position encoding (Whitney, 2001), it was proposed that a serial representation of letter order provides input to both the lexical and sublexical routes. This encoding of individual letters is instantiated in the posterior fusiform, while the VWFA (mid fusiform) encodes the spatial relationships between letter pairs (open bigrams) (Grainger & Whitney, 2004). The open-bigram representation is taken to be specific to the visual/ lexical route. Thus, the posterior fusiform representation provides input to both the IFG and the VWFA, with no requirement for VWFA activation to precede IFG activation.

This proposal is consistent with a range of evidence. Imaging studies have associated the middle fusiform with lexical retrieval and the posterior fusiform with pseudoword processing (Dietz et al., 2005; Mechelli et al., 2005; Mechelli, Gorno-Tempini, & Price, 2003). Lesion studies of Japanese kanji (ideograms) versus kana (phonetic writing) show that damage to the VWFA preferentially affects the interpretation of kanji, whereas damage to the posterior occipital gyri preferentially affects the reading of kana (Sakurai et al., 2006). These results indicate that the VWFA may be involved in mapping whole-word visual representations to lexical items, while the orthographic representation supporting phonological processing is located more posteriorly.

Non–phase-locked Activity

Intriguingly, we found a non–phase-locked component in both the left and right IFG that was apparent even during stimulus presentation. This suggests that there was some component of the experimental task that required ongoing neural processing, unrelated to the processing of the briefly presented stimuli themselves. The idea that the same ROI could pick up evoked and induced activity from the same site, and that different populations of neurones in the same region may therefore make different contributions to cognitive function is not new. For example, Simpson and associates (2005) used MEG to examine the dynamic patterns of neural activity underlying the auditory steady-state response. They examined the continuous time series of responses to a 32 Hz amplitude modulation. Simpson and associates (2005) used mutual information (i.e., the decrease in entropy [or uncertainty] when two distributions are considered jointly rather than in isolation) to measure nonlinear interdependence between frequency bands both within and between two dipole sources, one in each of the left and right primary auditory cortices. They found that fluctuations in the amplitude of the evoked response were mediated by nonlinear interactions with oscillatory processes both at the same source in separate α- and β-frequency bands, and in the opposite hemisphere. Thus, neurons in the left auditory cortex either shared information between the α- and β-frequency bands at the same site, or they shared information with the right auditory cortex in the same frequency band (α or β).

A number of recent studies have suggested that the posterior superior IFG serves other motor functions in addition to speech, and that "it may also play a more general role in motor control by interfacing external information on the external motor representations of hand/arm and mouth actions" (Fink et al., 2006). To support this claim, Fink and colleagues (2006) enumerate a number of neuroimaging experiments that showed activation of the IFG including: (a) both the overt and covert production of actions (Bonda et al., 1995; Parsons et al., 1995); (b) mental imagery of grasping movements (Decety et al., 1994); (c) preparation of finger movements to copy a target movement (Toni et al., 1998); and (d) during imagery and execution of visually guided movements (Binkoski et al., 2000; Stephan et al., 1995). In addition Fink and colleagues (2006) point out that, as part of the "mirror neurone" system, the pars opercularis of the IFG is activated "during the observation and recognition of actions performed by others (Rizzolatti et al., 1996) and in the observation and subsequent imitation of actions (Buccino et al., 2004)." Finally, not only has the pars opercularis of the IFG been demonstrated to play a role in "cognitive control" (Snyder, Feigenson, & Thompson-Schill, 2007) but also in local visual search tasks. In the latter example, participants were asked to judge whether a simple figure was embedded in a more complex figure, as compared with judging whether a simple figure matched a highlighted portion of a more complex figure (Fink et al., 2006). Therefore, we suggest that the non–phase-locked component of the IFG activity we saw may have been related to the task requirement to maintain fixation and monitor changes in the color of the fixation cross.

Conclusion

On the basis of this focused review, it is clear that MEG can reveal not only the sequence of cortical activations underlying visual word recognition, but also the dynamic interplay between the nodes of the cortical network. It is also clear that MEG data show both similarities and differences when compared to fMRI. This poses a challenge for integrating information from both modalities. Crucially, these recent results from MEG and EEG/ERP strongly suggest that visual word recognition involves very early interactions between the vision and language domains in skilled adult readers.

References

Achim, A., Alain, C., Richer, F., & Saint-Hilaire, J.M. (1988). A test of model adequacy applied to the dimensionality of multi-channel average auditory evoked potentials. In: D. Samson-Dollfus (Ed.). *Statistics and topography in quantitative EEG*, Amsterdam: Elsevier, 161–171.

Allison, T., McCarthy, G., Nobre, A., Puce, A., & Bolger, A. (1994). Human extrastriate visual cortex and the perception of faces, words, numbers and colors. *Cerebral Cortex, 4*, 544–554.

Assadollahi, R., & Pulvermüller, F. (2003). Early influences of word length and frequency: a group study using MEG. *NeuroReport, 14*, 1183–1187.

Auranen, T., Nummenmaa, A., Hämäläinen, M.S., Jääskeläinen, I.P., Lampinen, J., Vehtari, A., & Sama, M. (2005). Bayesian analysis of the neuromagnetic inverse problem with the l^p-norm priors, *Neuroimage, 26*, 870–884.

Awh, E., Jonides, J., Smith, E.E., Schumacher, E.H., Koeppe, R.A., & Katz, S. (1996). Dissociation of storage and rehearsal in verbal working memory: Evidence from positron emission tomography. *Psychological Science, 7*, 25–31.

Baddeley, A.D. (1986). *Working memory.* Oxford, UK: Oxford University Press.

Bar, M., Kassam, K.S., Ghuman, A.S., Boshyan, J., Schmid, A.M., Dale, A.M., et al. (2006). Top-down facilitation of visual recognition. *PNAS, 103*, 449–454.

Ben-Sachar, M., Dougherty, R.F., Deutsch, G.K., & Wandell, B.A. (2006). Differential sensitivity to words and shapes in ventral occipito-temporal cortex. *Cerebral Cortex* (in press).

Bokde, A.L., Tagamets, M. A., Friedman, R.B., & Horwitz, B. (2001). Functional interactions of the inferior frontal cortex during the processing of words and word-like stimuli. *Neuron, 30*, 609–617.

Bonda, E., Petrides, M., Frey, S., & Evans, A.C. (1995). Neural correlates of mental transformations of the body-ib-space, *PNAS, 92*, 11180–11184.

Bookheimer, S. (2002). Functional MRI of language: New approaches to understanding the cortical organization of semantic processing. *Annual Review of Neuroscience, 25*, 151–188.

Brewer, A.A., Liu, J.J., Wade, A.R., & Wandell, B.A. (2005). Visual field maps and stimulus selectivity in human ventral occipital cortex. *Nature Neuroscience, 8*, 1102–1109.

Buccino, G., Vogt, S., Ritzl, A., Fink, G.R., Zilles, K., Freund, H-J., & Rizzolatti, G. (2004) Neural circuits underlying imitation learning of hand actions: An event-related fMRI study. *Neuron, 42,* 2, 323–334.

Büchel, C., Price, C., & Friston, K. (1998). A multimodal language region in the ventral visual pathway. *Nature, 394,* , 6690, 274–277.

Bürgel, U., Amunts, K., Hoemke, L., Mohlberg, H., Gilsbach, J.M., & Zilles, K. (2006). White matter fibre tracts of the human brain: Three-dimensional mapping at microscopic resolution, topography and intersubject variability. *Neuroimage, 29,* 1092–1105.

Burton, M.W., LoCasto, P.C., Krebs-Noble, D., & Gullapalli, R.P. (2005). A systematic investigation of the functional neuroanatomy of auditory and visual phonological processing. *Neuroimage, 26,* 647–661.

Cohen, L., Dehaene, S., Naccache, L., Lehericy, S., Dehaene-Lambertz, G., Henaff, M.A., & Michel, F. (2000). The visual word form area: spatial and temporal characterization of an initial stage of reading in normal subjects and posterior split-brain patients. *Brain, 123* (Pt 2), 291–307.

Coltheart, M., Curtis, B., Atkins, P., & Haller, M. (1993). Models of Reading Aloud - Dual-Route and Parallel-Distributed-Processing Approaches. *Psychological Review, 100,* 589–608.

Conrad, R., & Hull, A. J. (1964). Information, acoustic confusion and memory span. *British Journal of Psychology, 55,* 429–432.

Cornelissen, P.L., Tarkiainen, A., Helenius, P., & Salmelin, R. (2003). Cortical effects of shifting letter-position in letter-strings of varying length. *Journal of Cognitive Neuroscience,* 15, 5, 731–748.

Davis, C. J. (1999). *The self-organising lexical acquisition and recognition (SOLAR) model of visual word recognition*. Unpublished doctoral dissertation, University of New South Wales.

Decety, J., Perani, D., Jeannerod, M., Bettinard, V., Tadardy, B., Woods, R., et al. (1994). Mapping motor representations with positron emission tomography. *Nature, 371,* 600–602.

Dehaene, S., Le Clec, H.G., Poline, J.B., Le Bihan, D., & Cohen, L. (2002). The visual word form area: a prelexical representation of visual words in the fusiform gyrus. *Neuroreport, 13,* 321–325.

Dehaene, S., Jobert, A., Naccache, L., Ciuciu, P., Poline, J.B., Le Bihan, D., & Cohen, L. (2004). Letter binding and invariant recognition of masked words: behavioral and neuroimaging evidence. *Psychological Science, 15,* 307–313.

Dehaene, S., Cohen, L., Sigman, M., & Vinckier, F. (2005). The neural code for written words: a proposal. *Trends in Cognitive Sciences, 9,* 335–341.

Dejerine, J. (1895). *Anatomie des centres nerveux*. Paris: Rueff et Cie (repr. 1980, Masson).

Devlin, J.T., Jamison, H.L., Gonnerman, L.M., & Matthew, P.M. (2006). The role of the posterior fusiform gyrus in reading. *Journal of Cognitive Neuroscience, 18,* 6, 911–922.

Dhond, R.P., Buckner, R.L., Dale, A.M., Marinkovic, K., & Halgren, E. (2001). Spatiotemporal maps of brain activity underlying word generation and their modification during repetition priming. *Journal of Neuroscience, 21,* 10, 3564–3571.

DiVirgilio, G., & Clarke, S. (1997). Direct interhemispheric visual input to human speech areas. *Human Brain Mapping, 5,* 347–354.

Dougherty, R.F., Koch, V.M., Brewer, A.A., Fischer, B., Modersitzki, J., & Wandell, B.A. (2003). Visual field representations and locations of visual areas V1/2/3 in human visual cortex. *Journal of Vision, 3,* 586–598.

Fiebach, C. J., Friederici, A.D., Muller, K., & von Cramon, D.Y. (2002). fMRI evidence for dual routes to the mental lexicon in visual word recognition. *Journal of Cognitive Neuroscience, 14*, 11–23.

Fiez, J.A., & Petersen, S.E. (1998). Neuroimaging studies of word reading. *Proceedings of the National Academy of Sciences of the United States of America, 95*, 914–921.

Fink, G.R., Manjaly, Z.M., Stephan, K.E., Gurd, J.M., Zilles, K., Amunts, K., & Marshall, J.C. (2006). A role for Broca's area beyond language processing: evidence from neuropsychology and fMRI. In Y. Grodzinsky & K. Amunts (Eds.). *Broca's Region.* New York: Oxford University Press.

Grainger, J., & Whitney, C. (2004). Does the huamn mnid raed wrods as a wlohe? *Trends in Cognitive Sciences, 8*, 58–59.

Greenlee, J.D. W., Oya, H., Kawasaki, H., Volkov, I.O., Kaufman, O.P., Kovach, C., et al. (2004). A functional connection between inferior frontal gyrus and orofacial motor cortex in human. *Journal of Neurophysiology, 92*, 1153–1164.

Hämäläinen, M., & Ilmoniemi, R. (1984). Interpreting measured magnetic fields of the brain: estimates of current distributions. Technical Report, Helsinki University of Technology, TKK-F-A559.

Harm, M.W., & Seidenberg, M.S. (2004). Computing the meanings of words in reading: Cooperative division of labor between visual and phonological processes. *Psychological Review, 111*, 662–720.

Hauk, O., Davis, M.H., Ford, M., Pulvermüller, F., & Marslen-Wilson W.D. (2006). The time course of visual word recognition as revealed by linear regression analysis of ERP data. *Neuroimage, 30*, 1383–1400.

Helenius, P., Tarkiainen, A., Cornelissen, P.L., Hansen, P.C., & Salmelin, R. (1999). Dissociation of normal feature analysis and deficient processing of letter-strings in dyslexic adults. *Cerebral Cortex, 9*, 476–483.

Helenius, P., Salmelin, R., Service, E., & Connolly, J.F. (1998). Distinct time courses of word and sentence comprehension in the left temporal cortex. *Brain, , 121*, 1133–42.

Henson, R.N.A., Burgess, N., & Frith, C.D. (2000). Recoding, storage, rehearsal and grouping in verbal short-term memory: an fMRI study. *Neuropsychologia, 38*, 426–440.

Hillebrand, A. & Barnes, G.R. (2005). Beamformer analysis of MEG data. *Magnetoencephalography International Review of Neurobiology, 68*: 149.

Hillis, A.E., Newhart, M., Heidler, J., Barker, P., Herskovits, E., & Degaonkar, M. (2005). The roles of the "visual word form area" in reading. *Neuroimage, 24*, 548–559.

Joubert, S., Beauregard, M., Walter, N., Bourgouin, P., Beaudoin, G., Leroux, J.M., et al. (2004). Neural correlates of lexical and sublexical processes in reading. *Brain and Language, 89*, 9–20.

Kober, H., Möller, M., Nimsky, C., Vieth, J., Fahlbusch, R., & Ganslandt, O. (2001). New approach to localize speech relevant brain areas and hemispheric dominance using spatially filtered magnetoencephalography. *Human Brain Mapping, 14*, 236–250.

Kujala, J., Pammer, K., Cornelissen, P.L., Roebroeck, P., Formisano, E., & Salmelin, R. (2007). Phase coupling in a cerebro-cerebellar network at 8–13Hz during reading. *Cerebral Cortex, 17*, 1476–1485.

Lavidor M., & Walsh, V. (2004). The nature of foveal representation. *Nature Reviews Neurosci., 5*, 729–735.

Lavidor, M., Ellis, A.W., Shillcock, R., & Bland, T. (2001). Evaluating a split processing model of visual word recognition: effect of word length. *Cognitive Brain Research, 12*, 265–272.

Lee, H.W., Rayner, K., & Pollatsek, A. (1999). The time course of phonological, semantic, and orthographic coding in reading: Evidence from the fast-priming technique. *Psychonomic Bulletin & Review, 6*, 624–634.

Lukatela, G., Carello, C., Savic, M., Urosevic, Z., & Turvey, M.T. (1998). When nonwords activate semantics better than words. *Cognition, 68*, B31-B40.

Lukatela, G., & Turvey, M.T. (1994). Visual lexical access is initially phonological. 2. Evidence from phonological priming by homophones and pseudohomophones. *Journal of Experimental Psychology-General, 123*, 331–353.

Makris, N., Kennedy, D.N., McInerney, S., Sorensen, G.A., Wang, R., Caviness, V.S., & Pandya, D.N. (2005). Segmentation of subcomponents within the superior long-itudinal fascicle in humans: a quantative, in vivo, DT-MRI study. *Cebrebral Cortex, 15*, 854–869.

Marinkovic, K., Dhond, R.P., Dale, A.M., Glessner, M., Carr, V., & Halgren, E. (2003). Spatiotemporal dynamics of modality specific and supramodel word processing. *Neuron, 38*, 487–497.

Martin-Loeches, M., Hinojosa, J.A., Gomez-Jarabo, G., & Rubia, F.J. (1999). The recognition potential: an ERP index of lexical access. *Brain & Language, , 70,* 364–384.

McCandliss, B.D., Cohen, L., & Dehaene, S. (2003). The visual word form area: expertise for reading in the fusiform gyrus. *Trends in Cognitive Sciences, 7*, 293–299.

Mechelli, A., Crinion, J.T., Lons, S., Friston, K.J., Lambon Ralph, M.A., Patterson, K., et al. (2005). Dissociating reading processes on the basis of neuronal interactions. *Journal of Cognitive Neuroscience, 17*, 1753–1765.

Monaghan, P., Shillcock, R., & McDonald, S. (2004). Hemispheric asymmetries in the split-fovea model of semantic processing. *Brain and Language, 88,* 3, 339–354.

Nazir, T.A., Ben-Boutayab, N., Decoppet, N., Deutsch, A., & Frost, R. (2004). Reading habits, perceptual learning, and recognition of printed words. *Brain and Language, 88*, 294–311.

Nobre, A.C., Allison, T., & McCarthy, G. (1994). Word Recognition in the Human Inferior Temporal-Lobe. *Nature, 372*, 260–263.

Pammer, K., Hansen, P.C., Kringelbach, M.L., Holliday, I., Barnes, G., Hillebrand, A., Singh, K.D., & Cornelissen, P.L. (2004). Visual word recognition: the first half second. *Neuroimage, 22*, 1819–1825.

Parsons, L.M., Fox, P.T., Hunter Downs, J., Glass, T., Hirsch, T.B., Martin, C.C., et al. (1995). Use of implicit motor imagery for visual shape discrimination as revealed by PET. *Nature, 375*, 54–58.

Patton, H.D. (1982). Special properties of nerve trunks and tracts, pp. 101–127. In T. Ruch & H.D. Patton (Eds.). *Physiology and biophysics.* Vol. 4. Philadelphia: WB Saunders.

Paulesu, E., Frith, C.D., & Frackowiak, R.S.J. (1993). The Neural Correlates of the Verbal Component of Working Memory. *Nature, 362*, 342–345.

Phillips, J.A., Humphreys, G.W., Noppeney, U., & Price, C.J. (2002). The neural substrates of action retrieval: an examination of semantic and visual routes to action. *Vision and Cognition, 9*(4), 662–684.

Polk, T.A., & Farah, M.J. (1998). The neural development and organization of letter recognition: Evidence from functional neuroimaging, computational modeling, and behavioral studies. *PNAS, 95*, 3, 847–852.

Price, C.J., & Devlin, J.T. (2003). The myth of the visual word form area. *Neuroimage, 19*, 473–481.

Price, C.J., Winterburn, D., Giraud, A.L., Moore, C.J., & Noppeney, U. (2003). Cortical localization of the visual and auditory word form areas: A reconsideration of the evidence. *Brain and Language, 86*, 2, 272–286.

Pugh, K.R., Shaywitz, B.A., Shaywitz, S.E., Constable, R.T., Skudlarski, P., Fulbright, R. K., et al. (1996). Cerebral organization of component processes in reading. *Brain, 119,* 1221–1238.

Pugh, K.R., Shaywitz, B.A., Shaywitz, S.E., Shankweiler, D.P., Katz, L., Fletcher, J.M., et al. (1997). Predicting reading performance from neuroimaging profiles: The cerebral basis of phonological effects in printed word identification. *Journal of Experimental Psychology-Human Perception and Performance, 23,* 299–318.

Pulvermüller, F., Lutzenberger, W., Birbaumer, N. (1995). Electrocortical distinction of vocabulary types. *Electroencephalogram in Clinical Neurophysiology, , 94,* 357–370.

Pulvermüller, F., Assadollahi, R., & Elbert, T. (2001). Neuromagnetic evidence for early semantic access in word recognition. *European Journal of Neuroscience, 13,* 201– 205.

Rizzolatti, G., Fadiga, L., Matelli, M., Bettinardi, V., Paulesu, E., Perani, D., et al. (1996) Location of grasp representations in humans by PET. 1. Observation versus execution. *Experimental Brain Research, 111,* 246–252.

Robinson, S.E., & Vrba, J. (1999). Functional neuroimaging by synthetic aperture magnetometry (SAM). In T. Yoshimoto, M. Kotani, S. Kuriki, H. Karibe, & N. Nakasato (Eds.). *Recent Advances in Biomagnetism,* pp. 302–305.. Sendai: Tohoku University Press.

Sakurai, Y., Yagashita, A., Goto, Y., Ohtsu, H., & Mannen, T. (2006). Fusiform type alexia: pure alexia for words in contrast to posterior occipital type pure alexia for letters. *Journal of Neurological Science, 247,* 81–92.

Salmelin, R., Service, E., Kiesila, P., Uutela, K., & Salonen, O. (1996). Impaired visual word processing in dyslexia revealed with magnetoencephalography. *Annals of Neurology,* 40, 157–162.

Salmelin R., Schnitzler, A., Schmitz, F., & Freund, H-J. (2000). Single word reading in developmental stutterers and fluent speakers. *Brain, 123,* 1184–1202.

Sekihara, K., Nagarajan, S.S., Poeppel, D., & Marantz, A. (2002). Performance of an MEG adaptive-beamformer technique in the presence of correlated neural activities: effects on signal intensity and time-course estimates. *IEEE Trans Biomedical Engineering, 49,* 1534–1546.

Sereno, S.C., Rayner, K., & Posner, M.I. (1998). Establishing a time-line of word recognition: evidence from eye movements and event-related potentials. *NeuroReport, 9,* 2195–2200.

Simpson, M.I.G., Hadjipapas, A., Barnes, G.R., Furlong, P.L., & Witton, C. (2005). Imaging the dynamics of the auditory steady-state evoked response. *Neuroscience Letters, , 385,* 195–197.

Snyder, H.R., Feigenson, K., & Thompson-Schill, S. (2007). Prefrontal cortical response to conflict during semantic and phonological tasks. *Journal of Cognitive Neuroscience, 19,* 5, 761–775.

Stephan, K.M., Fink, G.R., Passingham, R.E., Silbersweig, D.A., Ceballos-Baumann, A.O., Frith, C.D. et al. (1995). Imagining the execution of movements. Functional anatomy of the mental representation of upper extremity movements in healthy subjects. *Journal of Neurophysiology, 73,* 373–386.

Tarkiainen, A., Helenius, P., Hansen, P.C., Cornelissen, P.L. & Salmelin, R. (1999) Dynamics of letter-string perception in the human occipito-temporal cortex. *Brain, 122,* 11, 2119–2131.

Tarkiainen A., Cornelissen P.L., & Salmelin, R. (2002). Dynamics of visual feature analysis and object-level processing in face vs. letter-string perception. *Brain, 125,* 1125–1136.

Toni, I., Krams, M., Turner, R., & Passingham, R.E. (1998). The time course of changes during motor learning: a whole brain fMRI study. *Neuroimage*, *8*, 50–61.

Uutela, K., Hämäläinen, M., & Somersalo, E. (1999). Visualization of magnetoencephalographic data using minimum current estimates. *NeuroImage*, *10*, 173–180.

Van Veen, B.D., van Drongelen, W., Yuchtman, M., & Suzuki, A. (1997). Localization of brain electrical activity via linearly constrained minimum variance spatial filtering. *IEEE Trans Biomedical Engineering*, , *44*, 867–880.

Vigneau, M., Jobard, G., Mazoyer, B., & Tzourio-Mazoyer, N. (2005). Word and non-word reading: What role for the visual word form area? *Neuroimage*, *27*, 694–705.

Vrba, J., & Robinson, S.E. (2001). Signal processing in magnetoencephalography. *Methods*, *25*, 249–271.

Whitney, C. (2001). How the brain encodes the order of letters in a printed word: The SERIOL model and selective literature review. *Psychonomic Bulletin & Review*, *8*, 221–243.

Whitney, C., & Cornelissen, P. (2005). Letter-position encoding and dyslexia. *Journal of Research in Reading*, *28*, 274–301.

III

IMPAIRED READING

9

Anatomical and Functional Correlates of Acquired Peripheral Dyslexias

Laurent Cohen, Fabien Vinckier, and Stanislas Dehaene

The acquisition of literacy over years of education rests on the development of elaborate links between vision and language. On the one hand, the visual system learns to rapidly identify strings of ordered letters across a wide range of shapes and viewing conditions. On the other hand, the verbal system learns how to segment explicitly the speech stream into discrete units, such as syllables and phonemes (Morais & Kolinsky, 1994). Associations are established between letter strings and sounds, which allows the reader to sound out newly encountered letter combinations, and between letter strings and lexical entries in memory, which allows the reader to access the stored knowledge attached to familiar words. Moreover, beyond the processing of single words, reading expertise includes the ability to rapidly scan and integrate pages of connected text.

The efficiency of the visual system of literate adults during reading reflects its ability to identify rapidly and in parallel arrays of several letters. Indeed, reading latencies are fairly constant irrespective of word length, at least within a range of about three to six letters (Lavidor & Ellis, 2002; Weekes, 1997) (Fig. 9.1). This perceptual ability takes about 5 years of instruction to develop, and an effect of word length persists at least to the age of 10 (Aghababian & Nazir, 2000). In addition to the processing of foveal strings of letters, text reading also requires the ability to explore sequentially arrays of words, on the basis of parafoveal vision, attentional scanning, and oculomotor control (Sereno & Rayner, 2003).

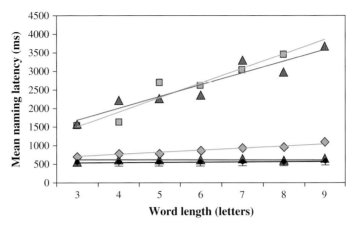

Figure 9.1 Normal controls (*black*) show almost no influence of word length on reading latencies. Patient D., who had a posterior callosal lesion, but an intact visual word form area (VWFA) and no hemianopia showed a normal pattern (*blue*). Patient M., who had an intact VWFA and right hemianopia, showed a moderate length effect (*green*). Patients F. (*magenta*) and A. (*yellow*), whose VWFA was lesioned, read words letter-by-letter, with a slope of over 300 ms per letter.

The breakdown of the visual component of expert reading following brain lesions in literate adults results in a variety of impairments collectively known as *peripheral dyslexias*, as opposed to the so-called *central dyslexias*. The latter affect later stages of word reading, such as grapheme–phoneme conversion or lexical access, and include cognitive syndromes such as surface and phonological dyslexia. As for peripheral dyslexias, they may be best understood by referring to the general principles of organization of the brain visual system, particularly to the gross dichotomy between the ventral "What" system devoted to shape processing and object recognition, and the dorsal "Where" system subtending spatial and attentional processing (Ungerleider & Mishkin, 1982). This dichotomy prompts a distinction between ventral and dorsal peripheral dyslexias, to which one may adjoin dyslexias caused by visual field defects following lesions of early visual pathways. Lesions affecting those systems may impinge on the processing of single foveal words, but also on the scanning of lines and pages of text.

Accounting for the behavioral diversity of peripheral dyslexias and for their anatomical and functional underpinnings is a benchmark for any model of word reading. The aim of this chapter is to confront a simple anatomical and functional scheme for the architecture of the reading system, with multimodal data from patients with various deficits affecting the visual stages of word processing. It should be clear that the proposed architecture is relevant only to the visual stages of reading and stops where central processes start. A further limitation to the scope of the chapter is that both our proposal and our empirical data are mostly concerned with word processing in the ventral visual system, and pure alexia will therefore receive disproportionate attention relative to other peripheral reading disorders. We will first outline the proposed architecture for reading, then sketch an overview of peripheral dyslexias, and eventually consider how the model may account for behavioral, anatomical, and functional observations in patients with varieties of alexia.

A Simple Scheme for the Cooperation of Ventral and Dorsal Visual Pathways During Reading

Early Retinotopic Processing and Perceptual Asymmetry

The first stage of visual word processing is the analysis of letters in retinotopic areas, with each half of foveal words being processed in the contralateral hemisphere (Fig. 9.2). Visual input is represented in increasingly abstract and invariant format through areas V1 to V4 (see Chapter 5 for a detailed neural model). The activation of such areas, located between about Talairach coordinates (TC) $y = -90$ and $y = -70$, is modulated by physical parameters such as word length, visual contrast (Mechelli , Humphreys, Mayall, Olson, & Price, 2000), stimulus degradation (Helenius, Tarkiainen, Cornelissen, Hansen, & Salmelin, 1999; Jernigan , Ostergaard, Law, Svarer, Gerlach, & Paulson., 1998), and stimulus rate and duration (Price & Friston, 1997; Price, Moore, & Frackowiak, 1996a).

There are indications, mostly behavioral, that perceptual word processing differs between the left and right hemifields, which may reflect differences between visual analysis in the right (RH) and in the left hemisphere (LH). At a basic level, the visual reading span of about ten letters (Rayner & Bertera, 1979) is not distributed equally across both hemifields, as letter identification performance decreases more slowly with eccentricity in the right visual field (RVF) than in the left visual field (LVF) (Nazir, Jacobs, & O'Regan, 1998). This asymmetry may contribute to the overall RVF advantage; that is, shorter latencies and higher accuracy with RVF than with LVF words (Chiarello, 1988; Cohen et al., 2002; Lavidor, Babkoff, & Faust, 2001a). Moreover, the absence of a word length effect on reading latencies is restricted to optimal viewing conditions, such as free foveal reading of horizontally displayed stimuli (Lavidor & Ellis, 2002; Lavidor, Ellis, Shillcock, & Bland, 2001b). In such conditions, the optimal gaze position for reading is slightly left of the word center (Nazir, 2000), suggesting that parallel processing is mostly a property of the RVF. Indeed, split-field studies show that, although there is no length effect for words displayed in the RVF, at least close to the fovea, such an effect emerges whenever words are displayed in the LVF (Lavidor & Ellis, 2002). Accordingly, when words extend across central fixation, only their left part induces a length effect (Lavidor et al., 2001b). As one possible correlate of this perceptual asymmetry, we found a left extrastriate

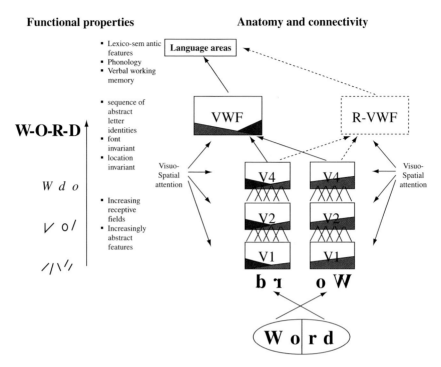

Figure 9.2 Model of the visual word processing system. Letters are first analyzed through a cascade of contralateral areas ranging from V1 to V4, which compute increasingly abstract representations. Eventually, an invariant representation of letter identities is created in the visual word form area (VWFA), located within the left occipitotemporal sulcus. The VWFA then projects to structures involved in phonological or lexico-semantic processing. Spatial attention (here represented by dark and light gray gradients) modulates the operation of all levels of word processing up to the VWFA, with a right-hemispheric predominance. The right-hemispheric region symmetrical to the VWFA (R-VWFA) is thought to subtend residual letter identification in patients with letter-by-letter reading. Letter identities are then transferred to language areas across the corpus callosum.

region (TC –24, –78, –12) only responsive to RVF stimuli, which showed stronger activation by alphabetic strings than by checkerboards, while no such difference was observed in corresponding RH extrastriate areas (Cohen et al., 2002). This may suggest that this LH region has developed greater perceptual abilities for RVF script than its RH counterpart for LVF stimuli.

The left and right visual systems also differ in their tendency to represent alphabetic characters in a format invariant for specific case and font. A number of studies, using mostly priming tasks with split-field stimuli, have shown that alphabetic strings are encoded in a format less dependent on physical shape and case when they are viewed in the RVF than in the LVF (Burgund & Marsolek, 1997; Marsolek, Kosslyn, & Squire, 1992; Marsolek, Schacter, & Nicholas,

1996), probably reflecting nonspecific processing asymmetries in the visual system (Burgund & Marsolek, 2000; Marsolek, 1995). Accordingly, using a masked priming paradigm, Dehaene and colleagues (2001) have evidenced case-specific physical repetition priming in the right extrastriate cortex (although similar regions were also present in left extrastriate at a lower threshold). In summary, there are indications that the left posterior visual system is crucial for important features of expert reading, namely the fast and parallel computation of abstract letter identities.

Left Visual Word Form Area

Invariant word recognition ultimately requires the computation of the *visual word form* (VWF), a representation of abstract letter identities invariant for parameters such as spatial position, size, font, or case. On the basis of brain imaging evidence, we have proposed that this representation is subtended by a definite cortical region in Brodmann's area 37, the so-called *visual word form area* (VWFA). Note that we refer to this region as the VWFA for the sake of simplicity, although it should be clear that this denomination rests on functional hypotheses that are still open to debate (McCandliss, Cohen, & Dehaene, 2003) and that it might comprise several hierarchically organized subregions (Vinckier et al., 2007) (see Chapter 5). This region, which activates about 170–200 ms after stimulation (Tarkiainen, Helenius, Hansen, Cornelissen, & Salmelin, 1999), is reproducibly located within the occipitotemporal sulcus bordering the left fusiform gyrus laterally (for a review of activations see Cohen et al., 2000). Following the scheme proposed by Malach and colleagues (2002), the VWFA is a subdivision of the ventral occipitotemporal cortex devoted to high-order object perception, with other subdivisions showing preferences for categories such as faces or buildings (Ishai, Ungerleider, Martin, Schouten, & Haxby, 1999; Kanwisher, McDermott, & Chun, 1997). Thus, the VWFA is activated by alphabetic strings relative to fixation but also relative to complex nonalphabetic stimuli such as false-fonts, faces, or geometrical patterns (e.g., Cohen et al., 2002; Price, Wise, & Frackowiak., 1996b; Puce, Allison, Asgari, Gore, & McCarthy, 1996). The VWFA is activated by visual words irrespective of their position in the visual field (Cohen et al., 2000) and represents alphabetic stimuli in an abstract graphemic format. Using the masked priming paradigm mentioned before, Dehaene and colleagues (2001) have shown a reduced activation of the VWFA whenever a target word is primed by the subliminal presentation of the same word. Importantly, this effect prevails whether the prime and the target are printed in the same or in different cases.

Those functional properties of the VWFA may result from more general features of inferotemporal neurons, already present in monkeys, such as preference for semicomplex shapes analogous to letters (Tanaka, 1996), invariance for viewing conditions (Booth & Rolls, 1998; Grill-Spector, Kushnir, Edelman, Avidan, Itzchak, & Malach, 1999), or preference for foveal stimuli (Levy, Hasson, Avidan, Hendler, & Malach, 2001). One may even speculate that the equivalence between upper- and lowercase letters is afforded by the property of inferotemporal neurons to establish links between stimuli with arbitrary but cognitively meaningful connections (Sakai & Miyashita, 1991). In the same vein, the binding of letters into words might be related to the representation of complex objects in inferotemporal cortex through the coactivation of neurons tuned to their elementary parts (Tsunoda, Yamane, Nishizaki, & Tanifuji, 2001).

Afferents and Efferents of the Visual Word Form Area

The transfer of visual information from lower-order retinotopic cortices to the VWFA takes place within the LH for stimuli displayed in the RVF. For LVF stimuli, information is conveyed from the right to the left ventral occipitotemporal cortex through interhemispheric fiber tracts that course in the splenium of the corpus callosum and over the posterior horns of the lateral ventricles (Binder & Mohr, 1992; Molko et al., 2002). The output projections of the VWFA to systems involved in lexical, semantic, motor, or phonological processes are less clearly defined. Following the observation of cases of alexia with agraphia, Dejerine (1892) suggested that the next step following visual word processing would be the angular gyrus, which he postulated to be the "visual center of letters." Indeed, the angular gyrus is among those regions that may be activated during reading tasks (Price, 1997), and there are indications of a functional connectivity between the angular gyrus and the left fusiform gyrus at coordinates matching the VWFA (Horwitz, Rumsey, & Donohue, 1998). There is also a correlated activity in the region of the VWFA and in the left inferior frontal areas (Bokde, Tagamets, Friedman, & Horwitz, 2001). A further potential output pathway is to temporal regions anterior to the VWFA. These regions, which have been difficult to image with functional magnetic resonance imaging (fMRI) due to magnetic suscept- ibility artifacts, are probably involved in supramodal semantic processing (for a review see Giraud & Price, 2001; see also Kreiman, Koch, & Fried, 2000; Lambon Ralph, McClelland, Patterson, Galton, & Hodges, 2001).

Top-down Influences from the Dorsal System

The operation of ventral visual regions during word reading depends not only on the intrinsic features of stimuli, but also on attentional influences that may impinge on all processing levels, from striate cortex (Chawla, Rees, & Friston, 1999; Somers, Dale, Seiffert, & Tootell, 1999) to the ventral occipitotemporal areas (Kastner, De Weerd, Desimone, & Ungerleider, 1998). For instance, an increased activation of the VWFA during the perception of written words, perhaps modulated by top-down signals from frontal cortex, predicts a better storage of those words in memory (Wagner et al., 1998). In order to understand the variety of peripheral reading impairments that may follow parietal lesions, several stages should be distinguished in the attentional control of word reading.

Engagement of Attention

Due to the limited processing resources of the visual system, attention must be engaged in a definite window, in which words benefit from enhanced processing, while external items are filtered out (for a review, see Kastner & Ungerleider, 2000). The shaping of this window results from combined bottom-up and top-down influences, both involving parietofrontal networks (see, e.g., Peelen, Hesenfeld, & Theeuwes, 2004). Bottom-up factors mostly reflect the perceptual salience of stimuli and depend on simple features such as contrast or size, on Gestalt structure, on dissimilarity from distractors, and the like (Parkhurst, Law, & Niebur, 2002). Attention can also be automatically attracted to a given region of space by visual cues presented before the target word (Posner, Walker, Frierich, & Rafal, 1984). As for top-down influences, they correspond to a priori expectations regarding the next relevant word, particularly its spatial location (Treisman & Souther, 1986), but possibly also other features, such as color (Nobre, Allison, & McCarthy, 1998). Note that a prerequisite for the orientation of attention toward the relevant region of space is an accurate binding of objects with spatial locations, a function that also depends on the integrity of the parietal lobes (Friedman-Hill, Robertson, & Treisman, 1995).

In normal subjects, one may expect that an optimal bottom-up engagement of attention should be disturbed by alphabetic stimuli with poor Gestalt features. For instance, words with widely spaced letters would not be automatically embraced in the attentional window. Individual letters would not be grouped into a perceptual whole, but rather stand out as distinct objects competing for the attraction of attention (Cohen, Dehaene, Vinckier, Jobert, & Montavont, 2008). Similarly, a single large letter made up of smaller letters ("Navon stimuli") generally has precedence for the attraction of attention, and therefore interferes with the identification of the small letters (Navon, 1977). In contrast to bottom-up processes, which are dependent on the physical properties of stimuli, the top-down allocation of attention may be disturbed by tasks that imply a nonoptimal shaping of the attentional window. For instance, one can force a spread of attention over several words and thereby interfere with the identification of each individual word (Davis & Bowers, 2004; Treisman & Souther, 1986).

Processing in the Ventral Pathway and Beyond

The alphabetic stimuli that fall within the attentional window are processed in the ventral visual stream, as described before, so as to compute an ordered representation of abstract letter identities, the VWF. In normal subjects, the visual degradation of stimuli may prevent optimal word processing in the ventral pathway. For instance, reading low-contrast words (Legge, Ahn, Klitz, & Luebker, 1997), words printed in mIxEd case (Lavidor, 2002), vertically presented words (Bub & Lewine, 1988), or words displayed in the LVF (Lavidor & Ellis, 2002), induces an effect of word length on reading latencies. We suggest that these word length effects reflect a failure of optimal parallel letter processing in the ventral pathway and indicate the deployment of a serial process based on a coordination of dorsal and ventral processes.

Exactly when serial attention needs to be deployed for word reading may be partially under strategic control. It is likely to depend on whether the first pass of processing through the ventral system yields enough evidence to achieve the requested task. Indeed, beyond the computation of the VWF, word stimuli gain access to other neural codes outside the visual system, including phonology and lexico-semantic knowledge. Various lexical parameters, such as frequency or neighborhood structure, may affect the activation thresholds of such post-visual representations (Grainger & Jacobs, 1996; Morton, 1969). This may explain the influence of length on reading latencies for low-frequency words (Weekes, 1997). As discussed later, such words may have high lexical thresholds and therefore require further serial attentive processing before a response is generated, in order to supplement their initial parallel analysis in the ventral pathway.

Response Evaluation

In any chronometric task, subjects must evaluate the amount of information available and decide whether to respond. This decision process can be highly dependent on the task (e.g., reading aloud or speeded lexical decision), as different tasks may engage different representation codes and response criteria. The Multiple Read-Out Model (MROM) has been developed as an explicit implementation of such a versatile decision process (Grainger & Jacobs, 1996). It states that "a response in a given experimental task is generated (read out) when at least one of the codes appropriate for responding in that task reaches a critical activation level" (Jacobs, Rey, Ziegler, & Grainger, 1998). For instance, according to the MROM, a positive response decision would be taken in a lexical decision task if some criteria of lexical activation are reached before a temporal response deadline. If not, a negative response is produced. Whatever the actual evaluation functions, the important point in the context of reading impairments is that if information is not sufficient to respond after a first pass in the ventral stream, more information must be gathered by way of appropriate attentional strategies.

Reorienting of Attention and Accrual of Evidence

If the initial attentional setting does not allow the subject to produce a response, attention should be reoriented from the top-down in order to gather additional information about the target word. This reorienting may consist in moving or reshaping the spatial attentional window, or in shifting from one representation level to another (e.g., from the level of words to the level of letters, or from a global to a local level of organization). Subjects thus loop over the three previous processing stages until a response can be generated. This overall process is based on working memory processes, as it requires the reader to maintain, accumulate, and assemble information over durations in the order of several seconds.

Such iterations define active reading strategies, the clearest instance of which is letter-by-letter reading, in normal subjects or in brain-damaged patients. Basically, whenever fast parallel letter identification does not allow the reader to reach a reliable response, subjects engage in a serial reading process, as revealed particularly by an effect of length on reading latencies. For instance, reading aloud pseudowords probably requires the serial left-to-right conversion of graphemes into phonemes and the progressive build-up of a phonological string. The visual input must therefore be scanned serially, as revealed by a length effect (Weekes, 1997). We reviewed earlier a number of other situations in which such an effect emerges in normal readers, due to difficulties in attentional orientation, in the computation of the VWF, or in the activation of the target word in the lexicon. We propose here a unitary account of all occurrences of a length effect. Note however that the existence of a length effect does not necessarily imply serial letter processing, and that alternative theories have been put forward to account for instances for the length effect normally occurring in the LVF (Whitney & Lavidor, 2004). As discussed later, the most dramatic letter-by-letter reading effects occur in patients with lesions to the left-hemispheric ventral pathway. As a final point, the efficacy of the various processing stages may differ across subjects in proportion to their reading expertise, a source of variability that should be kept in mind when interpreting the performance of individual patients.

Expected Consequences of Parietal Lesions on Visual
Word Processing

Parietal damage may be expected to interfere with the operation of the ventral reading pathway for various reasons related to spatial and attentional processing, yielding a potential diversity of dyslexic symptoms. Potentially dissociated impairments may be expected for the coding of object position in space, for the control of saccades (Bisley & Goldberg, 2003), for the control of space-oriented attention (Gitelman et al., 1999), of object-oriented attention (Scholl, 2001), and of attention to global versus local features (Fink, Halligan, Marshall, Frith, Frackowiak, & Dolan, 1996; Weissman & Woldorff, 2004). Moreover, there are indications of a right hemispheric predominance for the control of spatial attention and the processing of global features, and of a left-hemispheric predominance for object-oriented attention (Egly, Driver, & Rafal, 1994) and the processing of local features.

Overview of Acquired Peripheral Dyslexias

In agreement with the dissection of the cerebral visual system into early visual cortex, ventral stream, and dorsal stream, we will now sketch in turn the features of hemianopic, ventral, and dorsal dyslexias.

Hemianopic Dyslexia

Reading is highly dependent on the integrity of the central visual field. Thus, masking the central seven letters makes reading performance drop to about 12 words per minute, whereas masking the central 11 letters makes reading virtually impossible (Fine & Rubin, 1999; Rayner & Bertera, 1979). Therefore, central scotomas, mostly resulting from retinal lesions, yield major reading deficits (Legge et al., 1997). In contrast, unilateral brain lesions affecting the retrochiasmatic visual tract up to the primary cortex result in homonymous scotomas sparing at least one half of the visual field, including half of the fovea. The ensuing reading impairments are therefore relatively mild. Only right hemianopia without sparing of foveal vision induces noticeable reading difficulty (Zihl, 1995). First, the visual span of such patients is reduced, which may require several fixations in order to perceive long words. Second, as they rely only on their intact LVF, they lose the reading advantages specific to the normal RVF. Accordingly, they show an influence of word length on reading latencies, as normal subjects do with words displayed in their LVF (Fig. 9.1). Third, perception in the right parafoveal field, in an area spanning about 15 letters (Rayner & McConkie, 1976), is important for preparing the accurate landing of the gaze on subsequent words (Sereno & Rayner, 2003). Therefore, hemianopic patients make abnormally short and numerous saccades when reading word sequences (Fig. 9.3) (Leff et al., 2000; Zihl, 1995). Interestingly, Upton and colleagues (2003) studied a right hemianopic patient with macular sparing in his left eye and macular splitting in his right eye. Accordingly, symptoms of

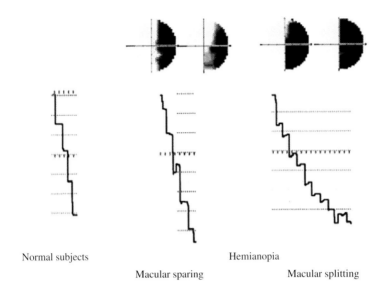

Normal subjects   Hemianopia

Macular sparing   Macular splitting

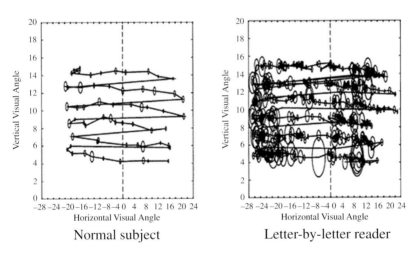

Normal subject   Letter-by-letter reader

Figure 9.3 *Upper panel*: Saccadic traces during the reading of a five-word array in normal subjects (*left*), and in right hemianopic patients with macular sparing (*middle*) or macular splitting (*right*), showing a substantial increase in the number and total duration of fixations in the latter case only. *Lower panel*: Fixations during the reading of a paragraph in a normal subject (*left*) and in a pure alexic patient with letter-by-letter reading. The size of ellipses represent the duration of fixations.

Upper panel is adapted from Leff, A.P., Scott, S.K., Crewes, H., Hodgson, T.L., Cowey, A., Howard, D., et al. (2000). Impaired reading in patients with right hemianopia. *Annals of Neurology, 47*, 171–178; lower panel is adapted from Behrmann, M., Shomstein, S.S., Black, S.E., & Barton, J.J. (2001). The eye movements of pure alexic patients during reading and nonreading tasks. *Neuropsychologia, 39*, 983–1002.

hemianopic dyslexia were restricted to conditions in which the patient was reading with his right eye only. The case of patient M. will be presented later as an illustration of hemianopic dyslexia with behavioral, anatomical, and functional data (Cohen et al., 2003).

Ventral Dyslexias

Apperceptive Agnosias and Reading

Visual agnosias following ventral visual lesions are commonly divided into apperceptive and associative agnosias (Humphreys & Riddoch, 1993; Lissauer, 1890). In apperceptive agnosias, early shape processing impairments interfere with the identification of any kind of stimuli. In associative agnosias, patients are unable to identify shapes for which they nevertheless demonstrate good, albeit not necessarily normal, perceptual abilities (e.g., in copying, matching, or description tasks) (Rubens & Benson, 1971). Patients with apperceptive agnosia following lesions of intermediate visual areas, such as V2 and V4, are impaired at word reading just as they are at identifying other types of shapes and objects (Heider, 2000; Michel, Henaff, & Bruckert, 1991; Rizzo, Nawrot, Blake, & Damasio, 1992).

Associative Agnosias and Pure Alexia

Associative agnosias for alphabetic stimuli correspond to the syndrome of pure alexia, also known as alexia without agraphia, word blindness, or agnosic alexia. Such patients typically have entirely preserved production and comprehension of oral language, and they can write normally either spontaneously or to dictation. However, they show various degrees of impairment of word reading. In the most severe cases, known as *global alexia*, they cannot identify single letters, let alone whole words (Dalmas & Dansilio, 2000; Dejerine, 1892). More frequently, patients show relatively preserved letter identification abilities and develop letter-by-letter reading strategies, as if only the most finely tuned mechanisms of word perception were affected, those allowing for rapid and parallel identification of letter strings. As an indication of this effortful reading strategy, such patients show a large increase in the number and the duration of fixations per word, relative to normals and even to patients with hemianopic dyslexia (Behrmann, Shomstein, Black, & Barton, 2001) (Fig. 9.3).

Beyond the distinction between global and letter-by-letter alexia, cases of pure alexia may vary along several dimensions. Is the visual field entirely affected, or is alexia restricted to one hemifield (Cohen et al., 2000; Dejerine, 1892)? Are there residual reading abilities in purely implicit reading tasks, such as lexical decision, beyond the apparent inability to identify words (Coslett & Saffran, 1989; Coslett, Saffran, Greenbaum, & Schwartz, 1993)?

Do patients have access to abstract letter identities, allowing them to decide that "a" and "A" are instances of the same grapheme (Dalmas & Dansilio, 2000; Miozzo & Caramazza, 1998; Mycroft, Hanley, & Kay, 2002), for example? Importantly, those diverse behavioral patterns all result from lesions confined to the territory of the left posterior cerebral artery (PCA). The crucial brain structures include the ventral occipitotemporal cortex, the underlying white matter, and, particularly, the posterior interhemispheric callosal connections (Binder & Mohr, 1992). This diversity will be illustrated later by the cases of patients with the main variants of pure alexia (letter-by-letter reading, global alexia, and left callosal hemialexia), and the underlying mechanisms will be discussed in greater detail thereafter.

Dorsal Dyslexias

Peripheral reading disorders that result from parietal lesions may be broadly divided into those that reflect an impaired localization of objects in space versus those that reflect an impaired attentional control on object processing. The latter may themselves encompass distinct impairments of space-oriented versus object-oriented attention. Those mechanisms may be, and often are, associated and difficult to disentangle in a given patient.

Spatial Dyslexia and Bálint's Syndrome

The basic symptom is an inability to read connected text due to chaotic scanning of the display. The patients' gaze wanders randomly from word to word, and the relative position of words cannot be appreciated. However, patients can read accurately the disconnected words on which they land. This disorder may be seen as a consequence, in the domain of reading, of two more general spatial impairments that are components of Bálint's syndrome (Rizzo & Vecera, 2002): *simultanagnosia*, which prevents the binding of objects with a stable localization in space and hence the computation of their relative positions; and possibly *ocular apraxia*, which precludes an accurate control of saccades toward peripheral targets, as required for the orderly scanning of word arrays.

Although the identification of single optimally printed words is not substantially affected, patients may have major difficulties reading words presented in unusual formats, such as vertically arrayed or widely spaced letters. This disrupts the automatic binding of letters into single visual objects, and therefore requires a scanning of each component letter, which Bálint patients cannot do. Those points are illustrated later by the case of a patient with bilateral parietal atrophy and severe Bálint's syndrome.

Bálint patients are often impaired at identifying large letters made of smaller letters ("Navon stimuli"), a task that may require the computation of the global shape on the basis of the relative position of the small letters

(Jackson, Swainson, Mot, Husain, & Jackson, 2004; Navon, 2003; Rizzo & Vecera, 2002). Impaired letter-by-letter scanning may also interfere with the task of reporting the components of letter strings, even with optimally displayed real words (Baylis, Driver, Baylis, & Rafal, , 1994)[1] A related phenomenon was reported by Humphreys (1998), who showed that patients with parietal lesions could read short words normally (i.e., without an effect of word length), but were abnormally slow at counting the letters of the same words. Conversely, patients with ventral lesions showed letter-by-letter reading, with a preserved subitizing (i.e., fast perception) of letter numerosity. A similar account may explain why Bálint patients are impaired at reading pseudowords, for which grapheme-to-phoneme conversion may require the sequential inspection of letters. For instance, a patient studied by Coslett and Saffran (1991) read accurately 29 out of 30 briefly presented words, whereas she identified only four out of 30 pseudowords.

Attention-related Dyslexias

Attention-related dyslexias are usually divided into attentional dyslexia and neglect dyslexia. The status of the so-called positional dyslexia (Katz & Sevush, 1989) and letter position dyslexia (Friedmann & Gvion, 2001), which have been much less studied, is still unclear, but may also be related to attentional impairments.

Attentional dyslexia.   The hallmark of attentional dyslexia is the contrast between preserved reading of words presented in isolation, and high error rates when the target is surrounded by other words (for a review see Davis & Coltheart, 2002). It is generally attributed to an impaired attentional selection of one among several concurrent stimuli (Shallice, 1988). Normally, an attended item benefits from enhanced perceptual processing, while surrounding stimuli are filtered out. Insufficient focusing of the attentional window would simultaneously result in an inaccurate processing of the target and in the intrusion of distractors into later stages of processing. As mentioned before, a similar situation can be brought about in normal subjects by briefly presenting two simultaneous words and specifying only afterward which word should be reported (Davis & Bowers, 2004; Treisman & Souther, 1986). This procedure forces a spread of attention over the two words and induces reading errors that are analogous to those observed in attentional dyslexia (for qualifications to this analogy see Davis & Bowers, 2004). Most errors are visually similar to the target, and result from substitutions, additions, or deletions of letters. Such errors may be attributed to a reduced processing of the target in the ventral visual pathway as a result of the competition by surrounding words. Much interest has been devoted to another kind of error, namely letter migration errors (i.e., significant intrusions of letters from distractor words into the response to the target). This kind of error may result from an insufficient suppression of letters from the surrounding words.[2] Such ideas are in good agreement with imaging data in normals, showing that when multiple object are presented simultaneously, they exert mutual inhibition, resulting in decreased ventral visual activations relative to sequential presentation (Kastner et al., 1998). Directing attention toward one of the stimuli compensates this reduction of activity. Moreover, the activation induced by distractors in areas T4 and TEO is reduced in proportion to the attention that is paid to the target and inversely correlated with frontoparietal activations (Pinsk, Doniger, & Kastner, 2004). It is thus plausible that in attentional dyslexics, impaired selection abilities, which are unmasked in the presence of flanker words, cause both visual errors due to a weakened representation of the target, and letter migrations due to an excessive activation of distractors.

The phenomenon of flanker interference is not restricted to words surrounded by words, but also prevails when patients are asked to read single letters surrounded by other letters. This leads to the paradoxical observation that patients may be good at reading isolated words, but not at naming their component letters. More generally, interference seems to occur only between items of the same category. In their seminal article, Shallice and Warrington (1977) showed that flanking letters but not flanking digits interfered with letter identification. Similarly, no mutual interference occurs between letters and whole words (Warrington, Cipolotti, & McNeil, 1993). One may note that in some patients the interference between letters is the same whether the target and flankers are printed in the same case or not (Shallice & Warrington, 1977; Warrington et al., 1993). This suggests that the parietal impairment underlying attentional dyslexia impinges on visual representations that already show some segregation among categories of objects. This property would fit the inferotemporal cortex, in which local preferences for faces, places, words, and the like have been repeatedly evidenced (Hasson, Harel, Levy, & Malach, 2003; Haxby, Gobbini, Furey, Ishai, Schouten, & Pietrini, 2001; Kanwisher et al., 1997). Moreover, attentional modulation has been demonstrated in those regions in normal subjects (Kanwisher & Wojciulik, 2000), as well as in parietal patients (Vuilleumier et al., 2001). Still, the irrelevance of case changes for attentional selection is not absolute. Indeed, letter migrations between words may be reduced by using different typographic cases (Saffran & Coslett, 1996). This suggests that, even in parietal patients, low-level visual features may help to focus the attention on the target word and to discard distractors.

In brief, attentional dyslexia may be due to insufficient attentional focusing on one among several concurrent letters or letter strings represented in the VWF system. Note that the few cases of attentional dyslexia with sufficient lesion data consistently point to a left parietal involvement (Friedmann & Gvion, 2001; Mayall & Humphreys, 2002; Shallice & Warrington, 1977; Warrington et al., 1993).[3] It is possible that attentional control of such language-related representations is more dependent on left-hemispheric parietofrontal structures. Such asymmetry may relate to a left-hemispheric bias for object-oriented attention (Egly et al., 1994), or to the left dominance for language.

Letter position dyslexia.   Friedmann and Gvion (2001) studied two patients with left occipitoparietal lesions, whose predominant errors consisted of letter migrations *within* words, mostly affecting middle letters. Using a variety of tasks, they demonstrated the perceptual origin of this phenomenon. The patients also made occasional *between*-word migration errors, and the authors proposed to relate letter position dyslexia to "classical" attentional dyslexia. Interestingly, the difference in the pattern of migration errors between the two syndromes may partly result from systematic differences between the Hebrew and the Latin writing systems. Thus, within-word migrations are more probable in Hebrew, due to the orthographic and morphological structure of the language, which makes it likely that random within-word letter migrations will result in real words. Other differences in the perceptual, attentional, and oculomotor strategies normally involved in Hebrew versus Latin reading (for a review, see Nazir, Ben-Boutayab, Decoppet, Deutsch, & Frost, 2004) might also contribute to the emergence of this particular pattern of deficit. At any rate, letter position dyslexia raises the possibility that some attentional focusing is necessary for the accurate encoding of letter order, even in optimal display condition.

Neglect dyslexia.   The defining feature of neglect dyslexia is the existence of a left–right spatial gradient in the rate of reading errors (for an overview and references, see Riddoch, 1990). As in attentional dyslexia, error rate is increased in the presence of concurrent stimuli. However, due to the asymmetry of neglect, this extinction phenomenon occurs only when distractors are located on the ipsilesional side of targets (Sieroff & Urbanski, 2002). Following the general pattern of hemispatial neglect, it is by far more common to observe left than right neglect dyslexia, although a number of right-sided cases have been reported. Neglect dyslexia is generally associated with signs of neglect outside the domain of reading, although patients with seemingly isolated neglect dyslexia have been reported. Although the mechanisms that are impaired in attentional dyslexia are not spatially lateralized, neglect is thought to result from associated impairments of both nonlateralized and lateralized components of attentional/spatial processing (Husain & Rorden, 2003). The latter may depend on maps of the opposite hemispace subtended by each posterior parietal lobe (Medendorp, Goltz, Vilis, & Crawford, 2003; Sereno, 2001). Assuming that those lateralized maps contribute to the top-down modulation of the ventral visual stream, one may expect that distinct varieties of neglect dyslexia may arise, depending on the side of the lesion, on the affected parietal structure, on the ventral regions that are deprived of attentional control, and the like. Indeed, there are numerous clinical observations to illustrate this fractionation of neglect dyslexia (Riddoch, 1990).

Neglect errors typically affect the leftmost letters when patients read single words, and the leftmost segment of lines when they read connected text. However, those two types of errors can be to some extent doubly dissociated, suggesting that neglect dyslexia is not a homogeneous syndrome (Costello & Warrington, 1987; Kartsounis & Warrington, 1989). This fractionation is best illustrated by the case of patient J.R., who suffered from bilateral occipitoparietal lesions (Humphreys, 1998). When presented with words scattered on a page, he omitted the rightmost words, but he made reading errors affecting the leftmost letters of the words that he picked out. Likewise, he showed left neglect when he was asked to read single words, while he showed right neglect when trying to name the component letters of the same stimuli. This suggests that J.R.'s left lesion yielded right between-object neglect, whereas his right lesion yielded left within-object neglect.

A clarifying framework was proposed by Hillis and Caramazza (1995), who suggested that the varieties of neglect dyslexia may be attributed to spatial attentional biases acting on one or more of progressively more abstract word representations, derived from Marr's theory of object perception (Marr, 1982): a peripheral retinocentric feature representation, a stimulus-centered letter-shape level, and a word-centered graphemic representation akin to the VWF (for a review of supportive data, see Haywood & Coltheart, 2000). Thus, in a deficit at the retinocentric level, error rate for a given letter should depend on its position in the visual field relative to central fixation, and not on its rank within the target word. In contrast, in a deficit at the stimulus-centered level, error rate should depend on the distance from the center of the word, irrespective of the position of the word in the visual field. Naturally, both parameters may be relevant in some if not in the majority of patients. More remote from neglect in its usual sense, neglect at the graphemic level yields errors affecting one end of words, irrespective of their spatial position or orientation. Thus, patient N.G. made errors with the last letters (e.g., hound → house) when reading standard words, but also vertical words and mirror-reversed words, as well as when naming orally spelled words and when performing other lexical tasks such as spelling (Caramazza & Hillis, 1990). Note, however, that there are alternative accounts of word-centered neglect dyslexia in frameworks that refute the existence of object-centered neural representations (Deneve & Pouget, 2003; Mozer, 2002).

Finally, there is behavioral evidence that letter strings that are neglected in standard reading tasks may nevertheless be processed to higher representation levels. This is suggested, for instance, by preserved performance in lexical decision (Arduino, Burani, & Vallar, 2003), by the fact that erroneous responses often tend to have the same length as the actual targets (Kinsbourne & Warrington, 1962), or by higher error rates observed with nonwords than with real words (Sieroff, Pollatsek, & Posner, 1988). The interpretation of such findings is still debated (Riddoch, 1990), but it is plausible that neglected words can be processed in the ventral visual pathway in the absence of conscious awareness, as has also been shown in normal subjects (Dehaene et al., 2001; Devlin et al., 2003), and with other types of visual stimuli such as faces or houses in neglect patients (Rees, Wojciulik, Clarke, Husain, Frith, & Driver, 2000).

Studies of Alexic Patients

We will now illustrate the model proposed earlier with case studies of patients suffering from acquired peripheral dyslexia. We first concentrate on the operation of the ventral visual pathway. We start by describing the normal pattern of activation observed during reading, with an emphasis on the VWFA and the right-hemispheric symmetrical region. We then validate the link between lesions of the VWFA and the occurrence of pure alexia by a study of lesion overlap in a small series of patients. We then summarize individual data from patients with hemianopic alexia, letter-by-letter reading, global alexia, and variants of pure alexia resulting from an intact but deafferented VWFA. Finally, we turn to the contribution of the dorsal visual pathway and report the case of a patient with dorsal dyslexia following bilateral parietal atrophy.

Normal Occipitotemporal Activations During Reading

Several patients described here were tested, in addition to standard neuropsychological assessment, with simple letter and word reading tasks. In particular, we studied the influence of word length on reading latencies. Lesion topography was studied on the basis of normalized anatomical MRI. Moreover, we documented the properties of the ventral occipitotemporal reading pathway using a functional MRI protocol that was also studied in normal controls (Cohen et al., 2003). In this protocol, subjects were presented with four types of stimuli: a fixation point, real words, consonant strings, and checkerboards covering approximately the same field as letter strings. They were instructed to pay attention equally to all types of stimuli, and to read real words covertly.

In normal subjects, relative to fixation, alphabetic stimuli activated a bihemispheric network, with a left-sided predominance (Fig. 9.4). This network included activations in the left ventral occipitotemporal cortex corresponding to the VWFA (TC –42, –63, –15). There were right-sided symmetrical activations (TC 36, –63, –18), but the functional properties of those symmetrical regions appeared quite different: The VWFA was activated by alphabetic stimuli relative to checkerboards, whereas the right-hemispheric region symmetrical to the VWFA (R-VWFA) reacted identically to both, confirming that the VWFA has some degree of specialization for alphabetic

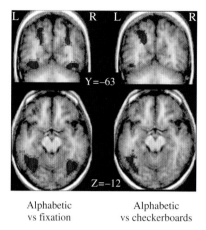

Alphabetic   Alphabetic
vs fixation   vs checkerboards

Figure 9.4 In normal subjects, bilateral ventral temporal areas are activated by alphabetic stimuli relative to fixation. When contrasting alphabetic stimuli versus checkerboards, activations are restricted to the left hemisphere, and correspond to the visual word form area (VWFA).

processing. We now show how lesions affecting the VWFA are associated with the occurrence of pure alexia.

Pure Alexia and the VWFA: Study of Lesion Overlap

Brain lesions were analyzed in six patients with lesions in the territory of the left PCA (see below for some of the case histories) (Fig. 9.5). Lesions were reconstructed manually, smoothed, and then added, with a positive weight for the three patients *with* pure alexia and an equal negative weight for the three patients *without* pure alexia. The resulting image (Fig. 9.6) is proportional to the log likelihood ratio, log[P(pure alexia | lesion) / P(no pure alexia | lesion)], which expresses for each voxel the conditional link between the existence of a lesion and the occurrence of pure alexia. The critical area follows closely the left occipitotemporal sulcus, and overlaps with the VWFA, as identified on fMRI in normal subjects by contrasting alphabetic stimuli versus checkerboards. We will now illustrate the link between the VWFA and pure alexia in more detail with the cases of individual patients.

Right Hemianopic Dyslexia: Patient M.

Case History

Patient M. was a 54-year-old right-handed building engineer (Cohen et al., 2003). Eight months before the present study, he suffered from an infarct in the territory of the left PCA, revealed by sudden right homonymous

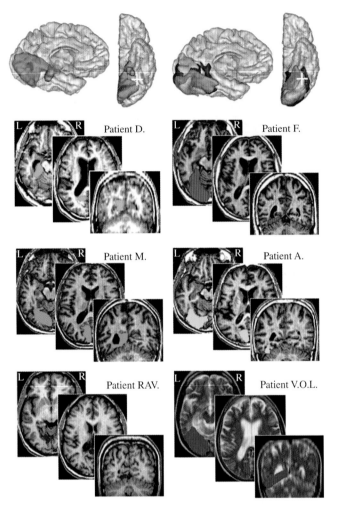

Figure 9.5 Reconstruction of lesions in Talairach space, compared to the average normal location of the visual word form area (VWFA; *white cross*). *Left column*: The lesions of patients without pure alexia did not affect the critical VWFA region. *Right column*: The lesions of patients who showed letter-by-letter reading (patients A. and F.) or global alexia (patient V.O.L.), encroached on the VWFA, in the lateral occipitotemporal sulcus. The additional callosal lesion may be responsible for the left hemialexia in patient D., and for the lack of letter-by-letter reading abilities in patient V.O.L.

hemianopia. The anatomical MRI showed a left ventral and mesial occipito-temporal lesion, destroying both banks of the calcarine sulcus, the lingual gyrus, and extending to the mesial part of the fusiform gyrus. The peak of the normal VWFA fell in a region of intact cerebral tissue, lateral to the ischemic lesion and to the enlarged lateral ventricle (Fig. 9.5).

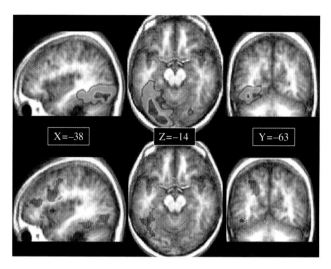

Figure 9.6 The normalized lesions from the six patients were combined to compute for each voxel an index of the conditional link between the existence of a lesion and the occurrence of pure alexia (*top row*). The critical area follows the left occipitotemporal sulcus, and overlaps neatly with the visual word form area (VWFA), as identified with functional magnetic resonance imaging (fMRI) in normal subjects by contrasting alphabetic stimuli versus checkerboards (*bottom row*).

Goldmann perimetry showed a complete right homonymous hemianopia with no sparing of the macula. Oral language production and comprehension, picture naming, writing to dictation, and identification of spelled-out words were normal. Story reading was errorless but slower than in normals (52 s in the patient versus a mean of 35 s in normals). The patient named flawlessly centrally presented words and single letters. However, word reading latencies increased by 64 ms per letter, a slope significantly steeper than in normal subjects (Fig. 9.1). As the patient had a complete right hemianopia, we compared this pattern to the performance of 15 control subjects reading words displayed in one hemifield. The patient's slope did not differ from the slope observed in controls for LVF words (average: 22 ms per letter), whereas it was significantly steeper than the normal slope for RVF words (average: 9 ms per letter). In sum, the word length effect exhibited by patient M. when reading stimuli in free-field could be considered as a consequence of his hemianopia, with an otherwise intact reading system.

The fMRI study of word reading showed an essentially normal pattern (Fig. 9.7). There were activations by alphabetic stimuli versus fixation in the VWFA (TC −39, −57, −9), as well as in the R-VWFA (TC 39, −57, −15). As in normals, the R-VWFA was also activated by checkerboards relative to fixation (TC 30, −54, −18), whereas the VWFA was not.

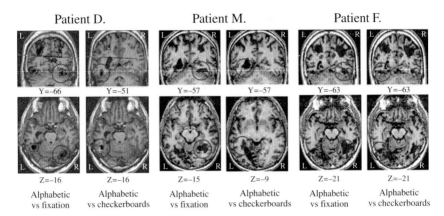

Patient D.   Patient M.   Patient F.

| Y=-66 | Y=-51 | Y=-57 | Y=-57 | Y=-63 | Y=-63 |

| Z=-16 | Z=-16 | Z=-15 | Z=-9 | Z=-21 | Z=-21 |

| Alphabetic vs fixation | Alphabetic vs checkerboards | Alphabetic vs fixation | Alphabetic vs checkerboards | Alphabetic vs fixation | Alphabetic vs checkerboards |

Figure 9.7 Ventral occipitotemporal activations in patients. The right column shows the contrast of alphabetic stimuli versus fixation, and the left column shows the contrast of alphabetic stimuli versus checkerboards ($p < 0.001$). In the two patients without pure alexia (D. and M.), the visual word form area (VWFA) was activated by letter strings relative to checkerboards, whereas both types of stimuli yielded an equivalent activation of the symmetrical right (R)-VWFA. In the letter-by-letter reader patient F., the VWFA was partially disrupted, and right-hemispheric regions discriminated alphabetic stimuli versus checkerboards, thus assuming functional properties generally specific to the VWFA.

Discussion

Despite a large cortical lesion and the resulting hemianopia, patient M. had no subjective reading difficulties. Nevertheless, the study of his reading latencies suggests that those were abnormally dependent on word length, and hence that the mechanisms that normally compute the identities of letter arrays in parallel were disrupted by the cortical lesion. Those mechanisms may be specific to the left-hemispheric visual system, explaining why in normal subjects only RVF words are read with no appreciable effect of word length, while there is such an effect with LVF words (Lavidor & Ellis, 2002). Leaving aside this subtle deviation from optimal performance, it is tempting to relate the sparing of patient M.'s reading abilities to the spared activation of the VWFA by words entering through the intact LVF. As in normals, we assume that the activations induced by both alphabetic stimuli and checkerboards in the R-VWFA did not play a crucial role in patient M.'s reading abilities. In short, we suggest that this patient read roughly like normal subjects read words displayed in their LVF.

We now turn to patients with lesions affecting later stages of visual word processing, yielding reading deficits that are not explainable in terms of a restricted visual field.

Pure Alexia with Letter-by-Letter Reading: Patient F.

Case History

Patient F. was a 68-year-old right-handed retired manager (Cohen et al., 2003) who suffered from an infarct in the territory of the left PCA, revealed by sudden right homonymous hemianopia and reading difficulties.

The anatomical MRI showed a left ventral occipitotemporal lesion (Fig. 9.5). It affected the inferior occipital cortex and the lingual gyrus, with no extension dorsal to the calcarine sulcus. It extended anteriorly to the fusiform and parahippocampal gyri. There was an additional small right inferior occipital lesion probably resulting from a previous overlooked cerebrovascular accident. The region of normal VWFA activation overlapped substantially with the left fusiform lesion.

Goldmann perimetry showed right superior homonymous quadrantanopia. Oral language production and comprehension, picture naming, writing to dictation, and identification of spelled-out words were normal. Story reading, although correct, was much slower than in normal subjects (over 4 minutes). Eight months after the infarct, word reading was still slow and effortful. When reading single words, the patient made 16% errors. Latencies on correct trials had a mean of 9,200 ms, and showed a major effect of word length, with a slope of 1,140 ms per letter. This slope decreased over the following months, down to a value of 311 ms per letter at the time of the imaging study. This is still much steeper than in normal subjects, but also steeper than in the hemianopic patient M. described earlier. In summary, patient F. qualified as a typical pure alexic with an efficient letter-by-letter reading strategy.

The fMRI study showed strong right ventral occipitotemporal activations by alphabetic stimuli at the coordinates of the R-VWFA (TC 39, –60, –18) (Fig. 9.7). This region was activated by alphabetic stimuli more strongly than by checkerboards, a pattern that differed significantly from normal subjects. In the left hemisphere, we found a small cluster of residual activation contiguous to the lesion, with the approximate location and properties of the normal VWFA (TC –42, –63, –24). Furthermore, a language-related network was activated more strongly by words versus consonant strings in patient F. as compared to normal subjects, presumably reflecting letter-by-letter reading: Left anterior insula/Broca's area (TC –36, 15, 3) and supramarginal gyrus (TC –42, –51, 33), but also left-predominant prefrontal cortex, bilateral rolandic cortex, and bilateral posterior middle temporal gyrus.

Discussion: The Underpinnings of Letter-by-Letter Reading

Contrary to the previous patient, patient F. was substantially impaired in his daily command of reading in the absence of other language deficit, including writing. In agreement with the proposed framework, patient F.'s lesion overlapped with the normal region of the VWFA. As for letter-by-letter reading, a classical hypothesis is that it consists of a kind of internal spelling of stimuli by the RH to the left-hemispheric language system. Anatomical and functional data are compatible with this hypothesis.

First, in patient F. the right-hemispheric R-VWFA activations showed a strong preference for alphabetic stimuli over checkerboards, a pattern specific to the VWFA in normal subjects as well as in patient M. This suggests that, indeed, the right-sided visual system assumed a function in reading normally devoted to the VWFA, namely letter identification. There is converging evidence that alphabetic identification is within the reach of the right-hemispheric visual system, even if this process is not needed for normal reading (for a review, see Coslett & Saffran, 1998). Such evidence comes from studies of split brains (Baynes & Eliassen, 1998), left-hemispherectomized patients (Patterson, Vargha-Khadem, & Polkey., 1989), deep dyslexic patients with extensive LH lesions (Coltheart, 1980), and patients with pure alexia. Bartolomeo and colleagues (1998) studied a pure alexic patient who lost her letter-by-letter reading abilities following a contralateral RH infarct. Similarly Coslett and Monsul (1994) transiently disrupted the residual reading abilities of a pure alexic patient by means of transcranial magnetic stimulation. Similar evidence exists on the identification of Arabic digits by the RH (Cohen & Dehaene, 1995; Cohen & Dehaene, 1996; Gazzaniga & Hillyard, 1971; Gazzaniga & Smylie, 1984; Seymour, Reuter-Lorenz, & Gazzaniga, 1994). In brief, the RH thus appears as a plausible source of alphabetic identification in letter-by-letter reading.

Second, callosal connections appeared to be intact in patient F., allowing for interhemispheric transfer of letter identities. Third, letter-by-letter word reading induced a stronger than normal activation of language-related areas, particularly in a network repeatedly associated with verbal working memory, including Broca's area (BA 44), the dorsolateral prefrontal cortex (BA 9), and the left supramarginal gyrus (BA 40) (for a review, see Cabeza & Nyberg, 2000). Those activations in language-related structures probably reflect the progressive identification of the target word in the LH, on the basis of incremental information arriving from the RH. Finally, one should note that residual activation was observed around the VWFA, suggesting that this structure was partially spared. However, it is unclear which role, if any, the residual activation of the VWFA played in the patient's behavior, considering that they were closely surrounded by lesioned cerebral tissue and possibly deprived of some of their connections. The crucial role of the connections leading to the VWFA is further illustrated by the next two cases.

Pure Alexia Due to Cortical Deafferentation: Patient C.Z.

The case of patient C.Z. will not be reported in any detail, as she was quite similar to patient F. in terms both of behavior (letter-by-letter reading) and of functional activation pattern (Cohen et al., 2004). However, patient C.Z.'s lesion, which resulted from the surgical resection of a neuroectodermal tumor, spared the VWFA but included the entire left primary visual cortex, as well as all fiber tracts leading to the VWFA from both the right and the left visual fields. As compared, for instance, to patient F., this case shows that deafferentation of the VWFA yields essentially the same clinical outcome as an actual cortical lesion.

The study of patient C.Z. also provided information on the mechanisms of the progressive improvement of reading speed in letter-by-letter readers. We had the opportunity to run the same behavioral testing and fMRI experiment a second time 8 months after collecting the first data. The overall topography of activations was mostly unchanged as compared to the first fMRI session, including left-predominant frontoparietal and right-predominant temporal areas. However, the activation level decreased in most of this network between the two sessions. This general trend contrasted with a focal increase restricted to specific left frontal and parietal areas. This pattern of evolution fits with the minimal hypothesis of preserved skill learning, reflected by a reduction in initially active regions, in parallel with a sharpening of responses in a better-tuned or more task-specific network (Poldrack, 2000).

Although complete deafferentation of the VWFA yields a pattern of alexia indistinguishable from that resulting from cortical lesions, partial deafferentation due to callosal lesions allows for a finer dissection of the early visual pathways involved in reading.

Pure Alexia in the Left Hemifield Due to Callosal Lesion: Patient D.

Case History

Patient D. was a 63-year-old retired computer engineer. One year before the present study, he suffered from an infarct in the territory of the left PCA, revealed by mild right-sided hemiparesis, a right homonymous visual scotoma, and transient word-finding difficulties. The anatomical MRI showed three small lesions in the territory of the left PCA, including one in the white matter of the forceps major, just contiguous to the splenium of the corpus callosum. The VWFA was intact (Fig. 9.5).

Goldmann perimetry showed a right superior homonymous peripheral scotoma completely sparing central vision. Oral language production and comprehension, picture naming, story reading, writing to dictation, identification of spelled-out words, and graphemic processing were normal. The patient named flawlessly and rapidly centrally presented words and single letters. On average, word reading latencies increased by a marginal 7 ms per additional letter, thus showing a normal pattern. As his visual field was largely intact, the patient was submitted to a tachistoscopic split-field word reading task. The patient named flawlessly and rapidly RVF words (0/40 errors; mean latency 623 ms). With LVF words, he made significantly more errors (16/40 errors) and responded more slowly (mean correct latency = 723 ms). The patient's asymmetry in error rates far exceeded the average 6.3% RVF reading advantage observed in controls (Fig. 9.8). In sum, the patient considered his reading skills as unimpaired, and the experimental assessment of central reading performance was normal. Nevertheless, split-field reading revealed a reduced performance with words displayed in the LVF.

The usual fMRI study of reading showed a normal pattern of activation, as was expected on the basis of lesion topography: The VWFA was preserved and responsive to alphabetic stimuli more so than to checkerboards. Conversely, the symmetrical R-VWFA was equally activated by both types of stimuli. However, this experiment did not allow us to study the differences between activations induced by LVF and RVF stimuli, and to study the mechanism of the patient's left hemialexia. Therefore, patient D. was submitted to an event-related lateralized reading protocol (Cohen et al., 2002). In summary, he was presented with randomly mixed words, consonant strings, and checkerboards displayed in the LVF or in the RVF.

The global contrast of alphabetic stimuli versus checkerboards showed results closely similar to those of the central reading experiment. We performed separate analyses of the activations induced by RVF and LVF stimuli, expecting to observe an abnormal pattern in the latter case, underlying the behavioral asymmetry. For RVF stimuli, the VWFA showed a normal pattern of activation. In contrast, LVF alphabetic stimuli did not significantly activate the VWFA relative to checkerboards at the usual threshold. At a lower threshold, the peak voxel was activated by consonant strings, but not by words. This pattern was clearly abnormal, as it showed no activation of the VWFA by words relative to checkerboards. Comparison to a group of nine normal subjects confirmed that the difference between the activation of the VWFA by RVF and LVF stimuli was significantly larger in the patient than in normal subjects (Fig. 9.8).

Discussion: Callosal Connections and Reading

The case of patient D. lends itself to a straightforward account within the framework that was proposed earlier. First, reading performance in ecological conditions was normal—rapid and with no significant effect of word length—attesting of the integrity of the core reading pathway leading from left V1 to the VWFA and thence to subsequent language areas. Accordingly, the temporal lesion was anterior and mesial to the VWFA, which was activated during

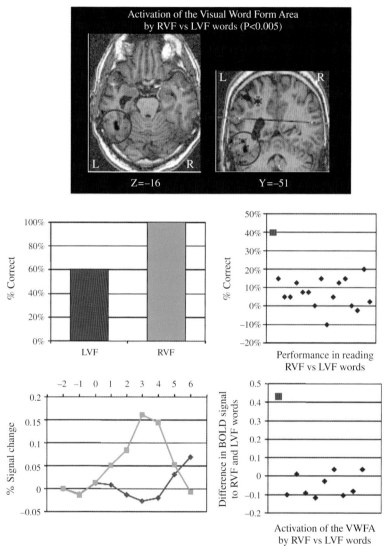

Figure 9.8 Lateralized word reading in patient D. *Top row*: The visual word form area (VWFA) was activated more strongly by right visual field (RVF) words than by left visual field (LVF) words ($p < 0.005$). *Middle row left*: Percent correct responses in the lateralized reading task, showing flawless performance for RVF words (*green*) and a high error rate for LVF words (*red*). *Middle row right*: The RVF advantage in lateralized reading was larger for the patient (*red square*) than in 15 controls (*blue diamonds*). *Bottom row left*: Plot of the percent change in BOLD signal for RVF words (*green curve*) and LVF words (*red curve*) in the VWFA. *Bottom row right*: The difference of BOLD signal for RVF versus LVF words was larger in patient D. (*red square*) than in nine controls. The patient thus showed an abnormal asymmetry in both his behavior and his activation pattern.

249

reading. Second, patient D.'s partial impairment in reading LVF words can be attributed to a partial interhemispheric disconnection due to a left-sided lesion of the splenium of the corpus callosum. We have shown previously using diffusion tensor imaging, although in a patient with much larger lesions, that the fiber tract critically affected by such lesions connects right and left ventral occipitotemporal regions, including probably connections from the right V4 area to the VWFA (Molko et al., 2002). Accordingly, patient D. showed an abnormally weak activation of the VWFA by LVF versus RVF words.

Letter-by-letter reading is the most frequent but certainly not the more dramatic form of pure alexia. As for left hemialexia, it generally goes undetected by patients themselves. Much more incapacitating is global alexia, as illustrated by the patient initially reported by Dejerine (1892), who remained entirely unable to read even years after his stroke. We now describe briefly a similar case of global alexia.

Global Alexia and Implicit Reading: Patient V.O.L.

Case History

Patient V.O.L. was a 66-year-old right-handed woman, who suffered from a left PCA infarct responsible for right hemianopia with macular sparing, severe alexia, and some degree of associative agnosia for objects (Cohen & Dehaene, 2000). The anatomical MRI showed an extensive ventral occipitotemporal lesion, also affecting the mesial occipital lobe both below and above the calcarine sulcus (Fig. 9.5). The infarct encompassed the left part of the splenium of the corpus callosum. After normalization in Talairach space, the anterior boundary of the temporal lesion reached about $y = -20$. In summary, patient V.O.L. had global alexia; her lesion included the VWFA and beyond, and it affected interhemispheric connections.

She made as many as 31% errors when trying to name isolated uppercase letters. She often reached the correct response by outlining the target letter with her finger. She was almost completely unable to read any word aloud. She tried to resort to an effortful and distressing letter-by-letter reading strategy, made many letter naming errors, and testing had to be discontinued after the first few items. In contrast, she did not make a single error in naming the same words when they were spelled out orally to her. She could write letters, words, and sentences normally, either spontaneously or to dictation.

In contrast with this severe deficit, residual implicit word processing abilities were evidenced using tasks requiring no explicit word identification. For instance, V.O.L. performed above chance level in lexical decision tasks. She was almost perfect at discriminating real words from consonant strings (4.4% errors). She then had the feeling that she was not responding randomly, but rather spotting out letter combinations that looked unusual or impossible in French. However, she said she had not been able to identify a single word. When real words were mixed with legal pseudowords, V.O.L.'s accuracy decreased to a 20–30% error rate, still far above chance level. Nevertheless, she had the feeling that she responded in an essentially random fashion, and reported that all items looked about as good to her. She denied having identified a single word. She was also quite fast, with mean reaction times ranging from 1,096 ms to 1,736 ms. Such fast reaction times confirm that, during lexical decision, the patient did not resort to a slow and error prone letter-by-letter reading strategy. This conclusion was reinforced by the fact that reaction times were never correlated with stimulus length. However, no evidence of implicit access to word meaning was found using semantic decision tasks. Indeed, while semantic access has been evidenced in some pure alexic patients, this type of residual ability is not universal in this condition (Arguin, Bub, & Bowers, 1998). Semantic access is easier to demonstrate using Arabic numerals than ordinary words, particularly using tasks requiring no verbal output. For instance, patient V.O.L. and other global alexic patients could easily decide which of two 2-digit Arabic numbers was larger, although they made massive errors when reading aloud the very same stimuli (Cohen & Dehaene, 1995; McNeil & Warrington, 1994).

Discussion

The case of patient V.O.L. raises two important questions: Why do some pure alexic patients enjoy effective letter-by-letter reading abilities, while others suffer from global alexia? What are the mechanisms of implicit word processing in global alexic patient?

We suggested before that letter-by-letter reading is based upon letter identification in the RH and transfer to the LH of letter identities, thus allowing for the eventual word identification. Hence, the development of letter-by-letter reading might depend on premorbid functional dispositions. There is indeed some variability among normal subjects in the functional properties of the R-VWFA. For instance, Cohen and colleagues (2002) found in two out of seven subjects an R-VWFA activation for alphabetic stimuli versus checkerboards, invariant for position in the visual field, although this activation was always weaker than in the VWFA proper. One may speculate that such an RH activation pattern could be a predisposition to the emergence of letter-by-letter reading in case of an LH lesion.

A second precondition to letter-by-letter reading is the ability of letters to reach the LH through direct or indirect links between the right ventral occipitotemporal cortex and speech areas. Di Virgilio and Clarke (1997) studied the brain of a patient with a right ventral occipitotemporal cortex lesion extending from TC $y = 5$ to $y = -52$ along the anteroposterior axis, overlapping with the putative R-VWFA. By staining anterograde degenerating axons, they evidenced monosynaptic projections from the lesioned area to left-hemispheric language areas, including Broca's and Wernicke's areas and the inferior parietal lobule. Such data help to flesh out the interhemispheric pathways that might be involved in letter-by-letter reading. In this context, an interhemispheric disconnection should be sufficient to shift a patient from letter-by-letter reading to global alexia. Accordingly, the global alexic patient V.O.L. had a callosal lesion, whereas interhemispheric connections were apparently intact in the letter-by-letter patient F. Similarly, Binder and Mohr (1992) concluded that the only area that is lesioned in global alexics as compared to letter-by-letter readers includes the left forceps major, and this extends into the left-hemispheric white matter above the posterior ventricular horn. As an aside, if we assume that the interhemispheric pathways involved in letter-by-letter reading project from the R-VWFA to language areas, they should differ from those normally involved in reading of LVF words, which are thought to project from the RH visual cortex to the VWFA (Molko et al., 2002). The callosal lesions that induce left hemialexia (patient D.) and those that prevent letter-by-letter reading in alexic patients (patient V.O.L.) appear to be similar. Whether two anatomically distinct transcallosal pathways can actually be identified remains an open question.

The cerebral pathways that support implicit reading abilities remain unclear. Implicit reading can be elicited in tasks with no overt verbal component, such as lexical or semantic decision (Coslett et al., 1993). Its emergence requires that explicit reading, particularly through letter-by-letter strategies, be absent or prevented, for example through the rapid presentation of masked stimuli. Coslett and Saffran have put forward a number of arguments supporting the hypothesis that implicit reading would reflect a lexical and semantic access within the RH, capable of driving nonverbal responses, and impeded by concurrent attempts of the LH to engage in verbal strategies (Coslett & Saffran, 1998). In some patients, implicit word identification may eventually be made available to overt verbal output, yielding deep dyslexic phenomena, such as fast reading of short, highly imageable words (Buxbaum & Coslett, 1996). Endorsing the right-hemispheric hypothesis, such deep dyslexic phenomena also require that semantic information be transferred to the LH. Sidtis and colleagues (1981) studied a patient who underwent a two-stage callosotomy. When only the posterior half of his corpus callosum was severed, the patient could not read aloud words presented in his LVF. However, he could still verbally approach their meaning, presumably owing to the transfer of semantic information through the intact anterior callosum. This suggests that, in addition to the transhemispheric pathway subtending letter-by-letter reading, a more anterior semantic route, perhaps available only in a few subjects with a strong premorbid contribution of the RH to reading, may help some patients to circumvent their pure alexia.

Interestingly, some empirical arguments suggest that implicit reading rests on parallel letter processing (Arguin et al., 1998), indicating that the serial character of letter-by-letter reading might not result from an intrinsic lack of parallel letter processing in the RH, but from the limited capacity of interhemispheric letter transfer, or from the letter-by-letter strategy of lexical access. It may also be that in some patients there is enough remaining ability in the left VWFA to support some parallel processing and above-chance performance in some tasks.

Reading Impairment in a Patient with Bilateral Parietal Atrophy

Case History

Patient B.O. was a 63-year-old woman who suffered from progressive biparietal atrophy (Benson, Davis, & Snyder, 1988), revealed by gestural and visual difficulties interfering with everyday life activities (Vinckier et al., 2006). Anatomical MRI showed brain atrophy predominating in dorsal regions, mostly visible in the parietal cortex (Fig. 9.9). In particular, a striking contrast was observed between the preserved ventral occipitotemporal cortex and the severely shrunken dorsal occipitoparietal cortex, with a dramatic enlargement of the intraparietal sulcus.

Patient B.O. showed a clear-cut dissociation between impaired dorsal and preserved ventral visual processing. Thus, she had severe simultanagnosia, as

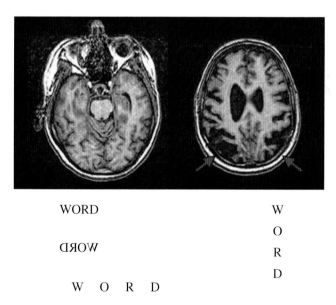

Figure 9.9 A patient with Bálint's syndrome due to bilateral parietal atrophy could read foveally presented words. However, she made 45% errors with horizontal words with spaced letters, 75% errors with vertical words, and 100% errors with mirror-printed words.

evidenced for instance by her piecemeal description of the Cookie Theft picture (Goodglass & Kaplan, 1972), and left spatial hemineglect. In contrast, she could flawlessly identify pictures of familiar objects, faces, and colors. In summary, visuospatial abilities ("where") seemed to be impaired whereas object recognition ("what") was largely preserved. In addition, patient B.O. suffered from limb apraxia and Gerstmann's syndrome.

The patient's reading abilities reflected her dissociated pattern of visual impairment. On the one hand, text reading was severely impeded by simultanagnosia and neglect. When presented with a page of text, B.O. read randomly scattered words, mostly picked out of the right half of the page. She could not consistently follow a given line nor jump to the beginning of the next one. On the other hand, and in agreement with her preserved object naming, the words that she selected were almost always read correctly. With isolated words, reading was rapid and fairly accurate (about 10% errors), with latencies of about half a second, and no effect of word length. The few errors mostly affected the left half of targets, a consequence of the left hemispatial neglect.

However, whenever words were presented using unusual displays, a major deficit emerged, even if no time limit was imposed (Fig. 9.9). Thus, the patient was entirely unable to read mirror-reversed words. With vertical words, she made almost 80% errors, a rate which increased with word length. Even correct responses required several seconds to be produced. When the patient was presented with rotated words, errors increased steeply from 50 degrees to 80 degrees, reaching a rate of 50%. As a final type of visual distortion, she was asked to read words with wide blank s p a c e s between letters. Based on the local combination detector (LCD) model of visual word recognition (see Chapter 5), we predicted that this manipulation should disrupt bigram coding in the ventral pathway whenever the amount of blank space exceeded a critical value. Indeed, error rates increased to 40% when two blank characters were inserted between contiguous letters. Finally, reading of pseudowords was severely impaired, with about 70% errors even with normal display conditions. Almost all erroneous responses to pseudowords consisted of real words with some visual similarity to the target.

Discussion

In a previous section, we proposed that an effect of word length on reading latencies is diagnostic of a failure to reach a response criterion on the basis of parallel letter identification. According to this idea, the length effect does not reflect an intrinsic property of the expert ventral visual pathway, but rather the serial scanning of letters whenever it is required to gather additional information on the target. Assuming that this attention-driven strategy involved the parietal lobes, we expected that tasks that induce a length effect in normal subjects should make reading impossible in patients with parietal lesions. This is precisely what we observed in patient B.O. using the unusual word displays described earlier (rotation, spacing, etc.), all of which are known to induce a length effect in normal subjects (Bub & Lewine, 1988; Cohen et al., 2008; Lavidor et al., 2001a). As for pseudowords, they induce a normal length effect probably not because of a failure of parallel letter processing, but because of the necessity to scan them serially to achieve grapheme-to-phoneme conversion (Weekes, 1997). At any rate, the patient's inability to read pseudowords presumably reflected the same impairment of serial attentional processing as with physically distorted displays. In brief, the study of patients with parietal lesions provides an opportunity to delineate the limits of the reading expertise of the ventral visual system. While it is attuned to the identification of letter strings in parallel across a variety of display conditions, this ability does not extend to settings that depart too much from the usual reading conditions in which the system was trained.

Conclusion

In this chapter, we tried to present a coherent picture of the brain mechanisms subtending visual word perception, as revealed by the study of brain-damaged patients. We first sketched a hypothetical view of the cerebral architecture for visual word recognition, emphasizing the interaction between bottom-up information flow in the ventral visual pathway and top-down input from the dorsal pathway. We then proposed an overview of acquired peripheral dyslexias derived from this model and from considerations on the gross organization of the visual system. Thus, we distinguished dyslexias related to visual scotomas, to ventral lesions (i.e., pure alexia), and to dorsal lesions. The latter include several still somewhat fuzzy syndromes, such as Balint's syndrome dyslexia, attentional dyslexia, and neglect dyslexia. Finally, we illustrated this approach with cases of patients suffering from hemianopia or from variants of pure alexia, combining behavioral, anatomical, and functional data. Those observations suggest that the cortical lesion responsible for pure alexia overlaps with the VWFA as activated in normal subjects. An equivalent impairment may result from white matter lesions deafferenting the critical cortical region. Similarly, deafferentation restricted to the left half of the visual field following posterior callosal lesions can result in left hemialexia. We also discussed the possible reasons why some patients show global alexia while others develop a compensatory letter-by-letter reading strategy, and what might be the cerebral bases of implicit reading abilities. Finally, we showed how the study of patients with lesions to the dorsal pathway can inform us on the role of spatial processing and attention on single word reading and clarify the limits of the perceptual expertise subtended by the ventral pathway.

Notes

1. However, impairments in the two latter tasks may be alternatively attributed to attentional deficits, two types of accounts that may be difficult to distinguish empirically. The lack of report of the large Navon letters may reflect an inability to pay attention to global features when there are competing local objects. As for the inability to report the component letters of single words, it may be related to attentional dyslexia.
2. Some letter migration errors could be attributed to spatial dyslexia; i.e., to an impaired serial scanning and localization of letters within words. This ineffective strategy, which probably explains the impairment of spatial dyslexics in reading pseudowords, could occasionally apply to real words and induce letter position errors. However, this mechanism cannot provide a full account of attentional dyslexia. For instance, Shallice & Warrington's (1977) patients did not have Balint's syndrome, and they could accurately scan large arrays of letters for a given target. A similar observation applies to patients with letter position dyslexia, who did not make position errors when processing character strings in a serial manner (e.g., reading Arabic numbers or spelling out printed words) (Friedmann & Gvion, 2001).
3. Anatomo-clinical correlations are difficult to draw for some patients described under the label of attentional dyslexia, but who show additional occipitotemporal lesions and intricate deficits, particularly major impairments in reading single letters or words (Hall, Humphreys, & Cooper, 2001; Mayall & Humphreys, 2002).

References

Aghababian, V., & Nazir, T.A. (2000). Developing normal reading skills: aspects of the visual processes underlying word recognition. *Journal of Experimental Child Psychology, 76,* 123–150.

Arduino, L.S., Burani, C., & Vallar, G. (2003). Reading aloud and lexical decision in neglect dyslexia patients: a dissociation. *Neuropsychologia, 41,* 877–85.

Arguin, M., Bub, D.N., & Bowers, J.S. (1998). Extent and limits of covert lexical activation in letter-by-letter reading. *Cognitive Neuropsychology, 15,* 53–92.

Bartolomeo, P., Bachoud-Levi, A.C., Degos, J.D., & Boller, F. (1998). Disruption of residual reading capacity in a pure alexic patient after a mirror-image right-hemispheric lesion. *Neurology, 50,* 286–8.

Baylis, G.C., Driver, J., Baylis, L.L., & Rafal, R.D. (1994). Reading of letters and words in a patient with Balint's syndrome. *Neuropsychologia, 32,* 1273–86.

Baynes, K., & Eliassen, J.C. (1998). The visual lexicon: Its access and organization in commissurotomy patients. In M. Beeman & C. Chiarello (Eds.). *Right hemisphere language comprehension,* 79–104. Mahwah, NJ: Lawrence Erlbaum Associates.

Behrmann, M., Shomstein, S.S., Black, S.E., & Barton, J.J. (2001). The eye movements of pure alexic patients during reading and nonreading tasks. *Neuropsychologia, 39,* 983–1002.

Benson, D.F., Davis, R.J., & Snyder, B.D. (1988). Posterior cortical atrophy. *Archives of Neurology, 45,* 789–93.

Binder, J.R., & Mohr, J.P. (1992). The topography of callosal reading pathways. A case-control analysis. *Brain, 115,* 1807–1826.

Bisley, J.W., & Goldberg, M.E. (2003). The role of the parietal cortex in the neural processing of saccadic eye movements. *Advances in Neurology, 93,* 141–157.

Bokde, A.L., Tagamets, M.A., Friedman, R.B., & Horwitz, B. (2001). Functional interactions of the inferior frontal cortex during the processing of words and word-like stimuli. *Neuron, 30,* 609–617.

Booth, M.C., & Rolls, E.T. (1998). View-invariant representations of familiar objects by neurons in the inferior temporal visual cortex. *Cerebral Cortex, 8,* 510–23.

Bub, D.N., & Lewine, J. (1988). Different modes of word recognition in the left and right visual fields. *Brain and Language, 33,* 161–88.

Burgund, E.D., & Marsolek, C.J. (1997). Letter-case-specific priming in the right cerebral hemisphere with a form-specific perceptual identification task. *Brain and Cognition, 35,* 239–58.

Burgund, E.D., & Marsolek, C.J. (2000). Viewpoint-invariant and viewpoint-dependent object recognition in dissociable neural subsystems. *Psychology Bulletin and Review 7,* 480–489.

Buxbaum, L.J., & Coslett, H.B. (1996). Deep dyslexic phenomena in a letter-by-letter reader. *Brain and Language, 54,* 136–167.

Cabeza, R., & Nyberg, L. (2000). Imaging cognition II: An empirical review of 275 PE.T. and fMRI studies. *Journal of Cognitive Neuroscience, 12,* 1–47.

Caramazza, A., & Hillis, A.E. (1990). Spatial representation of words in the brain implied by studies of a unilateral neglect patient. *Nature, 346,* 267–269.

Chawla, D., Rees, G., & Friston, K.J. (1999). The physiological basis of attentional modulation in extrastriate visual areas. *Nature and Neuroscience, 2,* 671–676.

Chiarello, C. (1988). Lateralization of lexical processes in the normal brain: a review of visual half-field research. In H.A. Whitaker (Ed.). *Contemporary reviews in neuropsychology.* New York: Springer-Verlag.

Cohen, L., & Dehaene, S. (1995). Number processing in pure alexia: the effect of hemispheric asymmetries and task demands. *NeuroCase, 1,* 121–137.

Cohen, L., & Dehaene, S. (1996). Cerebral networks for number processing: Evidence from a case of posterior callosal lesion. *NeuroCase, 2,* 155–174.

Cohen, L., & Dehaene, S. (2000). Calculating without reading: Unsuspected residual abilities in pure alexia. *Cognitive Neuropsychology, 17,* 563–583.

Cohen, L., Dehaene, S., Naccache, L., Lehéricy, S., Dehaene-Lambertz, G., Hénaff, M.A., et al. (2000). The visual word form area: Spatial and temporal characterization of an initial stage of reading in normal subjects and posterior split-brain patients. *Brain, 123,* 291–307.

Cohen, L., Dehaene, S., Vinckier, F., Jobert, A., & Montavont, A. (2008). Reading normal and degraded words: Contribution of the dorsal and ventral visual pathways. *Neuroimage, 40,* 353–366.

Cohen, L., Henry, C., Dehaene, S., Molko, N., Lehéricy, S., Martinaud, O., et al. (2004). The pathophysiology of letter-by-letter reading. *Neuropsychologia, 42,* 1768–1780.

Cohen, L., Lehericy, S., Chochon, F., Lemer, C., Rivaud, S., & Dehaene, S. (2002). Language-specific tuning of visual cortex? Functional properties of the Visual Word Form Area. *Brain, 125,* 1054–1069.

Cohen, L., Martinaud, O., Lemer, C., Lehericy, S., Samson, Y., Obadia, M., et al. (2003). Visual word recognition in the left and right hemispheres: anatomical and functional correlates of peripheral alexias. *Cerebral Cortex, 13,* 1313–1333.

Coltheart, M. (1980). Deep dyslexia: A. right-hemisphere hypothesis. In M. Coltheart, K. Patterson, & J.C. and Marshall (Eds.). *Deep dyslexia,* 326–380. London: Routledge.

Coslett, H.B., & Monsul, N. (1994). Reading with the right hemisphere: Evidence from transcranial magnetic stimulation. *Brain and Language, 46,* 198–211.

Coslett, H.B., & Saffran, E. (1991). Simultanagnosia: to see but not two see. *Brain, 114,* 1523–1545.

Coslett, H.B., & Saffran, E.M. (1989). Evidence for preserved reading in 'pure alexia'. *Brain, 112,* 327–359.

Coslett, H.B., & Saffran, E.M. (1998). Reading and the right hemisphere: Evidence from acquired dyslexia. In M. Beeman M. & C. Chiarello (Eds.). *Right hemisphere language comprehension,* 105–132. Mahwah, NJ: Lawrence Erlbaum Associates.

Coslett, H.B., Saffran, E.M., Greenbaum, S., & Schwartz, H. (1993). Reading in pure alexia: the effect of strategy. *Brain, 116,* 21–37.

Costello, A., & Warrington, E.K. (1987). The dissociation of visuospatial neglect and neglect dyslexia. *Journal of Neurology, Neurosurgery, and Psychiatry, 50,* 1110–1116.

Dalmas, J.F., & Dansilio, S. (2000). Visuographemic alexia: a new form of a peripheral acquired dyslexia. *Brain and Language, 75,* 1–16.

Davis, C., & Coltheart, M. (2002). Paying attention to reading errors in acquired dyslexia. *Trends in Cognitive Science, 6,* 359.

Davis, C.J., & Bowers, J.S. (2004). What do letter migration errors reveal about letter position coding in visual word recognition? *Journal of Experimental Psychology, Human Perception and Performance, 30,* 923–41.

Dehaene, S., Naccache, L., Cohen, L., Bihan, D.L., Mangin, J.F., Poline, J.B., et al. (2001). Cerebral mechanisms of word masking and unconscious repetition priming. *Nature and Neuroscience, 4,* 752–758.

Dejerine, J. (1892). Contribution à l'étude anatomo-pathologique et clinique des différentes variétés de cécité verbale. *Mémoires de la Société de Biologie, 4,* 61–90.

Deneve, S., & Pouget, A. (2003). Basis functions for object-centered representations. *Neuron, 37,* 347–359.

Devlin, A.M., Cross, J.H., Harkness, W., Chong, W.K., Harding, B., Vargha-Khadem, F., et al. (2003). Clinical outcomes of hemispherectomy for epilepsy in childhood and adolescence. *Brain, 126,* 556–566.

Di Virgilio, G., & Clarke, S. (1997). Direct interhemispheric visual input to human speech areas. *Human Brain Mapping, 5,* 347–354.

Egly, R., Driver, J., & Rafal, R.D. (1994). Shifting visual attention between objects and locations: evidence from normal and parietal lesion subjects. *Journal of Experimental Psychology, General, 123,* 161–177.

Fine, E.M., & Rubin, G.S. (1999). Reading with central field loss: number of letters masked is more important than the size of the mask in degrees. *Vision Research, 39,* 747–756.

Fink, G.R., Halligan, P.W., Marshall, J.C., Frith, C.D., Frackowiak, R.S., & Dolan, R.J. (1996). Where in the brain does visual attention select the forest and the trees? *Nature, 382,* 626–628.

Friedman-Hill, S.R., Robertson, L.C., & Treisman, A. (1995). Parietal contributions to visual feature binding: evidence from a patient with bilateral lesions. *Science, 269,* 853–5.

Friedmann, N., & Gvion, A. (2001). Letter position dyslexia. *Cognitive Neuropsychology, 18,* 673–696.

Gazzaniga, M.S., & Hillyard, S.A. (1971). Language and speech capacity of the right hemisphere. *Neuropsychologia, 9,* 273–280.

Gazzaniga, M.S., & Smylie, C.E. (1984). Dissociation of language and cognition: A psychological profile of two disconnected right hemispheres. *Brain, 107,* 145–153.

Giraud, A.L., & Price, C.J. (2001). The constraints functional neuroanatomy places on classical models of auditory word processing. *Journal of Cognitive Neuroscience, 13,* 754–765.

Gitelman, D.R., Nobre, A.C., Parrish, T.B., LaBar, K.S., Kim, Y.H., Meyer, J.R., et al. (1999). A large-scale distributed network for covert spatial attention: further anatomical delineation based on stringent behavioral and cognitive controls. *Brain, 122,* 1093–1106.

Goodglass, H., & Kaplan, E. (1972). *The Boston diagnostic aphasia examination*. Lea & Febiger: Philadelphia.

Grainger, J., & Jacobs, A.M. (1996). Orthographic processing in visual word recognition: A multiple read-out model. *Psychology Review, 103,* 518–565.

Grill-Spector, K., Kushnir, T., Edelman, S., Avidan, G., Itzchak, Y., & Malach, R. (1999). Differential processing of objects under various viewing conditions in the human lateral occipital complex. *Neuron, 24,* 187–203.

Hall, D.A., Humphreys, G.W., & Cooper, A.G.C. (2001). Neuropsychological evidence for case-specific reading: Multi-letter units in visual word recognition. *The Quarterly Journal of Experimental Psychology, 54A:* 439–467.

Hasson, U., Harel, M., Levy, I., & Malach, R. (2003). Large-scale mirror-symmetry organization of human occipito-temporal object areas. *Neuron*, 37, 1027–1041.

Haxby, J.V., Gobbini, M.I., Furey, M.L., Ishai, A., Schouten, J.L., & Pietrini, P. (2001). Distributed and overlapping representations of faces and objects in ventral temporal cortex. *Science, 293,* 2425–2430.

Haywood, M., & Coltheart, M. (2000). Neglect dyslexia and the early stages of visual word recognition. *Neurocase, 6,* 33–44.

Heider, B. (2000). Visual form agnosia: Neural mechanisms and anatomical foundations. *Neurocase, 6,* 1–12.

Helenius, P., Tarkiainen, A., Cornelissen, P., Hansen, P.C., & Salmelin, R. (1999). Dissociation of normal feature analysis and deficient processing of letter-strings in dyslexic adults. *Cerebral Cortex, 9,* 476–483.

Hillis, A.E., & Caramazza, A. (1995). A framework for interpreting distinct patterns of hemispatial neglect. *Neurocase, 1,* 189–207.

Horwitz B.,, Rumsey, J.M., & Donohue, B.C. (1998). Functional connectivity of the angular gyrus in normal reading and dyslexia. *Proceedings of the National Academy of Sciences, USA, 95,* 8939–8944.

Humphreys, G.W. (1998). Neural representation of objects in space: a dual coding account. *Philosophical Transactions of the Royal Society, London, B 353,* 1341–1351.

Humphreys, G.W., & Riddoch, M.J. (1993). Object agnosias. In C. Kennard (Ed.). *Visual perceptual defects*. London: Baillière Tindall,.

Husain, M., & Rorden, C. (2003). Non-spatially lateralized mechanisms in hemispatial neglect. *Nature Reviews Neuroscience, 4,* 26–36.

Ishai, A., Ungerleider, L.G., Martin, A., Schouten, J.L., & Haxby, J.V. (1999). Distributed representation of objects in the human ventral visual pathway. *Proceedings of the National Academy of Sciences, USA, 96,* 9379–9384.

Jackson, G.M., Swainson, R., Mort, D., Husain, M., & Jackson S.R. (2004). Implicit processing of global information in Balint's syndrome. *Cortex, 40,* 179–180.

Jacobs, A.M., Rey, A., Ziegler, J.C., & Grainger, J. (1998). MROM-P: An interactive activation, multiple read-out model of orthographic and phonological processes in visual word recognition. In J. Grainger & A. M. Jacobs (Eds.). *Symbolic connectionist approaches to human cognition,* 147–188. Hillsdale, NJ: Lawrence Erlbaum Associates.

Jernigan, T.L., Ostergaard, A.L., Law, I., Svarer, C., Gerlach, C., & Paulson, O.B. (1998). Brain activation during word identification and word recognition. *Neuroimage, 8,* 93–105.

Kanwisher, N., McDermott, J., & Chun, M.M. (1997). The fusiform face area: a module in human extrastriate cortex specialized for face perception. *Journal of Neuroscience 17,* 4302–4311.

Kanwisher, N., & Wojciulik, E. (2000). Visual attention: insights from brain imaging. *Nature Review Neuroscience, 1,* 91–100.

Kartsounis, L.D., & Warrington, E.K. (1989). Unilateral neglect overcome by cues implicit in stimulus displays. *Journal of Neurology, Neurosurgery, and Psychiatry, 52,* 1253–1259.

Kastner, S., De Weerd, P., Desimone, R., & Ungerleider, L.G. (1998). Mechanisms of directed attention in the human extrastriate cortex as revealed by functional MRI. *Science, 282,* 108–111.

Kastner, S., & Ungerleider, L.G. (2000). Mechanisms of visual attention in the human cortex. *Annual Review of Neuroscience, 23,* 315–341.

Katz, R.B., & Sevush, S. (1989). Positional dyslexia. *Brain and Language, 37,* 266–289.

Kinsbourne, K., & Warrington, E.K. (1962). A. variety of reading disability associated with right hemisphere lesions. *Journal of Neurology, 25,* 339–344.

Kreiman, G., Koch, C., & Fried I. (2000). Category-specific visual responses of single neurons in the human medial temporal lobe. *Nature Neuroscience, 3,* 946–953.

Lambon Ralph, M.A., McClelland, J.L., Patterson, K., Galton, C.J., & Hodges J.R. (2001). No right to speak? The relationship between object naming and semantic impairment: neuropsychological evidence and a computational model. *Journal of Cognitive Neuroscience, 13,* 341–356.

Lavidor, M. (2002). An examination of the lateralized abstractive/form specific model using MiXeD-CaSe primes. *Brain and Cognition,* 48, 413–417.

Lavidor, M., Babkoff, H., & Faust, M. (2001a). Analysis of standard and non-standard visual word format in the two hemispheres. *Neuropsychologia, 39,* 430–439.

Lavidor, M., & Ellis, A.W. (2002). Word length and orthographic neighborhood size effects in the left and right cerebral hemispheres. *Brain and Language, 80,* 45–62.

Lavidor, M., Ellis, A.W., Shillcock, R., & Bland T. (2001b). Evaluating a split processing model of visual word recognition: effects of word length. *Brain Research Cognitive Brain Research, 12,* 265–272.

Leff, A.P., Scott, S.K., Crewes, H., Hodgson, T.L., Cowey, A., Howard, D., et al. (2000). Impaired reading in patients with right hemianopia. *Annals of Neurology, 47,* 171–178.

Legge, G.E., Ahn, S.J., Klitz, T.S., & Luebker, A. (1997). Psychophysics of reading, XVI. The visual span in normal and low vision. *Vision Research, 37,* 1999–2010.

Levy, I., Hasson, U., Avidan, G., Hendler, T., & Malach R. (2001). Center-periphery organization of human object areas. *Nature Neuroscience, 4,* 533–539.

Lissauer, H. (1890). Ein Fall von Seelenblindheit nebst einen Beitrage zur Theorie der-selben. *Archiv für Psychiatrie und Nervenkrankheiten, 21,* 222–270.

Malach, R., Levy, I., & Hasson, U. (2002). The topography of high-order human object areas. *Trends in Cognitive Science, 6,* 176–184.

Marr, D. (1982). *Vision: A computational investigation into the human representation and processing of visual information.* New York: W.H. Freeman.

Marsolek, C.J. (1995). Abstract visual-form representations in the left cerebral hemi-sphere. *Journal of Experimental Psychology, Human Perception and Performance, 21,* 375–386.

Marsolek, C.J., Kosslyn, S.M., & Squire, L.R. (1992). Form-specific visual priming in the right cerebral hemisphere. *Journal of Experimental Psychology, Learning, Memory, and Cognition, 18,* 492–508.

Marsolek, C.J., Schacter, D.L., & Nicholas, C.D. (1996). Form-specific visual priming for new associations in the right cerebral hemisphere. *Memory and Cognition, 24,* 539 556.

Mayall, K., & Humphreys, G.W. (2002). Presentation and task effects on migration errors in attentional dyslexia. *Neuropsychologia, 40,* 1506–1515.

McCandliss, B.D., Cohen, L., & Dehaene, S. (2003). The Visual Word Form Area: Expertise for reading in the fusiform gyrus. *Trends in Cognitive Science, 7,* 293–299.

McNeil, J.E., & Warrington, E.K. (1994). A. dissociation between addition and subtraction within written calculation. *Neuropsychologia, 32,* 717–728.

Mechelli, A., Humphreys, G.W., Mayall, K., Olson, A., & Price, C.J. (2000). Differential effects of word length and visual contrast in the fusiform and lingual gyri during reading. *Proceedings of the Royal Society, London, B, 267,* 1909–1913.

Medendorp, W.P., Goltz, H.C., Vilis, T., & Crawford, J.D. (2003). Gaze-centered updating of visual space in human parietal cortex. *The Journal of Neuroscience, 23,* 6209–6214.

Michel, F., Henaff, M.A., & Bruckert, R. (1991). Unmasking of visual deficits following unilateral prestriate lesions in man. *Neuroreport, 2,* 341–344.

Miozzo, M., & Caramazza, A. (1998). Varieties of pure alexia: The case of failure to access graphemic representations. *Cognitive Neuropsychology, 15,* 203–238.

Molko, N., Cohen, L., Mangin, J.F., Chochon, F., Lehéricy, S., Le Bihan, D., et al. (2002). Visualizing the neural bases of a disconnection syndrome with diffusion tensor imaging. *Journal of Cognitive Neuroscience, 14,* 629–636.

Morais, J., & Kolinsky, R. (1994). Perception and awareness in phonological processing: the case of the phoneme. *Cognition, 50,* 287–297.

Morton, J. (1969). The interaction of information in word recognition. *Psychological Review, 76,* 165–178.

Mozer, M.C. (2002). Frames of reference in unilateral neglect and visual perception: A computational perspective. *Psychological Review, 109,* 156–185.

Mycroft, R., Hanley, J.R., & Kay, J. (2002). Preserved access to abstract letter identities despite abolished letter naming in a case of pure alexia. *Journal of Neurolinguistics, 15,* 99–108.

Navon, D. (1977). Forest before the trees: The precedence of global features in visual perception. *Cognitive Psychology, 9,* 353–383.

Navon, D. (2003). What does a compound letter tell the psychologist's mind? *Acta Psychologica (Amst), 114,* 273–309.

Nazir, TA. (2000). Traces of print along the visual pathway. In A. Kennedy, R. Radach, D. Heller, & J. Pynte (Eds.). *Reading as a perceptual process,* 3–22. Amsterdam: Elsevier.

Nazir, T.A., Ben-Boutayab, N., Decoppet, N., Deutsch, A., & Frost R. (2004). Reading habits, perceptual learning, and recognition of printed words. *Brain and Language, 88,* 294–311.

Nazir, T.A., Jacobs, A.M., & O'Regan, J.K. (1998). Letter legibility and visual word recognition. *Memory and Cognition, 26,* 810–821.

Nobre, A.C., Allison. T., & McCarthy, G. (1998). Modulation of human extrastriate visual processing by selective attention to colours and words. *Brain, 121,* 1357–1368.

Parkhurst, D., Law K., & Niebur, E. (2002). Modeling the role of salience in the allocation of overt visual attention. *Vision Research, 42,* 107–123.

Patterson, K., Vargha-Khadem, F., & Polkey, C.E. (1989). Reading with one hemisphere. *Brain, 112,* 39–63.

Peelen, M.V., Heslenfeld, D.J., & Theeuwes, J. (2004). Endogenous and exogenous attention shifts are mediated by the same large-scale neural network. *Neuroimage, 22,* 822–830.

Pinsk, M.A., Doniger, G.M., & Kastner, S. (2004). Push-pull mechanism of selective attention in human extrastriate cortex. *Journal of Neurophysiology, 92,* 622–629.

Poldrack, R.A. (2000). Imaging brain plasticity: conceptual and methodological issues. a theoretical review. *Neuroimage, 12,* 1–13.

Posner, M.I., Walker, J.A., Frierich, F.J., & Rafal, R.D. (1984). Effects of parietal injury on covert orienting of attention. *The Journal of Neuroscience, 4,* 1863–1874.

Price, C.J. (1997). Functional anatomy of reading. In R.S.J. Frackowiak, K.J. Friston, C.D. Frith, R.J. Dolan, & J.C. Mazziotta (Eds.). *Human brain function*, 301–328. San Diego: Academic Press.

Price, C.J., & Friston, K.J. (1997). The temporal dynamics of reading: a PET study. *Proceedings of the Royal Society, London, B, 264*, 1785–1791.

Price, C.J., & Moore, C.J., & Frackowiak R.S. (1996a). The effect of varying stimulus rate and duration on brain activity during reading. *Neuroimage, 3,* 40–52.

Price, C.J., Wise, R.J.S., & Frackowiak, R.S.J. (1996b). Demonstrating the implicit processing of visually presented words and pseudowords. *Cerebral Cortex, 6,* 62–70.

Puce, A., Allison, T., Asgari, M., Gore, J.C., & McCarthy, G. (1996). Differential sensitivity of human visual cortex to faces, letterstrings, and textures: a functional magnetic resonance imaging study. *Journal of Neuroscience, 16,* 5205–5215.

Rayner, K., & Bertera, JH. (1979). Reading without a fovea. *Science*, *206*, 468–469.

Rayner, K., & McConkie, G.W. (1976). What guides a reader's eye movements? *Vision Research, 16*, 829–837.

Rees, G., Wojciulik, E., Clarke, K., Husain, M., Frith, C., & Driver, J. (2000). Unconscious activation of visual cortex in the damaged right hemisphere of a parietal patient with extinction. *Brain, 123*, Pt 8, 1624–1633.

Riddoch, J. (1990). Neglect and the peripheral dyslexias. *Cognitive Neuropsychology, 7,* 369–389.

Rizzo, M., Nawrot, M., Blake, R., & Damasio, A. (1992). A human visual disorder resembling area V4 dysfunction in the monkey. *Neurology, 42,* 1175–1180.

Rizzo, M., & Vecera, S.P. (2002). Psychoanatomical substrates of Balint's syndrome. *Journal of Neurology, Neurosurgery and Psychiatry, 72,* 162–78.

Rubens, A.B., & Benson, D.F. (1971). Associative visual agnosia. *Archives of Neurology, 24,* 305–316.

Saffran, E.M., & Coslett H.B. (1996). "Attentional dyslexia" in Alzheimer's disease: A case study. *Cognitive Neuropsychology, 13*, 205–228.

Sakai, K., & Miyashita, Y. (1991). Neural organization for the long-term memory of paired associates. *Nature, 354,* 152–155.

Scholl, B.J. (2001). Objects and attention: the state of the art. *Cognition, 80,* 1–46.

Sereno, M.I. (2001). Mapping of contralateral space in retinotopic coordinates by a parietal cortical area in humans. *Science, 294,* 1350–1354.

Sereno, S.C., & Rayner, K. (2003). Measuring word recognition in reading: eye movements and event-related potentials. *Trends in Cognitive Science, 7,* 489–493.

Seymour, S.E., Reuter-Lorenz, P.A., & Gazzaniga, M.S. (1994). The disconnection syndrome: basic findings reaffirmed. *Brain, 117,* 105–115.

Shallice, T. (1988). *From neuropsychology to mental structure.* Cambridge: Cambridge University Press.

Shallice, T., & Warrington, E.K. (1977). The possible role of selective attention in acquired dyslexia. *Neuropsychologia, 15,* 31–41.

Sidtis, J.J., Volpe, B.T., Holtzman, J.D., Wilson, D.H., & Gazzaniga, M.S. (1981). Cognitive interaction after staged callosal section: Evidence for transfer of semantic activation. *Science, 212,* 344–346.

Sieroff, E., Pollatsek, A., & Posner, MI. (1988). Recognition of visual letter strings following injury to the posterior visual spatial attention system. *Cognitive Neuropsychology, 5,* 427–449.

Sieroff, E., & Urbanski, M. (2002). Conditions of visual verbal extinction: does the ipsilesional stimulus have to be identified? *Brain and Cognition, 48,* 563–569.

Somers, D.C., Dale, A.M., Seiffert A.E., & Tootell, R.B.H. (1999). Functional MRI reveals spatially specific attentional modulation in human primary visual cortex. *Proceedings of the National Academy of Sciences USA, 96,* 1663–1668.

Tanaka, K. (1996). Inferotemporal cortex and object vision. *Annual Review of Neuroscience, 19,* 109–139.

Tarkiainen, A., Helenius, P., Hansen P.C., Cornelissen, P.L., & Salmelin R. (1999). Dynamics of letter string perception in the human occipitotemporal cortex. *Brain, 122,* 2119–32.

Treisman, A., & Souther, J. (1986). Illusory words: the roles of attention and of top-down constraints in conjoining letters to form words. *Journal of Experimental Psychology Human Perception and Performance, 12,* 3–17.

Tsunoda, K., Yamane, Y., Nishizaki, M., & Tanifuji, M. (2001). Complex objects are represented in macaque inferotemporal cortex by the combination of feature columns. *Nature Neuroscience, 4,* 832–838.

Ungerleider, L.G., & Mishkin, M. (1982). Two cortical visual systems. In D.J. Ingle, M.A. Goodale & R.J. Mansfield (Eds.). *Analysis of visual behavior,* 549–586. Cambridge: MIT Press.

Upton, N.J., Hodgson, T.L., Plant, G.T., Wise, R.J., & Leff, A.P. (2003). "Bottom-up" and "top-down" effects on reading saccades: a case study. *Journal of Neurology, Neurosurgery and Psychiatry, 74,* 1423–1428.

Vinckier F, Dehaene S, Jobert A, Dubus JP, Sigman M, Cohen L. (2007). Hierarchical coding of letter strings in the ventral stream: Dissecting the inner organization of the visual word-form system. *Neuron, 55,* 143–156.

Vinckier, F., Naccache, L., Papeix, C., Forget, J., Hahn-Barma, V., Dehaene, S., et al. (2006). "What" and "where" in word reading: ventral coding of written words revealed by parietal atrophy. *Journal of Cognitive Neuroscience, 18,* 1998–2012.

Vuilleumier, P., Sagiv, N., Hazeltine, E., Poldrack, R.A., Swick, D., Rafal, R.D., et al. (2001). Neural fate of seen and unseen faces in visuospatial neglect: a combined event-related functional MRI and event-related potential study. *Proceedings of the National Academy of Sciences USA, 98,* 3, 495–500.

Wagner, A.D., Schacter, D.L., Rotte, M., Koutstaal W., Maril A., Dale A.M., et al. (1998). Building memories: remembering and forgetting of verbal experiences as predicted by brain activity. *Science, 281,* 1188–1191.

Warrington, E.K., Cipolotti, L., & McNeil, J. (1993). Attentional dyslexia: a single case study. *Neuropsychologia, 34,* 871–885.

Weekes, B.S. (1997). Differential effects of number of letters on word and nonword naming latency. *Quarterly Journal of Experimental Psychology, 50A,* 439–456.

Weissman, D.H., & Woldorff, M.G. (2004). Hemispheric asymmetries for different components of global/local attention occur in distinct temporo-parietal loci. *Cerebral Cortex.*

Whitney, C., & Lavidor, M. (2004). Why word length only matters in the left visual field. *Neuropsychologia, 42,* 1680–1688.

Zihl, J. (1995). Eye movement patterns in hemianopic dyslexia. *Brain, 118,* Pt 4, 891–912.

10

Neural Correlates of the Cognitive Processes Underlying Reading

Evidence from Magnetic Resonance Perfusion Imaging

Argye E. Hillis

Both lesion studies and functional neuroimaging studies have provided evidence for specific neural substrates underlying certain components of the reading process. Some of the evidence both within and across methodologies converges in support of specific structure–function relationships, whereas other evidence appears to be conflicting. The focus of this chapter is to review data from a single methodology—acute functional lesion–deficit correlation—that has been used to evaluate specific hypotheses regarding the neural basis of reading. The hypotheses were generated from functional imaging and/or chronic lesion studies and then tested in patients with acute stroke. This method involves both detailed assessment of reading (and other lexical tasks) and identifying the acute functional lesion (structurally damaged plus dysfunctional but undamaged brain tissue) within 24 hours of the onset of stroke symptoms. The goal of this methodology is to determine those areas of the brain responsible for impairments of specific components of the reading process, before reorganization or recovery. The acute functional brain lesion is identified with magnetic resonance diffusion-weighted imaging (MRI-DWI), which reveals densely ischemic or infarcted tissue within minutes to hours after onset of stroke, together with perfusion-weighted imaging (PWI), which reveals areas of low blood flow surrounding the core infarct, which also contribute to the patient's deficit. The underlying assumption of this type of study is that if an area is necessary for a particular component of the reading process, damage or dysfunction of the tissue in that area should disrupt that component, at least acutely (before reorganization or recovery). Another important aspect of this methodology is that patients are selected only on the basis of having an acute, supratentorial ischemic stroke (in some studies referable to the left hemisphere), so that patients with and without some deficit of interest and patients with and without damage or dysfunction of some region of interest are studied. This inclusion criterion prevents a selection bias and allows identification of both the probability that a deficit is associated with damage to or dysfunction of a particular region and the probability that damage to or dysfunction of the region results in the deficit. Both probabilities are important, because certain areas of the brain are particularly vulnerable to damage in stroke, so that they are over-represented in many chronic lesion–deficit association studies. The acute functional lesion–deficit methodology identifies both the sensitivity and the specificity of a deficit for predicting damage to a given area of brain.

The various hypotheses about the neural basis of reading that have been evaluated with this methodology will be reviewed. These hypotheses are framed in terms of an architecture of the cognitive processes underlying reading, based on the computational requirements of the reading task and evidence from patients with selective deficits in reading that can be explained by proposing damage to one of the postulated components, as outlined below.

An Architecture of the Reading Task

Reading a familiar printed word, such as *height*, must begin by matching a printed stimulus to learned information about the sequence of letters that comprise that word. This initial step of word recognition must accommodate variations in font, case, size, location, and even orientation of the word, so that HEIGHT, *height,* or even height written upside down or vertically, printed on either side of the page, are all recognized as the same word. This recognition process likely requires computation of a sequence of spatial representations of the printed stimulus that are increasingly abstracted away from the physical form (Monk, 1985; based on a more general theory of vision proposed by Marr, 1982). The first visual representation of, say, the word HEIGHT in the upper left corner of the page would specify the variations in light intensities of the physical stimulus and would retain information about the location of the stimulus in the visual field, as well as about the size and shape of the letters. This representation, labeled the *retinocentric feature map* (Hillis & Caramazza, 1990; Caramazza & Hillis, 1990a & b) or *viewer-centered spatial representation* (Hillis, Newhart, Heidler, Marsh, Barker & Dagonkar, 2005), roughly corresponds to Marr's "primal sketch." Evidence for this level of representation comes from neurologically impaired patients whose reading errors increase further to the side of the viewer contralateral to the lesion (the "contralesional" side; Hillis, Rapp, Benzing, & Caramazza, 1998). A subsequent representation likely retains information about letter shape, including case and orientation, but not location or size, of the stimulus. This *stimulus-centered letter shape map* roughly corresponds to Marr's "2 ½-D sketch." Evidence for the independence of this level of representation is provided by patients who make errors specifically on the contralesional side of the physical stimulus, irrespective of the location or size of the stimulus. Thus, some patients with right cortical lesions make errors only on the left side of the stimulus (H in the word HEIGHT, but T in the word HEIGHT rotated 180 degrees) (Arguin & Bub, 1993; Hillis & Caramazza, 1991a, 1995a; Subbiah & Caramazza, 2000; Haywood & Coltheart, 2000). A final computed representation of the stimulus would retain only information about the letter identities—graphemes—and their relative order, without information about location, font, case, or orientation. This *word-centered grapheme description*, akin to Marr's object-centered 3-D model, would be identical for the stimuli HEIGHT, *height*, or even the word h-e-i-g-h-t spelled aloud. This location-, orientation-, case-, and modality-independent representation would specify the sequence of graphemes that comprise the stimulus, irrespective of whether the stimulus is a familiar or novel word. Evidence that this level of representation has spatial extent with a canonical left–right orientation (initial letters on the left, final letters on the right), comes from patients who make errors on the side of the canonical word contralateral to the brain lesion (e.g., H in both the word HEIGHT and in the word HEIGHT rotated 180 degrees or spelled aloud; Barbut & Gazzaniga, 1987; Hillis & Caramazza, 1990, 1995a & b; Warrington, 1991).

Once a grapheme description of the word is computed, it can be used to match a stored representation of the sequence of graphemes that comprise the spelling of a familiar word (an orthographic lexical representation), or it can be held in a buffer while each grapheme or small group of graphemes is converted to a phonological segment (using orthography-to-phonology correspondence, or OPC, mechanisms; Coltheart, Patterson, & Marshall, 1980). The former would allow one to recognize that HEIGHT is a familiar word (because it matches an orthographic lexical representation), while HYTE is not (because it does not match an entry in the lexicon). The activated orthographic lexical representation of HEIGHT would access the meaning, or semantic representation, and the phonological lexical representation (learned pronunciation) of HEIGHT. Thus, the reader would know that HEIGHT is a vertical dimension and pronounced /halt/ (rhyming with fight). Use of OPC mechanisms alone would as likely result in pronunciation of the word HEIGHT as "hate" (rhyming with eight). Although these mechanisms are

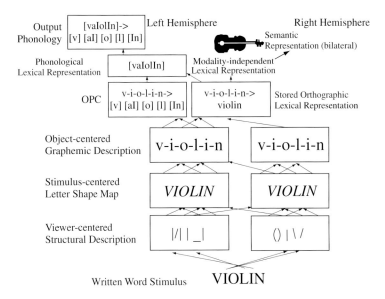

Figure 10.1 Schematic representation of proposed component representations and processes underlying reading.

represented as relatively independent in the schematic representation of the reading process in Figure 10.1, there is evidence that semantic and OPC mechanisms interact in accessing phonological lexical representations (Hillis & Caramazza, 1991b, 1995c; Nickels, 1992; Patterson & Hodges, 1992). Some types of models do not postulate separate lexical representations and sublexical OPC mechanisms, but propose that semantic and OPC mechanisms interact in computing a correct pronunciation (Plaut, 1996). However, the strengths and weaknesses of this sort of computational model are beyond the scope of this chapter. For heuristic purposes, it will be assumed that orthographic and phonological lexical representations of learned words are "stored" relatively independently of one another and independently of OPC mechanisms. This proposal would explain the performance of patients who make errors in reading irregular familiar words (e.g., height) but not regular words (e.g., bite) or pseudowords (pite) by assuming selectively impaired access to lexical representations and preserved OPC mechanisms (see Patterson, Coltheart, & Marshall, 1985 for review). It would also account for the reading performance of patients who are impaired in reading pseudowords but not in reading familiar words, by assuming selective impairment of OPC mechanisms and spared access to lexical representations (Beauvois & Derouesne, 1979). Hypotheses about the neural correlates of the proposed components of the reading task, and evidence from studies of reading and MRI (DWI and PWI) in acute stroke supporting these hypotheses, are discussed below.

Neural Regions Necessary for Each Component of the Reading Process: Evidence from Acute Functional Lesion–Deficit Studies

Computation of Early Visual Representations of Words Depends on Right Occipitoparietal Cortex and Left/Right Striate Cortex

Obviously, reading a printed word depends on first seeing the word, which requires visual pathways terminating in striate cortex. Although the striate cortex in each hemisphere is responsible only for computing visual stimuli in the opposite visual field, damage to the striate cortex on one side does not normally affect reading, because compensatory eye movements shift the entire stimulus word into the intact visual hemifield. However, it has been proposed that subsequent processing or attention to spatial representations of any visual stimulus depends predominantly on right temporoparietal cortex (Vallar & Perani, 1985). Alternatively, evidence from functional imaging and lesion studies suggests that spatial attention for reading and other tasks depends on spatially specific attentional mechanisms in the temporoparietal junction/angular gyrus bilaterally and sustained attention mechanisms in the right intraparietal sulcus (Corbetta & Shulman, 2002).

Evidence from patterns of performance of stroke patients on a variety of visual tasks indicates that computation of a viewer-centered spatial representation depends on the right parietal cortex (angular gyrus and intraparietal sulcus), whereas computation of a stimulus-centered spatial representation depends predominantly on the right superior temporal cortex. A study of 50 patients showed that acute right parietal dysfunction (revealed by hypoperfusion on PWI) was associated with left viewer-centered hemispatial neglect—errors on the contralesional side of the viewer on both sides of stimuli (Fisher's exact: $p <.0001$) (Hillis, Newhart, Heidler, Barker, & Degaonkar, 2005). See Figure 10.2. In contrast, right superior temporal dysfunction was strongly associated with left stimulus-centered hemispatial neglect—errors on the contralesional side of each stimulus, irrespective of the side of the viewer (Fisher's exact: $p <.0001$). To test the hypothesis that these types of spatial representations are also computed in reading and depend on the same neural correlates in reading as in other visuospatial tasks, we studied 95 patients with acute ischemic stroke within 48 hours of onset on a variety of reading tasks and with DWI and PWI (Hillis, Newhart, Heidler, Marsh, Barker, & Degaonkar, 2005). Damage or dysfunction of the right inferior parietal lobule or visual association cortex was strongly associated with impaired computation of the viewer-centered spatial representation on the left (contralesional) side—viewer-centered neglect dyslexia. That is, production of errors on the left side of words (e.g., height read as "eight" or "fight") that increased further to the left of the viewer was associated with infarct and/or

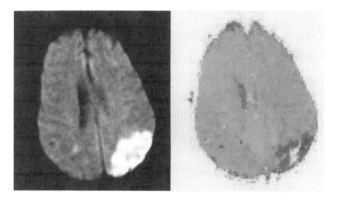

Figure 10.2 Diffusion-weighted image (DWI) (*left*) and perfusion-weighted image (PWI) (*right*) of a patient with hypoperfusion and infarct of left angular gyrus associated with impaired oral reading of pseudowords and words, impaired written lexical decision, and impaired reading comprehension (but spared auditory comprehension).

hypoperfusion of the right angular gyrus ($\chi^2 = 23.2$; $df = 1$; $p < .00001$), right supramarginal gyrus ($\chi^2 = 12.0$; $df = 1$; $p < .0004$), and visual association cortex ($\chi^2 = 43.5$; $df = 1$; $p < .0001$). In contrast, damage to or dysfunction of the right superior temporal cortex was strongly associated with stimulus-centered neglect dyslexia ($\chi^2 = 15.2$; $df = 1$; $p < .0001$) and not with viewer-centered neglect dyslexia. In these patients, errors increased further toward the left side of the stimulus word (e.g., more errors on the initial H than E and no errors on the final letters in HEIGHT), irrespective of the side of the viewer (Hillis, Newhart, Heidler, et al. 2005). These contrasting patterns of neglect, and their corresponding areas of dysfunctional tissue, are illustrated in Figure 10.3.

Right or Left Mid-fusiform Gyrus Is Essential for Computing Word-centered Grapheme Descriptions

There is robust evidence from functional MRI (fMRI) studies of reading that the bilateral (left > right) mid-fusiform gyri are activated in response to viewing written words and pseudowords, as well as letters, relative to other visual stimuli. The area of activation is quite consistent across studies and across printed stimuli, irrespective of location, font, or size (Price et al., 1996; Puce, Allison, Asgari, Gore, & McCarthy 1996; Uchida et al., 1999; Cohen et al., 2000, 2002; Polk et al., 2002; Polk & Farah, 2002; Cohen & Dehaene, 2004 for review). These results have been taken as evidence that the left mid-fusiform gyrus has a specialized role in reading, and in particular, in computing location- and font-independent visual word forms, akin to the graphemic description level of representation in reading discussed earlier

A. Viewer-centered neglect dyslexia   B. Stimulus-centered neglect dyslexia

Reading: *There is nothing unfair about it.->*   *There is nothing unfair about it.->*
about it."   "There is... washing hair without it"

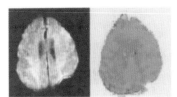 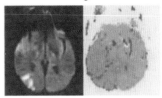

Figure 10.3 A: Diffusion-weighted image (DWI) (*left*) and perfusion-weighted image (PWI) (*right*) scans of a patient with viewer-centered neglect dyslexia associated with hypoperfusion (but no infarct) of right inferior parietal lobule, along with representative reading errors. B: DWI (*left*) and PWI (*right*) scans of a patient with stimulus-centered neglect dyslexia associated with hypoperfusion (but not infarct) in right superior temporal gyrus, along with representative reading errors. Hypoperfused areas appear blue. Note that hypoperfusion without infarct cause tissue dysfunction in the area.

(McCandliss, Cohen, & Dehaene., 2003; Cohen et al., 2003). This area has thus been dubbed, the *visual word form area* (VWFA) (Cohen et al., 2000, 2002). However, based on activation of the same or nearby area during a variety of nonreading lexical tasks, and on the fact that lesions in this area are associated with a variety of lexical deficits, other investigators have objected to the label. These opponents of the label of "visual word form area" have proposed that the left mid-fusiform gyrus has a specialized role in modality-independent lexical processing, rather than reading specifically (Büchel, Price, & Friston, 1998; Price, Winterburn, Giraud, Moore, & Noppeney, 2003; Price & Devlin, 2003, 2004).

To evaluate these two proposals, we studied 80 patients with acute, left hemisphere ischemic stroke on two reading tasks that require access to a graphemic description or visual word form but do not require lexical output; that is, written lexical decision and written word–picture verification (verifying whether or not a written word and picture have the same referent, using semantically and phonologically related foils). In addition, patients were administered other lexical tasks, including oral and written naming of pictures, oral naming of objects from tactile exploration, oral reading, spelling to dictation, and spoken word/picture verification. Patients underwent MRI, including DWI and PWI, the same day. It was assumed that if the left mid-fusiform were critical to accessing visual word forms, then damage to or dysfunction of this area would, at least at the onset of stroke (before reorganization and recovery), reliably cause impaired performance on written lexical decision and written word–picture verification.

Results of this study did not support the hypothesis that the left mid-fusiform gyrus is necessary for accessing visual word forms, since there was not a significant association between damage to or dysfunction of this region and impaired written lexical decision or written word–picture verification (Hillis, Newhart, Heidler, Barker, Herskovits, & Degaonkar, 2005). Of 53 patients who showed hypoperfusion (severe enough to cause dysfunction) and/or infarct that included the left mid-fusiform gyrus, 22 subjects had intact written word comprehension and 15 had intact written lexical decision, indicating that these tasks can be accomplished without function of this region.

How, then can we explain the reliable activation of the left mid-fusiform gyrus during reading? On one account, the activation represents modality-independent lexical processing, rather than a reading-specific process (Price & Devlin, 2003, 2004). There is some evidence that this (or a nearby) region is essential for modality-independent lexical processing (as discussed later). However, other evidence suggests that either the left or right mid-fusiform gyrus *and* access to other language areas from the intact mid-fusiform gyrus are both essential for computing a location-, font-, and orientation-independent graphemic description (one potential meaning of a visual word form). The primary evidence in support of this latter account comes from patients with alexia without agraphia or "letter-by-letter reading." These patients typically have two lesions: one in the left occipital lobe (preventing direct visual input to the left mid-fusiform gyrus) or in the left mid-fusiform gyrus itself, and the other in the splenium of the corpus callosum (preventing visual input from the right hemisphere to the left mid-fusiform gyrus) (Binder & Mohr, 1992; Chialant & Caramazza, 1998; Dejerine, 1981 & 1982; Miozzo & Caramazza, 1998; Saffran & Coslett, 1998; Marsh & Hillis, 2005). In one case of acute alexia without agraphia, written word recognition was impaired when the left mid-fusiform gyrus was infarcted and the splenium was hypoperfused, but recovered when the splenium was reperfused (despite persistent damage to the left mid-fusiform gyrus). These results were interpreted as evidence that the patient was able to rely on the right mid-fusiform gyrus to compute graphemic descriptions; but these graphemic descriptions could not be used for reading until the function of the splenium was restored. Reperfusion of the splenium apparently allowed information from the right mid-fusiform gyrus to access language cortex for additional components of the reading process (Marsh & Hillis, 2005). This proposal of a critical role of either the left or right mid-fusiform gyrus in computing graphemic descriptions is consistent with the reliable activation of this area in response to written words, pseudo-words, and letters in functional imaging, consistent with evidence of bilateral mid-fusiform gyrus in written lexical decision (Fiebach et al., 2002), and consistent with electrophysiological evidence of a mid-fusiform activity early in the reading process (Salmelin et al., 1996; Tarkiainen et al., 1999).

Part of Brodmann's Area 37/Fusiform Gyrus Is Essential for Modality-independent Lexical Processing

As noted, an alternative (or complementary) account of left mid-fusiform gyrus activation during reading, based predominantly on positron emission tomography (PET) and fMRI studies, is that this region is engaged in modality-independent lexical processing, including Braille reading, sign language, oral reading, and naming (Price & Devlin, 2003, 2004). In support of this proposal, in the study of lexical processing along with DWI and PWI in the 80 acute stroke patients described in the preceding section, there was a strong association between damage to or dysfunction of this area and impairment in oral reading ($\chi^2 = 10.8$; $df = 1$; $p = .001$), spoken picture naming ($\chi^2 = 18.9$; $df = 1$; $p < .0001$), spoken object naming to tactile exploration ($\chi^2 = 8.2$; $df = 1$; $p < .004$), and written picture naming ($\chi^2 = 13.5$; $df = 1$; $p < .0002$) (Hillis, Newhart, Heidler, Barker, Herskovits, et al., 2005). That is, structural damage or tissue dysfunction of mid-fusiform gyrus was associated with impaired lexical processing, irrespective of the input or output modality. In this study, the infarct or hypoperfusion that included the left mid-fusiform gyrus generally also included adjacent areas of the left fusiform gyrus/ BA 37. Therefore, it is possible that dysfunction of areas nearby the left mid-fusiform gyrus, such as the lateral inferotemporal multimodality area (LIMA: Cohen, Jobert, Le Bihan, & Dehaene, 2004) was critical to modality-independent lexical processing. Further support for the essential role of at least a portion of the left fusiform gyrus in modality-independent lexical access comes from patients who show impaired naming (with visual or tactile input) and oral reading when this region is hypoperfused, and improved naming and oral reading when this region is reperfused (Hillis, Kane, et al., 2002, Hillis, Newhart, Heidler, Barker, Herskovits, et al., 2005). Previous studies have also reported impaired oral naming and oral reading in association with lesions to this region (e.g., Raymer et al., 1997; Foundas, Daniels, & Vasterling, 1998; Hillis, Tuffiash, et al., 2002; Sakurai, Sakai, Sakuta, & Iwata, 1994).

Involvement of the left BA 37/fusiform gyrus in lexical access in the reading process is also supported by recent functional imaging studies of reading development. For example, several studies suggest that children who read by the slower, sublexical process of assembling pronunciations (before recognizing whole words) show activation primarily in the left angular gyrus. However, as they begin to read familiar irregular words by the faster process of accessing lexical representations, activation shifts to the left fusiform gyrus and extra-striate cortex (Pugh et al., 2001). Consistent with this proposed role of the left fusiform gyrus in lexical access, this area shows greater activation during familiar word reading relative to pseudoword reading (Tagamets et al., 2000), and greater activation with age and reading skill (Pugh et al. 2001).

Left Inferior Parietal Lobule (Angular Gyrus and Supramarginal Gyrus) in Sublexical OPC Mechanisms

Pugh and colleagues (2001) also reviewed evidence from functional imaging of reading in normal and developmentally delayed readers that the left inferior parietal lobule (which is composed of angular and supramarginal gyri and part of the "dorsal stream" of reading) is involved in sublexical reading. Studies have shown greater activation in the left dorsal regions (including the inferior parietal lobule) during pseudoword relative to word reading, increased activation during phonological analysis, and decreased activation with faster presentation rates (Pugh et al., 2001). Reading is also associated with activation in the left inferior parietal lobule in some functional imaging studies of adults (Binder, McKiernan, Parsons, Westbury, Possing, Kaufman, Buchanan, 2003 Jobard, Crivello, & Tzourio-Mazoyer, 2003; Joubert et al., 2004). An important role of the left angular gyrus is also indicated by the frequent association between lesions in this area and impaired reading (Dejerine, 1891; Benson, 1979; Vanier & Caplan, 1985; Black & Behrmann, 1994; Hillis, Kane, Barker, et al., 2001), but most lesion studies have not defined the component of reading that was impaired. Furthermore, reading-disabled subjects show less connectivity in PET studies between the left BA 37 and left angular gyrus during oral reading than do normal readers (Horwitz et al., 1998). Most of these functional imaging studies and lesion studies indicate that the left angular gyrus and/or supramarginal gyrus play a role in reading, but only the evidence reviewed by Pugh and colleagues (2001) and Jobard and colleagues (2003) indicates a specific component of reading (OPC mechanisms) that may depend on the left inferior parietal lobule.

Two studies of reading with concurrent DWI and PWI in acute stroke have evaluated the role of the left inferior parietal lobule in reading. In the study of 80 patients described earlier, we found that hypoperfusion/infarct of the left angular gyrus was associated with impaired written word comprehension ($\chi^2 = 32.7$; $df = 1$; $p < .0001$) and lexical decision ($\chi^2 = 29.2$; $df = 1$; $p < .0001$), indicating that it may be essential for accessing lexical orthographic representations or some other aspect of learned orthography essential to accessing orthographic lexical representations. Reading of pseudowords was not specifically evaluated in this study. In an earlier study of 40 acute stroke patients, areas of neural dysfunction associated with impairments of specific components of the reading process were identified (Hillis, Kane, Barker, Beauchamp, & Wityk, 2001). In this study, impaired application of OPC mechanisms was defined as significantly more impaired reading of pseudowords relative to words, and was associated with hypoperfusion/ infarct of both the left angular gyrus ($\chi^2 = 5.9$; $df = 1$; $p < .02$) and the supramarginal gyrus ($\chi^2 = 5.5$; $df = 1$; $p < .02$). However, impaired access to orthographic lexical representations for reading comprehension and reading of irregular words was also associated with hypoperfusion/ infarct of the left angular gyrus ($\chi^2 = 7.1$; $df = 1$; $p < .01$) in that study. Together, these results suggest that the left inferior parietal lobule may be critical in accessing some aspect of learned orthography necessary for reading both familiar and unfamiliar words. Whether these roles depend on a common cognitive and/or neural mechanism or on separate processes that are subserved by adjacent areas within the left inferior parietal lobule is unclear. These data are consistent with models of reading that do not specify separate "routes" for reading familiar and unfamiliar words (e.g., Plaut & Shallice, 1993), but can also be accommodated within models that do specify separate "routes" or representations/processes for reading familiar versus unfamiliar words.

Left Posterior, Inferior Frontal Gyrus Is Critical for Sublexical OPC Mechanisms in Reading Aloud

Functional imaging of normal and impaired reading development also implicates the left posterior, inferior frontal gyrus in later stages of OPC that require assembly of a phonological representation for articulatory output (Pugh et al., 2001). Likewise, several functional imaging studies of healthy adults have indicated that the left posterior inferior frontal gyrus is engaged in tasks that require recoding of phonological representations into articulatory gestures (see Burton & Small, 2002, for review) or phonological recoding required for rhyming judgments (Burton, Locasto, Krebs-Noble, & Gullapalli, 2005). Some studies have specifically shown that activation during phonological recoding (e.g., for judgments of rhyming of written stimuli) is greater for pseudowords than words (Jobard et al., 2003; Mechelli, Gorno-Tempini, & Price, 2003; Xu, Grafman, Gaillard, Ishii, Vega-Bermudez, Pietrini, Reeves-Tyer, & DiCamillo, 2001).

The hypothesis that the left posterior inferior frontal gyrus (Broca's area) is not only engaged, but also necessary, for sublexically reading aloud unfamiliar words and pseudowords is provided by studies that demonstrate an association between lesions in the posterior inferior frontal gyrus and impaired pseudoword reading (Hillis & Caramazza, 1995c). Although damage to this area typically disrupts orchestration of speech articulation for all verbal tasks acutely after stroke (Mohr, 1976; Hillis, Work, Breese, Barker, Jacobs, & Maurer, 2004), it seems to have a more prolonged effect on sublexical reading. Thus, patients with chronic Broca's aphasia often have a severe impairment in reading aloud pseudowords even when they can repeat them (e.g., Matthews, 1991; Schweiger, Zaidel, Field & Dobkin, 1989; see Goldberg & Benjamins, 1982, for review). Even in acute stroke, some patients with an infarct and hypoperfusion in Broca's area are more impaired in oral reading of

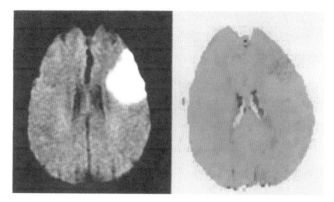

Figure 10.4 Diffusion-weighted image (DWI) (*left*) and perfusion-weighted image (PWI) (*right*) of a patient with impaired oral reading of pseudowords relative to words. DWI shows an infarct that includes Broca's area. PWI shows hypoperfusion of part of Broca's area. The smaller area of hypoperfusion illustrates "luxury perfusion"—reperfusion of an area of tissue that already shows infarction.

pseudowords than words, and have trouble reading aloud pseudowords that they can repeat (e.g., single syllable pseudowords, indicating a specific impairment in OPC, beyond the motor speech impairment). For example, the patient whose scans are shown in Figure 10.4 was more impaired in oral reading of monosyllabic pseudowords (79% correct) than words (94% correct), although he showed normal performance in repetition of the same words and pseudowords. These results indicate that his Broca's area lesion resulted in impaired OPC mechanisms, even for monosyllables. He did have impaired planning and programming of speech articulation in oral naming, oral reading, and repetition of polysyllabic words and pseudowords.

Because of the impairment in orchestrating speech articulation for all verbal tasks produced by dysfunction of Broca's area, it has been difficult to evaluate more specific effects of damage to this area on OPC mechanisms. Future studies that include tests of rhyme judgments about word and pseudoword pairs might help to determine whether this region is necessary for converting orthographic codes to sublexical phonological representations or for holding sequences of phonemes in a "buffer" while each phoneme is converted, or for converting sublexical phonological representations to articulatory programs.

Conclusion

Functional neuroimaging studies of reading have been invaluable for identifying the networks of brain regions engaged in various aspects of reading. Evidence that acute dysfunction (damage or hypoperfusion) in each of these brain regions reliably disrupts some aspect of reading can confirm that each of these areas is essential for a particular component process underlying reading. Studies of acute functional lesions (using DWI and PWI) and reading complement the functional imaging studies, by testing hypotheses generated from functional imaging studies concerning the role of particular areas (right and left inferior parietal lobule, right and left mid-fusiform gyrus, and Broca's area) in reading.

Acknowledgment

The research reported in this paper was supported by NIH R01: NS047691.

References

Arguin, M., & Bub, D. N. (1993). Evidence for an independent stimulus-centered spatial reference frame from a case of visual hemineglect. *Cortex, 29,* 349–357.

Barbut, D., & Gazzaniga, M. S. (1987). Disturbances in conceptual space involve language and speech. *Brain, 110,* 1487–1496.

Beauvois, M. F., & Derouesne, J. (1979). Phenological alexia: Three dissociations. *Journal of Neurology, Neurosurgery, and Psychiatry, 42,* 115–1124.

Benson, D.F. (1979). *Aphasia, Alexia and Agraphia.* Chrchill Livingstone: New York.

Binder, J.R., McKiernan, K.A., Parsons, M.E., Westbury, C.F., Possing, E.T., Kaufman, J.N., Buchanan, L. (2003). Neural correlates of lexical access during visual word recognition. Journal of Cognitive Neuroscience, 15, 372–393.

Binder, J. R., & Mohr, J. P. (1992). The topography of callosal reading pathways. A case-control analysis. *Brain, 115,* 1807–1826.

Black, S., & Behrmann, M. (1994). Localization in alexia. In A. Kertesz (Ed.). *Localization and Neuroimaging in Neuropsychology.* San Diego: Academic Press.

Büchel, C., Price, C. & Friston, K. (1998). A multimodal language region in the ventral visual pathway. *Nature, 394,* 274–277.

Burton, M., & Small, S. (2002). Models of speech processing. In A.E. Hillis (Ed.) *Handbook of Adult Language Disorders: Integrating Cognitive Neuropsychology, Neurology, and Rehabilitation,* pp. 253–268. Philadelphia: Psychology Press.

Burton, M.W., LoCasto, P.C., Krebs-Noble, D., Gullapalli, R.P. (2005). A systematic investigation of the functional neuroanatomy of auditory and visual phonological processing. *NeuroImage,* 26, 647–661.

Caramazza, A., & Hillis, A. E. (1990a). Spatial representations of words in the brain implied by studies of a unilateral neglect patient. *Nature, 346,* 267–269.

Caramazza, A., & Hillis, A. E. (1990b). Levels of representation, coordinate frames, and unilateral neglect. *Cognitive Neuropsychology, 7,* 391–445.

Chialant, D., & Caramazza, A. (1998). Perceptual and lexical factors in a case of letter-by-letter reading. *Cognitive Neuropsychology, 15,* 167–201.

Cohen, L., & Dehaene, S. (2004). Distinct unimodal and multimodal regions for word processing in the left temporal cortex. *Neuroimage, 23,* 4, 1256–1270.

Cohen, L., & Dehaene, S. (2004). Specialization within the ventral stream: The case for the visual word form area. *Neuroimage, 22,* 466–476.

Cohen, L., Dehaene, S., Naccache, L., Lehéricy, S., Dehaene-Lambertz, G., Hénaff, M. A., & Michel, F. (2000). The visual word form area: Spatial and temporal characterization of an initial stage of reading in normal subjects and posterior split brain patients. *Brain, 123,* 291–307.

Cohen, L., Henry, C., Dehaene, S., O., M., Lehéricy, S., Martinaud, O., C., L., & Ferrieux, S. (2004). The pathophysiology of letter-by-letter reading. *Neuropsychologia, 42,* 13, 1768–1780.

Cohen, L., Jobert, A., Le Bihan, D., Dehaene, S. (2004). *Distinct unimodal and multimodal regions for word processing in the left temporal cortex. Neuroimage*, 23, 1256–1270.

Cohen, L., Lehericy, S., Chochon, F., Lemer, C., Rivaud, S., & Dehaene, S. (2002). Language-specific tuning of visual cortex? Functional properties of the visual word form area. *Brain, 125,* 1054–1069.

Cohen, L., Martinaud, O., Lemer, C., Lehericy, S., Samson, Y., Obadia, M., et al. (2003). Visual word recognition in the left and right hemispheres: anatomical and functional correlates of peripheral alexias. *Cerebral Cortex, 13,* 1313–1333.

Coltheart, M., Patterson, K., & Marshall, J. C. (1980). *Deep dyslexia.* London: Routeledge and Kegan Paul.

Corbetta, M., & Shulman, G. L. (2002). Control of goal-directed and stimulus-driven attention in the brain. *Nature Reviews. Neuroscience, 3,* 3, 201–215.

Dejerine, J. (1891). Sur un cas de cécité verbale avec agraphie, suivi d'autopsie. *Comptes Rendus Hebdomadaires des Séances et Mémoires de la Société de Biologie, Ninth series, 3,* 197–201.

Cohen, L., Martinaud, O., Lemer, C., Lehéricy, S., Samson, Y., Obadia, M., et al. (2003). Visual word recognition in the left and right hemispheres: anatomical and functional correlates of peripheral alexias. *Cerebral Cortex, 13,* 1313–1333.

Dejerine, J. (1892). Contribution à l'étude anatomo-pathologique et clinique des différentes variétés de cécité verbale. *Memoires Societe Biologique, 4,* 61–90.

Fiebach, C.J., Friederici, A.D., Müller, K, von Cramon, D.Y, (2002). *fMRI evidence for dual routes to the mental lexicon in visual word recognition.* Journal Cognitive Neuroscience. 1,14(1), 11–23.

Foundas, A., Daniels, S. K., & Vasterling, J. J. (1998). Anomia: Case studies with lesion localization. *Neurocase, 4,* 35–43.

Goldberg, T., & Benjamins, D. (1982). The possible existence of phonemic reading in the presence of Broca's aphasia: a case report. *Neuropsychologia, 20,*5, 547–558.

Haywood, M., & Coltheart, M. (2000). Neglect dyslexia and the early stages of visual word recognition. *Neurocase, 6,* 33–44.

Hillis, A. E., & Caramazza, A. (1990). The effects of attentional deficits on reading and spelling. In A. Caramazza (Ed.). *Cognitive neuropsychology and neurolinguistics: advances in models of cognitive function and impairment,* pp. 211–275. London: Lawrence Erlbaum Associates.

Hillis, A. E., & Caramazza, A. (1991a). Spatially-specific deficit to stimulus-centered letter shape representations in a case of "neglect dyslexia". *Neuropsychologia, 29,* 1223–1240.

Hillis, A. E., & Caramazza, A. (1991b). Mechanisms for accessing lexical representations for output. Evidence from a category-specific semantic deficit. *Brain and Language, 40,* 106–144.

Hillis, A. E., & Caramazza, A. (1995a). A framework for interpreting distinct patterns of hemispatial neglect. *Neurocase, 1,* 189–207.

Hillis, A. E., & Caramazza, A. (1995b). Spatially-specific deficits in processing graphemic representations in reading and writing. *Brain and Language, 48,* 263–308.

Hillis, A. E., & Caramazza, A. (1995c). Converging evidence for the interaction of semantic and phonological information in accessing lexical information for spoken output. *Cognitive Neuropsychology, 12,* 187–227.

Hillis, A. E., Kane, A., Barker, P., Beauchamp, N., & Wityk, R. (2001). Neural substrates of the cognitive processes underlying reading: Evidence from magnetic resonance imaging in hyperacute stroke. *Aphasiology, 15,* 919–931.

Hillis, A. E., Kane, A., Tuffiash, E., Ulatowski, J. A., Barker, P., Beauchamp, N., & Wityk, R. (2002). Reperfusion of specific brain regions by raising blood pressure restores selective language functions in subacute stroke. *Brain and Language, 79,* 495–510.

Hillis, A. E., Newhart, M., Heidler, J., Barker, P. B., & Degaonkar, M. (2005). Anatomy of spatial attention: insights from perfusion imaging and hemispatial neglect in acute stroke. *Journal of Neuroscience, 25,* 3161–3167.

Hillis, A. E., Newhart, M., Heidler, J., Barker, P. B., Herskovits, E., & Degaonkar, M. (2005). The roles of the "visual word form area" in reading. *Neuroimage, 24,* 548–559.

Hillis, A. E., Newhart, M., Heidler, J., Marsh, E. B., Barker, P. B., & Degaonkar, M. (2005). The neglected role of the right hemisphere in spatial representation of words for reading. *Aphasiology, 19,* 225–238.

Hillis, A. E., Rapp, B., Benzing, L., & Caramazza, A. (1998). Dissociable coordinate frames of unilateral spatial neglect: Viewer-centered neglect. *Brain and Cognition, 37,* 491–526.

Hillis, A. E., & Rapp, B. S. (2004). Cognitive and neural substrates of written language comprehension and production. In M. Gazzaniga (Ed.). *The new cognitive neurosciences,* 3rd ed. Cambridge, MA: MIT Press pp. 755–788.

Hillis, A. E., Wityk, R. J., Tuffiash, E., Beauchamp, N. J., Jacobs, M. A., Barker, P. B., & Selnes, O. A. (2001). Hypoperfusion of Wernicke's area predicts severity of semantic deficit in acute stroke. *Annals of Neurology, 50,* 561–566.

Hillis, A. E., Work, M., Breese, E. L., Barker, P. B., Jacobs, M. A., & Maurer, K. (2004). Re-examining the brain regions crucial for orchestrating speech articulation. *Brain, 127,* 1479–1487.

Horwitz, B., Rumsey, J. M., & Donohue, B. C. (1998). Functional connectivity of the angular gyrus in normal reading and dyslexia. *Proceedings of the National Academy of Sciences, USA, 95,* 8939–8944.

Jobard, G., Crivello, F., & Tzourio-Mazoyer, N. (2003). Evaluation of the dual route theory of reading: a metanalysis of 35 neuroimaging studies. *Neuroimage, 20,* 2, 693–712.

Joubert, S., Beauregard, M., Walter, N., Bourgouin, P., Beaudoin, G., Leroux, J.-M., Karama, S., & Lecours, A. R. (2004). Neural correlates of lexical and sublexical processes in reading. *Brain and Language, 89,* 9–20.

Marr, D. (1982). *Vision.* New York: W.H. Freeman and Co.

Marsh, E. B., & Hillis, A. E. (2005). Cognitive and neural mechanisms underlying reading and naming: evidence from letter-by-letter reading and optic aphasia. *Neurocase, 11,* 325–318.

Matthews, C. (1991). Serial processing and the "phonetic route:" lessons learned in the functional reorganization of deep dyslexia. *Journal of Communication Disorders, 24,* 1, 21–39.

McCandliss, B. D., Cohen, L., & Dehaene, S. (2003). The visual word form area: Expertise for reading in the fusiform gyrus. *Trends in Cognitive Science, 7,* 293–299.

Mechelll, A., Gorno-Tempini, M. L., & Price, C. J. (2003). Neuroimaging studies of word and pseudoword reading: consistencies, inconsistencies, and limitations. *Journal of Cognitive Neuroscience, 15,* 2, 260–271.

Miozzo, M., & Caramazza, A. (1998). Varieties of pure alexia: The case of failure to access graphemic representations. *Cognitive Neuropsychology, 15,* 203–238.

Mohr, J. P. (1976). Broca's area and Broca's aphasia. In H. Whitaker (Ed.). *Studies in Neurolinguistics* (Vol. 1). New York: Academic Press.

Monk, A. F. (1985). Co-ordinate systems in visual word recognition. *Quarterly Journal of Experimental Psychology, 37A,* 613–625.

Nickels, L. (1992). The autocue? Self-generated phonemic cues in the treatment of a disorder of reading and naming. *Cognitive Neuropsychology, 9,* 155–182.

Patterson, K., & Hodges, J. (1992). Deterioration of word meaning implications for reading. *Neuropsychologia, 30,* 125–140.

Patterson, K. E., Coltheart, M., & Marshall, J. C. (1985). *Surface Dyslexia.* London: LEA.

Plaut, D. (1996). Relearning after damage in connectionist networks: toward a theory of rehabilitation. *Brain and Language,* 52, 25–82.

Plaut, D., & Shallice, T. (1993). Deep dyslexia: A case study of connectionist neuro-psychology. *Cognitive Neuropsychology, 10,* 77–500.

Price, C. J., & Devlin, J. T. (2003). The myth of the visual word form area. *Neuroimage, 19,* 473–481.

Price, C. J., & Devlin, J. T. (2004). The pros and cons of labeling a left occipitotemporal region: "The visual word form area". *Neuroimage, 22,* 477–479.

Price, C. J., Winterburn, D., Giraud, A. L., Moore, C. J., & Noppeney, U. (2003). Cortical localization of the visual word form areas: A reconsideration of the evidence. *Brain and Language, 86,* 272–286.

Polk, T.A, Stallcup, M., Aguirre, G.K, et al. (2002) Neural specialization for letter recognition. Journal of Cognitive Neuroscience, 14, 145–159.

Polk, T.A., Farah, M.J. (2002) *Functional MRI evidence for an abstract, not perceptual, word-form area.* Journal of Experimental Psychology General, 131, 65–72.

Price, C. J., Wise, R. J., Warburton, E. A., Moore, C. J., Howard, D., Patterson, K., et al. (1996). Hearing and saying. The functional neuro-anatomy of auditory word processing. *Brain, 119,* 919–931.

Puce, A., Allison, T., Asgari, M., Gore, J. C., & McCarthy, G. (1996). Differential sensitivity of human visual cortex to faces, letterstrings, and textures: A functional magnetic resonance imaging study. *Journal of Neuroscience, 16,* 5205–5215.

Pugh, K. R., Mencl, W. E., Jenner, A. R., Katz, L., Frost, S. J., Lee, J. R., Shaywitz, S. E., & Shaywitz, B. A. (2001). Neurobiological studies of reading and reading disability. *Journal of Communication Disorders, 34,* 479–402.

Raymer, A., Foundas, A. L., Maher, L. M., Greenwald, M. L., Morris, M., Rothi, L. G., & Heilman, K. M. (1997). Cognitive neuropsychological analysis and neuroanatomical correlates in a case of acute anomia. *Brain and Language, 58,* 137–156.

Saffran, E. M., & Coslett, H. B. (1998). Implicit vs. letter-by-letter reading in pure alexia: A tale of two systems. *Cognitive Neuropsychology, 15,* 141–165.

Sakurai, Y., Sakai, K., Sakuta, M., & Iwata, M. (1994). Naming difficulties in alexia with agraphia for kanji after a left posterior inferior temporal lesion. *Journal of Neurology, Neurosurgery, and Psychiatry, 57,* 609–613.

Salmelin, R., Service, E., Kiesilä, P., Uutela, K., Salonen, O. (1996) *Impaired visual word processing in dyslexia revealed with magnetoencephalography.* Annals of Neurology. *40,* 157–162.

Schweiger, A., Zaidel, E., Field, T., & Dobkin, B. (1989). Right hemisphere contribution to lexical access in an aphasic with deep dyslexia. *Brain and Language, 37,* 1, 73–89.

Subbiah, I., & Caramazza, A. (2000). Stimulus-centered neglect in reading and object recognition. *Neurocase, 6,* 13–31.

Tagamets MA, Novick JM, Chalmers ML, Friedman RB. (2000). *A parametric approach to orthographic processing in the brain: an fMRI study.* Journal of Cognitive Neuroscience,12, 281–297.

Tarkiainen, A., Helenius, P., Hansen, P.C., Cornelissen, P.L., Salmelin, R. (1999). Dynamics of letter string perception in the human occipitotemporal cortex. Brain, 122, 2119–2132.

Vallar, G., & Perani, D. (1985). The anatomy of spatial neglect in humans. In M. Jeannerod (Ed.). *Neurological and neuropsychological aspects of spatial neglect.* New York: Elsevier/ North-Holland.

Uchida I, Kikyo H, Nakajima K, Konishi S, Sekihara K, Miyashita Y. (1999). *Activation of lateral extrastriate areas during orthographic processing of Japanese characters studied with fMRI.* Neuroimage, 9, 208–215.Vanier, M., & Caplan, D. (1985). CT correlates of surface dyslexia. In K. E. Patterson & J. C. Marshall & M. Coltheart (Eds.). *Surface dyslexia: neuropsychological and cognitive studies of phonological reading.* London: Laurence Erlbaum.

Warrington, E. K. (1991). Right neglect dyslexia: A single case study. *Cognitive Neuropsychology, 8,* 191–212.

Xu, B., Grafman, J., Gaillard, W. D., Ishii, K., Vega-Bermudez, Pietrini, P., Reeves-Tyer, P., DiCamillo, P., & Theodore, W. (2001). Conjoint and extended neural networks for the computation of speech codes: the neural basis of selective impairment in reading words and pseudowords. *Cerebral Cortex, 11,* 3, 267–277.

11

Mapping the Word Reading Circuitry in Skilled and Disabled Readers

Kenneth R. Pugh, Stephen J. Frost, Rebecca Sandak,
Nicole Landi, Dina Moore, Gina Della Porta,
Jay G. Rueckl, and W. Einar Mencl

Research on the neurocognitive foundations of reading in typically and atypically developing readers has benefited in recent years from rapid advances in several neuroimaging technologies (see Papanicolaou, Pugh, Simos, & Mencl, 2004 for a review). In this chapter,[1] we describe recent studies from our lab, and from others, that were designed to generate data not only on the localization of reading-related brain activation, but also to examine patterns of interactions and dynamic tradeoffs among these distributed reading-related systems. Acquiring data of this sort is necessary, in our view, if we are to begin to construct neurobiological models of skilled word identification that can speak to the complexities and dynamics of reading performance. Indeed, computational models of reading in the behavioral domain stand or fall, not by their capacity to account for main effects of isolated variables (e.g., lexicality, frequency, consistency, concreteness, and the like), but rather by whether they can seamlessly account for complex interactions among them (Harm & Seidenberg, 1999). Ultimately, the same criteria must be applied to neurobiologically grounded models as well. Thus, it is critical that we begin to look beyond simply more and more fine-tuned localization and consider also a systems-level approach. Research on systems appears to be a realistic possibility at this stage in the development of these new technologies, given the evidence that extant neurophysiological measures are amenable to sophisticated psycholinguistic designs (Frost et al., 2005; Sandak et al., 2004a;

Dehaene et al., 2004). When we add to all this the clinically oriented goal of better understanding what those demonstrated differences in activation patterns for struggling readers imply about core deficits and optimal remediation, the need to develop dynamic accounts becomes all the more pressing (Pugh et al., 2005). We focus here primarily on studies of word identification in reading, given that this stage of processing appears to be crucial in discriminating fluent from reading disabled (RD) cohorts (Pugh et al., 2000a).

We begin with a review of relevant behavioral studies of component processing in fluent reading, with particular emphasis on the role of early (sublexical) phonology; this operation appears to be most compromised in RD cohorts. We then discuss the current literature on the neurobiology of skilled and disabled reading, along with consideration of a series of recent studies from our lab that aim to capture brain correlates of component processing, again with an emphasis on phonological processing, adaptive learning, and complex tradeoffs and interactions. In each section we also note relevant cross-linguistic studies. Indeed, an adequate neurobiological theory will need to make sense of both cross-language variance and invariance in both typical and atypical reading trajectories. Finally, we take stock of what we consider to be crucial next steps (both technical and theoretical) in the emerging cognitive neuroscience of reading and its disorders.

Behavioral Studies of Skilled Reading

An important issue in studies of reading concerns the question of whether prelexical phonological processing plays an important role in printed skilled and fluent word identification. Clearly, acquiring behavioral data on this question is crucial if we are to correctly interpret observed patterns of activation across the reading circuitry. Different classes of models have been put forward to address this question. Purely orthographic access models (Baron, 1973), and phonological coherence models (Van Orden & Goldinger, 1994; Van Orden, Pennington, & Stone, 1990) each assume singular lexical access codes; graphemic in the former, and phonologically mediated in the latter. By contrast, dual-process accounts usually posit two independent mechanisms or routes for accessing meaning: (1) by mapping from spelling to the lexicon and then obtaining phonological information through a lexical lookup procedure or (2) by mapping from spelling to a phonological code and then to the lexicon ("phonologically mediated access") (Coltheart, 1978; Coltheart, Rastle, Perry, Langdon, & Ziegler, 2001; Paap & Noel, 1991). A number of alternative models do not assume multiple independent mechanisms, but instead posit interactive bidirectional links with a cooperative division of labor among orthographic, phonological, and semantic processes to support efficient word recognition (Harm & Seidenberg, 1999; Plaut, McClelland, Seidenberg, & Patterson, 1996; Seidenberg & McClelland, 1989).

With regard to the evidence for the role of prelexical phonology in skilled word recognition, many studies have now demonstrated that phonological access is early and automatic (see R. Frost, 1998 for review). Using a semantic categorization task, Van Orden found that participants produced more false-positive responses to words that were homophones or pseudohomophones of category exemplars than for spelling foils (e.g., categorizing ROWS/ROZE as a flower more often than the control foil ROBS/REEZ) (Van Orden, 1987; Van Orden et al., 1988). This effect persisted, even at brief exposure durations, indicating that phonological recoding occurred early in processing and mediated activation of meaning. Moreover, because pseudohomophones are not represented lexically, Van Orden and colleagues concluded that the effect must occur before lexical access.

Findings using brief exposure paradigms, such as backward masking and priming, point to an early and robust influence of phonology on lexical access (Lesch & Pollatsek, 1993; Lukatela, Frost, & Turvey, 1999; Lukatela & Turvey, 1994a, 1994b; Perfetti & Bell, 1991; Perfetti, Bell & Delany, 1988). For example, Perfetti and colleagues found significantly better identification rates when briefly presented target words were followed by pseudoword masks that were phonemically similar, than when they were graphemically similar, suggesting that phonological information was automatically extracted from the pseudoword mask and contributed to the identification of the target (Perfetti & Bell, 1991; Perfetti et al., 1988). Furthermore, Lukatela and Turvey (1994a; see also Lesch & Pollatsek, 1993) observed associative priming, pseudoassociative priming, and pseudohomophonic associative priming relative to matched controls. At a short prime-target interval, robust priming of the target word FROG was obtained for TOAD, TOWED, and TODE. At a long interval both TOAD and TODE effects were observed, but TOWED effects were eliminated. The authors concluded that the initial access code must be phonological in nature, with orthographic constraints coming into play relatively late.

Cross-language studies have provided additional evidence indicating that the assembly of prelexical phonological codes mediates lexical access. A unique feature of Serbo-Croatian is that it has one spoken form, but two written alphabets (the Roman and Cyrillic) that share characters, some of which are pronounced the same in both alphabets (i.e., common letters) and some of which are pronounced differently in the two alphabets (i.e., phonologically ambiguous letters). This feature allows researchers to combine the characters such that letter strings have one or more phonological interpretations, depending on whether the phonologically ambiguous characters are interpreted as Cyrillic or Roman. Studies of readers who are competent in both written forms produce slower word naming and lexical decision latencies for letter strings composed of phonologically ambiguous and common letters compared to letter strings composed of phonologically unique and common letters (Lukatela, Popadic, Ognjenovic, & Turvey, 1980), and the size of the effect is positively correlated with the number of phonologically ambiguous letters (Feldman & Turvey, 1983). Moreover, this phonological ambiguity effect can be reduced by using an alphabetic prime composed of phonologically unique letters that effectively specify the target's script (Lukatela, Feldman, et al., 1989). There is also growing evidence that readers of Mandarin are sensitive to the sublexical phonological information contained in the phonetic components of compound words (see Perfetti, Liu, & Tan, 2005 for review). Studies have shown that homophone characters that are unrelated in meaning produce slower decision latencies and higher error rates than control stimuli in semantic similarity judgments (Perfetti & Zhang, 1995). Experiments in Chinese using the backward masking paradigm have shown that briefly exposed target words are better identified when a following mask is a homophone (Tan, Hoosain, & Peng, 1995), paralleling results in English (Perfetti et al., 1988). Although language differences have been reported relative to the size or type of phonological unit that governs lexical access (e.g., see the German/English comparison study of Ziegler et al., 2001; Goswami, Ziegler, et al., 2003), the key point is that the findings converge to indicate that word recognition in skilled adult readers does not appear to differ in fundamental ways across languages and orthographies, despite differences in the complexity of the mapping between a language's written form and its spoken form (Carello, Turvey, & Lukatela, 1992; R. Frost, 1998; Perfetti, 1985). Such language invariance has direct implications for our expectations regarding neurobiological similarities across different orthographies (Pugh et al., 2005).

Behavioral Studies of Reading Disability

Significant progress has been made in understanding the cognitive and linguistic skills that must be in place to ensure adequate reading development in children (Brady & Shankweiler, 1991; Bruck, 1992; Fletcher et al., 1994; Liberman et al., 1974; Rieben & Perfetti, 1991; Shankweiler et al., 1995; Stanovich & Siegel, 1994). With regard to reading disability, it has been argued that the reading difficulties experienced by some children may result from difficulties with processing speed (Wolf & Bowers, 1999), rapid auditory processing (Tallal, 1980), general language deficits (Scarborough & Dobrich, 1990), or visual deficits (Cornelissen & Hansen, 1998). However, there is growing consensus that, for the majority of struggling readers, a core difficulty in reading manifests itself as a deficiency within the language system and, in particular, a deficiency at the level of phonological representation and processing (Liberman, 1992; Liberman et al., 1974; Goswami & Zeigler, 2005).

Deficits in behavioral performance are most evident at the level of single word and pseudoword reading; RD individuals are both slow and inaccurate relative to nonimpaired (NI) readers. Many lines of evidence converge on the conclusion that the word and pseudoword reading difficulties in RD individuals are, to a large extent, manifestations of more basic deficits at the level of rapidly assembling the phonological code represented by a token letter string (Bradley & Bryant, 1983; Liberman et al., 1989). *Phonological assembly* refers to the operations associated with mapping from the orthographic to the phonological form in printed word identification. The failure to develop efficient phonological assembly skills in word and pseudoword reading, in turn, appears to stem from difficulties—at the earliest stages of literacy training—in attaining fine-grained phonemic awareness. Phonological awareness in general is defined as the metalinguistic understanding that spoken words can be decomposed into phonological primitives, which in turn can be represented by alphabetic characters (Brady & Shankweiler, 1991; Bruck, 1992; Fletcher et al., 1994; Liberman et al., 1974; Rieben & Perfetti, 1991; Shankweiler et al., 1995; Stanovich & Siegel, 1994).

As for why RD readers should have exceptional difficulty developing phonological awareness, the etiological underpinnings of this difficulty are still actively being investigated and the question of whether such language-level challenges might, in some children at least, be linked to more basic deficits in one of the above-mentioned domains is much debated. Nonetheless, a large body of evidence directly relates deficits in phonological awareness to difficulties in learning to read: phonological awareness measures predict later reading achievement (Bradley & Bryant, 1983; Stanovich et al., 1984; Torgesen et al., 1994); deficits in phonological awareness consistently separate RD and NI children (Fletcher et al., 1994; Stanovich & Siegel, 1994); phonological deficits persist into adulthood (Bruck, 1992; Shaywitz et al. 1999); and instruction in phonological awareness promotes the acquisition of reading skills (Ball & Blachman, 1991; Bradley & Bryant, 1983; Foorman et al., 1998; Torgesen et al., 1992; Wise & Olson, 1995). For children with adequate phonological skills, the process of phonological assembly in word and pseudoword reading becomes highly automated, efficient, and, as the just-mentioned evidence suggests, continues to serve as an important component in rapid word identification even for mature skilled readers (R. Frost, 1998).

Despite some developmental variability across languages and orthographies, we anticipate that RD will likewise show universality. Regardless of the writing system, RD often has a genetic basis (Grigorenko, 2001) and has been associated with a common neurobiological marker—the failure to develop a functionally specialized visual word form area (VWFA) in the left hemisphere (LH) ventral cortex (Paulesu et al., 2001; Shaywitz, Shaywitz, Pugh et al., 2002). Behavioral manifestations of RD seem to differ somewhat across languages, however. Whereas slow word identification is a hallmark of RD in all orthographies, inaccuracy of mapping is seen predominantly in irregular systems like English (Wimmer & Mayringer, 2002; Zeigler & Goswami, 2005). This difference in manifest symptoms is nonetheless consistent with a common etiology. Given the virtually one-to-one mapping between phonemes and graphemes in highly regular alphabetic orthographies like Finnish and German, once a student is able to associate letters with their corresponding sounds (and to blend those sounds together), word recognition can be achieved. When reading accuracy is measured, therefore, errors are rare; wide individual differences occur in reading speed, however, and the slowest readers are considered to have RD (Landerl et al., 1997; Wimmer & Mayringer, 2002). Like disabled readers in English, many RD readers in orthographies with very consistent grapheme–phoneme correspondences: (a) have a family history of RD (Lyytinen, 2004a, 2004b); (b) show the larger lexicality, length, and grain size effects relative to typically developing (TD) controls that also characterizes RD in English (Ziegler et al. 2003); and (c) exhibit signs of reduced distinctiveness (precision) in their phonological representations in the lexicon (Elbro, 1998; Elbro et al., 1998; Goswami, 2000; Ziegler & Goswami, 2005). Furthermore, their reading difficulties are predicted from younger ages by measures of similar skills that antedate RD outcomes in English-speaking samples (e.g., letter knowledge, phonological awareness, vocabulary), except that rapid serial naming skill at age 5–6 years appears to be a somewhat stronger predictor in Finnish and German than in English (Lyytinen, et al., 2004a; Wimmer et al., 2002). Recall, however, that rapid naming becomes the strongest prognostic measure for RD in English-speaking learners by about age 8 years (Meyer et al., 1998; Scarborough, 1998b). Thus, it may be that naming speed becomes important for predicting fluency among children who have already learned the sounds of letters, an accomplishment that is attained earlier in development when regular orthographies are being acquired.

From the extant evidence showing many similarities and a few differences in profiles of RD across orthographies, the hypothesis that RD is attributable to the same core phonological deficit in all languages is tenable. Indeed, Goswami (2000; Ziegler & Goswami, 2005), in line with previous theoretical work at Haskins (Fowler, 1991), has proposed that reduced precision in representing and processing phonological information may be the universal hallmark of RD. As noted earlier, the development of fine-grained representations (tapped by phonemic awareness and naming tasks), necessary for linking letters with phonemes and spellings with known words, both shapes and is shaped by growth in literacy. The transparency of the O > P correspondences in regular orthographies like Finnish, allows the yoked processes of phonemic awareness and decoding to develop earlier and more fully (even in RD) than is possible given the additional challenges faced when a more irregular orthography must be deciphered. Even though decoding will be more accurate by RD children in regular orthographies, the imprecision (and potentially reduced accessibility) of their stored phonological knowledge about words still impedes routinization and subsequent fluency.

Functional Imaging Studies of Skilled Reading

Given the importance of phonological information evidenced from behavioral studies of skilled and impaired reading, identifying the neuroanatomical correlates of phonology and their interactions with orthographic, morphological, and lexico-semantic component processes represents an important step toward understanding the functional architecture of reading and reading failure. Evidence from functional imaging studies indicates that skilled word recognition in general requires the development of a highly organized cortical system that integrates the processing of orthographic, phonological, and lexico-semantic features of words (see Pugh et al., 2000a and Sarkari et al., 2002 for reviews). This system broadly appears to include two posterior subsystems in the left hemisphere: a ventral (occipitotemporal) and a dorsal (temporoparietal) system, and a third area, anterior to the other two, centered in and around the inferior frontal gyrus.

The ventral system includes extrastriate areas, a left inferior occipitotemporal/fusiform area, and appears to extend anteriorly into the middle and inferior temporal gyri (MTG, ITG). It has been suggested that the occipitotemporal region functions as a presemantic VWFA by some researchers (c.f., Cohen et al., 2002, but see Price et al., 2003 for an alternative conceptualization). Importantly, the functional specificity of sites along the ventral pathway for reading appears to be late developing and critically related to the acquisition of reading skill, as discussed later (Booth et al., 2001; see Shaywitz et al., 2002, discussed later). More anterior foci within the ventral system extending into the MTG to ITG appear to be semantically tuned (Fiebach et al., 2002; Simos et al., 2002; Tagamets et al., 2000). The ventral system, particularly the posterior aspects thought to be prelexical and presemantic, is also fast-acting in response to orthographic stimuli in skilled readers but not in RD individuals (Salmelin et al., 1996). There is still a good deal of disagreement in the literature about the precise taxonomy of critical subregions comprising the ventral system (Cornelissen et al., 2003; Dehaene et al., 2004; Price et al., 2003). Nevertheless, recent studies examining both timing and stimulus-type effects suggest in general terms that moving anteriorly along the ventral pathways, subregions respond to word and word-like stimuli in a progressively abstracted and linguistic manner (Dehaene et al., 2004; Tagamets et al., 2000; Tarkiainen et al., 2003). Later, we describe several experiments suggesting potential distinctions between phonological and lexical–semantic tuning along the ventral pathway.

The temporoparietal system responding to reading tasks broadly includes the angular gyrus (AG) and supramarginal gyrus (SMG) in the inferior parietal lobule, and the posterior aspect of the superior temporal gyrus (Wernicke's area). Among their other functions (e.g., attentionally controlled processing) subregions within this system seem to be involved in mapping visual percepts of print onto the phonological and semantic structures of language (Black & Behrmann 1994; Price et al., 2003). In skilled readers, certain regions within the LH temporoparietal system (particularly the SMG) respond with greater activity to pseudowords than to familiar words, and to print more than pictures (Price et al., 1996; Simos et al., 2002; Xu et al., 2001; Sandak et al., 2004b). This finding, along with our own developmental studies (Shaywitz et al., 2002) suggests that temporoparietal regions play a critical role in the types of phono-logical analyses that are relevant to learning new material (Pugh et al., 2000a).

The anterior system is centered in posterior aspects of the inferior frontal gyrus (IFG) and appears to be associated with phonological recoding during reading, among other functions (e.g., phonological memory, syntactic proces-sing); more anterior aspects of the IFG seem to play a role in semantic retrieval (Poldrack et al., 1999). The phonologically relevant components of this multi-functional system have been found to function in silent reading and in naming (see Fiez & Petersen, 1998 for review; Pugh et al., 1997) and, like the temporoparietal system, is more strongly engaged by low-frequency words (particularly, words with irregular/inconsistent spelling-to-sound mappings) and pseudowords than by high-frequency words (Fiebach et al., 2002; Fiez & Peterson, 1998). We have speculated that this anterior system operates in close conjunction with the temporoparietal system to decode new words during normal reading development (Pugh et al., 2000a).

Of these three systems, the dorsal and anterior systems appear to predomi-nate during initial reading acquisition in normally developing beginning readers, with an increased ventral response to print stimuli as proficiency in word recognition increases. We observed (Shaywitz, Shaywitz, Pugh et al., 2002) that normally developing children younger than 10.5 years of age show robust engagement of temporoparietal and anterior systems, but limited engagement of the ventral system during pseudoword and real-word reading tasks. In contrast, children older than 10.5 years of age tend to show increased engagement of the ventral system, which in turn is correlated with increas-ingly skilled reading. Indeed, when multiple regression analyses examined both age and reading skill (measured by performance on standard reading tests), the critical predictor was reading skill level: the higher the reading skill, the stronger the response in the LH ventral cortex (with several other areas including RH and frontal lobe sites showing age- and skill-related reductions). RD readers by contrast showed age-related increases in a widely distributed set of regions across both LH and RH. Based on these cross-sectional developmental findings, we suggest that a beginning reader on a successful trajectory employs a widely distributed cortical system for print processing, including temporoparietal, frontal, and RH posterior areas. As reading skill increases, LH ventral sites become more active, and presumably more central to the rapid recognition of printed (word) stimuli (see Booth et al., 2001; Turkeltaub et al., 2003; Tarkianien et al., 2003 for similar arguments).

Each writing system has unique challenges depending on how the script encodes phonology, morphology, and semantics. The functional neuroanatomy of visual word recognition in reading has also been investigated in mature readers in a variety of written languages (which employ both alphabetic and nonalphabetic writing systems) (e.g., Chee et al., 1999; Fiebach et al., 2002; Kuo et al., 2003, 2004; Paulesu et al., 2000; Salmelin et al., 1996). Neuroimaging studies of alphabetic languages broadly implicate the same set of LH cortical regions (including occipitotemporal, temporoparietal, and inferior frontal networks) identified in English-language studies (see Pugh et al., 2005). These common networks are almost always engaged by skilled readers irrespective of the specific language and/or writing system under investigation. Language-specific differences usually appear to be a matter of degree, not of kind. That is, in one language, the reading-relevant constituents of a neural network might be more or less activated than in another language, but the general circuitry appears similar in its taxonomic organization (Paulesu et al., 2000). Recent work with nonalphabetic writing systems also suggests similarities. For example, Kuo and colleagues (2003) examined covert naming of high- and low-frequency Chinese characters and observed greater activation in left premotor/inferior frontal regions and the left insula for low-frequency characters relative to high-frequency characters. These areas have been implicated in phonological processing in English; in particular, the inferior frontal gyrus is more strongly engaged by low-frequency words and pseudowords than by high-frequency words (Fiebach et al., 2002; Fiez & Peterson, 1998). Moreover, high-frequency characters produced greater activation in the middle temporal/angular gyrus, which have been implicated in lexical-semantic processing in neuroimaging studies of English word recognition (Fiebach et al., 2002; Price et al., 1997; Simos et al., 2002) and the precuneus, previously implicated in visual imagery (Fletcher et al., 1996). In a subsequent study, Kuo and colleagues had participants perform homophone judgments and physical judgments on real characters, pseudocharacters (novel combinations of legal semantic and phonetic radicals that follow the positional architecture of Chinese characters), and Korean-like nonsense figures

(Kuo et al., 2004). A number of regions important for orthographic-to-phonological mapping in English were also more active for the homophone judgment relative to the character judgment in Chinese. These regions included the inferior frontal gyrus, inferior parietal lobule/supramarginal gyrus, and the fusiform gyrus. Note that some important differences have been reported for Mandarin reading, with increased reading-related activation at both superior parietal (Kuo et al., 2003) and especially left middle frontal regions; the middle frontal region is also implicated in reading disability in Chinese (Tan et al., 2001; Siok et al., 2004). Nonetheless, overall the reading networks appear to be largely similar to those observed for alphabetic writing systems (Kuo et al., 2003, 2004) with a few key differences. Again, we would argue that the universal demand of rapid contact with phonological systems for print stimuli results in the brain "choosing" largely invariant pathways when constructing the reading circuitry.

Functional Imaging Studies of Reading Disability

Evidence for Altered Circuits in Reading Disability

Clear functional differences exist between NI and RD readers with regard to activation patterns in dorsal, ventral, and anterior sites during reading tasks. In disabled readers, a number of functional imaging studies have observed LH posterior functional disruption, at both dorsal and ventral sites during phonological processing tasks (Brunswick et al., 1999; Paulesu et al., 2001; Pugh et al., 2000b; Salmelin et al., 1996; Shaywitz et al., 1998; 2002; Temple et al., 2001). This disruption is instantiated as a relative under-engagement of these regions, specifically when processing linguistic stimuli (words and pseudowords) or during tasks that require decoding. This functional anomaly in posterior LH regions has been observed consistently in children (Shaywitz et al., 2002) and adults (Salmelin et al., 1996; Shaywitz et al., 1998). Hypoactivation in three key dorsal and ventral sites, including cortex within the temporoparietal region, the angular gyrus, and the ventral occipitotemporal skill zone is detectable as early as the end of kindergarten in children who have not reached important milestones in learning to read (Simos et al., 2002). Posterior disruption is evident both in measures of activation and in analysis of functional connectivity (Horwitz et al., 1998; Pugh et al., 2000b).

Because the evidence from neuroimaging studies of skilled reading indicates that different languages and orthographies engage common circuits during reading, and given the argument for common phonological deficits, we might expect language-invariant neurobiological signatures to be associated with reading disability as well. The evidence to date from alphabetic languages is supportive of this expectation (Paulesu et al., 2001; Salmelin et al., 1996;

Shaywitz et al., 2002). Functional disruptions in LH posterior cortex (particularly the occipitotemporal region) in RD individuals performing reading tasks during neuroimaging have been found in several languages that vary in the complexity of mappings between printed and spoken forms (English, Finnish, German, French, and Italian). This common neurobiological signature, within a largely language-invariant circuitry for reading in the LH, reinforces the notion of universality in RD. A recent study of Chinese RD readers (Siok et al., 2004) reported a language-specific difference in the RD signature (specifically, diminished activation of middle frontal regions for RD readers relative to controls). This finding has not been reported in alphabetic languages. However, these authors also found diminished activation in RD readers at the same LH ventral region previously reported by Paulesu and others in RD within alphabetic languages in their word reading task (Brunswick et al., 1999; Paulesu et al., 2001; Salmelin et al., 1996; Shaywitz et al., 2002).

Potentially Compensatory Processing in Reading Disability

Behaviorally, poor readers compensate for their inadequate phonological awareness and knowledge of letter–sound correspondences by over-relying on contextual cues to read individual words; their word reading errors tend to be visual or semantic rather than phonetic (see Perfetti, 1985 for review). These behavioral markers of reading impairment may be instantiated cortically by compensatory activation of frontal and RH regions. In our studies (Shaywitz et al., 1998, 2002), we observed processing in RD readers that we interpret as compensatory. We found that on tasks that made explicit demands on phonological processing (pseudoword and word reading tasks), RD readers showed a disproportionately greater engagement of IFG and prefrontal dorsolateral sites than did NI readers (see also Brunswick et al., 1999; Salmelin et al., 1996 for similar findings). Evidence of a second, potentially compensatory, shift—in this case to posterior RH regions—comes from several findings. Using magnetoencephalography (MEG), Sarkari and colleagues (2002) found an increase in the apparent engagement of the RH temporoparietal region in RD children. More detailed examination of this trend, using hemodynamic measures, indicates that hemispheric asymmetries in activity in posterior temporal and temporoparietal regions (MTG and AG) vary significantly among reading groups (Shaywitz et al., 1998): there was greater right than left hemispheric activation in RD readers but greater left than right hemispheric activation in NI readers. Rumsey and colleagues (1999) examined the relationship between RH activation and reading performance in their adult RD and NI participants and found that RH temporoparietal activation was correlated with standard measures of reading performance only for RD readers (see also Shaywitz et al., 2002). In summary, initial adult and cross-sectional developmental studies have identified reading group differences in both functional neuroanatomical and behavioral trajectories; NI children develop a left hemispheric posterior (ventral) reading system capable of supporting fluent word identification, whereas RD readers, failing to master component reading skills, demonstrate presumably compensatory trajectories toward both RH posterior and frontal lobe regions. Although imaging studies have established group differences in developmental trajectories at two correlated levels of analysis, they are nonetheless descriptive. We must begin to conduct studies aimed at gaining a better understanding of key behavioral, neurobiological, and genetic etiological factors that may be responsible for this divergence in circuitry between NI and RD cohorts; such work is critical to establish a proper causal account.

Refining Our Account of Neurobiology of Skilled Word Recognition

In a preliminary model (Pugh et al., 2000a), we speculated that the temporoparietal and anterior systems are critical in learning to integrate orthographic, phonological, and semantic features of words, whereas the ventral system develops, as a consequence of adequate learning during reading acquisition, to support fluent word identification in normally developing, but not RD, individuals. This general taxonomy however, is both coarse-grained and underspecified. To explore functional subspecialization further, we have recently conducted a series of experiments with skilled readers as participants (Frost et al., 2005; Katz et al., 2005; Mencl et al., 2002; Sandak et al., 2004a; summarized in depth by Sandak et al., 2004b). We examined: phonological priming (Mencl et al., 2002), phonological/semantic tradeoffs (Frost et al., 2005), and critical factors associated with repetition effects (Katz et al., 2005) and adaptive learning (Sandak et al, 2004a). This line of research is aimed at providing more information on both subspecialization with the major LH regions, and how different component systems modulate processing in relation to one another in response to varied stimuli and at different stages during adaptive learning. Given the importance of the ventral pathway in the development of fluent reading, we are particularly interested in assessing both the tuning characteristics of the skilled, correlated occipitotemporal region (along with remote areas most closely linked to processing within this ventral area).

Phonological Priming

We have recently completed a functional magnetic resonance imaging (fMRI) study of phonological and orthographic priming effects in printed word recognition (Mencl et al., 2002). Participants performed a primed lexical decision task. Word prime–target pairs were either (a) both orthographically and phonologically similar (bribe–TRIBE); (b) orthographically similar but phonologically dissimilar (couch–TOUCH); or (c) unrelated (lunch–SCREEN). Results revealed that targets primed by phonologically dissimilar words evoked more activation than did targets primed by phonologically similar words in several LH cortical areas hypothesized to underlie phonological processing: this modulation was seen in the IFG, Wernicke's area, and the SMG. Notably, this phonological priming effect was also obtained within the early-activating LH occipitotemporal skill zone, consistent with the claim from behavioral priming research that phonologically analytic processing occurs early in lexical access. Whether these phonological effects within the ventral word form system we have observed occur early or late in processing, however, awaits replication of this experiment with real-time measures such as electroencephalograph (EEG) or MEG, where more precise temporal relations between activated systems can be uncovered.

Tradeoffs Between Phonology and Semantics

Many previous studies have attempted to identify the neural substrates of orthographic, phonological, and semantic processes in NI (Fiebach et al., 2002) and RD (Rumsey et al., 1997) cohorts. RD readers have acute problems in mapping from orthography to phonology and appear to rely on semantic information to supplement deficient decoding skills (Plaut & Booth, 2000). NI readers too, appear to show a tradeoff between these component processes. Strain and colleagues (1996) provided behavioral confirmation of this, demonstrating that the standard consistency effect on low-frequency words (longer naming latencies for words with inconsistent spelling-to-sound mappings such as PINT relative to words with consistent mappings such as MILL) is attenuated for words that are highly imageable/concrete. Importantly, this interaction reveals that semantics can facilitate the processes associated with orthographic-to-phonological mapping in word recognition.

Using fMRI, we sought to identify the neurobiological correlates of this tradeoff between semantics and phonology (Frost et al., 2005). A go/no-go naming paradigm was employed in an event-related fMRI protocol, with word stimuli representing the crossing of frequency, imageability, and spelling-to-sound consistency. Higher activation for high-imageable words was found in middle temporal and posterior parietal sites. In contrast, higher activation for inconsistent relative to consistent words was found in the IFG, replicating findings by Fiez and colleagues (1999) and Herbster and colleagues (1997). Critically, analyses revealed that imageability was associated with reduced consistency-related activation in the IFG, SMG, and occipitotemporal, but increased posterior parietal (AG) and middle temporal activation; this appears to be the principal neural signature of the behavioral tradeoff between semantics and phonology revealed by Strain and colleagues. These findings provide clear evidence that skilled performance results from complementary, cooperative processing involving different components of the reading circuitry.

Adaptive Learning

Previous studies have demonstrated that both increased familiarity with specific words and increased reading skill are associated with a shift in the relative activation of the cortical systems involved in reading, from predominantly dorsal to predominantly ventral. In another line of research, we are carrying out functional neuroimaging experiments in order to provide a more precise characterization of the means by which practice with unfamiliar words results in this shift, and to gain insights into how these systems learn to read new words. In one study from our group (Katz et al., 2005), we found evidence for this shift as skilled readers acquired familiarity for words via repetition. In that study, we examined repetition effects (comparing activation for thrice-repeated tokens relative to unrepeated words) in both lexical decision and overt naming. Across tasks, repetition was associated with facilitated processing, as measured by reduced response latencies and errors. Many sites, including the IFG, SMG, supplementary motor area, and cerebellum, showed reduced activation for highly practiced tokens. Critically, a dissociation was observed within the ventral system: the occipitotemporal skill zone showed practice-related reduction (like the SMG and IFG sites), whereas more anterior ventral sites, particularly the MTG, were stable or even showed increased activation with repetition. Thus, we concluded that a neural signature of increased efficiency in word recognition signals more efficient processing in dorsal, anterior, and posterior ventral sites, with stable or increased activation in more anterior middle and inferior temporal sites.

A second experiment (Sandak et al., 2004a) examined whether the type of processing engaged in when learning a new word mediates how well that word is learned, and the cortical regions engaged when that word is subsequently read. We suspected that repetition alone is not sufficient to optimize learning; rather, we hypothesized that the quality of the lexical representations established when new words are learned is affected by the type of processing engaged in during learning. Specifically, we predicted that, relative to attending to the orthographic features of novel words, learning conditions that stress phonological or semantic analysis would speed naming and, in turn, cortical activation patterns similar to those characteristic of increased familiarity with words (as seen in Katz et al., 2005). Prior to MRI scanning, participants completed a behavioral session in which they acquired familiarity for three sets of pronounceable pseudowords while making orthographic (consonant/vowel pattern), phonological (rhyme), or semantic (category) judgments. Note that in the semantic condition, participants learned a novel semantic association for each pseudoword. Following training, participants completed an event-related fMRI session in which they overtly named trained pseudowords, untrained pseudowords, and real words.

As predicted, we found that the type of processing (orthographic, phonological, or semantic) engaged in when learning a new word influences both how well that word is learned and the cortical regions engaged when that word is subsequently read. Behaviorally, phonological and semantic training resulted in speeded naming times relative to orthographic training. Of the three training conditions, we found that only phonological training was associated with both facilitated naming and the pattern of cortical activations previously implicated as characteristic of increased efficiency for word recognition (Katz et al., 2005). We suggest that for phonologically trained items, learning was facilitated by engaging in phonological processing during training; this in turn resulted in efficient phonological processing (instantiated cortically as relatively reduced activation in IFG and SMG) and efficient retrieval of presemantic lexical representations during subsequent naming (instantiated cortically as relatively reduced activation in the occipitotemporal skill zone). Semantic training also facilitated naming but was associated with increased activation in areas previously implicated in semantic processing, suggesting that the establishment and retrieval of semantic representations compensated for less efficient phonological processing for these items.

Implications of Recent Findings

Our recent experiments examining phonological priming, phonological/ semantic tradeoffs, and critical factors associated with adaptive learning in reading have yielded findings that allow for the development of a more fine-grained picture of the functional neuroanatomy and subspecializations within these systems, and we have begun to acquire information on learning-related modulation and tradeoffs among component regions. Across these studies identical sites in the SMG (within the temporoparietal system), IFG (within the anterior system) and the occipitotemporal skill zone (within the ventral system) showed (a) increased activation for pseudowords relative to words, (b) strong phonological priming effects, and (c) repetition-related reductions that were most salient in the phonologically analytic training condition. This converging pattern with regard to phonological variables strongly suggests a phonological "tuning" in these subregions. (It is particularly noteworthy that the developmentally critical occipitotemporal skill zone—the putative VWFA—by these data, appears to be phonologically tuned. It makes good sense that this region should be so structured, given the failure to develop this system in RD when phonological deficits are one of the core features of this population). By contrast, the angular gyrus (within the temporoparietal system) and the MTG/ITG (within the ventral system) appear to have more abstract lexico-semantic functions across our studies (see Price et al. 1997 for similar claims).

From these findings, we speculate that subregions within the SMG and IFG operate in a yoked fashion to bind orthographic and phonological features of words during learning; these systems also operate in conjunction with the AG, in which these features are further yoked to semantic knowledge systems distributed across several cortical regions. Adequate binding, specifically adequate orthographic–phonological integration, enables the development of the presemantic occipitotemporal skill zone into a functional pattern identification system. As words become better learned, this area becomes capable of efficiently activating lexico-semantic subsystems in the MTG/ITG, thus enabling the development of a rapid ventral word identification system. RD individuals, with demonstrable anomalies in temporoparietal function (and associated difficulties with phonologically analytic processing on behavioral tests), fail to adequately "train" ventral subsystems (particularly the occipito-temporal skill zone) and thus develop compensatory responses in frontal and RH systems.

In our view, this developing account better lends itself to the architectural assumptions put forward in interactive models (e.g., Harm and Seidenberg, 1999) than to the classic dual-route models. The findings on stimulus-type effects, and especially the data on adaptive learning, do not readily support the notion of, for instance, independent dorsal and ventral reading pathways, with each coding different information. Instead, they suggest a set of phonologically or semantically tuned subsystems that are widely distributed across both dorsal and ventral cortex and appear to act cooperatively during fluent word reading and in adaptive learning. Developmentally, there is good evidence that a ventral reading specialization depends on the intactness of processing across this distributed system.

Cross-linguistic studies will be critical in expanding our account. In the newly funded study involving a collaboration between Haskins Laboratories, the University of Jyvaskyla, and the National Yang-Ming University, we will longitudinally contrast typical and atypical reading development in English with Finnish and Mandarin Chinese. Relative to English, Finnish has a rather transparent orthographic-to-phonological mapping, whereas Mandarin is more opaque with regard to how phonology is coded in the writing system. Importantly, as noted, data suggest that skilled adult readers in all three languages appear to develop a common neurobiological circuit for reading (Pugh et al., 2005), suggesting very strong biological constraints on the neural pathways that will emerge as reading competence is acquired (even for very different orthographies).

However, we might anticipate that the initial neurocircuitry for reading might be rather different in each language, reflecting the different challenges that these writing systems place on orthography, phonology, morphology, visual memory, and the like. This would imply that, whereas a common ventral reading specialization should eventually develop for each language, the computational organization of this common neural pathway will differ somewhat as a function of the language-specific challenges (statistical properties of the writing system) during early reading development. An adequate neurobiologically grounded reading theory must be able to account for both language variance (with respect to computational factors) and language invariance (with respect to common neural pathways) over the course of development. With regard to ventral cortex (VWFA), we might expect that the tuning of this region, as well as its developmental course, will vary somewhat in orthographies that differ in orthographic depth. These anticipated language differences, along with our progressive studies of component processing tradeoffs during adaptive learning, will continue to drive the conceptual and computational development of neurobiological theories in the next phase of our research.

Conclusion

We conclude with a note on next steps in our research. Although neurobiological studies of word recognition, particularly those identifying the neurobiological signatures of RD, have generated a good deal of enthusiasm, it should be remembered that functional neuroimaging measures are not intrinsically explanatory; they simply describe brain organization at a given point in development. Links between multiple indices of reading (dis)ability including genetic polymorphisms, brain structure and function, and cognitive deficits promise to constitute the core scientific foundation for our understanding of neurodevelopmental disorders in the coming years, which aims to progress from descriptive neurobiological findings to potentially explanatory models. To that end, in a new project in our lab we are using a longitudinal design to characterize reading development in NI and RD cohorts of children by measuring developmental changes in reading performance (obtained during the early stages of reading acquisition through to the point where fluent reading is anticipated) using multimodal functional imaging (fMRI and event-related potentials [ERPs]), neurochemistry measured with magnetic resonance spectroscopy (MRS), and genetic analyses. By establishing meaningful links between behavioral/cognitive skills that must be in place to read and neuroanatomical, neurochemical, and genetic measures, we can begin to develop an explanatory account of neurocognitive divergences in typically developing and RD children (Grigorenko, 2001; Pugh et al., 2000a). That is, we believe that designs of this type will allow specifications of the biological *pathways* predisposing for risk for the development of RD and explorations of elements of these pathways that might be most suitable for pharmacological and behavioral intervention. Although the goal of linking genetics, neurochemistry, functional neuroanatomy, and behavior in reading development is both ambitious and, to some extent, exploratory, the goal of developing an adequate explanatory model of observed divergences in RD with respect to brain and behavior requires such links to be made.

Finally, as discussed, much behavioral research supports the notion that word recognition engages common processes across languages and orthographies; however, at present there is much less cross-linguistic neuroimaging research on reading development, disability, and the effects of intervention. Although the initial evidence has provided support for a common neurobiological signature of both skilled and impaired reading, some differences have been observed (Siok et al., 2004). Given the significant variability in orthographic form, orthographic-to-phonological mappings, methods of reading instruction, and manifestations of RD across languages and cultures, more work needs to be done in the area of cross-linguistic studies of reading, both in order to identify the neurobiological universals of reading and to understand how the functional organization of reading varies with language-specific features. Cross-linguistic neurocognitive research has the potential, we believe, to enhance significantly our current understanding of universal influences on learning to read.

Acknowledgments

This research was funded by NICHD grants F32-HD42391 to Rebecca Sandak, R01-HD40411 to Kenneth R. Pugh, and P01-HD01994 to Haskins Laboratories.

Note

1. A few sections of this chapter have appeared recently in:
   Frost, S.J. et al. (2008). Neurobiological studies of skilled and impaired word reading. In E.L. Grigorenko & A.J. Naples (Eds.). *Single-word reading: Behavioral and biological perspectives,* pp. 355–376. New York: Lawrence Erlbaum.
   Pugh, K.R. et al. (2006). Neurobiological studies of skilled and impaired reading: A work in progress. In G.R. Rosen (Ed.). *The dyslexic brain: New pathways in neuroscience discovery,* 21–47. Mahwah, NJ: Lawrence Erlbaum.

References

Ball, E.W., & Blachman, B.A. (1991). Does phoneme awareness training in kindergarten make a difference in early word recognition and developmental spelling? *Reading Research Quarterly, 26*, 49–66.

Baron, J. (1973). Phonemic stage not necessary for reading. *Quarterly Journal of Experimental Psychology, 25*, 241–246.

Black, S.E., & Behrmann, M. (1994). Localization in alexia. In A. Kertesz (Ed.). *Localization and neuroimaging in neuropsychology*. New York: Academic Press.

Booth, J.R., Burman, D.D., Van Santen, F.W., Harasaki, Y., Gitelman, D.R., Parrish, T.B., & Mesulam, M.M. (2001). The development of specialized brain systems in reading and oral-language. *Neuropsychology, Developmental Cognition, Section C, Child Neuropsychology, 7 (3)*, 119–41.

Bradley, L., & Bryant, P. (1985). *Rhyme and reason in reading and spelling*. Ann Arbor: University of Michigan Press.

Bradley, L., & Bryant, P.E. (1983). Categorising sounds and learning to read - A causal connection. *Nature, 301*, 419–521.

Brady, S. & Shankweiler, D. (1991). (Eds). *Phonological processes in literacy: A tribute to Isabelle Y. Liberman*. Hillsdale, NJ, USA: Lawrence Erlbaum Associates, Inc.

Bruck, M. (1992). Persistence of dyslexics' phonological deficits. *Developmental Psychology, 28*, 874–886.

Brunswick, N., McCrory, E., Price C., Frith, C.D., & Frith, U. (1999). Explicit and implicit processing of words and pseudowords by adult developmental dyslexics: A search for Wernicke's Wortschatz. *Brain, 122*, 1901–1917.

Carello, C., Turvey, M. T., & Lukatela, G. (1992). Can theories of word recognition remain stubbornly nonphonological? In R. Frost & L. Katz (Eds.), *Orthography, phonology, morphology, and meaning* (pp. 211–226). Oxford: North-Holland.

Chee, M.W.L., O'Craven, K.M., Bergida, R., Rosen, B.R., Savoy, R.L., (1999). Auditory and visual word processing studied with fMRI. *Human Brain Mapping, 7*, 15–28.

Coltheart, M. (1978). Lexical access in simple reading tasks. In G. Underwood (Ed.), *Strategies of information processing* (pp. 151–216). London: Academic Press.

Coltheart, M., Curtis, B., Atkins, P., & Haller, M. (1993). Models of reading aloud: Dual-route and parallel-distributed-processing approaches. *Psychological Review, 100*, 589–608.

Coltheart, M., Rastle, K., Perry, C., Langdon, R., & Ziegler, J. (2001). DRC: A dual route cascaded model of visual word recognition and reading aloud. *Psychological Review, 108*, 204–256.

Cohen, L., Lehericy, S., Chochon, F., Lemer, C., Rivaud, S., & Dehaene, S. (2002). Language-specific tuning of visual cortex? Functional properties of the Visual Word Form Area. *Brain, 125*, 1054–1069.

Cornelissen, P.L., & Hansen, P.C. (1998). Motion detection, letter position encoding, and single word reading. *Annals of Dyslexia, 48*, 155–188.

Cornelissen, P., Tarkiainen, A., Helenius, P., & Salmelin, R. (2003). Cortical effects of shifting letter position in letter strings of varying length. *Journal of Cognitive Neuroscience, 15*, 731–746.

Dehaene, S., Jobert, A., Naccache, L, Ciuciu, P., Poline, J.B., Le-Bihan, D., & Cohen, L. (2004). Letter binding and invariant recognition of masked words: Behavioral and neuroimaging evidence. *Psychological Science, 15(5)*, 307–313.

Elbro, C. (1998). When reading is "readn" or somthn. Distinctness of phonological representations of lexical items in normal and disabled readers. *Scandinavian Journal of Psychology,39,* 149–153.

Elbro, C., Borstrom, I., & Petersen, D. K. (1998). Predicting dyslexia from kindergarten: The importance of distinctness of phonological representations of lexical items. *Reading Research Quarterly, 33 (1),* 36–60.

Feldman, L.B., Turvey, M. T. (1983). Word recognition in Serbo-Croatian is phonologically analytic. *Journal of Experimental Psychology: Human Perception and Performance. 9(2),* 288–298.

Fiebach, C.J., Friederici, A.D., Mueller, K., & von Cramon, D. Y. (2002). fMRI evidence for dual routes to the mental lexicon in visual word recognition. *Journal of Cognitive Neuroscience, 14,* 11–23.

Fiez, J.A., Balota, D.A., Raichle, M.E., & Petersen, S.E. (1999). Effects of lexicality, frequency, and spelling-to-sound consistency on the functional anatomy of reading. *Neuron, 24,* 205–218.

Fiez, J.A., & Peterson, S.E. (1998). Neuroimaging studies of word reading. *Proceedings of the National Academy Sciences, 95,* 914–921.

Fletcher, P. C., Shallice, T., Frith, C. D., Frackowiak, R. S. & Dolan, R. J. (1996). Brain activity during memory retrieval. The influence of imagery and semantic cueing. *Brain, 119,* 1587–1596.

Fletcher, J., Shaywitz, S.E., Shankweiler, D.P., Katz, L., Liberman, I.Y., Stuebing, K.K., Francis, D.J., Fowler, A.E., & Shaywitz, B.A. (1994). Cognitive profiles of reading disability: Comparisons of discrepancy and low achievement definitions. *Journal of Educational Psychology, 86,* 6–23.

Foorman, B.R., Francis, D., Fletcher, J.K., Schatschneider, C., & Mehta, P. (1998). The role of instruction in learning to reading: preventing reading failure in at-risk children. *Journal of Educational Psychology, 90,* 37–55.

Fowler, A. E. (1991). How early phonological development might set the stage for phoneme awareness. In S. Brady & D. P. Shankweiler (Eds.), *Phonological processes in literacy: A tribute to Isabelle Y. Liberman* (pp. 97–118). Hillsdale, NJ: Erlbaum.

Frost, R. (1998). Toward a strong phonological theory of visual word recognition: True issues and false trails. *Psychological Bulletin, 123,* 71–99.

Frost, S.J., Mencl, W.E., Sandak, R., Moore, D.L., Rueckl, J., Katz, L., Fulbright, R.K., & Pugh, K.R. (2005). An fMRI study of the trade-off between semantics and phonology in reading aloud. *Neuroreport, 16,* 621–624.

Goswami, U. (2000). Phonological representations, reading development and dyslexia: Towards a cross-linguistic theoretical framework. *Dyslexia, 6,* 133–151.

Goswami, U., Ziegler, J.C., Dalton, L., & Schneider, W. (2003). Nonword reading across orthographies: How flexible is the choice of reading units? *Applied Psycholinguistics 24,* 235–247.

Grigorenko, E.L. (2001). Developmental Dyslexia: An update on genes, brain, and environments. *Journal of Child Psychology and Psychiatry, 42,* 91–125.

Harm, M.W., & Seidenberg, M.S. (1999). Computing the meanings of words in reading: Cooperative division of labor between visual and phonological processes. *Psychological Review, 106,* 491–528.

Herbster, A., Mintun, M., Nebes, R., & Becker, J. (1997). Regional cerebral blood flow during word and nonword reading. *Human Brain Mapping, 5,* 84–92.

Horwitz, B., Rumsey, J.M., & Donohue, B.C. (1998). Functional connectivity of the angular gyrus in normal reading and dyslexia. *Proceedings of the National Academy Sciences, 95*, 8939–8944.

Katz, L., Lee, C.H., Tabor, W., Frost, S.J., Mencl, W.E., Sandak, R., Rueckl, J.G., & Pugh, K.R. (2005). Behavioral and neurobiological effects of printed word repetition in lexical decision and naming. *Neuropsychologia, 43*, 2068–2083.

Kuo, W.J., Yeh, T.C., Lee, C.Y., Wu, Y.T., Chou, C.C., Ho, L.T., Hung, D.L., Tzeng, O.J.L., & Hsieh, J.C., (2003). Frequency effects of Chinese character processing in the brain: an event-related fMRI study. *NeuroImage 18*, 720–730.

Kuo, W.-J., Yeh, T.-C., Lee, J.-R., Chen, L.-F., Lee, P.-L., Chen, S.-S., Ho, L.-T., Hung, D. L., Tzeng, O. J.-L., & Hsieh, J.-C. (2004). Orthographic and phonological processing of Chinese characters: An fMRI study. *NeuroImage, 21*, 1721–1731.

Landerl, K., Wimmer, H., & Frith, U. (1997). The impact of orthographic consistency on dyslexia: A German-English comparison. *Cognition, 63*, 315–334.

Lesch, M. F. & Pollatsek, A. (1993). Automatic access of semantic information by phonological codes in visual word recognition. *Journal of Experimental Psychology: Learning, Memory and Cognition, 19*, 285–294.

Liberman, A.M. (1992). The relation of speech to reading and writing. In R. Frost and L. Katz. (Eds.). *Orthography, phonology, morphology, and meaning*. Amsterdam: Elsevier.

Liberman, I.Y., Shankweiler, D., Fischer, W., & Carter, B. (1974). Explicit syllable and phoneme segmentation in the young child. *Journal of Child Psychology, 18*, 201–212.

Liberman, I. Y., Shankweiler, D., & Liberman, A. M. (1989). The alphabetic principle and learning to read. In D. Shankweiler, I. Y. Liberman, et al. (Eds.), *Phonology and reading disability: Solving the reading puzzle. International Academy for Research in Learning Disabilities monograph series, No. 6*. (pp. 1–33). Ann Arbor, MI, USA: University of Michigan Press.

Lukatela, G., Feldman, L.B., Turvey, M. T., Carello, C., Katz, L (1989). Context effects in bi-alphabetical word perception. *Journal of Memory and Language, 28(2)*, 214–236.

Lukatela, G., Frost, S. J., & Turvey, M. T. (1999). Identity priming in English is compromised by phonological ambiguity. *Journal of Experimental Psychology: Human Perception and Performance, 25*, 775–790.

Lukatela, G. Popadić, D., Ognjenović, P., & Turvey, M.T. (1980). Lexical decision in a phonologically shallow orthography. *Memory & Cognition, 8*, 124–132.

Lukatela, G., & Turvey, M.T. (1994). Visual lexical access is initially phonological: 1. Evidence from associative priming by words, homophones, and pseudohomophones. *Journal of Experimental Psychology: General, 123*, 107–128.

Lyytinen, H. et al. (2004a). Early development of children at familial risk for dyslexia: Follow-up from birth to school age. *Dyslexia, 10, 3*, 146–178.

Lyytinen, H. et al. (2004b). The development of children at familial risk for dyslexia: Birth to school age. *Annals of Dyslexia, 54*, 185–220.

Mencl, W.E., Frost, S.J., Sandak, R., Lee, J.R., Jenner, A.R., Mason, M.A., et al. (2002). *Effects of orthographic and phonological priming in printed word identification: an fMRI study*. Paper presented at the Organization for Human Brain Mapping Conference, Sendai, Japan.

Meyer, M. M., Wood, F. B., Hart, L. A., & Felton, R. H. (1998). Predictive value of rapid automatized naming for later reading. *Journal of Learning Disabilities, 31(2)*, 106–117.

Paap, K. R., & Noel, R. W. (1991). Dual route models of print to sound: Still a good horse race. *Psychological Research, 53*, 13–24.

Papanicolaou, A.C., Pugh, K.R., Simos, P.G., & Mencl, W.E. (2004). Functional brain imaging: An introduction to concepts and applications. In P. McCardle and V. Chhabra (Eds.). *The voice of evidence in reading research.* Baltimore: Paul H. Brookes Publishing Company.

Paulesu, E., Demonet, J.-F., Fazio, F., McCrory, E., Chanoine, V., Brunswick, N., Cappa, S.F., et al. (2001). Dyslexia: Cultural diversity and biological unity. *Science, 291,* 2165–2167.

Paulesu E, McCrory E, Fazio F, Menoncello L, Brunswick N, Cappa S.F., et al. (2000). A cultural effect on brian function. *Nature Neuroscience, 3,* 91–96.

Perfetti, C. A. (1985). *Reading ability.* New York: Oxford University Press.

Perfetti, C.A., & Bell, L. (1991). Phonemic activation during the first 40 ms of word identification: Evidence from backward masking and priming. *Journal of Memory & Language, 30,* 473–485.

Perfetti, C.A., Bell, L., & Delaney, S. (1988). Automatic phonetic activation in silent word reading: Evidence from backward masking. *Journal of Memory and Language, 27,* 59–70.

Perfetti, C.A., Liu, Y., & Tan, L.H. (2005). The lexical constituency model: Some implications of research on Chinese for general theories of reading. *Psychological Review,* 112, 43–59

Perfetti, C.A., Zhang, S. (1995). Very early phonological activation in Chinese reading. *Journal of Experimental Psychology: Learning, Memory, and Cognition, 21(1),* 24–33.

Plaut, D.C., & Booth, J.R. (2000). Individual and developmental differences in semantic priming: Empirical and computational support for a single-mechanism account of lexical processing. *Psychological Review, 107,* 786–823.

Plaut, D. C., McClelland, J. L., Seidenberg, M., & Patterson, K. E. (1996). Understanding normal and impaired word reading: Computational principles in quasi-regular domains. *Psychological Review, 103,* 56–115.

Poldrack, R.A., Wagner, A.D., Prull, M.W., Desmond, J.E., Glover, G.H., & Gabrieli, J. D. (1999). Functional specialization for semantic and phonological processing in the left inferior prefrontal cortex. *Neuroimage, 10,* 15–35.

Price, C.J., More, C.J., Humphreys, G.W., & Wise, R.J.S. (1997). Segregating semantic from phonological processes during reading. *Journal of Cognitive Neuroscience, 9,* 727–733.

Price, C.J., Winterburn, D., Giraud, A.L., Moore, C.J., & Noppeney, U. (2003). Cortical localization of the visual and auditory word form areas: A reconsideration of the evidence. *Brain and Language, 86,* 272–286.

Price, C.J., Wise, R.J.S., & Frackowiak, R.S.J. (1996). Demonstrating the implicit processing of visually presented words and pseudowords. *Cerebral Cortex, 6,* 62–70.

Pugh, K.R., Mencl, W.E., Jenner, A.R., Katz, L., Frost, S.J., Lee, J.R., Shaywitz, S.E., & Shaywitz, B.A. (2000a). Functional neuroimaging studies of reading and reading disability (developmental dyslexia). *Mental Retardation & Developmental Disabilities Research Reviews, 6,* 207–213.

Pugh, K., Mencl, E.W., Shaywitz, B.A., Shaywitz, S.E., Fulbright, R.K., Skudlarski, P., et al. (2000b). The angular gyrus in developmental dyslexia: Task-specific differences in functional connectivity in posterior cortex. *Psychological Science, 11,* 51–56.

Pugh, K.R., Shaywitz, B.A., Shaywitz, S.A., Shankweiler, D.P., Katz, L., Fletcher, J.M., et al. (1997). Predicting reading performance from neuroimaging profiles: The cerebral basis of phonological effects in printed word identification. *Journal of Experimental Psychology: Human Perception and Performance, 2,* 1–20.

Pugh, K. R., Sandak, R., Frost, S. J., Moore, D., & Mencl, W. E. (2005). Examining reading development and reading disability in English language learners: Potential contributions from functional neuroimaging. *Learning Disabilities Research & Practice, 20 (1),* 24–30.

Rieben, L. & Perfetti, C. A. (1991). *Learning to read: Basic research and its implications.* Hillsdale, NJ: Lawrence Erlbaum.

Rumsey J.M., Horwitz B., Donohue B.C., Nace K.L., Maisog J.M., & Andreason P.A. (1999). Functional lesion in developmental dyslexia: left angular gyral blood flow predicts severity. *Brain & Language, 70,* 187–204.

Rumsey, J.M., Nace, K., Donohue, B., Wise, D., Maisog, J.M., & Andreason, P. (1997). A positron emission tomographic study of impaired word recognition and phonological processing in dyslexic men. *Archives of Neurology, 54,* 562–573.

Salmelin, R., Service, E., Kiesila, P., Uutela, K., & Salonen, O. (1996). Impaired visual word processing in dyslexia revealed with magnetoencephalography. *Annals of Neurology, 40,* 157–162.

Sandak, R., Mencl, W.E., Frost, S.J., Mason, S.A., Rueckl, J.G., Katz, L., et al. (2004a). The neurobiology of adaptive learning in reading: A contrast of different training conditions. *Cognitive Affective and Behavioral Neuroscience, 4,* 67–88.

Sandak, R., Mencl, W. E., Frost, S. J., Mason, S. A., & Pugh, K. R. (2004b). The neurobiological basis of skilled and impaired reading: Recent findings and new directions. *Scientific Studies of Reading: Special Issue on Neurobiology of Reading.* R. Sandak, R. & R. Poldrack, (Eds.), 8, 273–292.

Sarkari, S., Simos, P.G., Fletcher, J.M., Castillo, E.M., Breier, J.I., & Papanicolaou, A.C. (2002). The emergence and treatment of developmental reading disability: Contributions of functional brain imaging. *Seminars in Pediatric Neurology, 9,* 227–236.

Scarborough, H. S. (1998a). Early identification of children at risk for disabilities: Phonological awareness and some other promising predictors. In B. K. Shapiro, P. J. Accardo, & A. J. Capute (Eds.) *Specific reading disability: A view of the spectrum* (pp. 75–119). Timonium, MD: York Press.

Scarborough, H. S. (1998b). Predicting the future achievement of second graders with reading disabilities: Contributions of phonemic awareness, verbal memory, rapid serial naming, and IQ. *Annals of Dyslexia, 48, 115–136.*

Scarborough, H., & Dobrich, W. (1990). Development of children with early language delay. *Journal of Speech and Hearing Research, 33,* 70–83.

Seidenberg, M. S., & McClelland, J. L. (1989). A distributed, developmental model of visual word recognition. *Psychological Review, 96,* 523–568.

Shankweiler, D., Crain, S., Katz, L., Fowler, A.E., Liberman, A.M., Brady, S.A., et al. (1995). Cognitive profiles of reading-disabled children: Comparison of language skills in phonology, morphology, and syntax. *Psychological Science, 6,* 149–156.

Shaywitz, S.E., Fletcher, J.M., Holahan, J.M., Shneider, A.E., Marchione, K.E., Stuebing, K.K., Francis, D.J., Pugh, K.R., Shaywitz, B.A. (1999). Persistence of dyslexia: the Connecticut Longitudinal Study at adolescence. *Pediatrics, 104(6),* 1351–1359.

Shaywitz, S.E., Shaywitz, B.A., Fulbright, R.K., Skudlarski, P., Mencl, W.E., Constable, R.T., et al. (2002). Disruption of posterior brain systems for reading in children with developmental dyslexia. *Biological Psychiatry, 52,* 101–110.

Shaywitz, S.E., Shaywitz, B.A., Pugh, K.R., Fulbright, R.K., Constable, R.T., Mencl, W.E., et al. (1998). Functional disruption in the organization of the brain for reading in dyslexia. *Proceedings of the National Academy of Sciences, 95,* 2636–2641.

Simos, P.G., Breier, J.I., Fletcher, J.M., Foorman, B.R., Castillo, E.M., & Papanicolaou, A.C. (2002). Brain mechanisms for reading words and pseudowords: an integrated approach. *Cerebral Cortex, 12,* 297–305.

Siok, W.T., Perfetti, C.A., Jin, Z. & Tan, L.H. (2004). Biological abnormality of impaired reading is constrained by culture. *Nature, 431,* 70–76.

Stanovich, K.E., Cunningham, A.E.& Cramer, B.B. (1984). Assessing phonological awareness in kindergarten children: issues of task comparability. *Journal of Experimental Child Psychology, 38,* 175–190.

Stanovich, K.E., & Siegel, L.S. (1994). Phenotypic performance profile of children with reading disabilities: A regression-based test of the phonological-core variable-difference model. *Journal of Educational Psychology, 86,* 24–53.

Strain, E., Patterson, K., & Seidenberg, M.S. (1996). Semantic effects in single-word naming. *Journal of Experimental Psychology: Learning, Memory, and Cognition, 21,* 1140–1154.

Tagamets, M.A., Novick, J.M., Chalmers, M.L., & Friedman, R.B. (2000). A parametric approach of orthographic processing in the brain: an fMRI study. *Journal of Cognitive Neuroscience, 1,* 281–297.

Tan, L.H. , Hoosain, R., Peng, D. (1995). Role of early presemantic phonological code in Chinese character identification. *Journal of Experimental Psychology: Learning, Memory, and Cognition, 21(1),* 43–54.

Tan, L.H., Liu, H.L., Perfetti, C.A., Spinks, J.A., Fox, P.T., Gao, J.H. (2001). The neural system underlying Chinese logograph reading. *NeuroImage, 13,* 836–846.

Tarkiainen, A., Cornelissen, P.L., & Salmelin, R. (2003). Dynamics of visual feature analysis and object-level processing in face versus letter-string perception. *Brain, 125,* 1125–1136.

Temple, E., Poldrack, R.A., Salidis, J., Deutsch, G.K., Tallal, P., Merzenich, M.M., & Gabrieli, J.D. (2001). Disrupted neural responses to phonological and orthographic processing in dyslexic children: an fMRI study. *NeuroReport, 12,* 299–307.

Torgesen, J.K., Morgan, S.T., & Davis, C. (1992). Effects of two types of phonological awareness training on word learning in kindergarten children. *Journal of Educational Psychology, 84,* 364–370.

Torgesen, J.K., Wagner, R.K., Rasshotte, C.A. (1994). Development of reading-related phonological processing abilities: New evidence of bidirectional causality from a latent variable longitudinal study. *Journal of Learning Disabilities, 27(5),* 276–286.

Turkeltaub, P.E., Gareau, L., Flowers, D.L., Zeffiro, T.A., & Eden, G.F. (2003). Development of neural mechanisms for reading. *Nature Neuroscience, 6,* 767–73.

Van Orden, G. C. (1987). A ROWS is a ROSE: Spelling, sound, and reading. *Memory and Cognition, 10,* 434–442.

Van Orden, G.C., Goldinger, S.D. (1994). Interdependence of form and function in cognitive systems explains perception of printed words. *Journal of Experimental Psychology: Human Perception and Performance, 20(6),* 1269–1291.

Van Orden, G.C., Johnston, J.C., & Hale, B.L. (1988). Word identification in reading proceeds from the spelling to sound to meaning. *Journal of Experimental Psychology: Memory, Language and Cognition, 14,* 371–386.

Van Orden, G.C., Pennington, B.F., & Stone, G.O. (1990). Word identification in reading and the promise of subsymbolic psycholinguistics. *Psychological Review, 97,* 488–522.

Wimmer, H., & Mayringer, H. (2002). Dysfluent reading in the absence of spelling difficulties: A specific disability in regular orthographies. *Journal of Educational Psychology, 94,* 272–277.

Wise, B.W., & Olsen, R.K. (1995). Computer-based phonological awareness and reading instruction. *Annals of Dyslexia, 45,* 99–122.

Xu, B., Grafman, J., Gaillard, W.D., Ishii, K., Vega-Bermudez, F., Pietrini, P., et al. (2001). Conjoint and extended neural networks for the computation of speech codes: The neural basis of selective impairment in reading words and pseudowords. *Cerebral Cortex, 11,* 267–277.

Ziegler, J. C. & Goswami, U. (2005). Reading acquisition, developmental dyslexia, and skilled reading across languages: A psycholinguistic grain size theory. *Psychological Bulletin, 131 1,* 3–29.

Ziegler, J. C., Perry, C., Jacobs, A. M., & Braun, M. (2001). Identical words are read differently in different languages. *Psychological Science, 12,* 379–384.

Ziegler, J. C., Perry, C., Ma-Wyatt, A., Ladner, D., & Schulte-Korne, G. (2003). Developmental dyslexia in different languages: Language-specific or universal? *Journal of Experimental Child Psychology, 86,* 169–193.

12

The Reading Networks and Dyslexia

John Stein

The late Alvin Lieberman used to say that reading is difficult because speaking is so easy. We have an "instinct" to learn to speak, probably developed when the brain size and connectivity in *Homo sapiens* increased sharply over that of our closest relatives, the chimpanzees, about 75,000 years ago; this enabled symbolic representation of the world (Stein 2003). Hence, we can learn to speak simply by imitating those around us; we do not have to be taught. But reading does not come so naturally. Because it is a cultural invention made only about 5,000 years ago rather than enshrined in our genome, we have to be taught the letters of the alphabet and how word sounds can be represented as a series of those letters. As few of us are mathematicians or champion chess players, reading remains the most difficult skill that most of us ever have to learn. Hence, it is not surprising that over a quarter of all children fail to learn to read properly.

Nevertheless, reading should still be seen as an extension of speaking as it relies on many of the same auditory symbolic processes, just as language skills are built on preexisting auditory and audiomotor processes that had evolved earlier. The new feature that reading brought to the scene was visual representation of words in written rather than auditory form. The first writing was probably developed for symbolizing quantities of foodstuffs and the money to pay for them. Then the alphabetic principle was invented by the Phoenicians, who discovered that even complicated word sounds can be broken down into a much smaller number of phonological units (40 phonemes in English), and that these could be represented by an even smaller number of letter symbols. This may have followed as a natural generalization from the simple sounds of number and food words.

Reading Models

Once the alphabetic principle had been invented and the visual, "orthographic," representations of words became familiar, there was no longer any need for phonological mediation to read them. The visual representations of words or even groups of words could reveal their meaning through translating directly into their meanings. Thus, the first requirement for skilled reading is rapid visual analysis of the letters and their order. We can then link this visual form directly with our semantic lexicon to retrieve meaning.

However, for unfamiliar words, we still need to go back to the alphabet and interpose extra stages of translating the letters into the sounds they stand for, then melding them together to reveal the auditory representation of the word, thence its meaning. Therefore behind the "phonological" route we need to build up a background knowledge of the way in which words can be broken down into their constituent phonemes to match with whatever the letter/sound decoding system presents us. Remember that few words are visually familiar to beginning readers, so that learning to read has to begin with "phonics" and letter sound translation, and early skill at this is the best predictor of rapidly learning to read.

Soon however, the child learns the visual form of several words, so that he no longer has to translate them into their auditory forms, but can immediately recognize the word visually and retrieve its meaning. A little later, he can extract meaning, not word by word, but from a whole group of words in a phrase or even in a whole sentence. Early on in this process of learning sentence structure, the child learns to move the eyes on to the next word, even before the last is fully understood. Thus, reading speedily becomes a hugely complex cognitive operation, and it is not so surprising that many people fail to master it properly.

Even in adults, these two different routes for reading are still distinguishable, although they are probably not entirely separate, as used to be thought (Seidenburg 1993). Familiar words already in the sight vocabulary can be read directly via the visual/semantic ("lexical") route, whereas the few words with which the person is still unfamiliar have to be translated into their sounds via the phonological (also known as the "sublexical") route. Of course the lexical route is much faster because it avoids the laborious and time-consuming stages of letter-by-letter conversion to sounds. Hence, the more often it can be used, the more fluent a person's reading is.

Visual Input to Reading

The visual system provides the input to both the lexical and the sublexical routes for reading. One would naturally assume therefore that vision is the most important sense for reading. This seems obvious to the layman, but it is strongly disputed by many experts. This is because the dominant theory in the field is that much more crucial for reading is the phonological skill of learning how words can be split down into their constituent letter sounds (phonemes); hence, it is argued that acquisition of phonological skill at the level of individual letter sounds is in fact the most important prerequisite for reading.

Nevertheless, vision is probably the important first step for learning about phonology at the phonemic level. Not until children have learned that words can be represented as a sequence of visual symbols do they discover that the syllables that they have learned to speak can actually be split down further into separate sounds, which are represented by the letters. This is the alphabetic principle; and there is now a lot of evidence that children do not begin to learn the phonemic structure of words until after they begin to learn about how words can be represented as a sequence of letters (Morais, Cary et al. 1979). Moreover, illiterate adults learning to read only begin to grasp the subsyllabic phonemic structure of their language when they are taught how the words can be represented by the letters of the alphabet (Castro-Caldas, Petersson et al. 1998). Furthermore, in ideographicscripts, such as Japanese Kana, children's phonological skills never become more detailed than the mora (syllabic) level. Japanese children do not have to learn to subdivide word sounds any further because the writing system does not require it. Indeed, Kanji does not even require syllabic phonology; readers only need to learn mora when they learn Kana, which represents speech at this level.

Therefore in this chapter, I emphasize the visual requirements of reading. This is not to imply that phonological skills are not important, but to show how important basic visual processes are for reading. We will even see how learning to analyze the letters in words can actually help children to acquire phonological skills.

Foveal Splitting

Because of the way the visual pathways from the retina to the occipital cortex are organized, the left side of each word is first projected to the right primary visual striate cortex in area 17, whereas the right side is projected to the left striate cortex, so that the representation of each word is divided in two at the fovea. The left-sided first three or four letters usually carry more information about a word than subsequent ones do. Furthermore, mutual inhibition exists between the right and left hemisphere primary visual representations. So, this initial foveal splitting means that, unexpectedly, the right hemisphere (RH) has the advantage at the earliest stages of visually processing a word (Shillcock and Monaghan 2001). But this advantage seems to be missing in very poor readers; they tend to attend less to the left-hand side of a word, thus exhibiting left "minineglect" (Hari 2001).

The influence of foveal splitting is probably not restricted just to an initial short time window before the information is projected forward to extrastriate regions. All these regions also project back to V1 by recurrent connections. The primary visual cortex is essential for conscious awareness of a visual image, probably because it contains the most detailed, authoritative cortical representation of the retinal image (Cowey and Stoerig 1992). Hence, its division into two halves and the mutual inhibition between them reasserts itself whenever V1 is reinterrogated by recurrent projections from further forward.

Magnocellular and Parvocellular Visual Neurones

Different qualities of visual targets are analyzed by separate, parallel pathways in the visual brain. This separation begins right out in the retina with the existence of two kinds of retinal ganglion cell, whose axons project all the visual information back to the brain. Ten percent of these ganglion cells are known as *magnocellular* because they are noticeably larger than the others, with thicker, more rapidly conducting axons and more extensive dendritic fields that cover an area approximately 50 times greater than those of the more numerous, but much smaller, *parvocells*.

In addition to their size magnocellular cells can be distinguished from other retinal ganglion cells by their surface signature molecules, which can be detected by specific magnocellular antibodies, such as CAT 301 (Hockfield and Sur 1990). The precise structure of these surface molecules is controlled by a set of histocompatibility genes situated on the short arm of human chromosome 6. For reasons that are not yet fully understood, magnocells seem to be particularly vulnerable; they mature later than parvocells, and their development has been found to be impaired in prematurity and in mosty neurodevelopmental diseases such as dyslexia, dyspraxia, dysphasia, ADHD and autistic spectrum disorders (ASD).

Their large dendritic trees that draw from a wide area of retinal receptors mean that magnocellular neurones are more sensitive to large (low spatial frequency), dim, low-contrast stimuli than are parvocells. So they can indicate where visual "blobs" are, but without being able to identify them.

Also magnocells respond only at the onset and offset of a light stimulus (they are "rapidly adapting"). They are therefore much more strongly excited by visual transients, changing, flickering, or moving stimuli that have high temporal frequencies, than by steady, stationary lights. Their main function is therefore to time visual events and to signal the movements of visual targets— *visual temporal processing*. The large diameter of their axons means that they conduct information about these visual transients very rapidly to the superior colliculus for the reflex control of eye movements and to the magnocellular layers of the lateral geniculate nucleus (LGN) in the thalamus, en route to the primary visual cortex. In fact, the magnocellular cell signal may arrive in the visual cortex as long as 20 ms ahead of the parvocell volley.

But magnocells are not so sensitive as the parvocells are to fine detail (high spatial frequencies), nor to color differences. This means that the magnocellular system provides the brain with rapid information about the location and broad outline of letters and words primarily for directing attention and eye movements to each one if necessary, as is required when learning to read a new word. But parallel processing by the parvocellular system and the ventral stream visual word form area (VWFA) is required to distinguish the details of letters, for example between "m" and "n" or "c" and "e".

Only at the level of the LGN are the magno- and parvocellular inputs from the retina completely separated anatomically. In V1, magnocellular axons arrive in cortical input layer 4Cα, whereas parvocells input to layer 4Cβ. Thereafter, however, the two kinds of input interconnect strongly. Nevertheless magnocell input dominates responses to coarse, low-contrast, low-spatial-frequency, moving, or flickering stimuli, whereas parvocells dominate responses to stationary, fine, high-spatial-frequency, coloured stimuli. But selective lesions of the magnocellular layers of the LGN only impair detecting visual transients and motion, whereas they leave contrast sensitivity to stationary stimuli, even large ones with low spatial frequencies, relatively unaffected (Merigan and Maunsell 1990). So magnocell input seems only to be absolutely essential for temporal processing.

Visual what and where pathways

From the primary visual cortex (striate cortex, V1, in Brodmann's area 17), visual information is projected forward into extrastriate visual areas, again by two separate pathways. These pass either dorsomedially or ventrolaterally and are known as the dorsal "where" and the ventral "what" streams, respectively. The "where" stream receives mainly visual magnocellular input and projects to the visual motion area (V5/MT), which is situated in the extension of the superior temporal sulcus into the parietal cortex. After this, the "where" stream projects onward via the posterior parietal cortex angular and supramarginal gyri, to the frontal eye fields and prefrontal cortex, including the inferior frontal gyrus. Importantly also, magnocellular fibres dominate the visual input to the cerebellum. The magnocellular neurones supply these areas with information about the timing and movements of things in the outside world. These signals are then used for the visual guidance of attention and of eye and limb movements. All the above areas are known to be important for visuomotor control functions that are important for reading.

Most of the neurons in this dorsal pathway are large, conduct rapidly and, at least in cats, express the same surface markers as the subcortical visual magnocellular neurons that are recognized by antibodies such as CAT 301 (Hockfield and Sur 1990). So, the dorsal stream can be considered a cortical extension of the subcortical visual magnocellularsystem.

In contrast, the ventrolateral "what" stream receives equally from magno- and parvocells and projects ventrolaterally towards the VWFA on the undersurface of the occipital cortex, at the anterior end of the fusiform gyrus. The function of this stream is to identify pattern, form, color, and fine detail, to indicate "what" something is—for example, to identify and distinguish between letters.

Magnocellular System, Eye Movements, and Reading

At first sight, we might think that the magnocell-dominated "where" stream might not play any very important role in reading. Its function is to locate targets as blobs, to time visual events, and to signal visual motion; yet, print is stationary most of the time, so their expertise might appear not to be needed. But this account neglects the eye movements required for reading. The magnocellular system seems to play the main role in controlling the eyes' saccades from one letter or word to the next. Treating words as blobs because of their low spatial resolution, the magnocellular system guides each saccade to land close to the center of gravity of the next word. Thus, high magnocell sensitivity is required for precisely positioning the eyes onto the next word when reading, and poor reading may ensue if the ability to make accurate saccades to complex targets is impaired (Crawford and Higham 2001).

Fixations

Perhaps more importantly, the magnocellular system plays a crucial role in stabilizing the eyes during fixations on each word. These fixations only last about a quarter of a second but the fine details of the letters in a word can only be processed during these, not during reading saccades. t; so it is especially important to keep the eyes stationary then. If the eyes stray off the letter being fixated, a *retinal slip* motion signal is generated by the magnocellular system, and this is fed back to the oculomotor control system to bring the eyes back on target. Hence a sensitive magnocellular system is essential to provide these feedback signals, and another cause of poor reading appears to be unstable control of fixation, often caused by impaired development of the visual magnocellular system (Fowler 1991; Fischer, Hartnegg et al. 2000).

Meanwhile, the magnocellular system also plays an important role in controlling attentional gating in the primary visual cortex. This swings the focus of attention onto a word and allows detailed information about its letters to be projected from the primary visual cortex through to the ventral system VWFA in the fusiform cortex, where they are identified (Vidyasagar 2004).

Letter Order

In addition, the motion signals generated by images swishing over the retina during each saccade to the next word are used to help signal how far the eyes have moved, even though we are not consciously aware of this. Together with signals about the size of the oculomotor command to move the eyes and probably proprioceptive information provided by the eye muscles about their change of length, magnocellular signals about how far images have moved across the retina during each saccade are used to determine how far the eyes have moved. This information can then also be used to locate each letter with respect to the previous one fixated. Thus, the magnocellular system not only controls reading saccades and stabilizes fixations, it also seems to be important for determining the positional order of letters and words (Cornelissen, Hansen et al. 1998), whereas the "what" stream is left to identify them.

Vergence Control

When reading small print at the normal reading distance of about 30 cm, the eyes are not parallel, but converged at approximately 10 degrees toward each other. Control of these vergence movements is dominated by the magnocellular system, and this is known to be highly vulnerable to drugs and disease. Some of us know this only too well from the double vision that ensues when vergence breaks down after too much alcohol! It has been suggested that delayed maturation leading to mild impairment of the magnocellular system might cause unstable vergence control (Fowler, Riddell et al. 1990). This might account for the problems with visual perceptual stability that many beginning readers describe: of letters and words appearing to split, reverse themselves, and move over each other, so that they find it difficult to decide what order they should be in. This is another reason why poor readers have such difficulties building up reliable memorized representations of the visual/ orthographic form of words.

Magnocellular System and Dyslexia

The idea that the magnocellular system is particularly important for reading originates from studying children who have exceptional difficulties learning to read (developmental dyslexics). A great deal of evidence now suggests that in many, but probably not all, dyslexics, development of their magnocellular systems is mildly impaired. Thus, in many dyslexics, their retinal magnocellular responses are sluggish (Pammer and Wheatley 2001), and the magnocell layers in the lateral geniculate nucleus are smaller and more disorganized post mortem (Livingstone, Rosen et al. 1991). Visual evoked potential studies have shown that the magnocell volley may arrive in the visual cortex up to 20 ms later in dyslexic compared with good readers. The magnocellular system is most sensitive to coarse (low spatial frequency), flickering (high temporal frequency) stimuli; hence, contrast sensitivity to these tends to be lower in dyslexics (Lovegrove, Bowling et al. 1980). The visual motion area V5/MT receives most of its input from the magnocellular system; it, too, is less activated by visual motion stimuli in dyslexics (Eden, VanMeter et al. 1996); hence, their sensitivity to visual motion is lower (Cornelissen, Richardson et al. 1995).

Indeed, sensitivity to visual motion measured either psychophysically (Talcott, Witton et al. 2000) or by functional magnetic resonance imaging (fMRI) (Demb, Boynton et al. 1997) predicts visual reading ability in everybody, not just in dyslexics but also in both good and bad readers. As might be expected from the role of the magnocellular system in determining the order of letters, this correlation is particularly strong with individuals' visual/orthographic skills. As we have seen, the dorsal visual stream projects to the angular and supramarginal gyri. Hence the degree of fMRI activation of these areas correlates with individuals' reading ability; this may well derive at least in part from the strength of their magnocellular input.

Magnocellular System and Attention

The fast-track magnocellular inputs to the dorsal stream are important for controlling the focus of visual attention as well as controlling eye movements.. As we have seen, the "where" stream probably feeds back magnocellular signals to the primary visual cortex that enable us to focus on particular inputs to the ventral stream VWFA by gating them on or off (Vidyasagar, 2004). During each fixation this "attentional spotlight" probably not only feeds letters, one after the other through for identification by the ventral stream, but it also defines their spatial location with respect to each other. Thus, during each fixation of about 250 ms, seven or eight letters are accessed sequentially without moving the eyes (Vidyasagar, 2004). Consistent with this, serial visual search has been found to be critically dependent upon activation of magnocellular pathways (Cheng, Eysel et al. 2004). These gating inputs are presumably also the means by which serial visual search is mediated: the dorsal stream uses its crude spatial resolution and information about the location of targets to select each one sequentially. Each is then analyzed in detail by the ventral stream. Hence, numerous studies have now shown that poor readers are significantly slower at serial visual search (Iles, Walsh et al. 2000) and greatly affected by distractors (Facoetti, A et al. 2001).

Thus, the main reason why it takes such a long time for children to learn to read fluently may be because training the visual attentional search mechanism to work properly for reading is a slow process. Normally, visual search is fairly random, concentrating on salient features, and is not systematically or sequentially deployed across the visual field (Horowitz and Wolfe 1998), but for reading the attentional spotlight must be taught instead to proceed in an unusual linear sequential manner from left to right, accessing each letter in a word in the correct order.

Auditory/Phonological Processing?

There is general agreement that another important skill required for reading is the ability to split the sounds of words down into separate phonemes (acquisition of phonological skill), and it is important to try to understand what neural processes underlie this. Whilst learning orthography plays an important part in teaching children about the phonemic structure of words, it seems obvious that phonological skill would also depend upon basic auditory processing capacities. Although logical, this suggestion has proved highly controversial (Talcott, Witton et al. 2000). An alternative view is that language is so special that the processing required to comprehend it is exclusively linguistic; hence, looking for contributions to phonological skill from lower down in the auditory system is sure to be fruitless.

However, it is becoming increasingly clear that language is not so special after all. Chomsky and Lieberman's view was that, evolutionarily, we developed so far in advance of our closest relatives, the chimpanzees, because a crucial genetic mutation endowed us with a unique "encapsulated linguistic processor" that provided us with the communication powers of language, and that reading makes use of this. But it has turned out that speech and language are not totally new; they built on evolutionary adaptations that arose for quite different purposes (Stein 2003). For example, hemispheric specialization probably developed in the RH for improving an animal's visuospatial skills to find its way to food and back to home. Likewise, descent of the larynx may well have been an adaptation for swimming, not speaking. Similarly, the mirror cells found in Broca's area in the inferior frontal gyrus (IFG) that enable us to learn our language probably developed not for speaking at all, but for learning how to imitate other's use of tools. Thus, language and reading came to be mediated by the left hemisphere (LH) system of interconnected regions almost by accident.

The essential auditory input for phonological analysis of speech comes from the division of the auditory system that responds to temporal changes in sound frequency and intensity. Accurate temporal processing of this sort is required to identify the subtle frequency and amplitude changes that distinguish phonemes. Tallal was the first to suggest that developmental dysphasics have such problems with language because they are particularly poor at the auditory temporal processing required for the discrimination of speech sounds (Tallal and Piercy 1973). In the last few years, several hundred studies have compared basic auditory processing capabilities with language and reading skills. Almost all have shown correlations between basic auditory temporal processing and phonological skills, suggesting that the former does indeed help to determine the development of the latter; low-level auditory temporal processing does indeed underlie the acquisition of language skills. Indeed, auditory sensitivity to frequency and amplitude modulations can account for nearly 50% of individual differences in phonological skill in both good and bad readers (Witton, Stein et al. 2002).

Auditory Magnocellular System?

Such auditory temporal analysis seems to be mediated particularly by large neurones with rapid processing capacities (Trussell 1997). These could be called *auditory magnocells*, because they are recognized by magnocellular antibodies, such as CAT 301. However, no such clear anatomical separation of magno- and parvocells exists in the auditory system as there is in the visual system, so the existence of an auditory magno system is not generally accepted. Nevertheless, as in the visual system, development of large auditory cells may be impaired in dyslexics, and in dyslexic brains the magnocellular division of the auditory medial geniculate nucleus is found to contain fewer large cells on the left (Galaburda, Menard et al. 1994), like those in the dyslexic LGN. Moreover, temporal processing abilities in both auditory and visual domains tend to be similar in individuals, for example, most dyslexics, have both lowered visual motion sensitivity and lowered sensitivity to changes in auditory frequency, suggesting a common basis for both.

As in the visual system therefore, individual differences in the development of large (magnocellular type?) cells in the auditory system might also underlie differences in the acquisition of phonological skills. However, not all those who show phonological problems appear to have either auditory or visual weaknesses (that is, they are neither necessary nor sufficient causes of phonological weakness). Some have argued from this that they cannot be considered causal. But this is like saying that because smoking is neither necessary nor sufficient to cause lung cancer it can never cause it—patently false. The probability is that impaired auditory and visual temporal processing are two of a number of possible causes of impaired phonological processing.

A Pansensory General Temporal Processing Magno System?

Thus, large magnocellular neurones specialized for temporal processing are not confined to the visual system. They are also found in the auditory, somatosensory, memory, and motor systems (i.e., throughout the brain), and all seem to be recognized by magnocell-specific antibodies, such as CAT 301 (Hockfield and Sur 1990). They seem to constitute a specialized subsystem, devoted to temporal processing, probably developing from common precursors. Magnocellular systems of all types throughout the brain may be important for reading, involving not only visual but also auditory, somatosensory, cerebellar motor, and even hippocampal memory magnocellular neurones as well.

Risk Factors for Poor Reading

Studying the factors that predict difficulties with learning to read can provide us with powerful insights into how the brain copes with the problems presented by reading, and how these processes can go wrong. It is also important that teachers encountering possible problems in the classroom be aware of these indicators of reading difficulty, so that they can institute help as early as possible and thus avoid the downward spiral of failure, loss of self-confidence, frustration, misery, and depression that failure to learn to read can so often lead to.

Heredity

The most important influence appears to be heredity. The similarity in reading ability between siblings living in the same family (familiality) is as high as 80 percent. Comparing dizygotic with monozygotic (identical) twins enables us to divide familiality into two components, namely genetic heritability (h^2) and common environmental (c^2) factors (Olson, Wise et al. 1989). Heritability turns out to explain around 60% of familial variance in reading, so that the environment that the twins share in common explains around 20%. Thus, more than half of the differences that children show in reading ability can be explained by their genetic inheritance, and this proportion does not change much even after allowing for the effect of nonverbal IQ. In other words, these large genetic effects on reading are highly specific for reading.

Recent genetic linkage studies have confirmed what had been widely suspected earlier, namely, that several genes are involved; to date 10 have been postulated. Interestingly, many of the genes discovered so far, alleles of which have been identified as associated with poor reading ability, have turned out to be involved in controlling neuronal migration during early in utero development of the cerebral cortex. The most widely replicated genetic linkage of reading problems is to a site on the short arm of chromosome 6. We have identified two genes close to each other that seem to help control neuronal migration (Francks 2004). After electroporating complementary inhibitory RNA derived from these two genes into the developing cerebral cortex of the mouse, neuronal migration is arrested.

One of these C6 genes, KIAA 0319, seems to control glycosylation of the cell surface molecules. These respond to extracellular control signals and also act as signatures indicating to other cells what lineage they derive from. Thus, it may be significant that the magnocells with rapid temporal processing, "transient" sensitivity that is so important for reading (Hockfield and Sur 1990), all express the same specific magnocell signature molecules, such as that recognised by CAT 301. As mentioned earlier, visual and auditory transient sensitivity tend to correlate with each other within individuals. Thus, all magnocells may be under the same general developmental control. It is possible therefore that the development of all the temporal processing visual, auditory, memory, and motor skills required for reading might be under the control of genes like KIAA 0319 (Stein 2001). Different alleles might affect different individuals more in one system than another, idiosyncratically, so that one person may be stronger visually, another auditorily, and so on.

IQ

The next most important influence on reading ability is general intelligence. Twenty-five percent of the variance in children's reading is accounted for by their IQ. About half of this effect survives controlling for genetic effects that are shared with both IQ and reading. But IQ does only explain one-quarter of reading variance; some children with Down syndrome, with an IQ of only around 50, can be taught to read successfully, although they have limited comprehension.

Teaching

Clearly, children must receive enough appropriate teaching to learn to read. Those who truant too much, although this is rare in primary school, usually fail to learn to read properly. By the time they are in secondary school, however, probably the main reason why they truant is, because they cannot read, they gain very little, apart from humiliation, by attending class. Their teaching has been so unsuccessful that they vote with their feet.

Good quality teaching can obviate these effects however. Yet the fashion for abandoning phonics teaching in favor of real books and flash cards of whole words that took hold in the 1960s may have done children without highly developed visual memories a profound disservice. Many think that the decline in average spelling ability that has occurred in the second half of the 20th century can be attributed to that trend. There is now a welcome return to phonics teaching in primary schools. But let us hope that this development will not be to the exclusion of attention to visual factors in reading as well.

However, teaching quality is clearly not the most important factor. Heredity remains far more important, independently of general intelligence. The genes involved affect the way the brain develops, and affect how it carries out the fundamental visual and auditory processing operations required for reading. Thus we find that individuals' visual and auditory temporal processing sensitivity together with their IQ accounts for over two-thirds of their differences in reading ability (Talcott et al. 2000). Hence, the quality of children's teaching whether at school or at home, in terms of how often their mothers read with them or how many books there are in the house, seems to be considerably less important than how well their brains' magnocellular systems are adapted for reading.

Developmental Speech Problems

Developmental speech problems include late talking, impaired pronunciation, difficulties learning to identify letter sounds, confusing sound order, and failure to identify rhymes. Persuasive evidence suggests that these problems are associated with impaired development of the basic temporal processing functions of the auditory system described earlier, together with poor articulatory coordination, which is probably associated with deficient operation of the cerebellum. Hence, we can conclude that particularly the component of reading ability that depends on acquiring accurate phonological skills is to a large extent determined by basic auditory temporal processing, whereas the motor side of speech depends on proper maturation of the cerebellum.

Developmental Motor Problems

Poor reading is therefore also associated with a variety of other motor symptoms: late crawling, late walking, poor balance, exceptional clumsiness, difficulty learning to ride a bicycle, and slow acquisition of consistent handedness. Again, these symptoms point to an important role for the cerebellum in developing the sensorimotor skills required for reading.

The Reading Network in the Brain

Has this chapter moved us any closer to understanding the neural basis of reading? It seems that, above all, reading requires the temporal processing skills mediated by magnocellular systems in the brain, whether visual, auditory, or motor. We now consider how this translates into the reading network in the LH, which is specialized for these temporal functions. Modern techniques for imaging cortical areas of increased blood flow by functional magnetic resonance imaging (fMRI) or positron emission tomography (PET) imaging have greatly advanced our understanding of this network, although actually much of what has been discovered was suspected earlier from the results of lesion studies. Dejerine had shown as early as 1891 that "word blindness" was associated with lesions of the left angular gyrus at the temporoparietal junction, whereas Liepman had shown that lesions of the fusiform gyrus on the underside of the occipital cortex were associated with visual agnosia of various kinds. Also, it was known that lesions of Broca's area in the left IFG were often associated with reading as well as motor speech problems. In severe dyslexics, these areas were found to exhibit *ectopias*; these are small outgrowths of neurones, "brain warts" 1 mm or so in diameter, that disobey stop signals and migrate beyond the outer limiting membrane during development. They are associated with disorganized connectivity both beneath them and extending across the corpus callosum to homotopic areas in the contralateral hemisphere (Galaburda, Sherman et al. 1985).

But there are many problems with interpreting the results of lesions. Brain damage caused by maldevelopment, strokes, tumours, or trauma seldom removes just one function, partly because the lesions do not neatly dissect out one anatomical region, but also because reading, like language in general, is mediated not by a single structure, but by a distributed system of interconnected areas. Hence, removing one node alters the performance of the whole network, and it is therefore difficult to interpret what that one node contributes.

Unfortunately, this problem applies equally to the activations recorded by functional imaging as well. Observing increased blood flow in an area during a particular task merely shows that the area is more active than under other conditions, but it is silent about how other areas in the network are contributing to the function. Without this knowledge, functional imaging reduces to mere "modern phrenology"; knowing *what* areas are more active does not tell us *how* the network is carrying out the function.

The fact that the reading network is built on to that responsible for language makes interpretation of results specifically in terms of reading even more problematical. Nevertheless, the results of lesions and functional imaging concur in showing that the reading network is centered, although not exclusively, in the LH. As for language, the reading network comprises Wernicke's area at the back of the temporal lobe together with the supramarginal and angular gyri and their connections with the IFG via the arcuate fasciculus (see Fig. 12.1).

Fusiform Visual Word Form Area

The only completely new region that seems to have developed specifically for reading is an area known as the VWFA, which is situated in the anterior part of the left fusiform gyrus on the undersurface of the occipital lobe and extends forward into the back of the middle temporal gyrus (Cohen, Henry et al. 2004)). This is at the culmination of the ventrolateral visual "what" processing stream. Nevertheless access of visual signals to it seems to be under control of the magnocellular-dominated dorsal visual attentional focusing system.

Further back in the ventral visual stream, in the posterior fusiform gyrus, letters seem to be represented by their visual features, not by whether they are

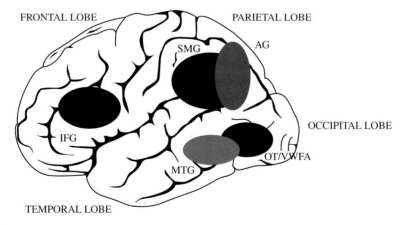

Figure 12.1 Cortical areas that are underactivated in dyslexic readers (AG = angular gyrus; IFG = inferior frontal gyrus; MTG = middle temporal gyrus; OT/VWFA = occipito temporal visual word form area; SMG = supramarginal gyrus).

orthographic symbols. But more anteriorly, the VWFA comes to represent their visual forms as orthographic symbols at a more abstract level than the lines and curves of which they are constructed. Thus, the VWFA is activated equally by upper- or lowercase versions of a word, but less so by pronounceable nonsense words and not at all by meaningless strings of letter like symbols. Its degree of activation seems to mirror the degree of orthographic skill possessed by the subject. Therefore, one can consider the VWFA as an important node on the pathway translating visual symbols into their meaning, still representing them visually but not as letters as such, but with respect to their orthographic coding. Further forward in the middle temporal gyrus, this visual representation seems to meet with the phonological representation of the word.

Temporoparietal Junction

Perhaps the most important region for reading, however, lies at the temporoparietal junction, where the posterior part of Wernicke's speech comprehension area meets the angular and supramarginal gyri (SMG), Brodmann areas 39 and 40. Here visual/orthographic and auditory/phonological information seem to communicate with the semantic lexicon, the store of word meanings. Thus, this important junction probably translates the visual forms of letters and words into their sounds, and hence into their meanings. In skilled readers, this region (particularly the SMG) seems to activate most when dealing with unfamiliar words (e.g., low-frequency or pronounceable nonwords) rather than familiar words (Simos, Breier et al. 2002). In contrast to the VWFA's orthographical representation, its degree of activation seems to correlate with an individual's phonological skill. Hence, the fMRI results confirm that the main role of the VWFA is to convert visual symbols into their sounds and thereby extract their meaning. It is not surprising therefore to find that these angular and supramarginal areas are particularly active in children learning to read, and their degree of activation predicts how successfully children will learn to read.

Inferior Frontal Gyrus

In addition, it is now clear that a number of areas around and including Broca's speech production area in the IFG are activated even during silent reading. The more posterior areas appear to be associated with phonological rehearsal during reading; hence, they mediate important metalinguistic functions dependent upon phonological short-term memory. For example holding the first words of a sentence in your phonological short-term memory is crucial for extracting the meaning of the whole sentence, represented by the order of words and their grammatical relationships (syntax).

The more anterior aspects of the IFG seem to play a role in semantic retrieval (Poldrack, Wagner et al. 1999). Like the temporoparietal system, they are more strongly engaged by low-frequency words and pronounceable nonwords than by high-frequency words. Like the temporoparietal system also, the anterior IFG is probably particularly important in children learning to read, for helping them to decode new words (Pugh, Sandak et al. 2005). Later on however, its degree of activation seems to become inversely related to children's reading ability. It is more active the worse the reader, probably because poorer readers have to rely more on the slower letter/sound phonological translation route for reading.

Cerebellum

The cerebellum is the brain's autopilot, responsible for coordinating the precise timing of muscle contractions, but also for planning such movements. Since accurate timing of sensory feedback and motor outflow is an essential requirement for these functions, the cerebellum receives a rich input of visual, auditory, proprioceptive, and motor magnocellular-mediated timing signals (Stein 1986). Purely on theoretical grounds therefore, it was likely to play an important role in reading. In particular, it receives a very large input from the visual magnocellular system, particularly from the parietal supramarginal and angular gyri (Stein and Glickstein 1992), and its main function is to mediate the acquisition of automatic skills. It does this by predicting the outcome of upcoming movements in terms of their sensory consequences. If the cerebellum predicts that the outcome of a movement will not occur as intended, the motor program can be modified before emission. Also, if the program, once executed, turns out to have failed to achieve its intended objective, it can be changed afterward to improve its outcome next time. In this way the cerebellum learns motor skills.

Importantly, this machinery is probably put to use not only for executing actual movements, such as the eye movements used for reading, the vocal tract movements used for speaking, and the hand movements used for writing, but accumulating evidence now suggests that cerebellar prediction is also used for planning movements and other cognitive operations, such as silent reading and silent speech (Schmahmann 2004).

Thus, the cerebellum probably plays a crucial role in the guidance of eye movements during reading, in visuomotor control for writing, and in mental rehearsal of word sounds for phonological analysis. So, it is not at all surprising to find that it is highly active during reading. A substantial body of evidence now suggests that particularly the right cerebellar hemisphere (linked to the LH of the cerebral cortex) plays a very important role in reading. Lesions there, particularly in children, are often accompanied by reading problems (Scott, Stoodley et al. 2001). This area is activated in functional imaging studies during reading tasks, even when single words are used and no eye movements are required. In several studies, the degree of cerebellar activation has been found to correlate with an individual's facility at the reading tasks employed. In anatomical studies, it has been shown that the size of the right cerebellar hemisphere predicts the extent of readers' phono-logical and orthographic skills (Rae, Harasty et al. 2002). In short, there is now very little doubt that cerebellar computations contribute significantly to reading.

Individual differences in cerebellar function may be assessed using tasks such as balancing, visually guided peg moving from one set of holes to another, and implicit learning. Numerous studies have shown that poor readers are worse than good readers at simply balancing on one leg with eyes open; moreover children's balancing ability correlates with their reading ability (Stoodley, Fawcett et al. 2005). Nobody claims that balancing is entirely a cerebellar function; clearly the vestibular and other systems are also involved. Nor do we think that the correlation between balance and reading indicates that balancing is directly required for reading. What it suggests is that cere-bellar precision may help to determine both balancing skill *and* aspects of the motor control required for reading, such as control of visual and auditory attention and eye fixations. This conclusion likewise explains why people's dexterity at visually guided peg moving correlates strongly with their reading ability.

When a complex sequence of finger movements is repeated, even when the subject is unaware of the repetition, performance of the sequence improves very significantly (and unconsciously), and this is associated with cerebellar activation. The amount of this implicit learning has also been found to correlate with reading ability (Stoodley, Harrison et al. 2005). Again, this suggests that the quality of an individual's cerebellar processing helps to determine her ability to develop the skills necessary for reading.

Conclusion

The most important theme of this chapter is that the ability to read depends greatly on the temporal processing systems of the brain: the visual magnocel-lular system for sequencing letters and words accurately and gating their access to the visual ventral stream for their identification; its auditory equiva-lent, which responds to the frequency and amplitude transients that distinguish letter sounds; together with motor timing systems, particularly those supplying and mediated by the cerebellum, which coordinate reading eye movements, speaking, and writing. These supply the reading network, which overlays similar processing modules used for speech and language comprehension.

Four main linked components of the reading network exist in the LH. The first is the VWFA situated in the left anterior fusiform gyrus, where letters are identified by the ventral visual stream. The second consists of Wernicke's area communicating with the supramarginal and angular gyri at the left temporoparietal junction. Here, auditory and visual representations are integrated with the meaning of words stored in the semantic lexicon. These project via the arcuate fasciculus to the third main component, which is located in the left IFG, including Broca's area. These areas are activated even for silent reading as well as reading out loud. The fourth important component is the right cerebellar hemisphere, which coordinates the other three.

References

Castro-Caldas, A., Petersson, K. M., Reis, A., Stone-Elander, S., & Ingvar, M. (1998). The illiterate brain. Learning to read and write during childhood influences the functional organization of the adult brain. *Brain, 121*, 1053–1063.

Cheng, A., Eysel, U., & Vidyasagar, T. (2004). The role of the magnocellular pathway in serial deployment of visual attention. *European Journal of Neuroscience, 20*, 2188–2192.

Cohen, L., Henry, C., Dehaene, S., Martinaud, O., Lehericy, S., Lemer, C., et al. (2004). The pathophysiology of letter-by-letter reading. *Neuropsychologia, 42*, 13, 1768–1780.

Cornelissen, P., Hansen, P. C., Hutton, J. L., Evangelinou, T. V., & Stein, J. F. (1998). Magnocellular visual function and children's single word reading. *Vision Research, 38*, 3, 471–482.

Cornelissen, P., Richardson, A., Mason, A., Fowler, S., & Stein, J. (1995). Contrast sensitivity and coherent motion detection measured at photopic luminance levels in dyslexics and controls. *Vision Research, 35*, 10, 1483–1494.

Cowey, A., & Stoerig, P. (1992). Reflections on blindsight. In A. D. Milner & M. D. Rugg (Eds.). *The neuropsychology of consciousness.* London, Academic Press.

Crawford, T., & Higham, M. (2001). Dyslexia and centre of gravity effect. *Experimental British Research, 137*, 122–126.

Demb, J. B., Boynton, G. M., et al. (1997). Brain activity in visual cortex predicts individual differences in reading performance. *Proceedings of the National Academy of Sciences, USA, 94*, 24, 13363–13366.

Eden, G. F., VanMeter, J. W., Rumsey, J. M., Maisog, J. M., Woods, R. P., & Zeffiro, T. A. (1996). Abnormal processing of visual motion in dyslexia revealed by functional brain imaging. *Nature, 382*, 6586, 66–69.

Facoetti, A. et al. (2001). Orienting visual attention in dyslexia. *Experimental British Research, 138*, 46–53.

Fischer, B., Hartnegg, K., et al. (2000). Dynamic visual perception of dyslexic children. *Perception, 29*, 5, 523–530.

Fowler, M. S. (1991). Binocular instability in dyslexics. In J. F. Stein (Ed.). *Vision and visual dysfunction,* Vol. 13. New York: Macmillan Press.

Fowler, M. S., Riddell, P. M., & Stein, J. F. (1990). Vergence eye movement control and spatial discrimination in normal and dyslexic children. In G. T. Pavlidis (Ed.) *Perspectives on dyslexia,* Vol. 1. New York: Wiley: 253–274.

Francks, C., Paracchini, S., Smith, S. D., Richardson, A. J., Scerri, T. S., Cardon, L. R., et al. (2004). A 77-kilobase region of chromosome 6p22.2 is associated with dyslexia in families from the United Kingdom and from the United States. *American Journal of Human Genetics, 75*, 6, 1046–1058.

Galaburda, A. M., Menard, M. T., & Rosen, G. D. (1994). Evidence for aberrant auditory anatomy in developmental dyslexia. *Proceedings of the National Academy of Sciences, USA, 91*, 17, 8010–8013.

Galaburda, A. M., Sherman, G. F., Rosen, G. D., Aboitiz, F., & Geschwind, N. (1985). Developmental dyslexia: four consecutive patients with cortical anomalies. *Annals of Neurology, 18*, 2, 222–233.

Hari, R. (2001). Left minineglect in dyslexic adults. *Brain, 124*, 1373–1380.

Hockfield, S., & Sur, M. (1990). Monoclonal Cat-301 identifies Y cells in cat LGN. *Journal of Comprehensive Neurology, 300*, 320–330.

Horowitz, T., & Wolfe, J. (1998). Visual search has no memory. *Nature, 394*, 575–577.

Iles, J., Walsh, V., & Richardson, A. (2000). Visual search performance in dyslexia. *Dyslexia, 6*, 3, 163–177.

Livingstone, M. S., Rosen, G. D., Drislane, F. W., & Galaburda, A. M. (1991). Physiological and anatomical evidence for a magnocellular deficit in developmental dyslexia. *Proceedings of the National Academy of Sciences, USA, 88*, 7943–7947.

Lovegrove, W. J., Bowling, A., Badcock, D., & Blackwood, M. (1980). Specific reading disability: Differences in contrast sensitivity as a function of spatial frequency. *Science, 210*, 4468, 439–440.

Merigan, W. H., & Maunsell, J. H. (1990). Macaque vision after magnocellular lateral geniculate lesions. *Vision and Neuroscience, 5*, 4, 347–352.

Morais, J., Cary, J., Alegria, J., & Bertelson, P. (1979). Does awareness of speech as a sequence of phones arise spontaneously? *Cognition, 7*, 323–332.

Olson, R., Wise, B., Conners, F., Rack, J., & Fulker, D. (1989). Specific deficits in component reading and language skills: genetic and environmental influences. *Journal of Learning Disabilities, 22*, 6, 339–348.

Pammer, K., & Wheatley, C. (2001). Isolating the M(y)-cell response in dyslexia using the spatial frequency doubling illusion. *Vision Research, 41*, 2139.

Poldrack, R. A., Wagner, A. D., Prull, M. W., Desmond, J. E., Glover, G. H., & Gabrieli, J. D. (1999). Functional specialization for semantic and phonological processing in the left inferior prefrontal cortex. *Neuroimage, 10*, 15–35.

Pugh, K. R., Sandak, R., Frost, S. J., Moore, D., & Mencl, W. E. (2005). Examining reading development and reading disability in English language learners: Potential contributions form functional neuroimaging. *Learning Disabilities Research & Practice, 20*, 1, 24–30.

Rae, C., Harasty, J., Dzendrowsky, T., Talcott, J., Simpson, J., Blamire, A., et al. (2002). Cerebellar morphology in developmental dyslexia. *Neuropsychologia, 40*, 1285–1292.

Schmahmann, J. D. (2004). Disorders of the cerebellum: ataxia, dysmetria of thought, and the cerebellar cognitive affective syndrome. *Journal of Neuropsychiatry and Clinical Neuroscience, 16*, 3, 367–378.

Scott, R., Stoodley, C., Anslow, P., Paul, C., Stein, J. F., Sugden, E. M., et al. (2001). Lateralised cognitive deficits in children following cerebellar lesions. *Developmental Medicine and Child Neurology, 43*, 685–691.

Seidenburg, M. (1993). Connectionist modelling of word recognition and dyslexia. *Psychological Science, 4*, 523–568.

Shillcock, R. C., & Monaghan, P. (2001). The computational exploration of visual word recognition in a split model. *Neural Computation, 13*, 1171–1198.

Simos, P. G., Breier, J. I., Fletcher, J. M., Foorman, B. R., Castillo, E. M., & Papanicolaou, A. C. (2002). Brain mechanisms for reading words and pseudowords: an integrated approach. *Cerebral Cortex, 12*, 297–305.

Stein, J. (2001). The magnocellular theory of developmental dyslexia. *Dyslexia, 7*, 12–36.

Stein, J. (2003). Why did language develop? *International Journal of Pediatric Otorhinolaryngology, 67*, S1–9.

Stein, J. F. (1986). Role of the cerebellum in the visual guidance of movement. *Nature, 323*, 6085, 217–221.

Stein, J. & Glickstein (1992). Role of the cerebellum in the visual guidance of movement. *Physiological Reviews, 72*, 967–1018.

Stoodley, C. J., Fawcett, A. J., Nicolson, R. I., & Stein, J. F. (2005). Impaired balancing ability in dyslexic children. *Experimental Brain Research,* 1–11.

Stoodley, C. J., Harrison, E. P., Stein, J. F., Stoodley, C. J., Fawcett, A. J., Nicolson, R. I., et al. (2005). Implicit motor learning deficits in dyslexic adults. *Neuropsychologia.*

Talcott, J., Witton, C., McLean, M., Hansen, P., Rees, A., Green, G., et al. (2000). Dynamic sensory sensitivity and children's word decoding skills. *Proceedings of the National Academy of Sciences, USA, 97*, 2952–2962.

Tallal, P., & Piercy, M. (1973). Defects of non-verbal auditory perception in children with developmental aphasia. *Nature, 241*, 5390, 468–469.

Trussell, L. O. (1997). Cellular mechanisms for preservation of timing in central auditory pathways. *Current Opinions in Neurobiology, 7*, 4, 487–492.

Vidyasagar, T. R. (2004). Neural underpinnings of dyslexia as a disorder of visuo-spatial attention. *Clinics in Experimental Opthomology, 87*, 1, 4–10.

Witton, C., Stein, J. F., Stoodley, C. J., Rosner, B. S., & Talcott, J. B. (2002). Separate influences of acoustic AM and FM sensitivity on the phonological decoding skills of impaired and normal readers. *Journal of Cognitive Neuroscience, 14*, 866–874.

Author Index

Subject Index

Note: Page numbers followed by *f* denote figures.